CW00739257

Explorer San Francisco

Mick Sinclair

Publishing

Front cover
Top: *San Francisco Bridge illuminated in the early evening* (K. Paterson).
Centre (left to right): *(a) Sculpture, Embarcadero Center* (K. Paterson); *(b) Fisherman's Wharf* (B. Smith); *(c) Wild flowers, Napa Valley* (K. Paterson); *(d) Transamerica Pyramid* (K. Paterson); *(e) The Stars and Stripes* (K. Paterson)
Spine
United States flag in front of the Golden Gate Bridge (K. Paterson)
Back Cover
Left: *Victorian houses against teh highrise blocks of the financial district* (K. Paterson);
Right: A cable car tourist bus (K. Paterson)

All pictures from AA World Travel Library

Page 3: *Golden Gate Bridge*
Page 4: *Street car*
Page 5: *(a) Fairmont Hotel*
Pages 5: *(b) Transamerica Pyramid*
Page 6/7: *San Francisco viewed from Marin*
Page 6: *(b) North Beach pastry shop*
Page 7: *Victorian house*
Page 9: *Alamo Square*
Page 27: *(a) Victorian architectural detail*
Page 27: *(b) Statue, Pacific Stock Exchange Building*
Page 247: *Old St. Mary's Church, Chinatown*
Page 267: *Washington Square Inn*

Written by Mick Sinclair

Published by AA Publishing, a trading name of Automobile Association Developments Limited, whose registered office is Fanum House, Basing View, Basingstoke, Hampshire, RG21 4EA. Registered number 1878835.

ISBN-10: 0 7495 47545
ISBN 13: 978-07495-475-47

The contents of this publication are believed correct at the time of printing. Nevertheless, AA Publishing accepts no responsibility for errors, omissions or changes in the details given, or for the consequences of readers' reliance on this information. This does not affect your statutory rights. Assessments of the attractions, hotels and restaurants are based upon the author's own experience, and contain subjective opinions that may not reflect the publisher's opinion or a reader's experience. We have tried to ensure accuracy, but things do change, so please let us know if you have any comments or corrections.

A CIP catalogue record for this book is available from the British Library.

Color separation by KDP, Kingsclere, UK
Printed and bound in Italy by Printer Trento Srl

Find out more about AA Publishing and the wide range of travel publications and services the AA provides by visiting our website at www.theAA.com/bookshop.

Revised fifth edition Jan 2006
First published 1995

Titles in the Explorer series:
Australia • Boston & New England • Britain • Brittany
California • Canada • Caribbean • China • Costa Rica • Crete
Cuba • Cyprus • Egypt • Florence & Tuscany • Florida
France • Germany • Greek Islands • Hawaii • India • Ireland
Italy • Japan • London • Mallorca • Mexico • New York
New Zealand • Paris • Portugal • Provence • Rome
San Francisco • Scotland • South Africa • Spain • Thailand
Tunisia • Turkey • Venice • Vietnam

A02413

How to use this book

ORGANIZATION

San Francisco Is, San Francisco Was

Discusses aspects of life and living today, from environmental concerns to politics, and details the history of America's favorite city.

A–Z

Covers places to visit, with suggested walks and excursions, and lists itineraries, tips for those on a tight budget and sightseeing ideas for children. Check out the Focus On articles, which consider a variety of topics in greater detail.

Travel Facts

Contains the practical information necessary for a successful trip.

Accommodations and Restaurants

Lists recommended establishments in San Francisco, giving a brief description of their high points. Entries are graded budget, moderate or expensive.

Admission charges

Inexpensive: under $7
Moderate: $7–$15
Expensive: over $15

ABOUT THE RATINGS

Most places described in this book have been given a separate rating:

▶▶▶ **Do not miss**

▶▶ **Highly recommended**

▶ **Worth seeing**

MAP REFERENCES

To make the location of a particular place easier to find, every main entry in this book is given a map reference, such as 176B3. The first number (176) indicates the page on which the map can be found; the letter (B) and the second number (3) pinpoint the square in which the main entry is located. The maps on the inside front cover and inside back cover are referred to as IFC and IBC respectively.

Contents

A–Z

Focus On

Walks

Mick Sinclair has made a career out of homing in on the nooks and crannies of America's major cities. The author of guidebooks to Chicago, Miami and New York, he has contributed travel articles and features on culture and the arts to magazines and newspapers all over the world.

My San Francisco

Hacking a route through the undergrowth, as the treacherous Golden Gate loomed hundreds of feet below and the ocean wind whipped around my ears, was an odd way to spend a day in San Francisco. Yet a hike along a coastal trail is as much a part of the City by the Bay as browsing the department stores around Union Square or ogling the Transamerica Pyramid. Packed onto the head of a peninsula, San Francisco may be small, but it is immeasurably varied.

I found that a few minutes' walk could take me from the herbalists of Chinatown to the elegant hotels of Nob Hill, from the cherry trees of Japantown to the *MTV*-lifestyles of the Lower Haight. Or, indeed, to the many acres of unspoiled and undeveloped land that culminate in slender beaches beside the Golden Gate or the Pacific Ocean.

From bed and breakfast in the Castro to a Financial District hotel suite 27 floors up, I moved from base to base within San Francisco. In doing so, I passed through changes in history, architecture and ethnicity to a degree hard to imagine existing in any other city.

San Franciscans themselves generally come from anywhere except San Francisco. Evidence of myriad nationalities pervades the city, from a French church or Buddhist temple to a Cambodian café. The large Asian population in particular is a reminder that San Francisco sits on America's West Coast, created not by colonial settlement but through the multicultural opportunism of the Gold Rush. That sense of seizing the moment still prevails in San Francisco, not least perhaps because of the ever-present threat of another major earthquake.

If there is one constant—other than earthquakes—to be found in this city, it is cafés. Yet I never found any two alike, or any two customers to order quite the same combination of coffee, milk, water and spices (and whatever else) in this health-conscious but caffeine-fueled city, where the lengthy lexicon of coffee types has become a form of *lingua franca*.

Mick Sinclair

San Francisco Is

San Francisco's striking mix of nationalities, cultures, languages and religions has been a feature of the city since the Gold Rush days. However, with 39 percent of its 750,000 population born outside the US, it is still easy to be surprised by the diversity of ethnic groups, of which those described below represent only the most visible—or the most unexpected.

ITALIANS San Francisco has the largest concentration of Italian-Americans in the US, and their impact on the city has been incalculable. Since the first wave of immigration in the 1880s, Italian names have become dominant in city politics and business. The Italian population is now spread throughout the city, but scores of Italian restaurants and cafés still remain in North Beach, the original Italian district.

THE CHINESE Largely through the racist restrictions which forced them into Chinatown during the late 1800s, San Francisco's Chinese have long been one of the largest and most visible elements in the city's ethnic mosaic. Traditionally, almost all have been of Cantonese origin, although the easing of Chinese immigration restrictions by the US in 1965 brought settlers from some of the country's far-flung regions—a fact evinced by the expanding selection of regional Chinese cuisines offered in Chinatown's many restaurants.

Chinatown may provide a spiritual home for San Francisco's Chinese, but many have departed for middle-class lifestyles in the Richmond District, where Clement Street offers some of the city's best Chinese bakeries and restaurants.

Elbow to elbow, discerning Chinatown shoppers

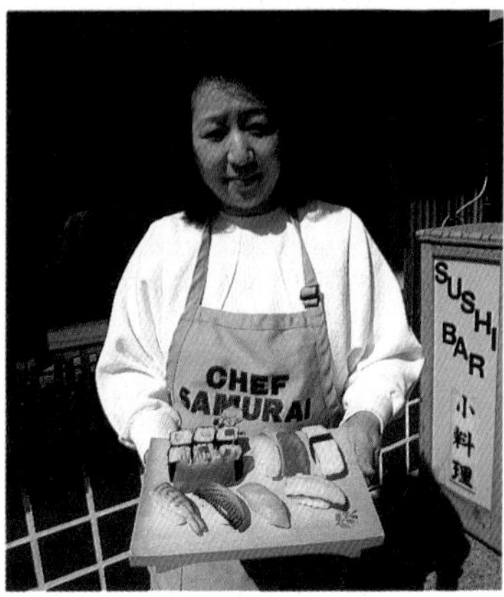

Fish at its best: Japantown sushi bar

FILIPINOS Strong links between the US and the Philippines enabled Filipinos to study and work in America in comparatively large numbers. Many arrived during the 1920s to labor on California farms, while others achieved American academic qualifications which led to powerful positions in their homeland. Those in San Francisco are seldom visible as a group except during Mass at St. Patrick's Church.

❑ Of America's 7.2 million Asians, 35 percent live in California, with San Francisco boasting one of the largest Asian communities outside Asia. ❑

THE JAPANESE Since the end of World War II, when its Japanese-American population returned from internment camps, the Japanese community of San Francisco has consistently numbered just under 1.6 percent of the city's total population, currently around 12,000. Few of them, however, actually live in Japantown, where Shinto and Buddhist temples, Japanese shops, restaurants and social centers nevertheless provide a focal point for the community and a site for its many festivals.

SOUTHEAST ASIANS California's Asian population increased by a startling 127 percent in the 1980s, a significant proportion of which came from the countries of Southeast Asia. Recent waves of Vietnamese, Cambodian, and Laotian immigration have resulted in a proliferation of new businesses—mostly restaurants—in the Tenderloin, carrying the promise of regeneration in this run-down neighborhood.

LATIN AMERICANS Spanish is more prevalent than English on the busy streets of the Mission District, which was settled in the 1940s by a Latin American population lured northward by the prospect of work in shipyards and in other industries stimulated by the war. Latin

A Latin American bakery in the Mission District

Americans now comprise 14 percent of the total population; around 50,000 live in the Mission District.

RUSSIANS The livestock of 19th-century Russian peasants who migrated to escape religious persecution became a feature of the Potrero Hill area until the late 1950s. More in evidence today are the cafés and bakeries dispensing Russian specialties in the Richmond District, where a significant community of urbanized Russians settled during the Soviet era. Its magnificent Cathedral of the Holy Virgin is the main Russian Orthodox church in the western US.

Enjoying Golden Gate Park

Chain-smoking couch potatoes are firmly in the minority among San Franciscans, who typically sport well-tuned bodies and engage in athletic activities with enough energy to make even spectators feel exhausted. Furthermore, San Francisco has frequently been the birthplace of cult sports that have gone on to become international obsessions.

FOOT POWER As walking and jogging became *de rigueur* across the US in the 1970s, San Franciscans quickly developed a desire for something more challenging. Their love of walking grew into a mania for "striding" or "power-walking," both popular terms for athletic walking—a brisk 4mph (6.5kph) trot. In 1985, the participants in the first San Francisco Hill Stride (held each August) made mincemeat of a 7-mile (11km) route around the city, barely breaking stride as steep streets, and even flights of stairs, loomed before them.

Another event in which San Franciscans pit themselves against the city's heights is October's California Infiniti mile: an ascent to the top of Nob Hill, with walkers, runners, cyclists—and even formally dressed waiters carrying trays of drinks—competing.

CYCLING Also undeterred by the city's hills are legions of devoted cyclists. One way San Franciscans beat rush-hour traffic is by taking their bikes to work: More than a few Financial District employees swap their bicycle clips for business suits in their office restrooms.

"Critical Mass," a communal cycle ride through the city began in 1992 with 45 riders and quickly escalated into a monthly event attracting

Stereo joggers

Rollerblades (opposite) are the smart way to move. Above: Tiburon

❑ "Like a swarm of killer bees"—the approach of a group of rollerblade skaters described by a *San Francisco Chronicle* journalist. ❑

thousands. By 1997, it was prompting newspaper headlines such as "Anarchy on Wheels," but its popularity spread: Many other cities in the US and beyond subsequently staged their own "Critical Mass."

For pleasure cycling, Golden Gate Park has many miles of bike paths and is included on one of the city's two marked bike routes. More rugged trails are being developed across the Presido.

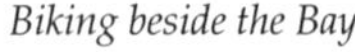

Biking beside the Bay

The brush-covered hills and protected wilderness of the Bay Area are also exploited by cyclists, often on well-supported guided bike tours—some lasting for two or three days. Many of these rural routes were made accessible by the advent of the mountain bike, which evolved from ad-hoc hillside races held by locals on the slopes of Marin County, north of San Francisco Bay, during the mid-1970s.

While the popularity of mountain bikes—with their innovative design—has swept the world, the hills of Marin County have been damaged by cyclists' wheels. Biking across them is only permitted in certain areas and within a 15mph (25kph) speed limit—rules upheld by patrols.

ROLLERBLADING The rollerblade revolutionized roller-skating in the early 1990s and San Francisco was among the first to embrace it with communal "skates around the city." Large numbers of rollerbladers also descend on Golden Gate Park each Sunday, and lone skaters can often be spotted weaving through the traffic.

SNOWBOARDING The winter snows that coat the mountains of the Sierra Nevada draw thousands of skiers from San Francisco. The innovative snow-sports enthusiast, however, is finding regular skiing increasingly passé compared to snowboarding: essentially a fast trip across the snow with one's feet attached to a glorified skateboard. The relative newness of the sport and the tough initiation that beginners endure, sometimes sustaining many injuries, have lent snowboarding cult status.

Like any city, San Francisco is in a constant ferment over political issues and intrigues, although the matters raising the hottest passions are often those which relate to California rather than just the city. Nonetheless, San Francisco is frequently gripped by local issues that few people could imagine coming to the forefront anywhere else.

NORTH VERSUS SOUTH Rare is the San Franciscan who has anything good to say about Los Angeles, 400 miles (6.5km) to the south. LA is popularly viewed as a flat, smog-infested basin criss-crossed by car-jammed freeways, whose population fears to walk the streets. San Francisco, though, is regarded as a beautiful city of hills and bay views where cultured and sociable residents mingle in cafés, and walk the streets rather than drive or use public transportation. Anything tainted by Southern California—such as the Transamerica Pyramid, built by an LA-based architectural firm—is met, initially at least, with some suspicion.

The antipathy between LA and San Francisco echoes a wider north–south division within California. North of San Francisco, the state continues for 300 miles (484km) and is host to a sparse population living amid the rivers and forests which provide the state with the bulk of its natural resources.

By contrast, heavily populated Southern California, behind its sun-and-surf image, has evolved into a vast industrial and suburban sprawl whose water supply comes from damming and diverting the northern rivers. This tampering with nature brings endless ecological headaches and upsets rural economies.

As the social problems of the south place an increasing burden on state funds, the rising taxes that result are resented in the north. A poll conducted in 1992, immediately following LA's Rodney King riots, found that all the state's northern counties wanted to break with the south and become America's 51st state—a scenario that one analyst described as "the Balkanization of California."

❑ In 1993, as part of a campaign to improve public transportation in the city, a law was passed attempting to compel all city officials to travel to work by public transportation at least twice a week. ❑

NEIGHBORHOOD POWER The e-economy boom of the 1990s raised rents in SoMa and the adjoining Mission District as hundreds of new technology companies were founded, bringing 35,000 new workers into the neighborhoods. Many long-established family-run businesses and residents on low incomes were driven out as juice bars and gyms appeared to cater to the influx of dotcom workers.

As San Francisco appeared to be turning into a suburb of Silicon

Top and below: Appealing to the voters

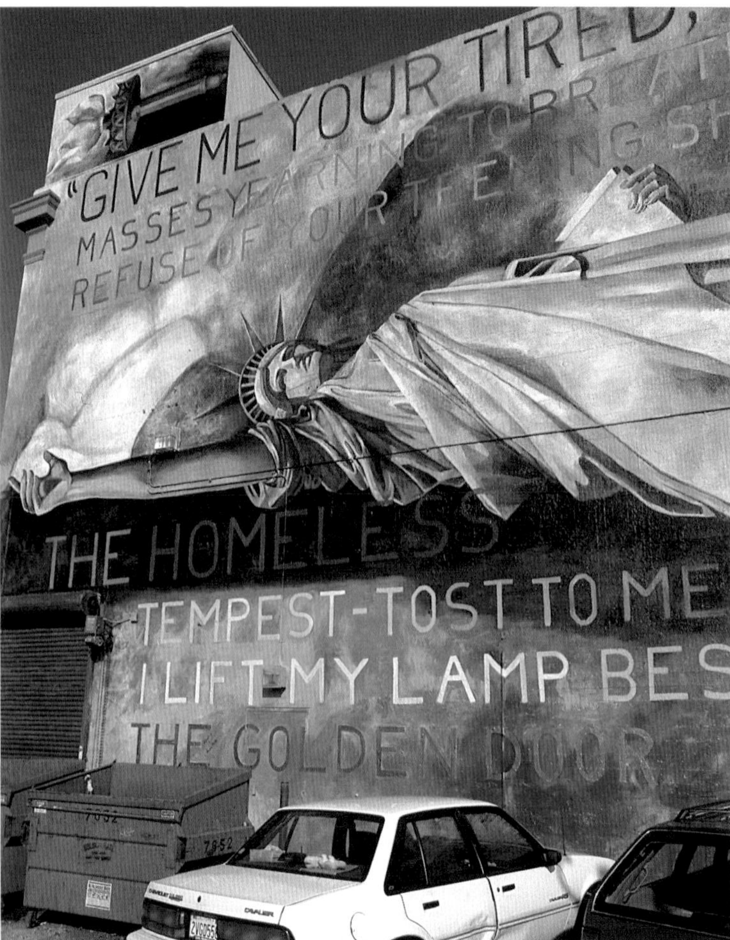

Lady Liberty reaches out...to SoMa

Valley, the Mission Anti-Displacement Coalition was created to oppose further change; another was the Mission Yuppie Eradication Displacement Project, which declared war on prestige cars found parked in the area. More successful than either, though, in removing the newcomers was the dot-com crash of 2000.

Another form of people power—or perhaps more accurately small-business power—has been seen in the troubled Tenderloin area. Lobbying from local store and restaurant owners resulted in the removal of several public telephones which drug dealers and prostitutes were using for business purposes. In another move to reduce the neighborhood's crime, owners of local tourist hotels proposed taxing local businesses to finance a private security force to patrol the streets.

GAY POWER As in no other city, gay issues are part of San Francisco's political agenda; and this returned to national attention in 2004 when the mayor permitted marriage licences to be issued to 4000 same-sex couples, thereby igniting moral debate and sharply dividing opinion throughout the country, which lead to the California Supreme Court voiding such marriages.

San Francisco may not be able to match New York or Los Angeles as an in-demand film set, but its distinctive architecture, climate, natural setting and cosmopolitan population have helped the city win a starring role in some memorable movies. The following is a highly selective list of some of the most thrilling, entertaining, or just plain strange films to have cast the city in a prominent role.

Basic Instinct (1992). Controversial San Francisco-based big-budget feature that found Michael Douglas and Sharon Stone tormenting each other, and the city's gay population hitting the streets to protest the unsympathetic portrayal of lesbians.

Bullitt (1968). Steve McQueen turns in an outstanding performance as a San Francisco cop embroiled in Mafia shenanigans. But what every action-movie fan remembers best is the car-chase climax along some of the city's steepest streets. Real-life reenactments are not possible, as the route was pieced together in the editing room.

Chan Is Missing (1982). Wayne Wang went on to bigger things with *The Joy Luck Club* (see opposite) but cut his directorial teeth on this low-budget exploration of contemporary Chinatown and San Francisco-Chinese society, based on a search for an elusive taxi driver.

The Conversation (1974). A brilliant Gene Hackman stars as the cynical private detective who eavesdrops on a Union Square conversation from a gadget-packed room at the St. Francis Hotel; his descent into paranoia as a major conspiracy unfolds around him is played out against various city locations.

Above, left: The Maltese Falcon

Dark Passage (1947). Humphrey Bogart's second major outing (see *The Maltese Falcon*, opposite) into the San Francisco fog comes after he escapes from San Quentin Prison and enlists the aid of Lauren Bacall in proving his innocence. The art deco apartment house that features in the film as Bacall's home is on Montgomery Street, just below Telegraph Hill.

Dirty Harry (1971). In the first and best of the Dirty Harry series, Clint Eastwood established his superstar credentials as a lone-wolf San Francisco cop stalking a demented kidnapper to an unforgettable finale at Candlestick (now known as 3Com) Park.

Frisco Kid (1935). The city's notorious Barbary Coast—which appears as a highly sanitized Hollywood version—gives James Cagney a vehicle to brawl his way to the top of the waterfront pecking order.

Invasion of

Harry's day... being made

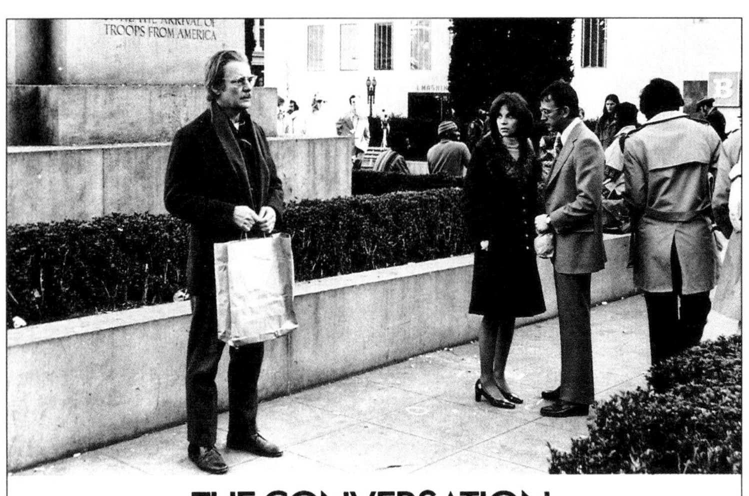

TROOPS FROM AMERICA
THE CONVERSATION
directed by Francis Ford Coppola starring Gene Hackman DISTRIBUTED BY CINEGATE

❑ Seldom mentioned in accounts of cinematic San Francisco, *The Subterraneans* (1960) is an abysmal screen version of Jack Kerouac's novel which inadvertently provides plenty of laughs in its attempts to capture the city's late-1950s beatnik scene. ❑

the Bodysnatchers (1978). In this clever remake of the 1950s sci-fi classic, it is not small-town Americans but the entire population of 1970s San Francisco who are replaced by zombie look-alikes from outer space. The main characters amusingly epitomize the era's alternative lifestyles.

The Joy Luck Club (1993). The director of *Chan Is Missing* (see opposite), Wayne Wang, used major Hollywood funding to great effect in this adaptation of Amy Tan's best-selling novel; opening in modern-day Chinatown, the film evolves into a classy tear-jerker about the trials and tribulations of several generations of Asian-American women.

The Maltese Falcon (1941). The third screen version of the Dashiell Hammett story could well be the best—and most influential—private detective film ever made; an electrifying Humphrey Bogart leads the quest for the bird, beginning on the fog-covered steps of the Stockton Tunnel.

Pacific Heights (1990). One of San Francisco's venerable Victorian houses (actually located on Potrero Hill) is the setting of this engaging thriller in which a young professional couple inadvertently rents a room to a tenant with severe antisocial tendencies.

Vertigo (1958). Alfred Hitchcock's complex—or perhaps just confusing—psychological thriller draws a San Francisco private eye (James Stewart) out of retirement and into a doomed affair with Kim Novak.

Vertiginous: Stewart and Novak

San Francisco's exquisite natural setting is enhanced immeasurably by a wealth of distinctive architectural styles, varying in design from playful Victorian gingerbread homes to uniquely contoured, dramatic high-rise office buildings.

EARLY STRUCTURES Protected from earthquake damage by its thick adobe walls, Mission Dolores dates with dignity from the 18th-century Spanish settlement and is easily the city's oldest structure (see page 124). The only other evidence of Spanish-era building survives as a small section of adobe wall which forms part of the Presidio's Officers' Club (see page 155).

HANDSOME VICTORIANS
Architectural refinement was the last thing on most people's minds in Gold-Rush San Francisco. But among the great influx of arrivals was a number of highly trained architects who, when fortune eluded them, plied their trade in the growing city.

As new residential areas sprang up to house the booming city's more affluent population, innovations in mechanized carpentry were allowing wood to be shaped in ways that were previously impossible. San Francisco, by now the West Coast's major port, received shiploads of mail-order building materials, and pretty wood-built Italianate homes—modeled on Italian villas and commonly marked by extended porches and Corinthian columns—arose during the 1860s as the favored dwellings of the wealthy.

Top: Levi Plaza, North Beach
Below: The straight-line Stick style

A notable feature of many of San Francisco's Victorian houses, bay windows are not only attractive but also make the most of the sunshine in this foggy city

STICK AND QUEEN ANNE Through the 1870s and 1880s, the Stick style—which involved the use of flat wooden boards to emphasize the building's vertical lines—was increasingly favored over simple Italianate. Desire for greater ornamentation led to a prevalence of Stick-Eastlake homes, so named for their elaborate decoration inspired by the work of British designer Charles Eastlake.

By the 1880s, the extravagant towers, turrets and sharply gabled roofs of the Queen Anne style were popular in high society. Each decorative flourish—stained-glass windows were a definite plus—was seen as an indication of the owner's financial standing.

Approximately 14,000 Victorian houses survived the 1906 earthquake and fire, and roughly half have been fully restored by their owners. The main groupings of these wood-built houses are found in Pacific Heights (see pages 148–150), the Western Addition (see page 179), Haight-Ashbury (see pages 106–109), the Mission District (see pages 124–125) and Russian Hill (see page 157).

COMMERCIAL BUILDING The fire that followed the 1906 earthquake destroyed much of the city, including the Financial District and the area around it. Forsaking stone walls for terra-cotta facades and adapting classical themes, the rebuilding of the Financial District was characterized by ground-level glass fronts intended for retail purposes and upper stories holding office space. Of numerous remaining examples, some of the best are on the lower sections of Sutter Street and Grant Avenue (see pages 86–88).

In 1925, the completion of the Pacific Telephone Building, its cultured profile still visible just south of Market Street, heralded another new look—one of set-back towers and art deco decoration echoing Eliel Saarinen's award-winning Tribune Tower in Chicago.

MODERN TOWERS The forest of high-rise buildings that appeared in the 1970s (such as the Transamerica Pyramid, see page 177) stimulated tighter building controls and monetary rewards for the preservation and adaptation of existing landmark structures. Levi's Plaza provides a widely acclaimed example of how to adapt existing buildings—in this case, 19th-century warehouses—to modern commercial use (see page 115).

By the 1990s, the Yerba Buena Gardens complex (see page 168) had transformed part of SoMa with a series of arts-related buildings, such as the new Museum of Modern Art with its truncated cylinder emerging from a brickwork facade and the immense hunk of red rock housing the Mexican Museum (page 117). A landscaped walkway dotted with sculptures and a waterfall picks a route through the architectural styles, and is overlooked by the Sony Metreon, rising for five glass-walled stories above Fourth Street.

Two Alamo Square "painted ladies"

The Financial District: then and now

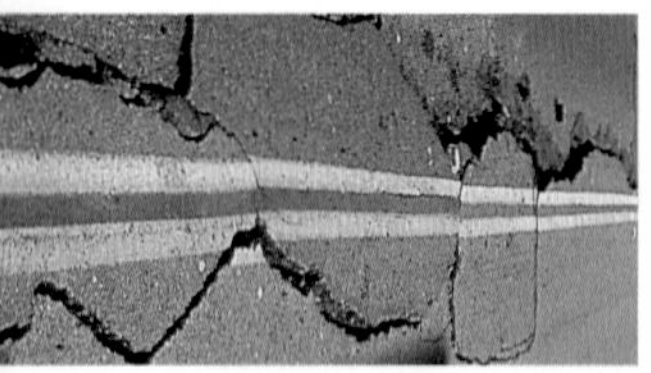

Living on top of one of the world's most notorious geological fault lines cannot fail to instill a sense of the earth's mighty powers in San Franciscans. But the ground opening up and swallowing the city is only one of a host of natural dangers that threatens them.

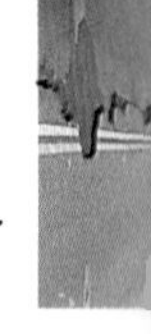

EARTHQUAKES Earthquakes are a fact of life all over California (which experiences 15,000 a year), and many occur each week in the San Francisco area. The majority of these measure less than 3 on the Richter scale and are too small to cause damage or even to be noticed in the city. For anyone who grows complacent, however, the Friday edition of the *San Francisco Chronicle* carries details and maps of the past week's earthquakes, while seismologists predict that a major quake will hit the Bay Area within the next 30 years.

For all the trepidation they inspire, earthquakes can have their advantages. The 1906 earthquake destroyed the city's notorious red-light area, while the 1989 Loma Prieta quake (7.1 on the Richter scale) resulted in the razing of the loathed Embarcadero Freeway, which had separated the Ferry Building and eastern waterfront from the rest of the city. One practical concern for San Franciscans is the extraordinarily high cost of insuring their homes and possessions against earthquake damage.

Earthquake damage in San Francisco. Top: A buckled street; in the Marina District, attempts to save a house (below) and domestic devastation (opposite)

FOREST FIRES In October 1991, fire swept across the Berkeley and Oakland hills (above the cities of Berkeley and Oakland, see pages 58–59 and 140–144), claiming 25 lives, destroying 3,000 homes, sending dark clouds of smoke over the bay and depositing several inches of ash on San Francisco's streets. California living, particularly in hillside "dream homes," means accepting a high-risk environment. In the tinderbox conditions of a hot summer, the smallest spark can cause a blaze to rage across an area where there are no natural firebreaks, where the homes are made of wood, and where narrow, winding roads can often make access difficult for firefighters.

THE BAY Besides providing a scenic backdrop to the city, San Francisco Bay plays a crucial ecological role. In the bay's marshes, microscopic marine creatures thrive and provide food for migratory waterfowl or, after being swept out to sea, for large ocean-dwelling creatures such as the California gray whale.

Commercial development has seen 75 percent of the marshlands disappear beneath new housing districts and industrial sites, while the diversion of the Sacramento and San Joaquin rivers to the farms of California's Central Valley has severely reduced the amount of fresh water entering the bay to temper its salty environment.

In the mid-1960s, in one of the state's first modern conservation campaigns, lobbyists forced the state government to stop pumping raw sewage into the bay, and to introduce laws to restrict landfill.

The largest city-owned solar array in the country covers 60,000sq ft (5,574sq m) atop the Moscone Convention Center and is hoped to reduce carbon dioxide emissions over thirty years equivalent to removing 7,000 cars from local roads. In 2005, meanwhile, San Francisco became the fist US city to host UN World Environment Day.

Currently, the future of the San Francisco Bay is largely in the hands of CALFED, a state-federal body advised by a citizens' group in which environmental lobbies are represented as well as agricultural and business interests.

❑ "A vanishing wonder of the world"—a Californian journalist describing San Francisco Bay in 1965. ❑

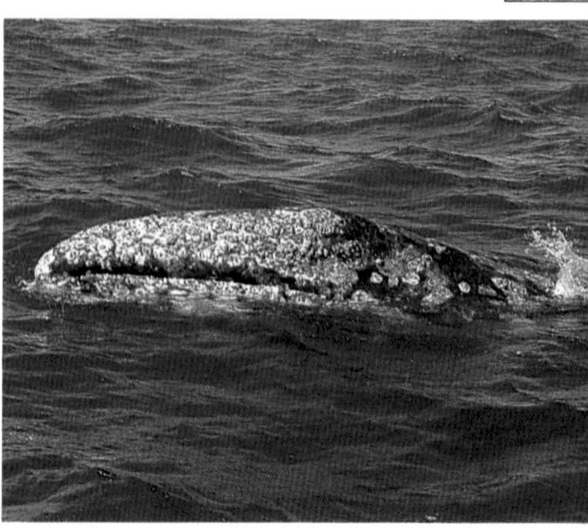

California gray whales (complete with barnacles) often visit in winter

THE OCEAN Much of San Francisco's Pacific shoreline is wild and rugged, and enjoys federal protection as the Golden Gate National Recreation Area (see page 99). Widely supported volunteer efforts help keep the coastline clean and have contributed to the restoration of the Bay Area's brown pelican population.

Meanwhile, few San Franciscans ever get tired of keeping a look out for California gray whales, which migrate between the Arctic and Baja California and can usually be spotted between December and March.

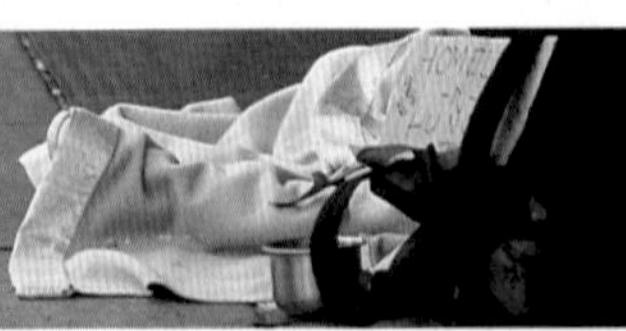

To varying degrees, San Francisco has its share of all the problems that any modern American city faces. The most highly charged issue and one which polarizes local opinion like no other, however, is homelessness.

ON THE STREETS With up to 15,000 homeless in San Francisco on any given day, the city has one of the worst homeless situations of any comparable city in the country. The fact that many spend their days around City Hall and the neighboring Civic Center makes their plight highly visible to anyone who lives or works in, or visits, San Francisco, and it is an issue that continues to divide both established politicians and grass roots support groups.

An all too-common scene around the Tenderloin

Anyone returning to San Francisco for the first time since the 1990s, however, might well be struck by an apparent change for the better, suggested by far fewer numbers of homeless people readily visible. Looks can be deceiving, though, as various initiatives have changed the approach to dealing with homelessness but have failed to resolve it.

THE MATRIX AND BEYOND Few plans to ease homelessness have been without controversy but one that polarized opinion more than most was the Matrix (also known as Operation Quality of Life) program of the 1990s. Under this, anyone sleeping in the street or using a shopping trolley to carry their possessions was liable for a police citation and fine, failure to pay which would lead to imprisonment. The city's religious leaders declared Matrix as heralding "new levels of inhumanity and heartlessness" and distaste, and it contributed to the failure of mayor Frank Jordan to win a second term in 1996.

Jordan's successor, Willie Brown, pledged to create jobs and low-income housing but instead presided over "sweeps" to move the homeless from particular sections of the city and a dot-com boom where the new jobs were for well-heeled cyberspace workers.

RISING RENTS As prices rose in the city through the late 1990s dot-com boom, low-income housing became increasingly rare and it was even suggested that the city charge for the right to sleep on mattresses on the floors of its homeless shelters. The decommissioning of the Presidio army base (see page 155) raised hopes that some of its accommodations may be

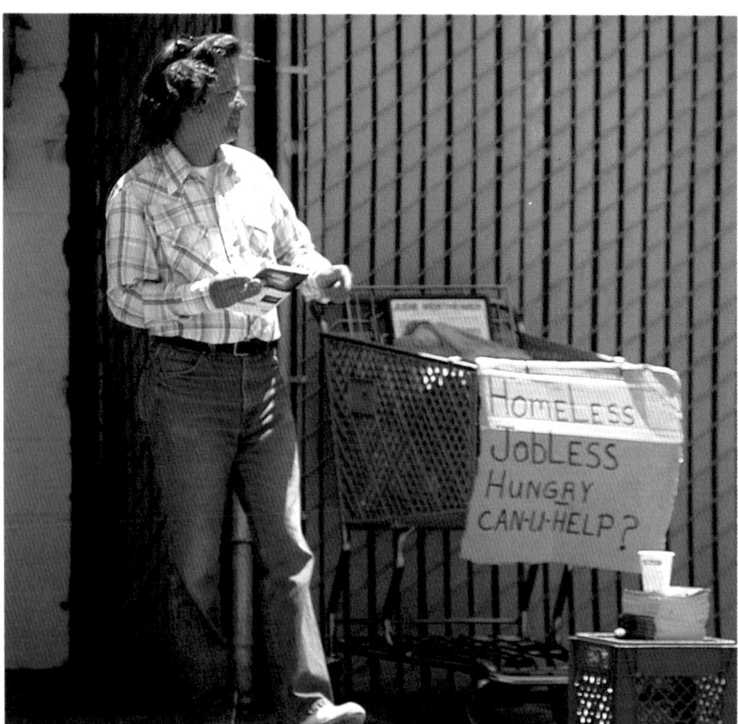

Passersby can be a godsend to those without a home or a job

made available but this was not to be. Meanwhile change, if slow, seemed to be in the hands of volunteer groups such as the Coalition on Homelessness, which provided a voice for street people and raised funds and public awareness through the Street Sheet newspaper. Some churches allowed the homeless to use their facilities and volunteers manned soup kitchens.

CARE NOT CASH In 2003, a five-part series based on four months of research appeared in the San Francisco Chronicle describing the horror and sadness of life on the city's streets. With another new mayor, Gavin Newsome, came another initiative to tackle the issue. Introduced in May 2004, "Care Not Cash" drastically cut welfare payments to homeless people with the intention that money saved would be spent on providing healthcare and long-term housing for the needy.

In early 2005, Mayor Newsome reported a 28 percent drop in the city's homeless over the previous two years, seemingly a signal of the success of past initiatives as well as "Care Not Cash" itself. Critics pointed to an apparent discrepancy between the amount saved and the amount spent on providing accommodations and facilities, and suggested that many homeless had simply been coerced to move elsewhere in the city or outside it to neighboring counties.

FUTURE Though not without opposition, and bringing even greater difficulties than before for those who remain homeless with sharply reduced financial support, by May 2005 some 800 formerly homeless people had been accommodated in "supportive housing," and formed part of a change dubbed by the Chronicle as the city's "most significant transformation in years in the landscape of homelessness."

San Francisco has more festivals than it knows what to do with, and barely a weekend passes without a neighborhood street fair, an ethnic celebration or a display of arts or crafts enlivening some portion of the city. The free weeklies and the Friday editions of daily newspapers carry current festival details, and the Visitor Information Center (tel: 415/283-0177) can provide information on special events taking place during your stay.

JANUARY

Chinese New Year Two weeks of events in and around Chinatown mark the Chinese New Year, the climax of which is a parade—complete with costumed characters, dragons and firecrackers—beginning on Market Street. The New Year is based on the lunar cycle and sometimes falls in February or March.

Tet Festival The Chinese community stages the largest, but not the only, Asian New Year celebration; another is the Vietnamese Tet Festival, lasting a weekend, held along two blocks of the Tenderloin.

Martin Luther King Birthday Celebration Events across the city recording African-American history and achievements mark the birthday of the Civil Rights leader.

San Francisco Sports & Boat Show San Francisco's weekend sailors descend on this week-long display of the latest in yachts and yachting.

Top: Gay Freedom Parade
Below: Mission District Carnaval

FEBRUARY

Russian Festival At the Russian Center, 2450 Sutter Street, the culture and cuisines of Russia's diverse regions are enjoyed and devoured over a weekend.

Pacific Orchid Exposition At Fort Mason Center, an intensely colorful display of the very best orchids, lovingly grown and cultivated by devotees throughout the Bay Area.

MARCH

St. Patrick's Day Parade Begins at Market and Second streets. Irish and

would-be-Irish San Franciscans dress in green for this brash and noisy parade; the day is also marked by special services at St. Patrick's Church, and events at the Irish Cultural Center (2700 45th Street).
Bay Area Music Awards Bill Graham Civic Auditorium. The region's biggest celebration of contemporary music and presentation of the coveted "Bammie" awards.

APRIL
Cherry Blossom Festival Japan Center, Japantown. Be it sumo wrestling or flower arranging, few aspects of Japanese culture are missing from this weekend fling. The main event is a parade from the Civic Center to Japantown, and further activities take place in Golden Gate Park's Japanese Tea Garden (see page 102).
Yachting Season Opening Day San Francisco Bay. On the last Saturday of the month, thousands of tiny—and not so tiny—private boats fill San Francisco Bay. The colorful spectacle is best observed from any suitable hillside spot.

MAY
Cinco de Mayo Mission District. Two-day celebration of the Mexican victory over the French in 1867, featuring Mexican arts, crafts and cooking, and a colorful parade from Mission Street to the Civic Center.
Bay to Breakers A few serious runners and 100,000 exhibitionists participate in this 7.5-mile (12km)

A regular visitor to Chinese New Year celebrations

run from the edge of San Francisco Bay to the Pacific Ocean.
Mural Awareness Month Various locations. Talks, tours and exhibitions are given on the city's many murals.
Carnaval Mission District. One of the city's most colorful and crowded events, with floats, costume contests and highly infectious dance music.

JUNE
Lesbian/Gay Freedom Day A massive display of gay and lesbian pride, on a route that varies from year to year, with food stalls and live entertainment. The same month brings a gay and lesbian film festival and the Annual Dyke March of lesbian and bisexual women.
Stern Grove Midsummer Music Festival The first of several successive Sundays of free music and arts events at Stern Grove, off Sloat Boulevard at 19th Street.

JULY
Independence Day The focal point of the city's 4th of July festivities at Crissy Field, on the northern waterfront, scene of picnics, fireworks and a 50-cannon salute.
San Francisco Marathon The third-largest and certainly the most scenic marathon in America takes its participants across the Golden Gate Bridge to a finish line in Golden Gate Park.

Carnaval rhythms on the Mission District streets

Cable Car Bell-Ringing Contest Union Square. Clangs resound as expert cable car bell-ringers compete to become this year's champion.

AUGUST

ACC Craft Fair Fort Mason Center. All manner of handicrafts displayed while in competition for a range of prestigious awards.

SEPTEMBER

San Francisco Blues Festival Fort Mason Center and Justin Herman Plaza. A weekend of top blues artists playing in the open air.

OCTOBER

Italian Heritage Month Mostly North Beach and Fisherman's Wharf. Special church services and wreath-laying ceremonies in the bay to commemorate lost fishermen. There are other events, often with Sicilian roots, celebrating one of the largest ethnic groups to make its presence felt in the early city.

Halloween Humorous celebrations of witchcraft and the supernatural occur throughout the city, but the date, with particular significance for the city's gay community (see page 70), brings special events—most notably to Castro and Polk streets. An official Halloween march takes place in Civic Center.

NOVEMBER

Day of the Dead Mission District. The Mexican tribute to the spirits of the dead celebrated with macabre art exhibitions and a parade along Mission Street.

San Francisco Book Festival Concourse Exhibition Center, 8th and Brannan streets. Vast gathering of publishers, authors and the very latest books, enlivened by readings, signings, discussions and other book-related events.

Tree lightings The city prepares for the season's festivities with Christmas tree lightings across the city, the last and biggest of them in Union Square.

DECEMBER

Santa Claus Parade Mission District. A gift-laden Saint Nick makes a three-hour trip along Mission and 24th streets.

❑ The following street fairs offer a chance to eat, drink and generally celebrate the neighborhood: Castro Street (October); Dore Alley (SoMa, July); Folsom Street (SoMa, September); Haight Street (June); Nihonmachi (Japantown, August); Potrero Hill (October); Union Street (June); Upper Grant Avenue (North Beach, June). ❑

San Francisco Was

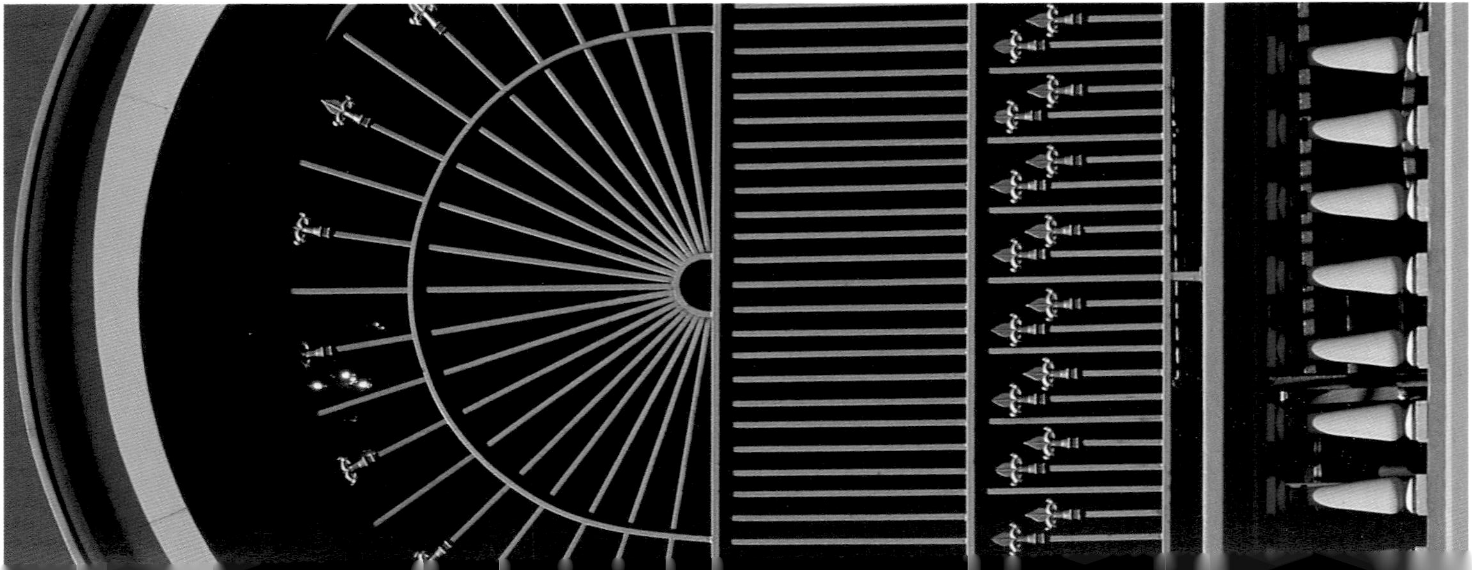

The geological upheaval which led to the formation of the San Francisco Peninsula—blessing the city with a spectacular natural setting but cursing it with frequent earthquakes—began millions of years ago and shows no signs of abating.

FROM THE OCEAN The land that is now California was beneath the Pacific Ocean when, 200 million years ago, the Pacific plate and the North American plate (two of the 20 tectonic plates which form the earth's crust) began moving, the heavier ocean plate sliding beneath the continental plate and pushing against it. The buckling which ensued created huge undersea mountains, which surfaced 10 million years ago and eventually became the mountains of present-day California. The future site of San Francisco also surfaced at this time, forming part of a vast valley.

THE PENINSULA As storm water from the mountains washed downward, it took the lowest and most direct course to the ocean. In doing so, deep channels, one of which became the strait known as the Golden Gate, were created. Successive Ice Ages (the last occurred about 10,000 years ago) caused ocean levels to rise, and the Pacific pushed inland to form San Francisco Bay. A ridge of high ground—the San Francisco Peninsula—was left above water between the bay and the ocean.

❑ Geologically, San Francisco is not part of North America; as with everything west of the San Andreas Fault, it sits on the Pacific plate, which is pushing steadily northward at the rate of 2in (5cm) a year. ❑

FAULT LINES Two major geological fault lines, among hundreds in the region, run beneath San Francisco (the San Andreas) and Berkeley (the Hayward). Frequent earthquakes in the area, caused by pressure along the faults, prove that the two tectonic plates are still continuing to push against each other.

Top: The San Andreas Fault
Below: Carved by storm water—San Francisco Bay, seen from Sausalito

A socially and culturally diverse Native American population, descendants of Asian tribes who crossed the Bering Strait into Alaska, had lived in the Bay Area for thousands of years. With the arrival of Europeans, their way of life came to an abrupt end.

FIRST CALIFORNIANS At the time of European discovery, an estimated 300,000 Native Americans lived in California, made up of many small ethnic groupings (too small to be termed "tribes"), each with a particular way of life and belief system. With its hills and sand dunes, the future site of San Francisco was not attractive territory, although approximately 3,000 Miwok people lived on the north side of the bay, and some 10,000 Ohlone to the south.

NATIVE LIFESTYLES Miwok and Ohlone people, divided into self-contained communities, hunted the region's abundant wildlife to supplement their staple diet of acorns. Basketmaking occupied much of their time. Apart from their practical use, baskets allowed each group to express artistry, and distinct and recognizable styles evolved. Peaceful coexistence was a characteristic of the native Californians; the region saw none of the great conflicts that occurred between tribes elsewhere in North America.

❑ Some 400 shell mounds have been located around San Francisco Bay; these comprised the discarded remains of shellfish and other animals eaten by many generations of Ohlone. ❑

EUROPEAN IMPACT With the Spanish settlement of California in the late 1700s came not only a new civilization and religion—which eroded native cultures—but also European diseases, such as chicken pox and measles, to which the indigenous people had no immunity. In the Bay Area, surviving natives also bore the brunt of the mid-1800s Gold Rush, which brought tens of thousands of white settlers with an insatiable desire for land.

Top and below: Miwok Indians

The Spanish had become established in South and Central America but the North American continent remained a barely charted territory, where just a few bold seafarers and adventurers carried the flags of European colonial powers, eager to strengthen their empires by locating the fabled "northwest passage" to the spice islands of the East.

CALIFORNIA SIGHTED Juan Rodriguez Cabrillo, a Portuguese navigator employed by Spain, sailed along the California coast in 1542, briefly dropping anchor off what is now San Diego. The first European known to step ashore in California was a Briton, Sir Francis Drake, who in 1579 berthed his *Golden Hind* for 36 days at a (much-disputed) point close to Point Reyes. Drake claimed the land for Queen Elizabeth I of England.

An early visitor: Sir Francis Drake and (top) his ship, the Golden Hind

❑ Not only were the members of the de Portola expedition the first Europeans to see San Francisco Bay, but they were also the first Europeans known to have experienced a California earthquake. At the time, they were camped by the Santa Ana River in present-day Orange County, near Los Angeles. ❑

SPANISH FOOTHOLD The British colonies took root on America's East Coast rather than the West Coast, however, and it was the Spanish who established the first European settlements in California, making Monterey, south of San Francisco, their capital. The Spanish founded a chain of missions in California, ostensibly to convert the indigenous population to Christianity, but also to cement their territorial claim (Russia was a rival) and gain native support in any potential colonial conflict.

SAN FRANCISCO BAY Although San Francisco Bay makes an excellent natural harbor, it cannot be seen from the ocean. Consequently, the first European sighting of the bay was by Gaspar de Portola's overland expedition of 1769. The first navigation by ship occurred six years later, led by Juan Manuel de Ayala, who mapped the bay and gave Spanish names to many of its features.

SAN FRANCISCO BORN Part of de Ayala's assignment, as his ship became the first to sail through the

Mission Dolores: the city's oldest building and earthquake survivor

Golden Gate Strait into San Francisco Bay, was to meet an overland party led by Juan Bautista de Anza. In March 1775, de Anza reached the tip of the San Francisco Peninsula and planted a cross to mark the site of a future presidio (or garrison, see page 155). Three miles (5km) south in a more sheltered location, the mission of San Francisco de Asis (soon better known as Mission Dolores, see page 124) was founded. Neither the mission nor the presidio stimulated growth in this distant outpost of the Spanish empire, however, and the expected threat from rival colonial powers failed to materialize.

THE CALIFORNIOS In 1821, newly independent Mexico acquired California from Spain. Uninterested in this distant land, the Mexican government permitted large sections of California to pass into the hands of the Californios (Californians of Spanish or Mexican descent), who effectively governed themselves. The wealthy and easy-going Californios left business administration to foreign settlers. From a cove on the eastern side of the peninsula, US ships would be loaded with California hides and tallow. Around the cove grew the settlement of Yerba Buena, later renamed San Francisco for the bay on which it sits.

❑ "I am afraid we shall see a great deal of trouble in California this year. There are seven or eight thousand emigrants from the USA expected."—W. D. M. Howard, San Francisco merchant and landowner, 1846. ❑

US ACQUISITION As the US pushed westward, waging war with Mexico and establishing an overland route into California, the territory inevitably fell into American hands. On July 9, 1846, the USS *Portsmouth* berthed at Yerba Buena and the Stars and Stripes was unfurled across the plaza (today's Portsmouth Square; see page 75).

Renaissance Faire, Marin County, a re-creation of 16th-century England

The discovery of gold in California in 1848 was the making of San Francisco, turning a remote and sleepy trading post with a few hundred inhabitants into a major city—and doing so almost overnight.

THE DISCOVERY On January 24, 1848, a farmhand discovered gold 50 miles (81km) west of present-day Sacramento. Although the find would transform California, word spread slowly because many people did not believe what they heard. Nonetheless, the handful of fortune-seekers who made their way to the site of the alleged discovery found that the rivers did indeed hold easily panned gold, washed down over millions of years from the Sierra Nevada Mountains.

In San Francisco, the discovery was not made known until May 12. When it came, the proclamation was made in theatrical style: Newspaper owner Sam Brannan strode through Portsmouth Square brandishing a bottle of the precious substance. There was no doubting Brannan's belief in the find. Besides the newspaper, he owned a hardware store which he had recently equipped with everything a prospective gold seeker could wish for, all for sale at inflated prices (see page 37).

A monument in Coloma dedicated to James Marshall, whose discovery led to the California Gold Rush

A prospector strikes lucky

THE 49ERS By the end of 1848, news of the discovery had spread across the US and beyond. The following year saw the arrival of the "49ers," mostly single men in pursuit of an instant fortune. While some 49ers made the perilous overland journey from the east, others arrived by ship, and San Francisco Bay became blocked with abandoned vessels as their crews headed inland to the

❏ San Francisco's booming population:

1847	500
1848	812
1849	20,000
1852	34,776
1860	56,802
1870	149,473
1880	233,959

Getting rich—or not—the hard way

gold-bearing areas (known as "the Diggins"). During 1849, the population of San Francisco rocketed from 812 to 20,000. Many of the new arrivals lived in makeshift tents and stayed long enough to equip themselves for a crack at the Diggins, alleviating their boredom at the countless saloons and gambling halls that had sprung up in the chaotic shanty town.

CHANGING FORTUNES Many who effortlessly plucked gold from California's rivers in the early days believed that it would always be as easy to find, and squandered their riches on riotous bouts of drinking and gambling in San Francisco before returning to the Diggins.

The rivers quickly yielded all the gold they had, however, and mines had to be dug to reach the seams beneath ground. Finding gold quickly became an industry dominated by mining companies, and—far from becoming rich overnight—many of the 49ers found themselves providing manual labor in the mines. The lasting riches resulting from the Gold Rush were made by the merchants who supplied the 49ers with tools, food, shelter and liquor, often accepting gold dust as currency. Prices in San Francisco had risen as rapidly as the population, often ten times higher than the equivalent in New York. As they grew wealthy, many merchants also bought plots of San Francisco land, which were soon to become valuable assets.

Opposite, top: Gold-washing
Below: Hopeful panners, 1849

The Gold Rush made an instant city out of San Francisco, but only in succeeding years—and not without much anger and anguish—did it acquire an infrastructure commensurate with its size and economic importance.

LAW AND DISORDER The vast majority of people in 1850s San Francisco had arrived solely to get rich quick, and seldom was concern for the law allowed to interfere with this pursuit. A series of fires razed substantial sections of the largely wood-built city. Some fires were started deliberately by criminal gangs—one of which was the Sydney Ducks, a notorious group of former convicts from Australia—who looted unattended shops and warehouses as their owners tackled the blazes.

An ineffectual police force (which, in 1850, numbered just 12 men) and endless legal conundrums (brought about by California's change from Mexican to US rule) set the scene for vigilante committees, first formed in 1851 by disgruntled merchants and property owners. Several public hangings later, the city's crime rate dropped dramatically.

❑ On land created by the filling in of the shallow Yerba Buena Cove in the 1850s, the city's Financial District was born in 1866 when the Bank of California moved to a site at the corner of California and Sansome streets. Ships abandoned in the bay were used in the landfill operation, and their remains still lie beneath the district's modern skyscrapers. ❑

FINANCIAL INSECURITIES Although by 1851 San Francisco was the fourth busiest trading port in the US, it still lacked a reliable banking system. To replace gold as currency, San Francisco's banks began minting their own coins (a practice then permitted under federal law) and made considerable profits by using less

San Francisco burning in the 1850s

Opposite, top: Nob Hill, where the Big Four built their opulent homes
Above: A Chinatown street in 1927

❑ The 120ft (37m) wide Market Street was laid out in 1847 by an Irish engineer, Jasper O'Farrell. For no apparent reason, O'Farrell cut through the city's existing grid-pattern streets at a 36-degree angle, inadvertently contributing to modern-day San Francisco's traffic congestion. ❑

gold in the manufacture of a particular coin than its face value stated. The banks used their profits to finance new gold-mining operations and later invested heavily in the silver mines of Nevada's Comstock Lode.

COMSTOCK BOOM AND BUST By the 1860s, San Francisco was reaping the profits of the Comstock Lode, and a building boom swept the city. On Nob Hill, recently made accessible by the creation of the cable car, the Big Four—the four merchants-turned-railroad-tycoons whose monopolistic business practices allowed them to dominate California (see page 37)—enraged the working classes by building extravagant mansions.

The linking of the city's economy to mining was to prove disastrous, however. The Comstock Lode was quickly exhausted, banks closed and a depression hit the city. It was thought that the opening in 1869 of the transcontinental railroad—California's first link to the eastern US—would alleviate this. Instead, the cheap goods the railroad carried from the east destroyed local markets. As jobs became scarce, the Chinese were unjustly blamed and banded together within the confines of Chinatown.

THE BARBARY COAST Drinking and gambling were major activities in 1850s San Francisco and, as soon as enough women had arrived, so too was prostitution. Along the waterfront were brothels of such unbridled sleaziness that sailors nicknamed the area "the Barbary Coast," after an infamous part of North Africa. Quick and casual sex could be found for as little as 25¢, although classier "parlors" aimed at "gentlemen" charged much more.

Faced with such distractions, ship captains had a constant problem finding crews for their next voyage. The practice that became known as "shanghaiing" began in San Francisco's waterfront bars, and involved knocking out a customer with a spiked drink and ferrying his unconscious body to a ship, on which he would have to work off his passage to some distant port.

A cast of larger-than-life characters emerged during San Francisco's formative years, some achieving prominence through their suddenly acquired wealth and power, others becoming notorious for their eccentricities or opinions. Loved or loathed, many of them earned lasting places in city folklore.

EMPEROR NORTON (1818?–1880) Joshua Norton was a successful entrepreneur until 1853, when his attempt to corner the rice market caused him to lose not only his money but also his mind. Wearing a cockaded hat, epaulettes and a ceremonial sword, he proclaimed himself "Emperor of the United States and Protector of Mexico." Norton spent the rest of his life wandering the city's streets issuing proclamations. He also demanded a 50¢-a-month levy (for "court expenses") from businesses, many of which not only paid, but also honored his handwritten promissory notes. On his death, flags flew at half-mast. He was buried with the mayor and a military band in attendance.

Eccentric Emperor Norton

Bonanza King John Mackay
Top: the transcontinental railroad

CLAUS SPRECKELS (1828–1908) A Prussian who settled in San Francisco in 1856, Claus Spreckels founded a sugar refinery to end dependence on expensive supplies imported from the East Coast via Cape Horn. Spreckels' sugar monopoly was the root of a vast fortune, which was later increased by his sons. One of them, Adolph, erected the French Renaissance mansion (one of several Spreckels-family homes popularly dubbed "sugar palaces") which still overlooks Lafayette Park. With his wife, Adolph founded the California Palace of the Legion of Honor.

❑ Other significant early San Franciscans, described elsewhere:
Lillie Coit (page 174)
John McLaren (page 101)
William C. Ralston (page 127)
Adolph Sutro (page 171) ❑

SAM BRANNAN (1818–1889) A convert to the Mormon faith (excommunicated as his greater devotion to money than to God became clear), Sam Brannan arrived in San Francisco in 1856. After opening California's first flour mill and founding its first newspaper, Brannan bought city plots and deliberately delayed the news of the gold discovery until he had equipped his own hardware store with prospectors' tools (see page 32). Brannan spent his wealth on champagne and developing the spa town of Calistoga in the Wine Country (see page 209). His investment in the Mexican Revolution proved his undoing, however, and he ended his days as a penniless alcoholic in a boarding house near San Diego.

Rags to riches to rags, Sam Brannan

AMBROSE BIERCE (1842–1914?) By the 1880s, his sharp wit and cynicism had made Ohio-born Ambrose Bierce the city's most frequently read newspaper columnist. "Bitter Bierce" was given a job on the *San Francisco Examiner*, but was later posted to Washington DC, and disappeared during a trip to Mexico. He became legendary for his apparent contempt for San Francisco, which he famously described as a "moral penal colony."

THE BIG FOUR Charles Crocker (1822–1888), Mark Hopkins (1813–1878), Collis P. Huntington (1821–1900), and Leland Stanford (1824–1893) joined forces to channel their money (and dubiously obtained federal grants) into the construction of the transcontinental railroad. Its completion in 1869 gave the Big Four a monopoly on transportation routes in California, through which they acquired unprecedented political power and amassed monumental wealth—some of which created the first Nob Hill mansions.

The columnist they loved to hate, Ambrose Bierce

THE BONANZA KINGS The discovery of Nevada's silver-rich Comstock Lode made millionaires of James G. Fair (1831–1894), James C. Flood (1826–1898), John Mackay (1831–1902) and William S. O'Brien (1826–1878). All Irish-born settlers, they became known as the Bonanza Kings and earned $500,000 a month each at the height of the boom. Flood and O'Brien's mining investments began with tips from the stockbrokers who patronized their saloon; Flood built the only Nob Hill mansion to survive the 1906 fire (now the Pacific Union Club, see page 131). The Fairmont Hotel nearby was built by Fair's daughter and named in his honor.

Fires and earthquakes were a regular feature of San Francisco life in the 1850s and 1860s, and hardy settlers learned to take such things in their stride. The geological calm enjoyed through subsequent decades ended suddenly on April 18, 1906, when an earthquake (and subsequent fire) reduced the city to ruins.

THE QUAKE At 5.12am, the infamous 1906 earthquake, measuring 8.3 on the modern Richter scale and lasting approximately a minute, rumbled along a section of the San Andreas Fault in Northern California. San Francisco was some distance from the epicenter, but the city (by now the ninth largest in the US with nearly 400,000 inhabitants) was the only major seat of population in the vicinity of the quake and suffered the most obvious damage.

The worst-affected areas were the Financial District and North Beach, where many buildings collapsed, as did the recently completed City Hall. Streets and cable-car lines buckled, chimneys fell through roofs, many buildings were left without their exterior walls and windows and crockery shattered throughout the city.

THE FIRE Although San Franciscans rose (or were thrown) from their beds in a state of shock, the damage the actual quake inflicted on the city was comparatively minor. Beneath the city's streets, however, many of the gas mains that carried power for lighting and heating ruptured, as did the water mains. As leaking gas (and electrical short circuits) caused fires to break out, there was insufficient water to contain them. Small fires burned uncontrolled and quickly turned into larger blazes. In a few hours, a single gigantic inferno was creeping steadily westward across the unprotected city.

THE FLAMES SPREAD As the blaze neared their homes, thousands of San Franciscans gathered their possessions and fled to the open spaces of Golden Gate Park or the Presidio, or escaped on ferries across the bay.

Without official sanction, the Presidio's commander declared martial law and ordered his troops into the city. In the ensuing confusion, soldiers shot or bayoneted innocent citizens who were assumed to be looting as they sought to retrieve their possessions from the gutted buildings.

After the earthquake—the three-day fire

❑ The 1906 earthquake revealed the corruption behind San Francisco's new City Hall, erected over a 20-year period at a cost of $8 million. By using cheap materials, construction costs had been cut on what should have been the emergent city's crowning glory, and the remaining funds had been diverted to private pockets. ❑

Scene of destruction in the Financial District

Efforts to stop the fire with dynamite failed dismally, and succeeded only in creating new fires and destroying some of the city's finest homes. By Friday, two days after the earthquake, the flames had left North Beach and Chinatown in ruins and were threatening to cross the wide Van Ness Avenue and engulf the Western Addition.

It was feared that the fire would sweep through the entire city, stopping only when it reached the ocean. Eventually, though, exhausted firefighters fought back the flames, and late on Saturday the fire burned itself out.

THE AFTERMATH The toll from the earthquake and fire was (officially) 300 dead and 250,000 homeless. The fire had razed 28,000 buildings on 490 city blocks across an area of almost 3,000 acres (1,215ha), and destroyed all of the city's public records. The problem of housing and feeding refugees became paramount, but a well-organized relief effort, bolstered by $100 million in donated supplies from all over the US, eased the difficulties. As life returned to normal, the most energetic San Franciscans set about rebuilding the city in the spirit of the phoenix depicted on the city's crest—a symbol of its recovery from earlier fires.

San Francisco quickly emerged from the devastation of the 1906 earthquake and fire and was ready to enjoy the booming 1920s as much as any other American city. However, the tumultuous and unpredictable events of the 1930s and 1940s were to have a longer-lasting influence on San Francisco's future.

A NEW CITY With 60,000 construction workers in the city, the rapid rebuilding of San Francisco echoed the lightning-paced development of the Gold Rush era. By 1909, 20,000 new buildings had arisen, many of them incorporating the new, earthquake-resistant steel frames. At the same time, a much-publicized court case attempted to rid the city of the corruption that had tainted its administration in past decades. The magnificent Civic Center complex and the new City Hall were completed, symbols of the city's hopes and aspirations for the future.

THE EXPO OF 1915 Ostensibly to celebrate the opening of the Panama Canal, the 10-month Panama–Pacific Exposition opened in 1915 with the intention of showing the world that San Francisco had fully recovered from the 1906 catastrophe. Across a 600-acre (243ha) site (now the Marina District), the best architects of the day erected beautiful beaux-arts pavilions to house exhibits ranging from classical art to the latest technology. (Although the buildings were intended as temporary, the Palace of Fine Arts survives today.) With exhibits from 35 countries, the Expo was a roaring success.

THE DEPRESSION San Francisco boomed in the nationally prosperous 1920s and reaped further benefits from California's growing agricultural and industrial economy, stimulated by World War I in Europe and improved by the discovery of oil at several sites. However, the rise of Los Angeles as California's most economically important city dented the optimism that followed the

Longshoremen's strike, 1934

rebuilding, while the Depression of the 1930s ended it almost completely.

GENERAL STRIKE In 1934, a three-month strike over pay and conditions by the city's International Longshoremen's Association paralyzed the city's economy. On July 5, a date remembered as "Bloody Thursday," police (supported by hired thugs) attempted to end the strike by firing tear gas into picket lines and, in the ensuing battles, shot dead two strikers. Widespread anger at the police action resulted in 150,000 city workers heeding the call for a general strike. As San Francisco ground to a halt, the Governor put the city under martial law and sent the National Guard into its streets. Although the general strike lasted just four days, it ended with the longshoremen winning many of their demands.

THE BAY BRIDGES The major event of the 1930s was the planning and

Opposite, top: The Palace of Fine Arts
Above: City Hall interior

completion of two enormous engineering projects: the Bay and Golden Gate bridges. These links to the East Bay and to Marin County gave a massive boost to the city's economy.

WORLD WAR II To celebrate the completion of the bridges, the Golden Gate International Exposition opened in 1939, hoping to repeat the success of the 1915 Expo. The outbreak of war in Europe provided a chilling backdrop, however, and the Japanese attack on Pearl Harbor in 1941 (which led to the internment of the city's Japanese-Americans) brought huge changes. The city gained a massive shipbuilding industry and a booming workforce, and became the embarkation point for over a million troops destined for war in the Pacific.

Golden Gate Bridge

San Francisco emerged from World War II with a strengthened economy and greatly increased population. In the next decades the city became a social laboratory, where many of the trends that would first shock, and then shape, the modern US saw the light of day.

BIRTH OF THE BEATS With its long history of nonconformity, San Francisco provided an obvious refuge for those who found themselves at odds with the materialist values of postwar America. By the mid-1950s, a ramshackle group of artists, writers and existentialists was colonizing the cafés of North Beach. In 1957, the publicity surrounding Allen Ginsberg's narrative poem *Howl* alerted the country to the city's new bohemians. Although the original protagonists moved on, the neighborhood was quickly awash with the sandals and bad poetry of the nation's first mass movement of disaffected youth.

❑ It was San Francisco newspaper columnist Herb Caen, who, mindful of the recently launched Sputnik satellite, coined the term "beatniks" as a derisory title for the Beats. ❑

Berkeley students rally against President Nixon in the 1960s, led by Mario Savio

CAMPUS REVOLTS In 1964, Berkeley students instigated the first of the campus protests which, a few years later, would escalate into massive, nationwide anti-Vietnam War revolts. Fronted by the besuited Mario Savio, the Free Speech Movement (FSM) arranged student sit-ins and rallies in response to the university authorities' efforts to ban the distribution of political material on campus. The occupation of an administrative building resulted in the largest mass arrest in California's history as 750 students, offering passive resistance, were dragged out by police.

Student demands for a role in the running of the university were eventually met, and the FSM's success encouraged nationwide student activism, which became increasingly confrontational and violent. In Berkeley in 1968, several days of rioting followed the blocking of a student march. At another protest a year later, a bystander was killed and

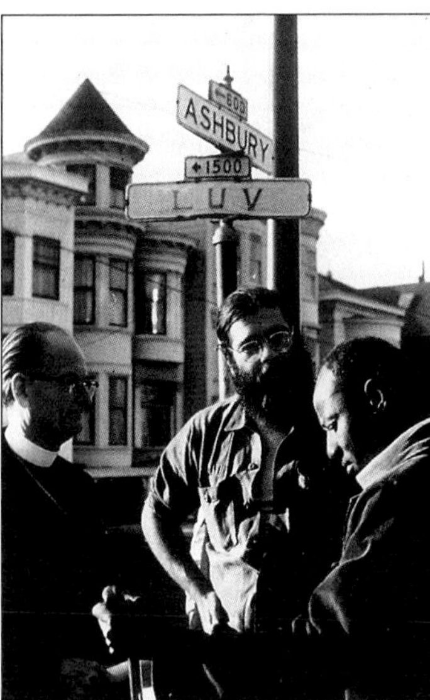

Luv conquers all on Haight Street

another blinded as the National Guard fired tear gas and buckshot.

BLACK PANTHERS Dressed in black jackets, black berets and dark glasses, and brandishing automatic weapons, the ultramilitant Black Panthers formed in Oakland in 1966, advocating self-determination for black Americans. As their message spread across the country, the FBI described them as "the gravest threat to domestic peace," but in reality the Black Panthers were fewer in number than their publicity suggested. Following shoot-outs with police and the imprisonment of many of their members, the Oakland Panthers grew less militant. They began concentrating on local community projects and canvasing black support for the Democratic Party.

HIPPIES By far the largest reaction against conventional social attitudes in the 1960s was provided by the hippies (see pages 110–111). What quickly spread around the world in a mass of tie-dyed T-shirts, rock music and burning incense, however, began with a disparate group of ex-Beats and others living in the low-rent, ethnically mixed Haight-Ashbury.

❑ One way the Black Panthers raised money for guns was by buying 20¢ copies of Mao Tse-tung's *Little Red Book* in Chinatown and reselling them to students for a dollar each. ❑

GAY LIBERATION Although San Francisco has a gay history stretching back to the Gold Rush, the city's gays had remained very much in the closet until the changing sexual attitudes of the 1960s and the 1970s' gay settlement of the Castro District. The emergence of openly gay city politicians was a national first and helped put San Francisco at the forefront of worldwide gay and lesbian consciousness. See also pages 70–71.

Berkeley now: less confrontational

▶▶▶ REGION HIGHLIGHTS

Alcatraz *pages 55–56*

Asian Art Museum *pages 122–123*

Berkeley *pages 58–61*

Chinatown *pages 72–75*

Golden Gate Bridge *page 98*

Golden Gate Park *pages 100–103*

Grace Cathedral *page 105*

M. H. de Young Memorial Museum *pages 118–121*

Nob Hill *pages 130–131*

North Beach *pages 134–137*

Oakland Museum of California *pages 142–143*

Palace of Fine Arts *page 152*

San Francisco Museum of Modern Art *pages 160–161*

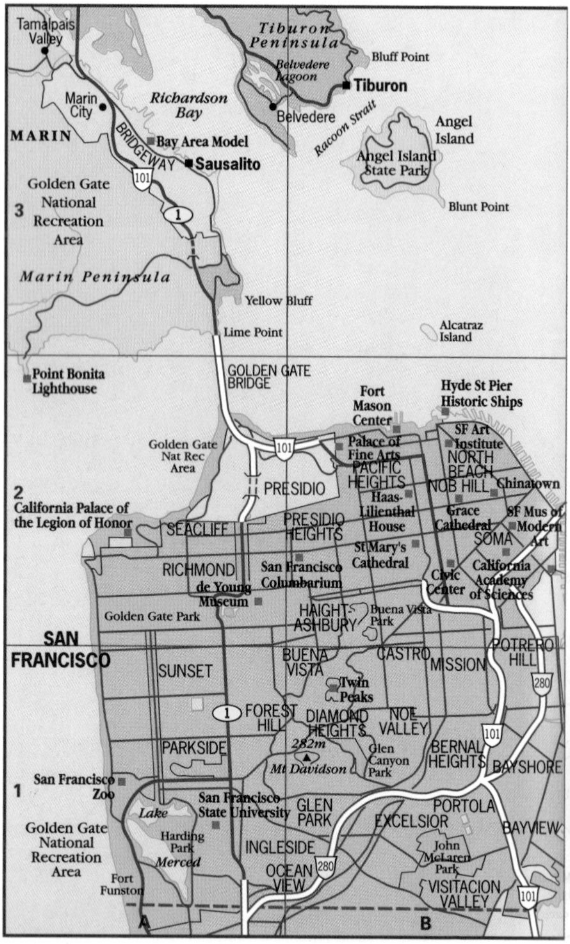

A nighttime view from Twin Peaks—at slightly over 900ft (274m) the highest point in San Francisco—across the city and bay to Oakland

Area Overview

Compact and well suited to walking, San Francisco occupies the tip of a peninsula that juts northward between San Francisco Bay and the Pacific Ocean. Splitting into a mosaic of clearly defined neighborhoods, the city's streets spread across hills and valleys and give spectacular views—of the bay or the city's skyline—from almost every corner.

FINANCIAL DISTRICT On the city's eastern side, the skyscrapers of the Financial District leave no doubt that this is where the city conducts its business. Here, the instantly recognizable Transamerica Pyramid looms above streets bustling with smartly suited office workers, and banks dating back to the Gold Rush line streets which once faced the busiest waterfront in the western US.

CHINATOWN AND NORTH BEACH Pushing hard against the Financial District, **Chinatown** may have fewer Chinese residents than it once did, but it is one of the largest Asian communities outside Asia, with 75,000 people crammed into its claustrophobic confines. Temples, herb stores and

fortune-cookie factories (see page 102) all play their part in Chinatown life, but most San Franciscans come here for the restaurants, which are, for the most part, inexpensive and excellent.

The rice and noodle shops of Chinatown are just a few steps away from the fresh pasta dishes served in the distinctly Italian-flavored **North Beach**. Besides its highly rated restaurants, North Beach has many of the cafés which helped make coffee drinking a favorite San Francisco pastime.

North Beach was once synonymous not only with Italians but also with struggling writers and artists. Many of the seminal figures of the Beat generation occupied low-rent apartments here or along the streets leading steeply upward to Coit Tower, which sits at the top of **Telegraph Hill**, now surrounded by expensive bay-view homes.

On the other side of North Beach, **Russian Hill** drew its share of literary notables during the 1920s. It is of greater contemporary renown for Lombard Street, hailed as the crookedest (and probably the most photogenic) of San Francisco's many crooked streets.

NOB HILL AND BEYOND For property owners, Telegraph and Russian are still both highly desirable hills, but it was **Nob Hill**, rising from the cacophonous streets of Chinatown, which was unrivaled as the city's most prestigious residential address in the late 19th century. Nob Hill's high social standing began when mining and railroad barons (whose shady business dealings made them millionaires and determined the course of California history) chose it as the site of their million-dollar homes.

All but one of the mansions perished in the calamitous 1906 earthquake and fire, and on their sites arose several fine hotels, the majestic Grace Cathedral and high-rise apartments with the best views in the city.

Above: Close-up of Chinatown, showing a detail from the Tien Hou (Tin How) Temple
Below: Lining the broad avenues of Pacific Heights are many eye-catching Victorian architectural curiosities

BUS ROUTES
The A–Z gazetteer gives the most useful bus routes to the location described, usually on the assumption that you are traveling from the Union Square area. As many routes criss-cross the city, however, there is usually a good choice of alternative routes which will drop you within a few minutes' walk of your destination. Inside the back cover of this book, a map shows the main routes; local telephone books also carry a bus map.

Leafy and literary, Russian Hill is also well stocked with elegant 19th-century homes

Today, the priciest homes and most coveted addresses are in **Pacific Heights**, a mixture of low-rise dwellings and elegant and expansive Victorian homes with "gingerbread" trim northwest of Nob Hill. Packed with antiques, ornaments and chic European designer fashions, the shops of Union and Fillmore streets reveal the consuming passions of Pacific Heights' wealthy residents.

NORTHERN WATERFRONT North of Pacific Heights, the city's northern waterfront holds the museum-packed **Fort Mason Center** and, to the east, **Fisherman's Wharf**. The one place in San Francisco where tourists outnumber locals, Fisherman's Wharf is the city's tackiest and most commercial area. Nevertheless, it can be fun, with some genuine history dispersed among the souvenir shops and overpriced seafood stands. Fisherman's Wharf is also the departure point for ferries to **Alcatraz Island**, the notorious former prison easily visible in the bay.

A mile or two west of Fisherman's Wharf, the engineering and esthetic perfection of **Golden Gate Bridge** links the city to the Marin Headlands, the strikingly undeveloped hills of Marin County. Near the bridge, on the city side, are the similarly wild woodlands of the **Presidio**, a former army base now increasingly a place of bike and walking trails, renovated historic builidngs and stunning overlooks.

SOUTH OF MARKET Socially as well as geographically, **Market Street** has long been a dividing line, keeping the well-to-do neighborhoods on its northern side apart from what until the late 1980s was industrial flatlands to the south, an area known as **SoMa** (short for South of Market). From the late 1980s, many of SoMa's unused warehouses

SAN FRANCISCO'S STEEPEST STREET
You might frequently find yourself thinking that San Francisco's steepest street must be the one you are running short of breath trying to climb. You will be correct only if you are laboring up the section of Filbert Street between Hyde and Leavenworth streets, in Russian Hill, which rises at an angle of 31.5 degrees.

DANGEROUS NEIGHBORHOODS
Compared to many major US cities, San Francisco is remarkably safe. Only four small areas might be considered dangerous. One is the Tenderloin (see page 176), between Union Square and the Civic Center, where most of the city's poor and homeless congregate. Another is the Western Addition (see page 179), between Haight-Ashbury and Japantown, where side streets are best avoided after dark. Parts of the Mission District and Sixth Street in SoMa are also best visited by day (see pages 124–125).

were converted to apartments and nightclubs, and in the late 1990s became the center of the dot0com boom. Yerba Buena Center—a gleaming modern complex of museums (including the stunningly designed Museum of Modern Art) and performance art venues laid out between green walkways and waterfalls—has cemented the district's rapid improvement.

West of SoMa, the **Mission District** takes its name from a mission founded here by the Spanish in 1776. The mission survives, but the area's ambience is determined not by history—though several side streets hold impressive examples of Victorian residential architecture—but by a sizeable Latino population, responsible for Latin-American bakeries and restaurants and the vivid murals that adorn many of the buildings. Low rents and social vitality made the Mission District attractive to a bohemian fringe of artists, writers and political activists; proximity to SoMa attracted dot-com workers through the late 1990s. Continuing west, the **Castro District** is probably the world's most famous gay neighborhood, with its businesses predominantly gay-run and its balconies draped with rainbow flags of gay solidarity.

HAIGHT-ASHBURY Booming gay culture may have been the big news of 1970s San Francisco, but a decade earlier it had been hippies that made the headlines, and it was in Haight-Ashbury, north of the Castro in the geographical heart of the city, that the flowers, beads and long hair reached their zenith. Reminders of the psychedelic days are easily found, as are Victorian homes tidily restored to become bed-and-breakfast inns. Meanwhile, vintage clothes shops and critically acclaimed restaurants are bringing a buzz to the neighborhood's Haight Street.

GOLDEN GATE PARK Between Haight-Ashbury and the ocean, the great green swath of Golden Gate Park stakes its claim to be one of the greatest—and certainly one of

Seen from the Marin Headlands, San Francisco looms up behind the cables of the Golden Gate Bridge

A short sail from Tiburon's harbor, Angel Island served as a fort, military hospital and immigration processing center, before becoming a state park

the biggest—urban parks anywhere in the world. Encompassing botanical gardens, statuary, a boating lake, a golf course, a herd of buffalo and a full-sized polo field, the park also finds room for one of the city's major art collections: the de Young Museum, which re-opened in 2005 with much expanded galleries.

THE BAY AREA Visitors quickly become aware that there is much more to San Francisco than the city on the tip of the peninsula. What locals call the Bay Area also includes the communities around San Francisco Bay, separated from the city by a bridge or a ferry ride.

On the bay's east side, Berkeley holds the vast University of California campus, which sprawls across the town and up the neighboring hillsides. Several campus museums and the campus itself justify a look, as do the plethora of bookshops and cafés, the haunts of lifelong Berkeley radicals and fresh-faced students alike.

Just south of Berkeley, Oakland became infamous during the late 1960s as the base of the ultramilitant Black Panthers. While poverty-stricken areas remain, much of Oakland has blossomed into a likeable, friendly town where the tacky shops of the newly developed waterfront do little to detract from the appeal of Oakland's Chinatown or the outstanding art and historical collections of the Oakland Museum.

SAUSALITO AND TIBURON On the north side of the bay, Sausalito climbs vertically from the waterside into tree-covered hills, where many expensive homes and a few expensive hotels offer a bucolic setting and fabulous views over the bay. Sausalito makes a great day-trip destination, but on busy days the village of Tiburon, also on the north side of the bay, can be a more attractive proposition. Beyond the quaint shops close to the dockside, much of Tiburon is a picture of pastoral tranquility.

SAN FRANCISCO'S TWINS

Many seasoned travelers share the opinion that there is little to rival San Francisco anywhere else in the world. Nonetheless, America's most liberal and beautiful metropolis is officially twinned with 15 cities: Abidjan, Assisi, Caracas, Cork, Esteli, Haifa, Ho Chi Minh City, Manila, Osaka, Paris, Seoul, Shanghai, Sydney, Thessaloniki and Taipei.

ITINERARY ASSUMPTIONS
These itineraries assume you are staying close to Union Square. Do not despair if this is not the case, however, as it is easy to travel between San Francisco's neighborhoods, either by bus or—less often—by cable car. If museums are your main interest, check that the ones you intend visiting are open on that particular day.

San Francisco offers great rewards for those who make judicious use of their time. Even with just a weekend to spare, a surprising amount of this varied but modestly sized city can be enjoyed, provided you plan ahead. With a full week available, there is no excuse for leaving without having every major sight and neighborhood—and some minor ones—under your belt. The itineraries below aim to provide a representative impression of San Francisco and its environs, but can easily be adapted to suit individual tastes.

Weekend itinerary

Day one On foot, explore the landmark buildings of the Financial District (see pages 86–88) and continue through the streets and alleyways of Chinatown (see pages 72–75), choosing one of its many restaurants for lunch. In the afternoon, head north by bus (or cable car through Russian Hill, see page 157) to spend an hour at Fisherman's Wharf (see pages 90–93). Continue into North Beach (see pages 134–137) to sample Italian cafés, the offbeat shops of Grant Avenue and the neighborhood's many dinner options.

Day two Take a bus to Haight-Ashbury (see pages 106–109) to discover the area's Victorian architecture and the funky shops and restaurants along Haight Street. Have lunch on Haight Street, or carry provisions for a picnic by Stow Lake in nearby Golden Gate Park (see pages 100–103). Spend the rest of the afternoon in the park, exploring the Japanese Tea Garden, the Rhododendron Dell, or the Strybing Arboretum and Botanical Gardens. Alternatively, allow several hours to explore the architecturally-striking galleries of the de Young Museum (see pages 118–121).

One-week itinerary

Day one Take a bus or cable car to Fisherman's Wharf (see pages 90–93) and catch an early ferry to Alcatraz (see pages 55–56). Return from Alcatraz to explore Fisherman's Wharf and indulge in an overpriced snack from a seafood stand. Continue to the area's less commercial sights such as Hyde Street Pier Historic Ships (see pages 112–113) and the National Maritime Museum (see page 128). If time permits, continue from Fisherman's Wharf to the museums of the Fort Mason Center (see page 96).

Day two In the morning, explore Union Square (see page 178), Maiden Lane (see page 116) and the architecture of the Financial District (see pages 86–88). Stroll around Jackson Square (see page 113) before going to Chinatown (see pages 72–75) for lunch. Spend the afternoon weaving around Chinatown's streets and alleyways.

Day three Walk or take a bus to North Beach (see pages 134–137) and explore the shops and cafés of the Italian community

The bright lights of the Mission District

and the haunts of the 1950s Beat poets. After lunch, climb Filbert Street to the top of Telegraph Hill for Coit Tower and its murals (see pages 174–175). From the tower walk a short way down the Filbert or Greenwich steps. Leave Telegraph Hill and take a bus from Washington Square to Pacific Heights (see pages 148–150) and the fashionable shops and restaurants of Union Street.

Day four In the morning, travel into SoMa (see pages 166–169) and explore the museums and architecture of the Yerba Buena Gardens complex. Have lunch and continue west by bus into the Mission District for Mission Dolores (see pages 124–125). If time allows, inspect some of the Mission District's murals. Take BART (the Bay Area Rapid Transit, see page 252) back to the city center.

Day five Travel by BART to Berkeley (see pages 58–61). Tour the university campus and its museums and have lunch on Telegraph Avenue or in one of the gourmet eateries of Shattuck Avenue. Take BART to Lake Merritt for the Oakland Museum of California (see pages 142–143). Depending on time, return to San Francisco either by BART or by ferry from Oakland's Jack London Square. For a less active day five, spend the day in Sausalito or Tiburon (see page 163 or 176).

Day six Same as day two of the weekend itinerary. Find time on your way to Haight-Ashbury to take a souvenir photo of Alamo Square's "painted ladies" (see page 54).

Day seven In the morning, stroll around the Civic Center (see pages 78–79). After lunch, visit the Cable Car Museum (see page 63) and take a cable car along California Street to Nob Hill (see pages 130–131). On Nob Hill, visit Grace Cathedral (see page 105) and relax over afternoon tea at the Renaissance Stanford Court Hotel.

SAN FRANCISCO BY CAR

San Francisco is not ideally seen by car, but if you are traveling beyond the city and have only a short time, you might spend a day following the blue and white seagull signs which mark the 49-mile (79km) Scenic Drive. This takes in all the city's major areas and many of its points of interest. A map of the drive is available free from most hotels and tourist information offices.

With countless hills and water on three sides, fabulous views are common in San Francisco. Whether a sweeping panorama of the Golden Gate or a postcard-perfect vista across the city's skyline, memorable views are often discovered by doing nothing more arduous than walking to the end of the street.

SAN FRANCISCO'S FOG
Visitors underestimate the view-spoiling capabilities of San Francisco's infamous fog at their peril. It may be bright and sunny where you stand, but the expansive panorama you are hoping to enjoy can still be obliterated by fog creeping stealthily through the city's valleys. However, fog is usually an early-morning phenomenon, which clears as the sun burns it off. Sometimes, though, the fog returns in the afternoon or early evening.

The view over San Francisco from Twin Peaks (top) and (below) from the Bank of America

Views from buildings The views from the summit of Coit Tower, at the top of Telegraph Hill, are not very different from those at its base, but both are worth savoring (see pages 174–175). To the north lies Fisherman's Wharf and San Francisco Bay, to the south is Chinatown and the Financial District, and immediately east is a steep drop to the Embarcadero and the East Bay.

The first-class hotels of Nob Hill (see pages 130–131) make the most of their settings. Both the Fairmont and the Mark Hopkins have cocktail lounges with stunning outlooks, and the glass-sided elevator that climbs the outside of the Fairmont to reach the 24th-floor Crown Room will test the mettle of anyone who claims they never suffer from vertigo. Some, but not all, rooms have views. Or opt for a scenic if expensive stay at the Financial District's Mandarin Oriental, where you can enjoy a vista that stretches beyond North Beach while luxuriating in your bath. For a view above SoMa, try the 39th floor cocktail lounge of the Marriott Hotel, or check-in to the Presidential Suite to gaze across Yerba Buena Gardens.

Floating views A sightseeing trip on San Francisco Bay (see page 89) takes in some of the city's major landmarks—including Coit Tower and the Golden Gate and Bay bridges—from an unusual sea-level angle. The ferry to Oakland passes under the Bay Bridge, and the return leg puts San Francisco's high-rise Financial District into sharp relief.

Palm trees add to the view along this Mission District street, which climbs into the neighborhood known as Bernal Heights

Street views Do not forget to look around whenever you climb one of the city's countless steep streets. The view to the rear will often take away what is left of your breath. Good areas for street views include Russian Hill (see page 157), Pacific Heights (where Lafayette and Alta Plaza parks are specifically designed to make the most of their high perches; see pages 148–150) and Potrero Hill (see page 153).

Juxtapositions As its brigades of shutter-clicking visitors attest, the sight of Alamo Square's "painted ladies" (a row of six well-preserved Victorian homes; see page 54) set against the modern towers of the Financial District in the background makes an excellent photograph, spanning almost a century of the city's architecture. Similar camera-worthy juxtapositions are found around Mission Dolores Park (see page 104), Haight-Ashbury (see pages 106–109) and SoMa (see pages 166–169).

Coastal views The Golden Gate National Recreation Area (see page 99) overlooks the Pacific and encompasses much of San Francisco's remarkably wild coastline. Walk the coastal trail and you will find the waters of the Golden Gate lapping at tiny beaches at the foot of treacherous hillsides, and enjoy the uncommonly glimpsed west side of Golden Gate Bridge from a point where the whole city is almost hidden behind hills.

The California Palace of the Legion of Honor (see pages 67–68) is memorable not only for its art, but also for the stirring ocean views from its Point Lobos Headland site.

Views from afar Some of the best views of the city can only be had by leaving it. From the UCB campus in Berkeley (see pages 60–61), the city sprouts evocatively from the peninsula, with the Golden Gate Bridge clearly visible. The Bridge offers some fine approach views, and the city is at its most photogenic when seen through the Bridge cables from the Marin County side of the Golden Gate National Recreation Area.

AERIAL VIEWS

When the outlook from terra firma fails to please, try looking down on San Francisco from an aerial tour (usually costing $80–$150 per person) operated by one of the following companies: San Francisco Helicopter Inc. (tel: 800/400-2404 or 650/635-4500; www.sfhelicopter.com); San Francisco Seaplane Tours (tel: 1-888/SEAPLANE; www.seaplane.com).

THE VIEW FROM ALCATRAZ

One of the best overall views of San Francisco is from the former prison on Alcatraz Island (see pages 55–56). While stepping ashore and enjoying the spectacle, consider for a moment the mental agony such a vision brought to the inmates who could often see (and hear) the city—so near and yet so far—from their cell blocks.

THE BIRDMAN OF ALCATRAZ
Murderer Robert Stroud was imprisoned in 1909 at the age of 19. In Leavenworth Jail, Kansas, he began keeping and studying birds and wrote the highly regarded Stroud's *Digest of the Diseases of Birds*. Not until 1942 was "the Bird Doctor of Leavenworth"—as Stroud was known—transferred to Alcatraz, and not until 1955 did a biography of Stroud first coin the phrase "Birdman of Alcatraz." This gave Stroud a lasting nickname and provided the title for the 1962 film about Stroud, which starred Burt Lancaster.

► African American Art & Cultural Complex *IBCE4*

762 Fulton Street (tel: 415/922-2049; www.aaacc.org)
Open Mon–Sat 12–5; exhibitions free
Bus: 24

Created through the union of several community cultural groups, and marked by a stunning mural depicting Louis Armstrong and Billie Holliday among others, on the building's east wall, the African American Art & Culture Complex provides a focal-point to the Fillmore Jazz Preservation District (see page 179). Diverse events are staged throughout the year at the complex's Buriel Clay Memorial Theater, while the Sargent Johnson Gallery hosts exhibitions by African American artists, predominantly from the Bay Area, and other changing shows drawing on African American themes.

►► Alamo Square *IBCE4*

Bordered by Fulton and Hayes, and Scott and Steiner streets
Bus: 21

When property developer Matthew Kavanaugh raised a row of pretty wooden homes overlooking Alamo Square in the mid-1890s, he could not have suspected that a century later they would be nicknamed "the painted ladies" and rank among the most photographed houses in San Francisco.

One of the city's most memorable and most widely reproduced images is the sight of the elaborate Victorian carpentry contrasting with the sleek towers of the Financial District in the distance. For the best camera angle, you will need to stand in Alamo Square itself, a compact patch of tree-fringed greenery located on a steep slope.

The classic shot of Alamo Square's Victorians backed by the towers of the Financial District

ALCATRAZ ATTITUDE
"Maximum security, minimum privilege"—the ethos of Alcatraz when it was chosen as a federal prison in 1934.

The island of Alcatraz north of Fisherman's Wharf, is easily sighted from any high vantage point in the city

▶▶▶ Alcatraz *IBCF6*

Ferry: from Fisherman's Wharf

The island of Alcatraz held what became the country's most feared place of incarceration from 1934, when the US government responded to fears of a national crime wave by creating a supposedly escape-proof prison with the harshest regime the law would allow.

The island's forbidding steep sides (on all but the sheltered eastern side where the small harbor that once landed supplies and prisoners now brings tourists) were landscaped by the army in the 1850s, to build an impenetrable fortress and deter enemy incursions into San Francisco Bay. For a time, a garrison of 200 soldiers was stationed on "the rock" (as the island became known) with enough food, water and equipment to withstand a four-month siege. As no attack was forthcoming, the island became a military prison and also housed, controversially, a group of Native Americans of the Hopi nation arrested for resisting attempts to forcibly remove their children to government-approved boarding schools where they would be "civilized."

Ironically, the running of the military jail became based on the concept of rehabilitation and trust; the reverse of the ethos that the government adopted when it took over Alcatraz. The island prison then became a top-security, strict-discipline penitentiary for "incorrigible" criminals—those deemed beyond salvation and considered too dangerous to be held in conventional jails.

At Alcatraz, even work was regarded as a privilege and had to be earned by a prisoner through good behavior. There was a guard for every three inmates, and any prisoners who did escape from their cells were faced with the prospect of crossing the freezing, swiftly-moving waters of the bay (regarded as unswimmable) to freedom. Already enduring the toughest prison regime in the US, the inmates of Alcatraz were further tormented by being able to see the bright lights of the city and hear its sounds drifting across the bay into their miserable cells.

Although stays at Alcatraz averaged nearly ten years, inmates were denied access to newspapers, radios and TVs, and 80 percent of them never received a visitor. Only 36 of the 1,576 convicts imprisoned here ever attempted to escape. All but five were recaptured within an hour; of the five nothing has been heard although their exploit did become the subject of the 1979 film, *Escape From Alcatraz.*

TOURS OF ALCATRAZ
Tours of Alcatraz (moderate) begin with a ferry from Pier 41 (at Fisherman's Wharf) with the Blue & Gold Fleet (tel: 415/705-5555; www.blueandgoldfleet.com/akcatraz). The fare includes the crossing, entry to the island's public areas and loan of an audiocassette guided tour and a cassette player. Departures are at 30-minute intervals throughout the day, and tickets go on sale at 8am. During the summer, it is advisable to reserve tickets well in advance.

Alcatraz tours allow visitors to view the former prison's canteen and recreation area, but the most powerful impression of the prison regime's harshness is provided by former cell blocks such as this

ALCATRAZ BY MISTAKE
Spanish navigators sailed around San Francisco Bay in 1775, naming its features and christening one of its islands, *Isla de los Alcatraces*, or Isle of Pelicans. This, however, is believed not to have been the island that bears that name today but to have applied to what subsequently became known as Yerba Buena Island. The discrepancy results from the work of Captain F. W. Beechey, a British seafarer who created the first detailed map of the bay in 1826, using many of the extant Spanish names.

Such conditions helped trigger what became known as the Battle of Alcatraz in 1946, when a group of prisoners overpowered their guards and seized their weapons. The resulting two-day stand-off saw the arrival of five coast guard ships and two naval destroyer escorts. Two guards and three prisoners lost their lives during the conflict, while two of the ringleaders were subsequently executed.

The high costs and logistical problems of running an island prison, and widespread opposition to the severity of the regime, not least because one of the last to be sent to the rock was a 19-year-old guilty of a relatively minor offence, led to the prison's closure in 1963. A year later, a group of Native Americans briefly occupied and claimed the island for the Lakota–Sioux nation under an 1868 treaty granting them rights to buy unused government land for a nominal fee.

Another Native American occupation of the island began in 1969 and would last for two years. Significantly, the second occupation—which began with 89 men, women and children, included the creation of a school, a clinic, an elected council and the broadcasts of Radio Free Alcatraz—was carried out on behalf of "Indians of all nations." As such, it was among the first direct actions bringing together native people of different tribal alliances. The occupation focused attention on the plight of Native Americans throughout the US, and inspired further high profile actions during the 1970s, notably those at Wounded Knee, South Dakota, and an occupation of the Bureau of Indian Affairs in Washington DC.

At Alcatraz, the occupation ended with heavily-armed FBI officers storming the island despite the fact that only 14 people remained there. Alcatraz became part of the Golden Gate National Recreation Area in 1972, opening its once tightly-guarded doors to the public the following year.

Most of the former prison, including the cellblock, mess hall with its tear-gas cylinders fixed to the ceiling, and prison hospital, can be seen, and there is a small museum and a short film. The audio-cassette tour (see panel, page 55), with commentary by former Alcatraz guards and inmates, is an excellent atmospheric accompaniment.

An essential link between the city and Oakland since 1936, the Bay Bridge was closed for a month after the 1989 Loma Prieta earthquake. Its reopening was a great relief to Bay Area residents

▶ Baker Beach *IFCB5*

Accessed from Lincoln Boulevard
Bus: 29
Fringed by rocky cliffs and stands of cypress and pine trees, mile-long (1.61km) Baker Beach makes an ideal break from the city's streets and draws anglers, joggers, picnickers and even a few nude sunbathers undeterred by the steady winds and lack of dependable sunshine (swimming here is dangerous). On weekends, history buffs arrive for talks about Battery Chamberlin, a defensive fortification begun in 1904, when a 95,000-lb (43,181kg) cannon was placed behind the beach, and continued during World War II with the digging of still-visible bunkers.

▶ Bay Bridge *IBCG5*

When completed in 1936, the Bay Bridge (formally known as the San Francisco–Oakland Bay Bridge) was the longest steel structure in the world. But it was to suffer a cruel twist of fate: Despite providing a vital transportation link across the bay, it was overshadowed by the more photogenic Golden Gate Bridge (see page 98), which opened in 1937. Nonetheless, the Bay Bridge—which, in 1933, consumed 18 percent of all the steel produced in the country—is fondly admired by the owners of the 250,000 vehicles which cross its 8-mile (13km) span each day and is one of the few bridges that include an underground tunnel as part of its length. The island of Yerba Buena provides a meeting place for the two above-water sections of the bridge.

In 1989, the month-long closure of the bridge following the Loma Prieta earthquake cost the city's businesses millions of dollars in lost revenue. In 1993, press reports suggested that the ability of the bridge to withstand another major quake was questionable. The simple answer was to build a new earthquake-resistant span alongside the extant one, but such a plan brought more controversy to the bridge, particularly so during 2004 when the only construction bid exceeded the legally set budget.

BAY BRIDGE: THE COST
$80 million was spent on the building of the Bay Bridge and 27 workers lost their lives during the three years of its construction. Once completed, one commentator described it as "the greatest expenditure of funds ever used for the construction of a single structure in the history of man."

The rustic entrance (above) to Chez Panisse. The acclaimed main courses are matched by similarly good desserts (below)...

▶▶ Berkeley *45D3*

BART: Berkeley

San Francisco may be regarded as America's most liberal city, but for left-wing local government, political activism and general anything-goes atmosphere, it is Berkeley which sets the pace. Sprawled across the hills of the East Bay, it is a 20-minute BART ride (see page 252) from the big city.

Berkeley owes much of its reputation for radicalism to its long-standing role as an academic center, the site of the University of California at Berkeley (UCB), the first of several campuses in the state's University of California system.

It was at UCB that the Free Speech Movement began in the early 1960s; that the earliest anti-Vietnam War protests were organized; and that Ronald Reagan (then Governor of California) ordered the National Guard to use tear gas against student demonstrators.

Bizarre as it may seem in retrospect, the origins of the university date back to the efforts of New England's Protestant churches to found a Christian educational center on the West Coast, partly inspired by a wish to contain the spread of Catholicism, introduced to native Californians by Spanish missionaries. A Christian college opened in the 1850s but, hindered by limited funds, it agreed to a takeover by the gold-rich state administration, and the University of California opened in 1873.

Arriving by BART brings you to Shattuck Avenue, the main thoroughfare of downtown Berkeley, offering little of interest beyond the expensive restaurants of the "Gourmet Ghetto" just north of Shattuck's intersection with Cedar Street. Among them, **Chez Panisse** (number 1517) is credited as being the birthplace of California cuisine.

...and by the attentive service and an ambience conducive to memorable eating

It is the university, just an easy walk east of the BART station, which brings most people to Berkeley, however. Drop by the Visitor Center, on the corner of University Avenue and Oxford Street, for a free campus map or to join a student-led walking tour (see panel).

The edge of the campus is directly across Oxford Street from the Visitor Center. The trees and winding footpaths which you will see initially, however, disguise the fact that the facility fills 100 acres (41ha) with confusingly arranged plazas, pathways, and often indistinguishable buildings. Designed to accommodate 5,000 students, UCB now has 30,000, and a map is essential to find your way around.

Several specific points of interest on the campus are detailed on pages 60 and 61, but be sure to take a stroll along **Sproul Plaza**, where many of the 1960s student actions originated. Its stalls still distribute information about ecological, social and political concerns.

Another site of dissent during the 1960s and 1970s was **Telegraph Avenue**, reached by crossing Bancroft Way. Lined by bookstores, restaurants, bakeries and cafés, Telegraph Avenue is a great place for feeling the pulse of present-day student life in Berkeley.

CAMPUS TOURS

Free, student-led walking tours of the campus depart from the Campanile on Saturday at 10am and Sunday at 1pm, and on weekdays at 10am from the Visitor Center, 101 University Hall (tel: 510/642-5215). Science buffs may prefer to concentrate on the Lawrence Berkeley Laboratory, where pioneering research has yielded nine Nobel prizes as well as paving the way for the atomic bomb. Free tours are conducted on Fridays from 10am to noon. Reservations must be made a week in advance (tel: 510/486-7292).

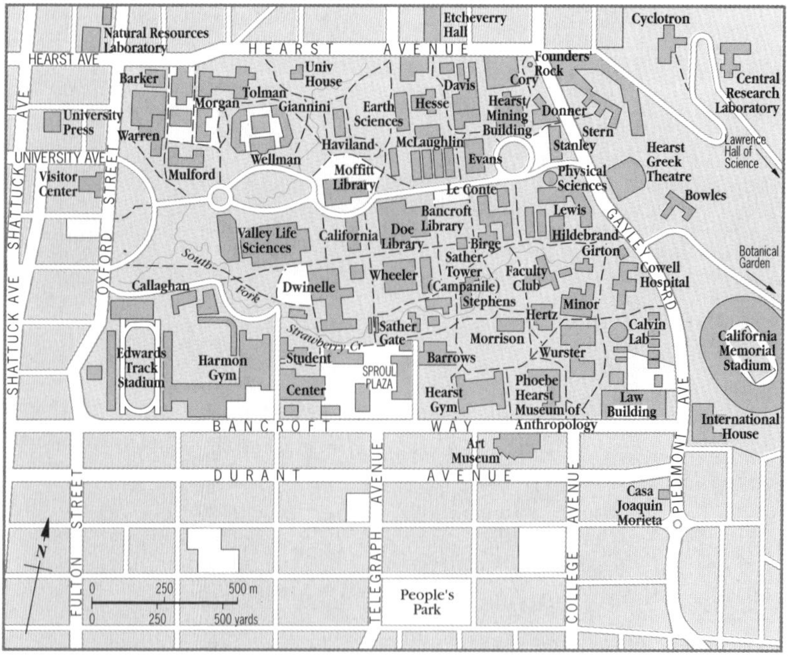

Finding your way around may be a headache, but the Berkeley campus has several buildings, historical collections and a number of museums that are well worth taking the trouble to locate, explore and enjoy.

SATHER GATE
Architect John Galen Howard gave the campus some of its finest features, including the outstanding Hearst Mining Building and Sather Gate. At the southern end of Sproul Plaza opposite Telegraph Avenue, Sather Gate has stood since 1911 and originally marked the main entrance to the campus. The gate has recently re-acquired some of its original decoration: a set of nude figures previously thought improper for a college campus.

The study of DNA, Lawrence Hall style

Gold and books You may not be able to borrow a book from the **Bancroft Library**, but you can study an 1849 gold nugget, allegedly the one that launched the Gold Rush, and admire the paintings of pioneer-era California on the walls. The library also mounts temporary exhibitions drawn from its 44 million books and manuscripts, which include a hoard of Mark Twain's notebooks, letters and publications. A few of these are likely to be on show.

The university's elegant **Doe Library** is next door, its **Map Room** holding everything cartographers dream about. Off the lobby is the entrance to the **Morrison Library**, where the temptation to grab a newspaper and fall into one of the inviting couches is hard to resist.

Anthropological troves Although it holds the largest stock of anthropological artifacts west of Chicago, the space-starved **Phoebe Hearst Museum of Anthropology** (tel: 415/643-3682; open: Wed–Sat 10–4.30, Sun 12–4.30; inexpensive) is only able to show off a comparative handful of its 4 million treasures at any one time. The holdings began with expeditions sponsored by Phoebe Hearst (wife of publisher George; mother of William Randolph) which, from 1899, enabled leading anthropologists to discover and plunder items of significance from sites of ancient civilization reaching from the Pacific to the Mediterranean.

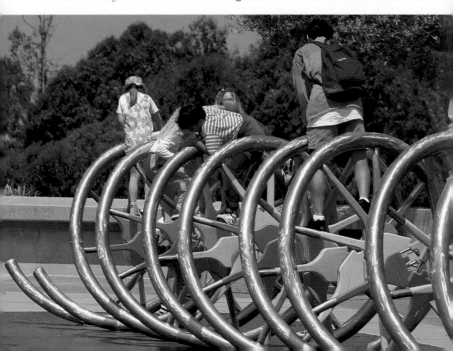

The changing exhibitions focus on diverse anthropological themes and may feature anything from Egyptian deities and Peruvian pots to carved Inuit ivories and Greek urns. The museum's permanent display documents the life of Ishi, a Native American believed to be the last surviving member of the Yahi tribe. Living at the museum (then in a different location) for five years until his death in 1916, Ishi passed on invaluable knowledge about his people's culture and lifestyle.

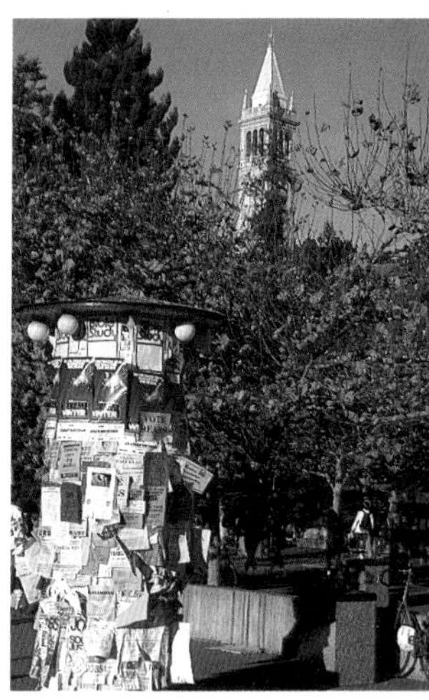

A noticeboard cluttered with student-aimed flyers on the campus at Berkeley; in the distance the Campanile soars aloft

Art and film Crossing Bancroft Way from the campus and entering the **Berkeley Art Museum** (tel: 510/642-0808; open: Wed–Sun 11–5, Thu until 7; inexpensive) is similar to stepping inside an immense concrete bunker. The museum, completed in 1970, has 11 galleries and an open-plan layout. This allows its exhibits, which include anything from ancient Japanese paintings to contemporary photography, to hang together with surprising cohesion.

The permanent collection includes 47 paintings by Hans Hoffman, a German-born abstract painter who settled in Berkeley and donated $250,000 (as well as the paintings) to get the museum off the ground. The building's basement houses the **Pacific Film Archive**, which frequently screens selections from its 6,000-strong collection of cinematic classics, oddities, obscurities and rarities.

Mining and beaux-arts The generally liberal air of the campus might be at odds with the eco-unfriendly world of petroleum engineering but students enrolled in such a course will well find themselves frequenting the exquisite beaux-arts Hearst Mining Building, designed by John Galen Howard (see panel, page 60) and opened in 1907. The building was raised to honor gold and silver mining baron George Hearst whose fortunes helped finance the university. George was husband to Phoebe (see facing page) and father to William Randolph, the newspaper magnate who became even richer than his parents.

Into the hills From outside the Mining Building, the campus bus climbs into the Berkeley hills, where the university's science laboratories are located. Although the public has limited access to the laboratories (see panel on page 59), the bus stops at the **Lawrence Hall of Science** (tel: 510/642-5132; open: daily 10–5) where talking computers and hands-on displays illustrate aspects of the natural world.

Even if you have no desire to put your hand through a laser beam or make a ghostlike appearance on a TV screen, Lawrence Hall is worth a visit for the view from its forecourt. On a fogless day, you can see across Berkeley to San Francisco and the Golden Gate.

THE CAMPANILE

Since 1914, the Campanile (officially called Sather Tower) has risen from the heart of the Berkeley campus. At the end of an inexpensive elevator ride, the Campanile's 200ft (61m) high observation tower offers fine views over Berkeley to San Francisco Bay. Each Sunday at 2pm, a carillon recital resounds from the Campanile across the campus and the neighboring streets.

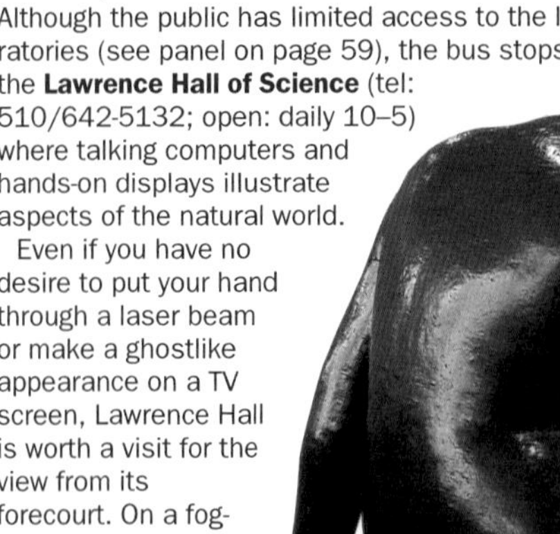

Deep thinking at the University Art Museum

BUENA VISTA'S FINE HOMES

Better known as the creator of Golden Gate Park (see panel, page 100), John McLaren oversaw the seeding of the barren peak that would become Buena Vista Park in the late 1800s. His efforts, coupled with the development of Haight-Ashbury, encouraged a flow of wealthy residents to the magnificent row of architecturally varied Victorian homes which were erected—and still remain—facing the park along Buena Vista Park West (see page 107).

▶ Buddha's Universal Church *IBCF5*

720 Washington Street (tel: 415/982-6116)
Bus: 15

The popular claim that Buddha's Universal Church, which opened in 1965, was financed by the proceeds of fortune cookie sales (see page 102) is not without foundation, although the cookies were just part of the fund-raising activities. The five-story church makes a striking contrast to Chinatown's compact 19th-century temples, although the finely decorated interior can be seen only on Sundays.

▶ Buddhist Church of San Francisco *IBCE5*

1881 Pine Street (tel: 415/776-3158)
Buses: 2, 3, 4

A few blocks from the heart of Japantown, the Buddhist Church of San Francisco opened in 1938, just a few years before many of its Japanese-American congregation found themselves relocated to internment camps for the duration of World War II. During the war years, the church was maintained by Western converts to Buddhism. While the church offices are always busy, the worship room—at the top of the staircase as you enter—is one of the most peaceful and evocative interiors in San Francisco. Services are conducted in English on Sunday mornings, and in Japanese on Sunday afternoons. Guided tours can be arranged by appointment.

▶▶ Buena Vista Park *IFCD4*

Corner of Haight and Baker streets
Buses: 6, 7, 66, 71

Branches of pine, redwood, cypress and eucalyptus trees entwine above the steep slopes of 36-acre (15ha) Buena Vista Park, creating an enticing pocket of wilderness just a few steps from busy Haight Street (best avoided at night). Visitors who weave upward along the park's footpaths and stairways—some of the walls are made from recycled tombstones—are rewarded with fine views reaching to the Financial District and San Francisco Bay.

The twin spires of St. Ignatius Church poke above the rampant shrubbery of Buena Vista Park

The winding machinery that pulls the 56,000ft (17,073m) of ever-moving cable, on which San Francisco's cable cars depend for their movement, can be seen in action in the basement of the Cable Car Museum

►► Cable Car Museum IBCF5

1201 Mason Street (tel: 415/474-1887)
Open: Oct–end Mar daily 10–5; Apr–end Sep daily 10–6; free
Cable car: Powell-Hyde & Powell-Mason lines

After the Transamerica Pyramid and Golden Gate Bridge, the cable car is the thing most people associate with San Francisco. Today's cable cars operate on only three routes and cover a limited area of the city.

Invented by a Scot, Andrew Hallidie, the first cable car ran along Clay Street on August 2, 1873. A safer way of negotiating the city's steep streets than horse-drawn wagons, the cable car also made possible the development of previously inaccessible high areas, most notably Nob Hill (see pages 130–131). By 1906, there were 600 cable cars in operation in San Francisco, but the earthquake and fire of that year, and the subsequent rise of motorized transportation, made them obsolete. Public demand encouraged the federal government to award the cable car National Historic Landmark status in 1964, and a proviso written into the San Francisco City Charter preserves the three existing lines.

The museum—housed in the 1907 cable car powerhouse—displays early cable cars, including the first, and provides a largely pictorial account of their development. It also demonstrates the clever engineering principle that keeps the cars working: Each one is pulled by an underground cable that never stops moving; the "gripman" on each car uses a lever to connect or disconnect the car to or from the cable through a slot in the road. (The heavy whirring sound, audible as you enter the museum, is the steel cable being pulled over 14ft wide winding wheels).

ANDREW S. HALLIDIE

Legend has it that the sight of a horse falling while trying to drag its load up one of San Francisco's hills inspired Andrew Smith Hallidie—an engineer and manufacturer of wire rope, who arrived in California in 1852—to invent the cable car. Wire rope had previously been used as a means of transporting materials in gold mines, but Hallidie was the first to develop the idea as a means of moving people.

San Francisco's famous cable cars are now used mainly by tourists

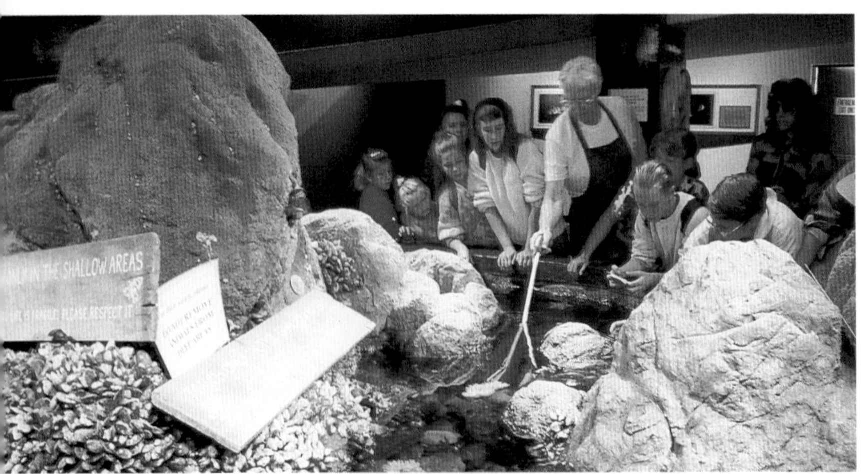

Exploring the tidepool

BOTANY AND ALICE EASTWOOD
The academy's Curator of Botany at the time of the 1906 fire was Alice Eastwood. Realizing that the collections—among the nation's foremost—might be lost, she climbed the exterior ironwork of the building (the interior stairway was destroyed) and carried what she could to safety. Ms. Eastwood, who lost all of her own belongings in the fire, spent 60 years in her job and died in 1953 aged 94.

Dolphin and admirer outside the California Academy of Sciences

►► California Academy of Sciences IFCC4

Golden Gate Park (tel: 415/750-7145); housed in a temporary location at 875 Howards Street
Open: summer daily 9–6, winter 10–5; moderate
Buses: 28, 29, 44

Directly across the expansive Music Concourse from the de Young and Asian Art museums (see pages 118–123), the California Academy of Sciences occupies a grandiose set of buildings, which do little to suggest its modest origins. Founded in 1853 by a small group of enthusiastic naturalists who held weekly meetings and published papers on the state's newly discovered species, the academy mounted its first exhibitions of natural history curiosities in any home which would have them.

Over the years the Academy has now evolved into a sizable museum and subsequently, the academy became established in a six-story building on Market Street, until the premises were destroyed by the 1906 fire (see panel). It was decided to move the academy—by then a popular feature among San Franciscans and known throughout the US—to Golden Gate Park, and the first section of the new building opened in 1916. The wonders of ants, astrobiolgy, the coral and the mysterious creatures of the deep are among the subjects innovatively tackled at this place of fun and learning.

The impact of 100 million visitors touring its galleries since its opening, and of the 1989 Loma Preita earthquake, led to the Academy's Golden Gate Park building being closed for renovation. It is due to re-open in bigger, bolder style in 2008. While its home at Golden Gate Park is being renovated, the California Academy of Science is temporarily housed in SoMa at 875 Howards Street, between 4th and 5th streets. The SoMa site is hardly an apologetic space, however, filling six floors of a former industrial site. Many of the features described here will re-appear in the revamped park home in bolder and better style.

The heart of the Academy continues to be the **Steinhart Aquarium►►►**, which is ingeniously designed to allow visitors to observe the life-support mechanisms, such as filters, oxygen tanks and heating and cooling tools as well as the occupants themselves, which include sturgeon, giant sea-bass, alligator snapping turtles and box turtles and moray eels. Side tanks reveal poison dart frogs, sea horses and the mysterious splitfin flashlight fish, which uses its own natural flashlight to find its way around the dark waters of the very, very deep. A colony of African Penguins can be observed preening themselves, and are particularly entertaining at feeding time around 11am and 3.30pm, when they are served up herring and capelin.

Adjacent to the aquarium is **SSsssnake Alley▶▶** in which lurk assorted boas and pythons, California Kingsnakes and what is claimed to be the world's only captive gunther's whipsnake, a tree-dwelling snake from Burma that eats only fish.

Among the academy's more daring ventures is the creation of a **Coral Reef▶▶▶**, composed of 4,000lb (1,819kg) of reef rock and hundreds of living coral colonies. A variety of colorful reef fish, not least the curiously patterned three spot damselfish, dart in and out of the rocky maze which also, within the protective tentacles of sea anemones, harbors two breeding colonies of downfish. Surgeonfish, meanwhile, earn their upkeep by consuming the algae that would otherwise cloud the tank. The exhibit reveals both the rich diversity of reef life and the threats that coral reefs are facing in the wild.

Astrobiology: Life in the Extreme▶▶ brings insights into how life at extreme points on Earth, such as the oceans depths, the very hot and the very cold, can be used to predict life elsewhere in the universe. Children can learn through interactive exhibits and the very young will enjoy the **Nature Nest▶** and the **Naturalist Center▶** that offers a science-based Story Time at 11am every Saturday.

African habitats re-created at the California Academy of Sciences

THE CHURCHES OF ST. IGNATIUS
With its twin spires rising from the junction of Fulton Street and Parker Avenue, St. Ignatius Church cost $300,000 to build and was completed in 1914, replacing the previous church, destroyed in the 1906 earthquake and fire. The original St. Ignatius was located on Market Street and became a college church in 1863, the root of the present-day University of San Francisco.

An imposing facade: California Palace of the Legion of Honor

► California Historical Society IBCJ7

678 Mission Street (tel: 415/357-1848)
Open: Wed–Sat 12–4.30; inexpensive
Buses: 15, 30, 45

The state-funded California Historical Society dates back to the 1870s, but not until 1922 did it acquire its lasting authority to collect and disseminate information on California's history. Housed at the grand Whittier House (see page 150) from 1956, the society now resides in a handsome wood-framed building which served as an office supply store from 1918 until the early 1990s.

Many of the society's most valuable holdings, such as the historical manuscripts and documents that fill its library, are reserved for bona fide researchers. There are, however, temporary exhibitions of historical artifacts and numerous selections from an excellent collection of 19th-century California art, with such late 19th- and early 20th-century luminaries as Edwin Deakin and Grace Hudson capturing scenes from the state's formative years.

►► California Palace of the Legion of Honor IFCA5

Lincoln Park (tel: 415/863-3330, 24-hour recording)
Open: Tue–Sun 9.30–4.45; moderate
Bus: 18

Auguste Rodin and San Francisco may seem strange bedfellows, but any fans of the sculptor visiting the city should make the ascent to the windswept hilltop—offering stunning views of the Golden Gate and the Pacific—where the California Palace of the Legion of Honor boasts an impressive number of the acclaimed Frenchman's works, as well as a strong general assemblage of European art.

The collection was started in the 1910s by Alma Spreckels, wife of millionaire sugar magnate Adolph. Impressed by the French pavilion at San Francisco's 1915 Panama–Pacific Exhibition and by the Legion d'Honneur on a visit to Paris (where Alma first met Rodin and developed a lasting interest in his work), the Spreckelses commissioned architect George Applegarth to build the California Palace of the Legion of Honor in a style modeled on its Parisian namesake.

While Alma's appreciation of European, and particularly French, art was real enough, the opening of the collection to the public was partly motivated by the Spreckelses' arch rivalry with another prominent San Francisco family, the de Youngs, who were behind the de Young Museum in Golden Gate Park. In 1884, Adolph Spreckels had shot and wounded Michael de Young following reports in the de Young-owned *San Francisco Chronicle* that Spreckels had defrauded shareholders in his sugar company.

On Armistice Day 1924, the California Palace of the Legion of Honor was formally donated to the city of San Francisco in memory of Californians killed in World War I.

Since the 1930s, the California Palace of the Legion of Honor and the de Young Museum have been under dual directorship, and in the 1970s they formally merged to become the Fine Arts Museums of San Francisco. A ticket at the Legion is also valid on the same day at the de Young Museum (and the Asian Art Museum) and vice versa.

Whatever your liking for other periods of art, it is the pieces by Rodin (1840–1917) that will stay with you. *The Shades* stands by the pathway from the parking lot and a "Thinker"—from an 1880 cast and one of the first pieces purchased by Alma Spreckels from the sculptor—sits just outside the columns which mark the building's entrance. Inside, some 70 Rodin works fill two spacious galleries and range from intriguing early experiments, such as *Man With a Broken Nose,* to the more confident and accomplished *Victor Hugo.*

The rest of the collection is arranged in a chronological sequence of galleries from medieval art onward. The best of the Dutch and Flemish rooms is Rubens' *The Tribute Money,* painted around 1612. Another major piece is El Greco's stirring *Saint John the Baptist* (*c*1600). By contrast, seek out a couple of early works (ca1618–1619) by Georges de la Tour, *Old Man*

THE *HOLOCAUST SCULPTURE*

While an hour or two at the Palace of the Legion of Honor should instill a sense of life's finer things, George Segal's *Holocaust Sculpture*, with its emaciated corpses and solitary figure looking despairingly through barbed wire toward the Golden Gate, intentionally does just the opposite. You will find this emotive work in the grounds of the Legion of Honor, beside the parking lot. Among the eleven corpses, re-created in a ghostly plaster form, are two biblical references: a Christ-like figure and a woman holding an apple.

Outside the Legion of Honor and high above the Golden Gate, a Rodin "Thinker" sits in meditation

HARVEY MILK
Although San Francisco is famously populated by oddballs, a Jewish-born camera shop owner is probably the last person who might be expected to feature prominently in the city's history—but Harvey Milk was exactly that. Arriving from New York in 1972, the 42-year-old Milk settled in the Castro and quickly became involved in gay activism. Milk's election to the city-governing Board of Supervisors in 1977 prompted extensive media coverage of gay issues in San Francisco and the US, as did his 1978 assassination and the subsequent "White Night Riots." In what some regard as a premonition of his own death, Milk once said, "Let the bullets that rip through my brain smash through every closet door in the country."

and *Old Woman*, and Seurat's *Eiffel Tower*, which stirred strong passions in 1890s Paris. Downstairs, the **Achenbach Foundation for Graphic Arts** (tel: 415/750-3679; reduced hours) holds 100,000 prints and 3,000 drawings from artists as diverse as Albrecht Dürer (1471–1528) and Georgia O'Keeffe (1887–1986). Selections are shown in short-term exhibitions.

▶ Cartoon Art Museum *IBCF5*

655 Mission Street (tel: 415/227-8666)
Open: Tue–Sun 11–5; inexpensive
Buses: 14, 41, 45

Galleries beside a busy artery of SoMa might be the last place you would expect to discover the secrets behind *Peanuts, Spiderman*, or any of the various cartoon strips and characters which have leapt from the printed page—or the movie or TV screen—to become icons of American popular culture. The Cartoon Art Museum is just such a place, however. The permanent stock of cartoon art—10,000 pieces of original artwork and drawings, rather than reproductions—reaches back to the 18th century and, along with items loaned from collectors and cartoon artists themselves, forms the core of the museum's changing exhibitions.

These eclectic shows have featured cartoon art from underground comics, highlighted work by female cartoonists, examined the realistic style of the original Flash Gordon strip, glimpsed the future with electronic comics, celebrated the past by displaying the original drawings from Disney classics, and the present with exhibitions devoted to literary comics such as MacSweeneys and the output of independent small presses.

The funny side of San Francisco sightseeing: above, the Gary Larson Gallery at the California Academy of Sciences; right, a warm welcome to the Cartoon Art Museum

With its striking Spanish baroque facade, the Castro Theatre has been a landmark on busy Castro Street since 1923

▶ The Castro *IBCE3*

Buses: 8, 24, 35, 37

The district known as the Castro (immediately south of Market Street and named for its main thoroughfare) was once known as Most Holy Redeemer Parish, and the lives of its working-class Irish population focused on the local Catholic church. But by the late 1970s the area had been transformed into the largest and most famous gay and lesbian neighborhood in the world. San Francisco's place in gay history dates back to the Gold Rush (see page 70), but the Castro was transformed as its former population decanted to the suburbs. Falling property values drew residents from nearby Haight-Ashbury, a traditionally ultra-liberal neighborhood where the sexual freedoms of the hippie era had attracted many gay and lesbian settlers during the 1960s and early 1970s. It was from the Castro that Harvey Milk set out on the road that would make him the country's first out-of-the-closet gay man elected to public office. Milk's energy and campaigning genius helped to politicize San Francisco's gay and lesbian community, while his assassination in 1978 inspired greater gay and lesbian assertiveness, and brought support from within the city's heterosexual population.

Financially prosperous, the Castro is a well-groomed neighborhood that takes great pride in its restored Victorian homes. Castro Street itself is rich with the landmarks of gay history—from the raised sidewalk on the corner with 18th Street, used by Harvey Milk and others as a public platform, to the site of Elephant Walk restaurant (see page 71). Be sure to visit the **Pink Triangle Park and Memorial▶** (17th and Markets streets), which commemorates the 15,000 gays and lesbians who died, were imprisoned or otherwise became victims of the Nazis in the 1930s and 1940s; the memorial comprises 15 granite pylons, one for each thousand. The Castro itself, while at times threatening to become a gay tourist trap, has evolved into a quiet and comfortable residential neighborhood.

THE CASTRO THEATRE

In terms of programming, the Castro is among the city's most innovative movie venues, with everything from classic to cult movies screened beneath its handsome ceiling.

CASTRO WALKING TOURS

For an excellent introduction to gay and lesbian San Francisco and the rise of the Castro, take the Cruisin' the Castro Tour; details are given on page 94.

In no other city do gays and lesbians enjoy such a high social profile or level of acceptance as they do in San Francisco. Even so, the city's gay roots go much deeper than many people realize, and the freedoms that many now take for granted have been hard won.

GAY AND LESBIAN CENTER
Housed at the city's Main Library, the Gay and Lesbian Center holds the world's largest collection of gay and lesbian books, videos and artwork. Whether for serious research, browsing or just to express solidarity, visitors are welcome at the facility—the only one of its kind in the world.

Top: Celebrations at the Gay Freedom Parade

GAY HALLOWEEN
Halloween remains an important date in the San Francisco gay calendar, and not just as an excuse to dress up and party. In the 1950s, when police regularly raided gay bars and made every effort to harass their users, October 31 was, bizarrely enough, recognized as a gay celebration and the San Francisco Police Department (very unofficially) observed a truce on that date.

Gold Rush days The mid-1800s Gold Rush transformed San Francisco from a barely populated outpost to a booming city almost overnight, and those who came to seek their fortune were mostly young males. The arrivals seldom struck it rich, but they did find themselves in a relatively lawless community where women were in short supply, and where the usual social restraints laid down by church, family and peer pressure were similarly absent. Legend has it that gold miners demonstrated their sexual preferences to other miners by the color of their bandana—part of their work attire. Meanwhile, the lack of leisure pursuits in the gold-mining communities encouraged miners to spend their earnings on drink, causing any sexual inhibitions to swiftly disappear.

After the Gold Rush, the widely publicized prostitution of the Barbary Coast deflected attention from the city's continuing role as a haven for gays and lesbians who, while forced to conceal their sexual identity in everyday life, were present in considerable numbers. Certain bars and nightclubs with drag acts became popular gay venues despite police raids encouraged by the illegality of same-sex dance partners and the serving of alcohol to homosexuals.

World War II and after During World War II, San Francisco became the embarkation point for military operations in the Pacific, giving many secret gays and lesbians their first taste of the city and its freedoms. At the end of the war, many gay men received a dishonorable discharge from the service; their papers, necessary for obtaining a civilian job, bore a large red "H" to denote "homosexual." With this social stigma awaiting them at home, and only a slim chance of finding work, many opted to stay in San Francisco.

By the 1950s, the city had an underground network of gay and lesbian meeting places: often windowless rooms operated by organized crime mobs who realized that the gay dollar was as valuable as anybody else's, and also that gay customers were unlikely to complain to the police about unfair business practices.

Police harassment was constant, and city politicians routinely ordered crackdowns on gay bars just prior to elections, encouraging the press to invent lurid accounts of the goings-on inside.

Gay politics San Francisco had acquired one of America's earliest gay organizations in the 1950s, but it took the upheavals of the 1960s, unease among the city's liberals about anti-gay discrimination, and the gay settlement of the Castro (see page 69)—where plate-glass windows

made the Elephant Walk the city's first gay bar visible from the street—to pave the way for gay concerns to enter the city's political agenda.

In 1977, a Castro camera store owner, Harvey Milk, ran for supervisor and became the country's first openly gay city official. While Milk's impact on the city's gay and lesbian communities was considerable, it was to be his assassination that galvanized them into direct action.

A year after his election, Milk, and the city's gay-supportive mayor, George Moscone, were shot and killed by Dan White, former right-wing supervisor. White's token five-year sentence so incensed the gay—and large sections of the heterosexual—population, that 50,000 people took part in a protest that culminated in police cars being overturned and City Hall being attacked; this event became known as the "White Night Riots."

Through the 1980s, San Francisco's gays helped the city take the lead in the fight against AIDS and by the 1990s gays and lesbians had attained an unprecedented level of acceptance in, and influence on, the city. Transexuals and the transgenderal have been less widely accepted, however.

Except for the higher-than-average proportion of males in its population, the Castro seems in every respect like any other affluent city neighborhood, a fact which might be a testament to the achievements of San Francisco's gays since the early 1970s, in two decades becoming a largely accepted and integrated section of the city's community

THE OLDEST STREET
In 1834, the Spanish settlement of Yerba Buena (today's San Francisco) acquired its first street, Calle de la Fundación (Foundation Street). When US rule was established, this was renamed Dupont Street to honor a naval captain. Dupont Street, with its many brothels, was razed by the 1906 earthquake and subsequently renamed Grant Avenue, ostensibly to commemorate President Ulysses S. Grant (1822–85). Actually it represented an effort to bury the street's reputation for debauchery.

THE RICKSHAW BAR
At 37 Ross Alley, the Rickshaw Bar was the epitome of the dark and hidden-away Chinatown drinking den. Consequently, Frank Sinatra made it one of his San Francisco haunts and, the story goes, the Beatles dropped by for a quiet drink after playing a concert in the city in 1964. Unfortunately for those who might want a drink, the bar has been closed for some years and various businesses have since occupied its site.

▶▶▶ Chinatown *IBCF5*

Buses: 15, 30, 45

Squeezed between the corporate high-rises of the Financial District and the Italian cafés of North Beach, Chinatown is San Francisco's most distinctive and energetic ethnic neighborhood. An estimated 75,000 people—Vietnamese, Laotian, Cambodian and Korean, as well as Chinese—form the largest Asian community outside Asia, crowded into an area of 24 blocks. Explore Chinatown slowly and on foot. The shops of Grant Avenue are aimed at visitors rather than locals. Intrepid shoppers should explore bustling Stockton Street and the many side streets and alleys. With space at a premium, Chinatown's buildings often have several uses, and it is not unusual to find a restaurant in a basement and a temple a few floors up.

For many San Franciscans, however, Chinatown simply means food. Some of the neighborhood's fare is described on page 216, its best restaurants on page 275. The symbolic entrance to Chinatown is the 1970 **Chinatown Gate**, decorated with dragons (representing fertility and power), fish (prosperity) and foo dogs (warding off evil spirits), which leads on to Grant Avenue from Bush Street.

A neighborhood landmark which has been around much longer is **Old St. Mary's Cathedral▶** (tel: 415/288-3800) at the corner of Grant Avenue and California Street. Completed in 1854, St. Mary's was the first Catholic cathedral on the West Coast and later housed the city's first language school, teaching English to local Chinese. The biblical quotation on the clock tower, "Son Observe the Time and Fly from Evil," was directed at the customers of the brothels which stood nearby during the first 50 years of the church's existence.

(*continued on page 74*)

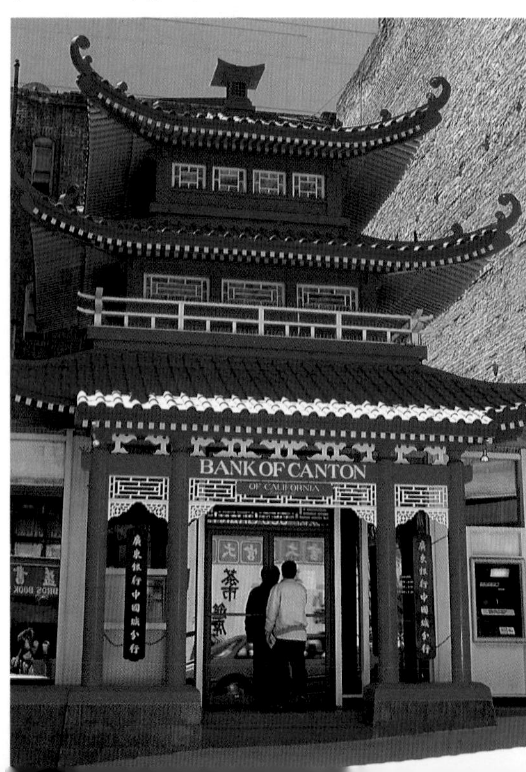

The pagoda-style Bank of Canton was once the Chinatown Telephone Exchange

Walk

Chinatown's main artery seething with pedestrians, street vendors and bemused tourists (see panel, page 72).

Grant Avenue: tourists' Chinatown

Chinatown

This walk through Chinatown begins at the Chinatown Gate and highlights the neighborhood's sights, sounds and smells, visits two temples and ends at the Chinese Historical Society of America.

The green-tiled **Chinatown Gate** (see page 72) leads onto **Grant Avenue**,

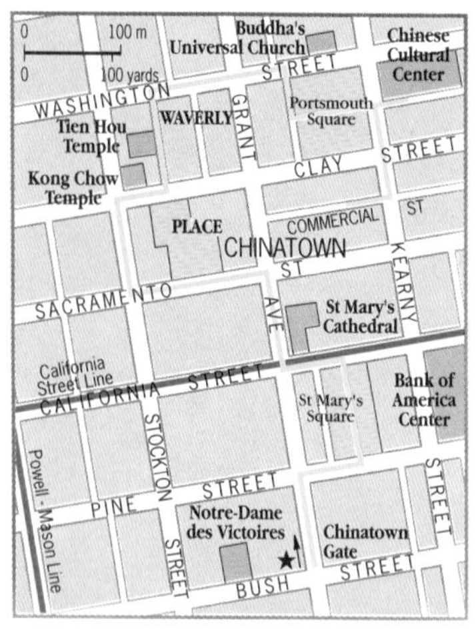

On the compact green space of **St. Mary's Square** (see page 74) stands an impressive stainless-steel and granite statue of Sun Yat-Sen (see page 74). The square takes its name from **Old St. Mary's Cathedral**, California's first cathedral (see pages 72 and 74).

A typical example of Chinatown's mixed-use buildings, the 1857 **Kong Chow Temple** (tel: 415/434-2513) occupies the top floor of the neighborhood's main post office. Another evocative religious site is the 1852 **Tien Hou Temple** on **Waverly Place** (see page 74).

Portsmouth Square once marked the city's waterfront (see page 75). Facing the square, the **Holiday Inn** is an unsuccessful attempt to blend high-rise architecture into the neighborhood. On the hotel's fourth floor are the exhibitions of the **Chinese Cultural Center** (see page 75). Permanent displays on Chinese life in San Francisco and California are offered by the **Chinese Historical Society of America**, on Clay Street (see page 74).

Exhibits at the Chinese Historical Society of America, on Broadway, as it passes through Chinatown

CHINATOWN ALLEYS
Once you grow accustomed to Chinatown's ceaseless bustle, take the time to stroll down some of the easy-to-miss alleys which lie between its busier and better-known streets. Exploring Spofford Street (between Sacramento and Washington streets), Hang Ah Place (between Sacramento and Clay streets; the only alley with a bend in it), or Ross Alley (between Washington and Jackson streets) will enable you to discover facets of this intriguing neighborhood which few tourists ever see.

(continued from page 72)

It was indeed an act of God—the 1906 earthquake—which left St. Mary's standing but razed the offending brothels, providing space for **St. Mary's Square▶**. A neat oblong of greenery which doubles as the roof of an underground parking lot, St. Mary's Square boasts a steel and granite statue of Sun Yat-Sen. He lived in Chinatown while raising funds and publishing a newspaper espousing his revolutionary ideals, which helped pave the way for the overthrow of China's Manchu dynasty and the founding of the Republic of China in 1911.

The **Chinese Historical Society of America▶▶** (965 Clay Street; tel: 415/391-1188; open: Tue–Fri 12–4, Sat and Sun 12–4; free, donation requested) uses archive newspaper cuttings and numerous artifacts to tell the turbulent story of the Chinese in California and their collective contribution to the state's development. Also detailed are some of the recent individual Chinese-American success stories.

Some Chinatown streetlights have been disguised as Chinese lanterns

Often referred to as "the Street of Painted Balconies" for its colorfully decorated facades, **Waverly Place▶▶▶** has a few restaurants and numerous family associations, churches and temples. From the late 1800s, many Chinese-Americans adopted Christianity because the churches offered them education—notably English-language classes—which the secular authorities denied them.

The Baptists were among the Western religious movements influential in Chinatown, and a sizeable Chinese congregation still attends Sunday services at the pagoda-topped Baptist Church located on the corner of Waverly Place and Sacramento Street. However, many present-day Chinese-Americans who consider themselves Christian retain at least some faith in the religions of their ancestral homeland.

Also on Waverly Place, Confucian and Buddhist temples occupy the top floors of several buildings, and visitors are welcome to look around these small, incense-charged rooms; a donation is appreciated. Most temples are open daily from 10am to 4pm. Those to see include **Jeng Sen** (number 146; tel: 415/397-2941), **Norras** (number 109) and, at number

125, Chinatown's oldest temple, **Tien Hou▶▶** (tel: 415/391-4841), founded in 1852; the sign gives the anglicized form, "Tin How."

Between Grant Avenue and Stockton Street are a handful of bustling alleys. Far in mood from the tourist-thronged streets, Ross Alley, Spofford Street and Old Chinatown Lane are lined by Chinese laundries, fortune cookie bakeries (see panel, page 102), social clubs, barber shops and a few food stalls. A sharp eye might also discover some of the secret doorways which were used in times past to flee approaching officials, who might be looking for illicit gambling or illegal employment practices.

In 1909 Chinatown acquired its own telephone exchange, raised in traditional style with a three-tier pagoda roof; the building is now used by the **Bank of Canton▶▶** (743 Washington Street). The Chinese disliked asking for people by number rather than by name, so the telephone operators not only memorized the details of Chinatown's 2,477 customers, but also knew where a person could be reached at any particular time of day. The exchange stayed in use until 1950.

Named for the ship which brought Commander John Montgomery ashore in 1846 to proclaim US rule in San Francisco and, two years later, used by Sam Brannan to announce the discovery of California gold (see pages 32 and 37), **Portsmouth Square▶** is now a favorite rendezvous for the hundreds of Chinatown males who enjoy furtively gambling on games of chance (as local police turn a blind eye), or go through Tai Chi routines.

From the square, a walkway leads across Kearny Street into the lobby of the **Holiday Inn**. The hotel is a brutal attempt to mimic the architectural themes of Chinatown, but its fourth floor holds the absorbing exhibitions of the **Chinese Cultural Center▶▶** (tel: 415/986-1822; open: Tue–Sun 10–4; free).

Chinatown guardian

ROBERT LOUIS STEVENSON
From late 1879, Scottish writer Robert Louis Stevenson would come to Portsmouth Square to relax and write, while waiting for his intended bride's divorce to become final. He is remembered with a granite plinth.

Items on show at the Chinese Cultural Center are selected to reflect the artistic traditions of different regions of China

Recent discoveries on the Southern California coast suggest that the Chinese reached North America long before Columbus set foot in the New World. Nevertheless, the city's present-day Chinese-American community traces its origins back to the mid-1800s Gold Rush.

The ubiquitous Chinese script and displays of exotic foods form part of Chinatown's colorful mystique

Mines and railroads Eager to escape their war-torn and famine-stricken homeland, the first large groups of Chinese arrived in San Francisco in the mid-1800s, pursuing the riches promised by what they called "Gum San," or Gold Mountain. Some became traders, but the majority made their way to California's gold mines. By 1851, one in ten of the state's 250,000 miners was Chinese, and they earned a reputation for being hardworking and dependable. Gold Rush California was, however, not a place of racial harmony, and it was the Chinese who were discriminated against by the Foreign Miners License Tax. Imposed in 1851, the tax placed a $20-a-month levy on all non-American miners; in practice, the money was collected only from the Chinese.

As labor-intensive mining declined, the chief source of Chinese employment became the transcontinental railroad, intended to link California with the rest of the US The railroad employed 20,000 Chinese and tested to the full their capacity for long hours of arduous, backbreaking work on difficult terrain and in appalling conditions.

Economic depression Contrary to expectations, the completion of the railroad in 1869 failed to alleviate the economic recession that followed the Gold Rush and the end of the Civil War. As jobs became scarce, labor unions blamed the Chinese for the work shortage, and the popular press stirred up "Yellow Peril" hysteria. Anti-Chinese racism was legitimized by the Exclusion Act of 1882, outlawing further Chinese immigration to the US for the purposes of finding work, and by the subsequent Scott Act prohibiting the immigration of Chinese women except as wives of merchants—thereby preventing the expansion of the Chinese-American population.

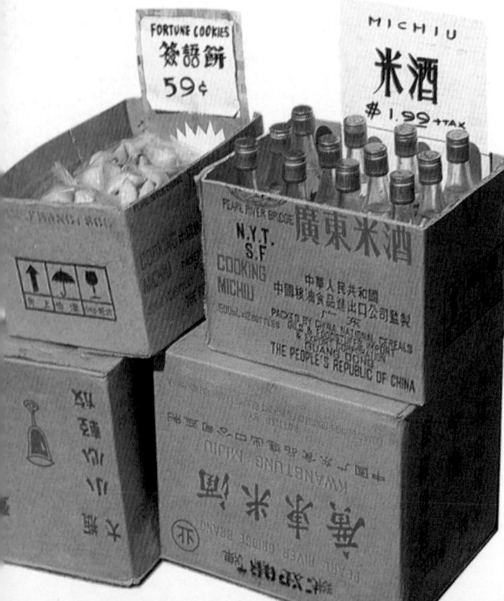

Chinatown life Barred from many towns and driven out of rural settlements, the Chinese community was forced into the Chinatown districts established in many large California communities. In San Francisco, 26,000 clustered into a 12-block area within the boundaries of present-day Chinatown. The smells of unusual herbs and vegetables, and the sight of traditionally dressed men with their hair in queues (ordered by China's ruling Manchu dynasty), made Chinatown a place of great exotica for white

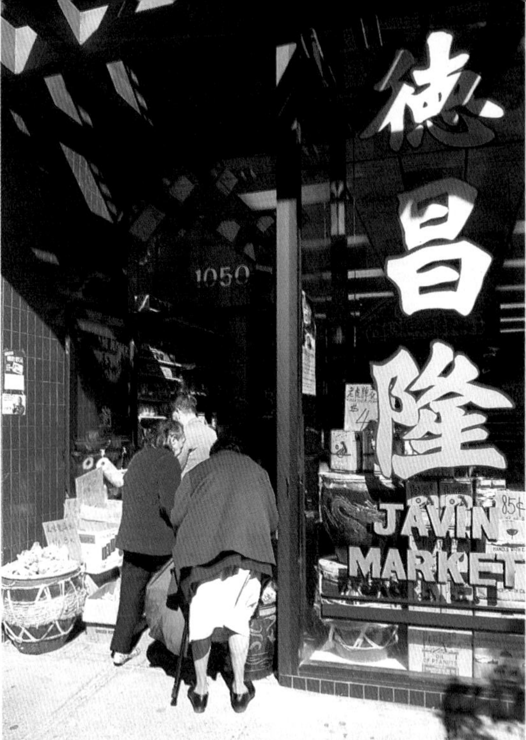

Americans. Denied the comforts of traditional family life, many Chinese men gambled, smoked opium and visited prostitutes—all of which added to the area's mystique. The Chinese faced violence if they ventured outside Chinatown's tight confines, and while merchants generally prospered, ordinary workers often slept in communal rooms and worked (if they were lucky) 20-hour days.

After the fire By 1900, the population of Chinatown had dropped to 11,000. Following the earthquake and fire of 1906, which destroyed the city's public records, many non-legal Chinatown residents claimed US citizenship and boosted their population by arranging the arrival of "paper" sons and daughters from China (see panel, page 176). In addition, the birthrate soared.

Meanwhile, the founding of the Republic of China by Sun Yat-Sen and others in 1911 ended 268 years of Manchu rule and enabled the Chinese to adopt Western ideas and modes of dress. By the 1920s, the restaurants and shops of Chinatown's Grant Avenue were becoming tourist attractions, and the Chinese were steadily becoming an accepted part of city life.

Although the Exclusion Act was not repealed until 1965, immigration became easier from 1940 as China and the US became war allies, and the fresh influx pushed Chinatown's boundaries outward, encouraging established Chinese to settle in other districts like the Richmond District.

While Chinatown remains the focal point of Chinese life, Chinese-Americans have become fully integrated into mainstream San Francisco society, successful in virtually every field of endeavor.

THE TONGS
Conflicts between Chinatown's affluent merchants and its downtrodden laborers were many and encouraged the creation of Tongs (a term for Chinese-American secret societies). Some Tongs claimed long histories to impress recruits, but their main purpose was to organize and control Chinatown's gambling, prostitution and opium use—regarded as immoral vices by merchants' organizations but seen as necessities by workers. With the Chinese excluded from the American justice system, Tong membership also provided a framework for avenging wrongs and settling disputes.

As Stockton Street passes through Chinatown, it becomes lined with busy market stalls and many of the stores, such as this one, where local people buy their food supplies

Holding the mayor's office and all the cogs of the civic machine, City Hall has been at the heart of San Francisco since 1915

CITY HALL GUIDED TOURS
Usually weekly the City Guides (tel: 415/557-4266) offer a free guided walking tour of the Civic Center (including City Hall), packed with facts and anecdotes on San Francisco history and politics. Each Monday at 10am and Tuesday to Friday at 10am, noon and 2pm, free tours of City Hall are run by the Office of the Building Manager; tel: 415/554-4933.

▶▶ Civic Center *IBCF5*

Buses: 10, 20, 21, 47, 49, 60, 70, 80

Although they date from the 1910s, the delightful beaux-arts buildings situated at the core of San Francisco's Civic Center have their origins in the classically inspired City Beautiful movement which began in the 1890s and greatly influenced American urban planning in the early 1900s.

Ironically, or perhaps fittingly for what might be considered the city's major public showplace, the Civic Center also bears evidence of San Francisco's major contemporary headache, with many of its vast homeless population milling listlessly all day around the plazas and gardens.

The centerpiece of the complex is the intricate and inspiring **City Hall▶▶▶** with its huge rotunda topped by a green copper dome, said to be modeled on St. Peter's in Rome and visible across much of the city.

Completed in 1915, City Hall was designed by the architectural firm of Arthur Brown and John Bakewell, both of whom had studied at the influential École des Beaux-Arts in Paris. A much-disputed story holds that, believing they had no chance of winning the commission, Brown and Bakewell submitted an extravagant design which they budgeted at an astronomical $3.5 million. The authorities were eager for a building to symbolize San Francisco's superiority over fast-growing Los Angeles, and so Brown and Bakewell's plan—based on the French baroque style and making generous use of marble—was accepted in spite of its cost.

Inside, the grand staircase is lined by ornate wrought-iron banisters and illuminated by freestanding and hanging lamps. The landings, decorated with porticoes and arches and guarded by neoclassical sculptures, give access to a labyrinthine complex of offices and official chambers. Since its opening, the building's sheer scale and majesty have served to eclipse the importance of the civic powerbrokers who have built careers by scurrying about its corridors. Various other art and history exhibits on aspects of San Francisco provide further interest.

City Hall has won greater affection in San Franciscans' hearts than its corruption-tainted predecessor (see page 39), which occupied the site of the former **Public Library** (now the Asian Art Museum), separated from City Hall by formal gardens and a neatly laid-out plaza.

A beautiful beaux-arts edifice erected in 1917, the library was proving unsuitable for the needs of the modern city—and suffered greatly from earthquake damage in 1989. The million or so tomes it held have been transferred a block south along Larkin Street to the new $98-million **Main Library▶** (tel: 415/557-4400).

Immediately to the west of City Hall across Van Ness Avenue is the **War Memorial Opera House**, which was opened in 1935, and formed the first of a group of buildings now grandly known as the Performing Arts Complex. The first United Nations charter was signed here, an event which was commemorated by the creation of **United Nations Plaza**, where Hyde Street meets Market Street (this is worth visiting to inspect the farmers' market which takes place on Wednesdays and Sundays). Besides operatic performances, for which the city's great and good arrive in all their finery on the season's opening night in September, the Opera House is also the home of the San Francisco Ballet. The streamlined, wraparound facade of glass and granite which faces the Opera House across Grove Street belongs to the city's most important classical music venue, the **Louise M. Davies Symphony Hall.**

THE HIBERNIA BANK BUILDING

Described by architect Willis Polk (see panel, page 112) as "the most beautiful building in the city," the Hibernia Bank building on the corner of McAllister and Market streets, close to the Civic Center, was San Francisco's earliest and most successful classically styled "temple of finance." With a copper dome above its porticoed entrance and its columned sides stretching along two streets, the building dates from 1892.

Louise M. Davies Symphony Hall, opened in 1980

Much less spectacular than its setting, the Cliff House sits on wave-lashed rocks above the Pacific, looking over sea-lion inhabited Seal Rock

Side by side: the Transamerica Pyramid and Columbus Tower

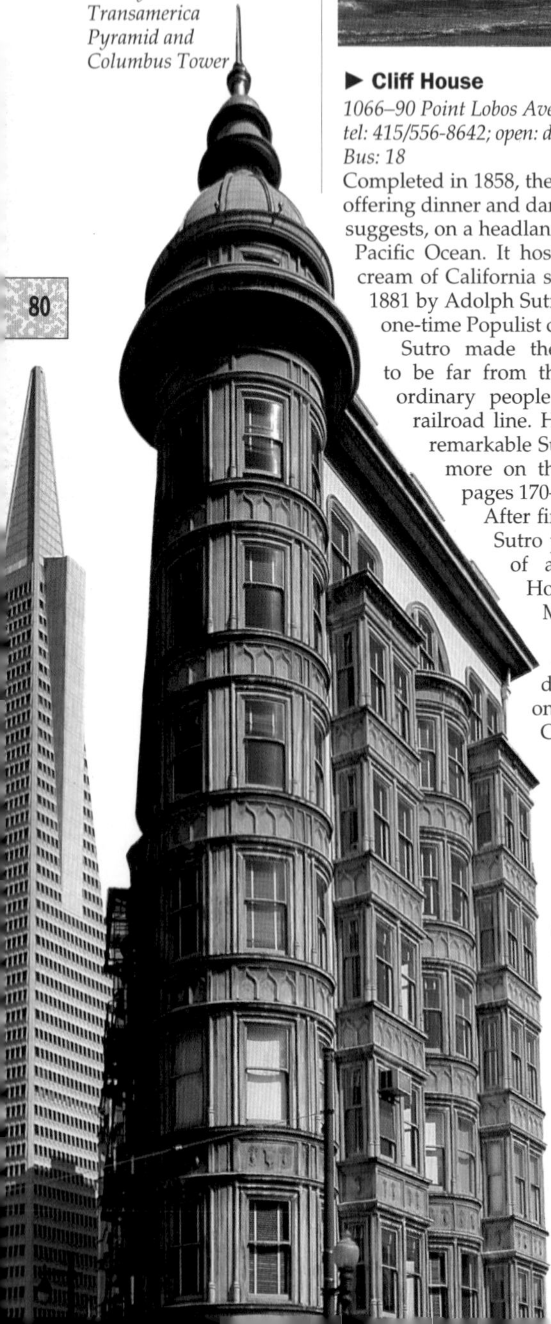

▶ Cliff House IFCA5

1066–90 Point Lobos Avenue (GGNRA Visitor Center; tel: 415/556-8642; open: daily 10–5; times may vary)
Bus: 18

Completed in 1858, the first Cliff House was a restaurant offering dinner and dancing, which perched, as the name suggests, on a headland above the crashing waves of the Pacific Ocean. It hosted three US presidents and the cream of California society before it was purchased in 1881 by Adolph Sutro, a wealthy philanthropist and a one-time Populist city mayor.

Sutro made the Cliff House, then considered to be far from the city proper, accessible to the ordinary people of San Francisco by laying a railroad line. He also began construction of the remarkable Sutro Baths on an adjacent site (for more on the baths, and Sutro himself, see pages 170–171).

After fire destroyed the building in 1894, Sutro pumped $50,000 into the creation of a sumptuous replacement Cliff House. The fancy spires and Mediterranean exuberance of the new eight-story Cliff House, opened in 1896, earned it the apt description of a "French-château-on-a-rock." Although the second Cliff House survived the 1906 earthquake and fire, it burned to the ground soon after, in 1907.

The present Cliff House, built by Sutro's daughter in 1909, and afterwards remodeled, has little charm and offers no suggestion of its predecessors' architectural glamour. It is, however, good for sea lion watching (see panel, page 81) and for picking up maps and information about the Golden Gate National Recreation Area, of which it forms a part.

▶ Columbus Tower IBCF5

906 Kearny Street
Buses: 15, 41

Logically enough, the triangular plot of land where Kearny Street meets Columbus Avenue is filled by a triangular building, Columbus Tower, completed in 1907. Threatened with demolition in the 1970s, the building was bought and restored by San Francisco-based film director Francis Ford Coppola.

The building, with its restored exterior, may now be dwarfed by the Transamerica Pyramid, but it wins many new admirers who see it as they approach Columbus Avenue from North Beach.

▶ Contemporary Jewish Museum *IBCK8*

121 Steuart Street (tel: 415/591-8800)
Open: Sun–Thu 12–6, free tours Sun, Wed at 12.30; inexpensive
Bus: 1

Founded in 1984, the Contemporary Jewish Museum claims to be the only such institution with a multicultural and artistic perspective. Its exhibitions bring diverse aspects of Jewish life and culture to not only Jewish audiences but to non-Jewish as well. Certainly, the museum has seldom been shy of staging stimulating and provocative shows. Exhibitions have included *Art and the Rosenberg Era*, which focused on the McCarthyism of the 1950s and the art inspired by the 1953 execution of the Rosenbergs as Communist spies.

▶ Embarcadero Center *IBCK8*

Between the Embarcadero and Battery Street
Buses: any Market Street bus

A complicated conglomeration of multi-level open-air walkways linking stores, restaurants, terraced cafés, several high-rise office buildings and new hotels, the Embarcadero Center takes up six city blocks and is part of a determined effort to improve the visitor appeal of the Financial District. It also gives office workers somewhere to go during their lunch breaks.

Begin at **Justin Herman Plaza**, across from the historic Ferry Building (see page 83) on the busy Embarcadero. (The Embarcadero Freeway which once dominated this stretch of waterfront was demolished after it had been damaged by the 1989 earthquake.) Here street musicians and roller-skaters add a human dimension to a broad concrete expanse. Select a snack from one of the many food outlets, find a place to sit down and contemplate the plaza's controversial **Vaillancourt Fountain** (see panel) or its equally opinion-splitting sculptural memorial to the 1934 strike of the International Longshoremen's Association (see page 40).

Before entering the center proper, be sure to pick up a free map. Without this vital aid, finding any of the 100-plus stores—which collectively offer such indispensable items as designer earrings and gourmet chocolates—can prove almost impossible. For shopping suggestions, see page 227.

THE VAILLANCOURT FOUNTAIN
Created by artist Armand Vaillancourt, the fountain consists of a series of large, crazily angled concrete tubes through which water (when available) flows and drops to lower levels.

Embarcadero Center

SEAL ROCKS
Adolph Sutro was among the first to protect California's seals, sought after for their skins and oil, by declaring Seal Rocks—beyond the Cliff House—off limits to hunters.

Most of the creatures living around Seal Rocks today are actually Stellars, a species of California sea lion which grows up to 14ft (4m) in length and is found along the coast between the Oregon border and Santa Barbara. For more on San Francisco sea lions, see panel on page 92.

▶▶ Exploratorium — IFCD6

3601 Lyon Street (tel: 415/EXP-LORE)
Open: Tue–Sun 10–5; inexpensive
Buses: 28, 30

Described as a "mad scientist's penny arcade," the Exploratorium is without doubt the best place in San Francisco to amuse young minds with low boredom thresholds. That said, it is no less pleasurable for adults, who could easily pass an hour or more in its entertaining interior.

Comprising a vast, curving hall built as part of the Palace of Fine Arts (see page 152), the Exploratorium is packed with over 650 hands-on, interactive exhibits designed to illustrate and explain the fundamentals of natural science and human perception.

Many of the exhibitions are temporary but among the permanent features are **Traits of Life▶▶** which, as its name suggests, examines the common links between all

Hands-on science at the Exploratorium, where learning can be fun—for everyone

living things, exploring the complexity of cells and DNA, how genes control the appearance of fruit flies, and lifting the lid on the remarkable adaptability of frogs. Be sure to allow time for the Microscope **Imaging Station▶▶**, for a close look at the very small, be it brain cells, muscle cells or the developing embryo of a tropical zebra fish. **Seeing▶** examines human perceptions through sight, making strong use of visual arts and including a variety of entertaining, as well as instructive, optical illusions.

▶ Federal Reserve Bank Building — IBCK8

101 Market Street
Bus: any Market Street bus

From the other side of Market Street, the Federal Reserve Bank's set-back facade makes a diverting sight in this section of the Financial District.

You can take a two-hour tour (Fri at noon; free; photo ID required) that provides whimsical explanations of banking processes and a chance to see the array of bills that comprise the American Currency Exhibit (see panel, page 87).

THE EXPLORATORIUM'S FOUNDER

The visionary founder of the Exploratorium was Frank Oppenheimer, brother of the more famous Robert. Both men worked on the development of the atomic bomb at Los Alamos in the 1940s; because Robert came to be remembered as the "father of the atomic bomb," Frank sometimes referred to himself in jest as the "uncle of the atomic bomb."

THE TACTILE DOME

The Exploratorium's most popular exhibit is the Tactile Dome, a completely dark enclosed space which participants can only leave by feeling their way along its walls and crawling out. This memorable experience requires an advance reservation (tel: 415/561-0362) and a separate admission fee.

ART IN RESIDENCE

Since its inception in 1969, the Exploratorium has encouraged examination of the relationship between art and science, and its artist-in-residence program has provided several intriguing pieces. Among these have been Ned Kahn's *Tornado*, a reservoir of fog continually pulled upward in an inverted vortex, and the more philosophically-centred work of Binh Danh, Claudia Hartm, Vanessa Renwick and John Slepian, gathered as Natural Reflections: pieces that invite meditation on various aspects of life and nature.

▶▶ Ferry Building *IBCG5*

East end of Market Street
Bus: any Market Street bus

Despite the neighboring skyscraping towers and the loss of its once-elegant interior to drab office space, the Ferry Building is perhaps the most enduring and romantic symbol of old San Francisco. Partly modeled on the Giralda Tower in Seville, Spain, by Bay Area architect Arthur Page Brown, the Ferry Building was completed in 1903 and 50 million people annually passed through its portals—mostly commuters from across the bay. With the opening of the Bay Bridge in 1937 and the shift to motorized transportation, use of the Ferry Building gradually declined. At 235ft (71m) it was the tallest building in the city for many years, miraculously remaining relatively unscathed by the earthquake and fire of 1906. An indication of the Ferry Building's seemingly charmed existence was the demolition in 1992 (following damage caused by the 1989 earthquake) of the Embarcadero Freeway, which had effectively partitioned the structure from the rest of the city. Nowadays, there is a good view of the Ferry Building from Justin Herman Plaza (see page 81).

San Franciscans relax beside the Ferry Building and its much-loved clock tower

FERRY BUILDING FERRIES

For old times' sake, you might be tempted to board one of the few ferries which these days depart from the Ferry Building's rear landing stage, bound for Larkspur, Sausalito, Tiburon or Oakland. While you wait, cast an eye over one of the city's lesser-known sculptures: a 1980s likeness of Mahatma Gandhi.

Caffeine may be the preferred fuel of most San Franciscans, but the city has no shortage of bars serving drinks with an alcoholic kick. Whether you want to sip a glass of locally brewed beer, drink with a view, imbibe beneath elegant chandeliers, spot the rich and famous or discover the latest hangout of the terminally hip, the city can deliver exactly what you need.

CHINATOWN BARS
It might go against the grain to drink rather than eat in restaurant-filled Chinatown, but doing so can have its rewards. A cavelike entrance is one interesting feature of LiPo (916 Grant Avenue), a long-serving local watering hole and one packed with tacky Chinese ornaments. Directly across Grant Avenue, the Buddha Lounge rarely has more than a handful of customers, but—on a good night—those who do enter its spartan interior are liable to be larger-than-life Chinatown characters.

Stone Age entrance to LiPo, a noted Chinatown bar

Top-rated taps The city boasts numerous microbreweries, which make their own beer on the premises and cater for a clientele that is increasingly knowledgeable about an ale's finer points. Among the oldest of these is North Beach's unpretentious **San Francisco Brewing Company** (155 Columbus Avenue), where four quality homemade beers are always on tap and attract capacity crowds on Friday and Saturday nights. Across the city, **Thirsty Bear Brewing Co.** (661 Howard Street) is a lively SoMa tapas spot that also brews its own beer. Large silver tanks hold gallons of the ale midway through the process. Another likely spot in the Embarcadero is the **Gordon Biersch Brewing Co.** (2 Harrison Street), while on the western edge of Golden Gate Park, **Beach Chalet Brewery and Restaurant** (1000 Great Highway) offers top-notch beers with ocean views in the impeccable setting of Willis Polk's Beach Chalet (see page 175).

Bars with views With a drink in your hand, in one of the city's high-elevation cocktail lounges, San Francisco's fine views can suddenly look even more spectacular.

On the 19th floor of Nob Hill's Mark Hopkins Hotel, the **Top of the Mark** combines great views with elegant surroundings. For the highest lookout over the city, however, you have to travel down the hill to the Financial District and the **Carnelian Room** (555 California Street); decorated with tapestries and antiques, the bar perches on the 52nd story of the Bank of America Building.

At **Harry Denton's Starlight Room** (450 Powell Street) mingle with cocktail-sipping nightowls against a background of jazz, Bay Bridge and the lights of the East Bay.

Upscale bars to be seen in Once the afternoon tea crowd (see pages 132–133) moves on, the **Ritz-Carlton Lobby Lounge** (600 Stockton Street) at the grand and stately hotel of the same name is a genteel place to sip a cocktail. As the teatime harpist exits, a jazz pianist takes over. For a more hip ambience amid original art-deco fittings, head for the **Redwood Room** at the Clift Hotel (495 Geary Street), which has been on the stylish drinkers' circuit ever since it opened following the repeal of Prohibition. Its days as the city's greatest singles bar may be long gone, but **Perry's** (1944 Union Street) still tempts regular Pacific Heights faces with its good service and wood paneling. Champagne lovers will be in heaven at brick-walled and elegant **Bubble Lounge** (714 Montgomery Street), which offers several hundred champagnes and sparkling wines.

Ovation, the comfortable bar of the Inn at the Opera (333 Fulton Street), offers the chance to spot world-famous opera stars engaged at the nearby Opera House and big names from the film and art worlds who savor the low-key atmosphere. Style-conscious rock stars are among the clientele of **Bambuddha Lounge** (at the Phoenix Hotel, 601 Eddy Street), with its Southeast Asian-inspired interior and its poolside area warmed by a slate fireplace.

Downscale bars to be seen in Patronized by the bright lights of the 1950s Beat generation, **Vesuvio** (255 Columbus Avenue) is still a favored meeting spot for embryonic writers and artists. Across the city, Haight-Ashbury's **Toronado** (547 Haight Street) is dark and dingy but has great beers and a convivial crowd. Serving a limited range of drinks but packed nightly with students, artists, posers and fashion victims, **Café Flore** (2298 Market Street) is worth a visit, if only to find out how it got its nickname ("Café Haircut"). The hippest hangout in the increasingly trendy Mission District is **Blondie's Bar & No Grill** (540 Valencia Street), where nattily dressed customers sip martinis and swap celebrity gossip.

Opposite (top) and above: Perry's on Union Street is a cozy niche for food, drink and the exchange of neighborhood gossip

THE OLDEST BAR

Dating from 1861, The Saloon (1232 Grant Avenue) is the oldest bar in California. Despite its pedigree, its wooden floorboards are shaken almost nightly by live rock and blues bands, which attract a beer-drinking clientele in plaid shirts and jeans.

The Brainwash: a SoMa venue for live music, poetry and comedy, eating, drinking, and washing your clothes

FORGOTTEN STREETS
Intrepid strollers can weave through almost the whole of the Financial District using only the short side streets, of which few people—even those who work in the neighborhood—are aware. Look for Trinity, Belden and Spring streets, or walk the three-block Liedesdorff Street, between Pine and Clay streets. This crosses the Gold Rush-era Commercial Street, which once extended into a 2,000-foot-long wharf and now provides a splendid view of the Ferry Building.

▶▶ Financial District

IBCF5

Buses: any Market Street bus

It may lack hard and sharp boundaries, but you can never forget where San Francisco keeps its Financial District: The forest of high-rise office buildings, located close to the eastern waterfront, is visible from all over the city. However, the pace of development has been tightly controlled in recent years, and the Financial District's modern architecture has in some cases—such as the **Transamerica Pyramid** (600 Montgomery Street, see page 177)—greatly enriched the skyline. A walk through the Financial District also reveals some slightly more venerable buildings. A few predate the calamitous 1906 earthquake and fire, others survive from the post-1906 construction frenzy, and many more date from the boom years of the 1920s.

Until the 1850s, the present Financial District's main north–south artery, Montgomery Street, marked the city's eastern shoreline, with the east–west streets terminating in wharves. The streets that now run east from Montgomery were created from landfill, and the city's earliest financial buildings spread steadily southward from the foot of Telegraph Hill to line them. Once the

Reaching for the sky

A stretch limo waits by the kerb in the heart of the Financial District

pacesetting Bank of California opened its new headquarters at the corner of California and Sansome streets in 1866, the location of the city's new commercial quarter was confirmed. It was the Gold Rush which made San Francisco, and made it rich, but following the opening of the transcontinental railroad in 1869 (see page 37), the city also became the unchallenged center of trans-Pacific trade. A lookout would be posted on the roof of the 1903 **Merchant Exchange Building▶▶▶** (465 California Street) to announce arriving ships to the traders and businessmen in the building's Grain Exchange Hall. Murals by William Coulter, who arrived in California in 1869 and became known for his paintings of the city's seafaring heritage, line the hall (peer through the glass-paneled doors of what is currently office space).

By contrast, one of the city's most acclaimed contemporary towers stands on the corner of California and Kearny streets. The clever, imposing **Bank of America Center▶** rises 52 stories above a plaza whose marble sculpture, *Transcendence*, is known informally as "Banker's Heart."

Contributions from Philip Johnson and John Burgee have sharply divided opinion in San Francisco. Their most intriguing San Francisco offering is **101 California Street▶▶**, a soaring silo with a garden theme.

Another bone of contention is Skidmore Owings & Merrill's **345 California Center▶** (345 California Street). Completed in 1987, it circumvented restrictions by incorporating two older buildings as well as a luxury hotel and shopping complex in its 48-story mass.

AMERICAN CURRENCY
American currency has appeared in many weird and wonderful forms, the proof is assembled at the Federal Reserve's American Currency Exhibit, which displays such curiosities from the free banking era as the Gold Dust Note, issued by the Miners Bank of Saving in the 1850s, and a the 3-cent note issued by a ladies clothing store in the 1860s.

A MEDIEVAL SKYSCRAPER?
For a final sample of Financial District architecture, step into the lobby of the Russ Building (235 Montgomery Street) to admire an inspired attempt to make a 1920s sky-scraper—the city's tallest building until 1964—resemble a medieval castle.

Where not to be when the next big earthquake hits

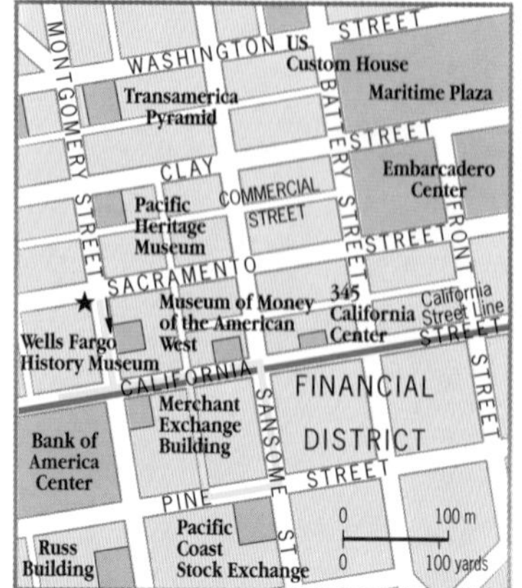

Financial District

Covering only a few blocks, this walk includes the most distinctive examples of the city's old and new commercial architecture, as well as two museums of Financial District history.

The **Bank of America Center** (see page 87) symbolizes the economic boom of the 1970s and is one of the few developments of the period to be warmly received. Close by, the **Wells Fargo History Museum** commemorates the company founded in 1852 to carry people and communications across the American frontier.

In the **Merchant Exchange Building** (see page 87) San Francisco's turn-of-the-20th-century importance as a center of seaborne trade is expressed by William Coulter's vast maritime paintings on the walls of the first-floor offices.

Art-deco sculptures and classical columns form a curious partnership on the exterior of the 1930 **Pacific Stock Exchange**.

At the Bank of California, the **Museum of Money of the American West** (see page 127) holds some of the gold nuggets that helped make San Francisco's Financial District what it is today.

Bank of America Center, sold in 1985 for $660 million, the largest sum paid for any building in the US

For visitors to San Francisco, a city bounded by water on three sides, boat trips—from a scenic hop across the bay to a leisurely dinner cruise—are an essential part of the experience.

Around the bay Two cruise companies offer enjoyable narrated tours daily around San Francisco Bay. The **Red & White Fleet's** one-hour cruise circles Alcatraz and Angel Island and passes beneath Golden Gate Bridge. Also lasting an hour longer, the **Blue & Gold Fleet's** bay cruise covers much of the same.

To Alcatraz The former prison of Alcatraz (see page 55) should be on everybody's San Francisco itinerary. The only way to reach Alcatraz Island is with the Blue & Gold Fleet's half-hourly departures from morning to mid-afternoon. In summer, catch an early ferry (the first is at 9.30am) to avoid the crowds and buy your ticket at least a day in advance, or two days in summer. The fare includes the loan of a prison-tour cassette and player. The same company operates evening tours (Thursday to Sunday) which include guided tours of the cellhouse and views of night-time San Francisco.

Dining and dancing Several companies offer the chance to combine floating with eating. On Fridays and Saturdays from May to December, the Blue & Gold Fleet operates three-hour dinner cruises which allow passengers to dance to a live band after eating all they can from an abundant buffet table. Every night is dine-and-dance time aboard the replica turn-of-the-20th-century bay steamer of **Hornblower Dining Yachts**, also the scene of lunch and Sunday brunch cruises.

Ferry travel One of the best—and least expensive—ways to enjoy the bay is simply to hop aboard a ferry. **Golden Gate Ferries** sail several times a day between the city and Sausalito and Larkspur. The Blue & Gold Fleet has a daily ferry link with Oakland's Jack London Square.

BOAT TRIP DETAILS
Blue & Gold Fleet (tel: 415/705-5555), departures from Pier 39 and Pier 41, Fisherman's Wharf, and the Ferry Building.
Golden Gate Ferries (tel: 415/455-2000), departures from the Ferry Building.
Hornblower Dining Yachts (tel: 1-888-MORN-BLOWER), departures from Pier 3, Embarcadero.
Red & White Fleet (tel: 415/673-2900), departures from Pier 43½, Fisherman's Wharf.

All aboard for Tiburon, Sausalito, Alcatraz

Assembled from scrap, Pier 39 is now a money-making tourist attraction

SAN FRANCISCO'S GHOST SHIP

On chilly nights when the waters of the bay are eerily shrouded in fog, watch out for a phantom clipper, the *Tennessee*, gliding effortlessly through the waves. The two-masted vessel sank in the bay 100 years ago but is regularly "sighted," most famously by several of the crew of a naval destroyer in 1942.

▶ Fisherman's Wharf *IBCF6*

Bus: 32
Cable car: Powell–Mason line

The only San Francisco neighborhood where locals are less prevalent than tourists, Fisherman's Wharf attracts 12 million visitors annually and covers a lengthy segment of the city's northern waterfront, immediately north of North Beach and east of Fort Mason Center.

Today, the only sign of commercial fishing is the modest catch unloaded in the early hours (usually 6–9am) at Pier 49. Earlier this century, though, it was a very different story, with 300 or more vessels daily disgorging tons of freshly caught sardine and crab along the bay. By the late 1950s, the fishing fleet was in decline, and it took a major urban renewal program to revitalize the area.

While much of present-day Fisherman's Wharf—be it street entertainers, bay cruises or endless opportunities to eat clam chowder from a bowl-shaped hunk of sourdough bread (see panels, pages 93 and 218)—is unapologetically geared toward tourists, few visitors leave completely disappointed. Do not expect to learn much about the real San Francisco, however, and bear in mind that the souvenirs sold here are more expensive than elsewhere.

Several of Fisherman's Wharf's genuinely historic sights are given their own separate accounts: Hyde Street Pier Historic Ships (see page 112), the National Maritime Museum and USS *Pampanito* (see page 128), and Alcatraz (see pages 55–56), for which ferries depart from Pier 41. You might combine a tour of Fisherman's Wharf with the museums of the Fort Mason Center (see page 96). With many national chain hotels located in Fisherman's Wharf, the area can make an affordable and geographically-sensible base for seeing the city. An easy downhill walk leads into North Beach (see pages 134–137) and Chinatown (see pages 72–75); slightly harder uphill treks reach Russian Hill (see page 157) and Tower Hill where Coits Tower (see pages 173–175) sits. With more energy, you could also tackle the bayside Golden Gate Promenade, which covers the 3 miles (5km) from Fisherman's Wharf to

(continued on page 92)

Walk

Fisherman's Wharf

This simple walk covers all the major free tourist attractions of Fisherman's Wharf, beginning at Ghirardelli Square and finishing at Pier 39.

Ghirardelli Square (see page 93) has been transformed from a chocolate factory into a strollable grouping of stores and restaurants without sacrificing its architectural integrity.

The Cannery (see page 93) was the world's largest fruit and vegetable canning center, but is now converted.

Frenchman Isadore Boudin was the first San Francisco baker to produce sourdough bread (see panel, page 218). Fisherman's Wharf has many outlets for this city specialty, but the best is a branch of the **Boudin Sourdough French Bread Bakery** (see panel, page 93) which allows a peek at the baking process.

Built of wood salvaged from abandoned piers and boats, **Pier 39** (see page 92) is another conglomeration of retail outlets, eating places and tourist amusements.

Completed in 1978 and intended to be a re-creation of a San Francisco street, Pier 39 is more successful as a place to indulge in a snack and relax while enjoying free entertainment.

Making Ghirardelli chocolate

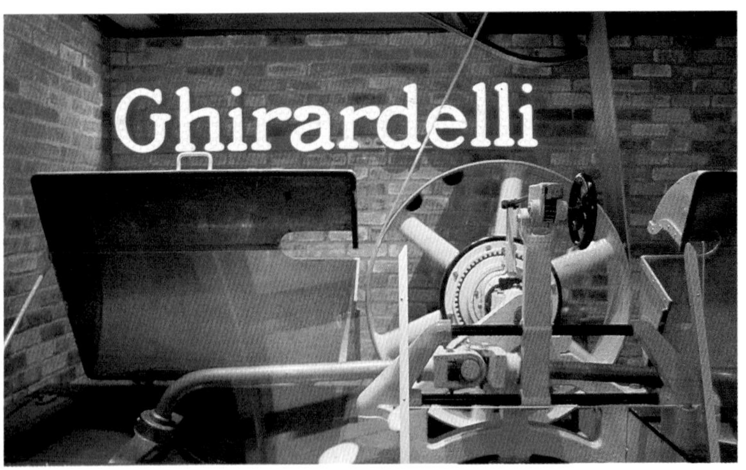

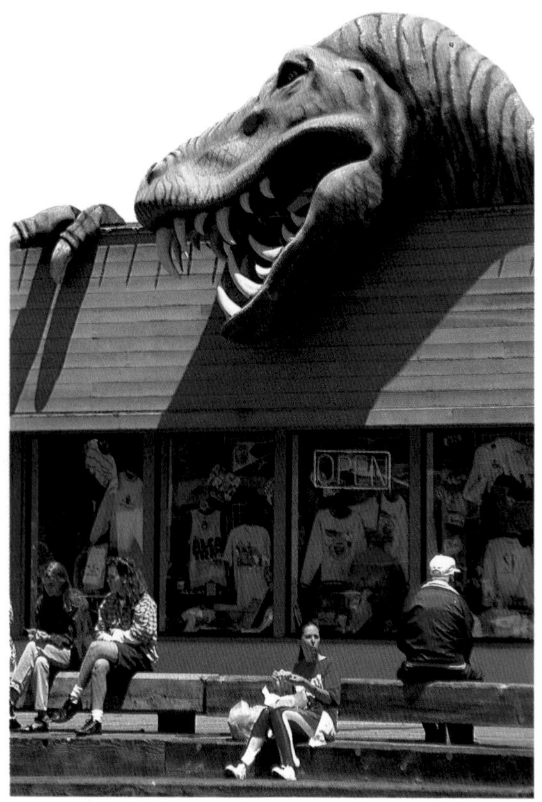

Fisherman's Wharf draws all kinds of visitors

PIER 39'S SEA LIONS
From an original group of 10 attracted by an abundant supply of herring, some 600 California sea lions are now believed to have made their homes beside Pier 39. The creatures can be observed from a viewing area. On Saturday and Sunday between 11am and 5pm a sea lion expert leads a question and answer session. You will need to listen closely: A distinguishing feature of the California sea lion is its very loud bark. The mammal center is open all year, with displays, amusements and staff on hand to answer questions. For more sea lions, see page 81.

A young visitor enjoys the sea-lion sculptures close to Pier 39, which celebrate the colony of the creatures that now lives here

(continued from page 90)
Fort Point (see page 96), beneath Golden Gate Bridge.

Built in the 1970s on the site of an abandoned cargo wharf, split-level **Pier 39▶** is packed with shops, restaurants and amusement arcades. If buying, eating or fighting for your life at a computer screen holds no appeal, a walk along the wooden boardwalk can be enjoyable. Structure your walk to include the west side of the pier and you will spot the colony of California sea lions which took up residence here in 1990 (see panel). On the pier's top deck, the **Marine Mammal Interpretive Center▶▶** provides information on the fish-crazed creatures, and the adjoining **National Park Store** has literature on other aspects of natural California.

Near the pier's entrance, **Aquarium of the Bay▶** (tel: 415/623-5300; open: summer daily 9–8, rest of year Mon–Fri 10–6, Sat–Sun 10–7) gathers an eclectic stock of aquatic life from the waters of the Pacific and allows visitors to peer at it while walking through a transparent underwater tunnel. For thrills and spills, continue along the pier to **Turbo Ride▶** (tel: 415/392-8313; open: Mon–Fri 10–6, Sat–Sun 10–7), where two flight-simulator journeys take participants on adventures through time and space.

Also on Pier 39, the **Eagle Café** is the antidote to Fisherman's Wharf's overpriced restaurants. The self-service café was lifted on stilts from its original location nearby and placed here in 1978, 50 years after it opened.

Neither of the major tourist attractions that interrupt the souvenir stores lining Jefferson Street offer great intellectual stimulation, but you might welcome them on a rainy day, or if you have restless children to entertain. The **Wax Museum** (number 145; tel: 800/439-4305; open: Mon–Fri 10–9, Sat–Sun 9–11; moderate) has plenty of waxen images of stage, screen and sports stars, and a Chamber of Horrors featuring Dracula, Al Capone and the founder of the Church of Satan. At number 175, **Ripley's Believe It or Not!▶** (tel: 415/771-6188; open: Sun–Thu 10–10, Fri–Sat 10–midnight; moderate) is more entertaining. Here the exhibits include an 8ft (2.5m) long cable car made of match-sticks and a room devoted to California earthquakes, which features a very disorienting moving wall.

The Del Monte fruit company once canned its peaches at what, in 1968, was imaginatively and expensively (the cost estimated at $5.5 million) transformed into **The Cannery▶**, on Leavenworth Street between Beach and Jefferson streets. An assortment of shops, eating places and galleries is now found throughout the brick-built factory, while the pretty, tree-lined courtyard is the scene of free entertainment. The Cannery is the start-point of 75-minute tours aboard a 13-seater fire engine, following a route to the Presidio, Fort Point, and across the Golden Gate Bridge to Sausalito before returning via Pacific Heights.

It was the success of an earlier conversion that inspired the creation of The Cannery and contributed greatly to the emergence of Fisherman's Wharf as a tourist center. The red-brick Ghirardelli chocolate factory (9800 North Point Street) had been a city landmark since its opening in 1893. At **Ghirardelli Square▶▶**, former work spaces are filled with specialty stores and restaurants offering breathtaking views of the bay. Visitors flock to its spacious plaza (its waterfall is by artist/street landscaper Ruth Asawa). The much-loved Ghirardelli chocolate, produced since Gold Rush days, can be sampled at the **Chocolate Manufactory and Soda Fountain** inside the Clock Tower building on the Plaza Level.

Boudin's Bakery

SOURDOUGH BREAD
The Boudin Sourdough French Bread Bakery (156 Jefferson Street) is one of 10 descended from Isadore Boudin's original sourdough bakery, opened in 1849. The crusty, no-yeast sourdough loaf was popular with gold-miners and subsequently became synonymous with the city. Some say that the quality of a sourdough loaf is dependent upon the local fog.

Moored at Fisherman's Wharf, some surviving members of San Francisco's much depleted fishing fleet

Unlike most US cities, San Francisco is best explored on foot. To get the most from an hour or two's walk, however, you should join one or more of the city's guided tours. Whether they look at Victorian homes, explore gay history, locate hippie hotspots or provide a beginner's guide to dim sum, these tours reveal landmarks and aspects of local life that are otherwise hidden. Most guided walks cost $20–$30 per person; the following are a small selection of the author's favorites.

Store signs are almost too many to read along Grant Avenue, Chinatown's showpiece thoroughfare

FREE AND INEXPENSIVE WALKS
A tight budget is no obstacle to joining a guided walking tour. Every day of the week, City Guides (tel: 415/557-4266) operates free tours—including City Hall, Victorian-era Haight-Ashbury, Nob Hill, Sutro Heights Park and the mansions of Pacific Heights. City Guides also offers a tour of the Mission District's murals, as (for a small charge) does the Precita Eyes Mural Arts Center (see panel, page 126).

Thorough research The enjoyment of a walk naturally depends on the quality of the guide's background research; the most conscientious among them will have pored for hours over dusty archives for the real stories behind the historic headlines.

One exceptionally well-researched walk is **Cruisin' the Castro** (by reservation only; tel: 415/550-8110). Visitors of every sexual persuasion often wonder why San Francisco has such a large and visible gay and lesbian population, and many of the answers are provided on this four-hour tour.

Covering only a few blocks of Castro Street, the walk involves very little legwork but provides fascinating insights into the city's underpublicized gay and lesbian history, which stretches back to the Gold Rush. The tour comes up-to-date by explaining the more recent importance of the Castro neighborhood and visiting the Names Project quilt (see page 69). The price includes brunch in a local restaurant.

To become an instant expert on the city's Victorian homes, their most colorful occupants and their architecture, join the **Victorian Homes Walk** (tel: 415/252-9485). The knowledgeable guide will outline the fine points of the city's Queen Anne, Edwardian and Italianate building styles while taking a route through parts of Pacific Heights, Russian Hill and the Western Addition, revealing notable houses that few visitors would be able to discover on their own.

Neighborhood walks The tucked-away temples and narrow alleyways of Chinatown may well seem daunting to first-time visitors, who might also lack the time to gain full enjoyment from one of the city's most vibrant ethnic enclaves. A crash course in Chinatown's history, culture and cuisine is provided by the **Wok Wiz** walk (tel: 650/355-9657), which spends over two hours weaving through the district's side streets, visiting a fortune cookie factory (see panel, page 102), a wok store, an herb store (at last, a chance to find out what bird's-nest soup is all about), a traditional Chinese brush-and-ink artist and a tea emporium. An optional lunch provides adventurous but shy diners with a demystification of dim sum (Chinese dumplings).

Covering similar ground and offering an equally good introduction to the neighborhood is **All About Chinatown** (tel: 415/982-8839) which also provides a list of selected Chinatown restaurants for later exploration and includes a 10-course dim-sum lunch. The Chinatown tours are among the city's most popular walks and should be booked a week or more in advance.

Many walking tours focus on the geographically close-knit Financial District, Chinatown and North Beach, but the twice-weekly **Haight-Ashbury Flower Power Walking Tour** (tel: 415/863-1621) examines the historical strands that make Haight-Ashbury one of San Francisco's most interesting districts. The walk uses vintage photographs and examples of local Victorian architecture to chart the neighborhood's origins as a weekend resort, and describes its 1960s transformation into the heart of the hippie movement while pausing at significant sites of the psychedelic era. The knowledge-able folk of San Francisco Architectural Heritage (tel: 415/441-3000) offer one of four walks on Saturday afternoons: the Beaux Arts treasures of the Civic Center; the Victorian homes found along Broadway; the 1850s to 1920s buildings of Cow Hollow, better-known as the Union Street area of Pacific Heights; and along Van Ness Avenue, the thoroughfare that served as a fire break during the disaster of 1906.

Spooky Walk San Francisco has its share of ghost stories. One way to find out about the tales is the two-hour Vampire Tour of San Francisco (1-866/424-8836), which is led by a vampress of 108 years standing and takes in the haunted past of Nob Hill beginning at the corner of Taylor and California streets, by Huntington Park. More from the after-life, including the spirits of dead rock stars, is found on the Haunted Haight Walking Tour (tel: 1-800/838 3806) commencing at 7pm from outside 1573 Haight Street.

BARBARY COAST TRAIL
Indicated by brass markers in the sidewalk, the Barbary Coast Trail is a 3.8-mile (6km) walk through the city's historic sites. Created by the San Francisco Historical Society (tel: 415/775-1111; www.sfhistory.org), the walk takes in such notable locations as the birth of the Gold Rush and North America's oldest Asian temple. Maps can be printed from the society's website.

The Castro District has seen many changes over the years, but Louie's Barber Shop, in business since 1947, has survived them all

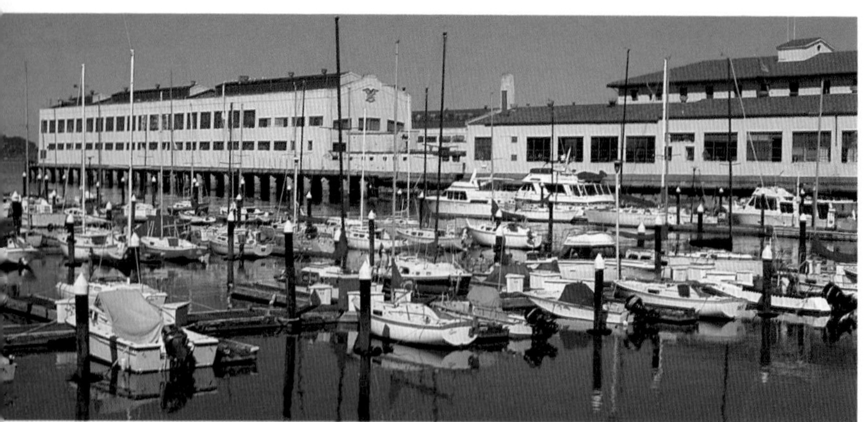

Culture by the bay: Fort Mason Center

FORT POINT'S CANNONS
Fort Point was decommissioned in 1914, although to all intents and purposes it was made obsolete a year after its completion with the advent of wall-piercing artillery. None of Fort Point's cannons was ever fired in anger, but one of them is kept in a fire-ready state and is used by park rangers to give cannon-loading demonstrations—a far more interesting and complex task than you might imagine.

Beneath Golden Gate Bridge: Fort Point

▶▶ Fort Mason Center *IBCE6*

Between Fisherman's Wharf and Golden Gate Bridge (tel: 415/556-1693)
Open: Wed–Sun 10–5; free
Bus: 28

From the time of San Francisco's 18th-century Spanish presidio (or garrison) to the Korean War of the 1950s, Fort Mason retained its military role. In 1972, however, it became part of the Golden Gate National Recreation Area. Its rambling hilltop Victorian office building housed the park's headquarters, and the waterfront barracks were earmarked for a cultural center. Today, some 50 nonprofit organizations, including art, music and broadcasting workshops, theaters and museums such as the Museo Italo-Americano (see page 127), and the San Francisco Craft & Folk Art Museum (see page 159), occupy the buildings.

Fort Mason also houses an offshoot of the San Francisco Museum of Modern Art: the **San Francisco Museum of Art Artists Gallery** (Building A), which enables prospective patrons of emerging Northern California artists to rent a work before buying or renting it. More rewarding for those on moderate budgets is the **Book Bay Bookstore**, operated by the Friends of the San Francisco Public Library (Building C), which has copiously stocked shelves of secondhand books at giveaway prices.

Also here is the award-winning vegetarian restaurant, **Greens** (Building A), unique among Fort Mason occupants for paying a percentage of its substantial profits as rent (others pay a token rental).

▶ Fort Point National Historic Site *IFCB6*

Southern end of Golden Gate Bridge (tel: 415/556-1693)
Open: Fri–Sun 10–5; inexpensive
Bus: 29

As the traffic on Golden Gate Bridge rumbles overhead, it is hard to imagine how diminutive Fort Point, completed in 1861, was ever expected to deter enemy incursions into San Francisco Bay. Some assistance in doing so, however, is provided by the displays of artillery housed in the rooms off the restored courtyard, alongside temporary exhibits covering diverse aspects of American military history.

The Irish have contributed as much as any ethnic group to the growth of San Francisco, but unlike the influence of the Italians and Chinese, their impact is not always obvious.

Early Irish Of the handful of Irish settlers that arrived in pre-US California, one, a certain John Read, settled in Marin County in 1826 as a land-owning *ranchero*, while another, Timothy Murphy ("Don Timoteo"), took charge of the secularized Mission San Rafael. In 1844, Irish priest Eugene McNamara received an enormous land grant from California's Mexican governor and intended to bring 10,000 Irish immigrants to settle it. However, the Gold Rush—combined with Ireland's potato famine—prompted a mass Irish migration to California. By the 1870s, the Irish accounted for 30 percent of the state's population.

Irish established In San Francisco, the Irish became preeminent in city affairs by the late 19th century, dominating the transportation and construction trades and the police force. The Irish-formed trade unions had a major impact on the city, and they organized popular protests against the elitist millionaires of Nob Hill and the monopolistic business practices of the railroad companies.

Irishman Dennis Kearney became president of the influential Workingmen's Party of California in 1877 and led 3,000 protesters up Nob Hill to show their contempt for Charles Crocker's "spite fence" (see panel, page 130). However, it was Kearney, and other Irish organizations, who stirred up the anti-Chinese feeling which contributed to the ghettoization of the Chinese community.

Later, Irish-American mayor James Phelan led an anti-corruption drive and championed the City Beautiful movement, which eventually created the Civic Center.

IRISH ORGANIZATIONS
The St. Patrick's Day Parade (see pages 24–25), a tide of green which sweeps along Market Street each March, is one unmistakable sign of the Irish presence. Less obvious markers can be found at the Irish Cultural Center (2700 45th Avenue) and by picking up the free monthly paper, *The Irish Herald*.

IRISH NEIGHBORHOODS
Before the earthquake of 1906, SoMa was the city's Irish neighborhood. Subsequently, the Irish moved west to the Mission District (now Latino) and the Castro (now gay), before spreading throughout the city.

Legend has it that America's first Irish coffee was served in San Francisco in 1952

THE COLOR SCHEME
Golden Gate Bridge is painted a reddish-orange shade formally known as International Orange, the color most distinguishable in fog. Things could have been different: During the construction a variety of golds were tested, and some students offered to paint the bridge royal blue with yellow polka dots.

►►► Golden Gate Bridge *IFCB6*

Buses: 28, 29, 76 (Sundays and holidays)

Of all the 575,000 bridges in the US, probably none is more instantly recognizable than San Francisco's Golden Gate Bridge, linking the city to Marin County.

Eager to create work in the gloom of the Depression, the federal government gave the go-ahead for the bridge in 1930 and authorized a bond issue of $35 million to finance its construction. The Golden Gate Bridge was not created without opposition, however, and there was a particularly angry outcry against an early design offered by the project's chief engineer, Joseph B. Strauss, which was likened to "two grotesque steel beetles emerging from either bank." Responsibility for the design which eventually became the bridge has been much disputed, but the work is thought to have been largely that of Strauss's locally appointed assistant, Irving Morrow.

At 1.7 miles (2.5km) long (including approaches) with towers as high as a 48-story building, the bridge was completed in 1937 and is still among the world's largest suspension bridges. It can be crossed by car, on foot and by bicycle, though the steady rumble of traffic tends to upset contemplation of the extraordinary views—as do the often ferocious winds zapping across the span.

Golden Gate Bridge: In 1987, to mark the 50th anniversary of its opening, the bridge was closed to traffic and 200,000 people filed onto it, causing the central span to drop by 10ft (3m)

▶▶Golden Gate National Recreation Area *IFCB5*

From the cliffs of Fort Funston in the south to the rugged hills of Marin County in the north, the Golden Gate National Recreation Area (GGNRA) bestows federal protection to a long, slender chunk of the San Francisco coastline. A large section of the land was once military-owned (abandoned forts are a common sight), and most of the GGNRA's 75,000 or so acres (30,364ha), which often lack marked boundaries, can be explored on foot (and some parts by bike). Information and maps are distributed at several sites, but the main headquarters are at Fort Mason Center (see page 96).

Between the ocean and Sunset District's Lake Merced, the tall cliffs of **Fort Funston▶** make a popular liftoff point for hang gliders, and footpaths weave around the area's sand dunes, once used to practice coastal assaults. The GGNRA's wildest and most hike-worthy section (on the city side) is the **coastal trail▶▶** which winds through the coarsely vegetated hillsides rising steeply above the tiny beach of **Land's End▶**. From the trail, often subject to blustery winds and frequently offering vertiginous views, you will also spot the pocket-sized **China Beach▶▶**, named for the Gold-Rush-era Chinese fishermen who lived in shacks beside it. Apart from a foolhardy clamber down the hillside, China Beach is accessible only from the affluent residential area around Seacliff Avenue. The coastal trail continues to **Baker Beach** (see page 57) and through a section of the Presidio before reaching the approach to Golden Gate Bridge. The GGNRA extends to parts of the northern waterfront, and continues on the north side of the Golden Gate.

Across the Golden Gate, the undulating hillsides which face the city form part of the **Marin Headlands▶**. The Marin Headlands Visitor Center (tel: 415/331-1540; open: 9.30–4.30), off Highway 101, is a worthwhile first stop before exploring this interesting and enticing mix of ridges, valleys and beaches.

One part of Golden Gate National Recreation Area

SWIMMING AT CHINA BEACH

After a long hike on a warm day, China Beach has special appeal. It is one of the few beaches in San Francisco where swimming is regarded as safe. The lifeguard post is manned from mid-April to mid-October.

POINT BONITA LIGHTHOUSE

Explore the Marin Headlands on a summer weekend and you will be able to visit Point Bonita Lighthouse, completed in 1855 and the oldest fixed beacon on the West Coast. The lighthouse is the prize at the end of an eventful half-mile (open: Sat–Mon 12.30–3.30) trail from Point Bonita.

JOHN MCLAREN
Born in Scotland in 1846, John McLaren trained at Edinburgh's Botanic Gardens and, having migrated to California, landscaped several Bay Area parks before becoming assistant supervisor, and then supervisor, of Golden Gate Park. McLaren became so involved in the park's development and so well-known in the city, that a special law was passed in 1917 enabling him to work beyond retirement age. McLaren continued as park supervisor until his death in 1943.

GOLDEN GATE PARK
For information contact the Beach Chalet Visitor Center (tel:415/751-2766) or Friends of Recreation and Parks (tel: 415/750-5105).

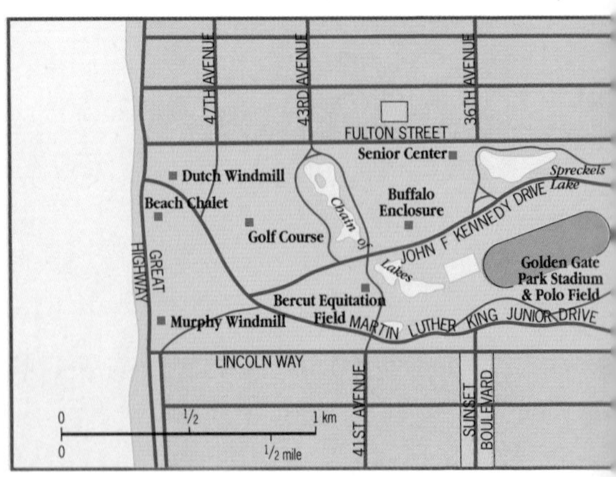

►►► Golden Gate Park *IFCB4*

Buses: 5, 7 (daytime), 18, 21, 28, 29, 44, 71

Three miles (5km) long and half a mile (1.5km) wide, Golden Gate Park stretches from Haight-Ashbury to the Pacific, providing San Francisco with one of the world's largest urban parks. Hidden among these 1,000 green acres (405ha) are a polo field, a golf course, an archery range, a botanical garden, two major museums, countless lakes, ponds and waterfalls, and even a few windmills. Yet Golden Gate Park still has sufficient space to enable anyone to become hopelessly lost—and quickly found again—amid its tree-lined lanes and walkways.

The park has given San Francisco a stage from which to show itself to the world (with events as diverse as the Midwinter International Exposition of 1894 and the

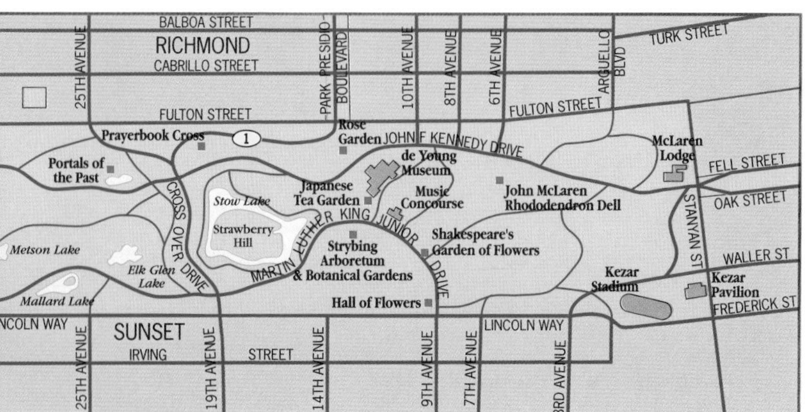

hippie Human Be-In of 1967) as well as a large and bucolic retreat for those who enjoy jogging, skateboarding, roller-skating and kite-flying.

Many San Franciscans were amused in 1869 when the city authorities announced that a wind-bitten area of sand dunes then known as the Outer Lands was to be the site of a new public park, a decision partly influenced by a desire to clear the area of its squatters' camps.

The ecological headache of transforming sand dunes into a lushly landscaped park caused the project to take shape slowly. Not until the appointment of John McLaren as park supervisor in 1890 did Golden Gate Park begin to assume the appearance it still largely retains.

The gifted and single-minded McLaren was to spend the rest of his life creating and shaping Golden Gate Park.

One of the park's many refreshing fountains

HAGIWARA'S FORTUNE COOKIE

Curiously, it was Makoto Hagiwara, creator of the Japanese Tea Garden, who, in 1909, devised the fortune cookie—a crisp disc of pastry folded while warm around a printed fortune-telling message—as a novelty to offer visitors to the garden. By the 1920s, his idea had been usurped by the restaurants of Chinatown, with whom it became synonymous.

You really can drink tea at the Japanese Tea Garden, which sits in Golden Gate Park close to the de Young Museum. The garden's tea pavilion (below) is designed in traditional Japanese style, and its jasmine and green teas are served with fortune cookies

Several entrances lead into Golden Gate Park, but the best approach is from Haight-Ashbury's Panhandle, a slender green strip facing the red sandstone **McLaren Lodge**, former home and office of John McLaren. Maps of the park can be obtained from here.

Lined by numerous walkways, John F. Kennedy Drive goes west into the park and quickly reaches the turn-off leading to the **AIDS Memorial Grove▶**, a 15-acre (6-ha) wooded grove adopted for private services following the death of a loved one to Aids. Ahead on JFK Drive, meanwhile, the Conservatory of Flowers is unlikely to re-open following 1989 earthquake damage.

Further on, the **John McLaren Rhododendron Dell▶** is the first of the park's many secluded gardens and groves and the only place in the park where you will find a likeness of John McLaren: a statue depicts him holding a pine cone. McLaren's gaze may be a serene one, but he fought tooth and nail against the decision to stage the 1894 Midwinter International Exposition in the park, after which one of the structures built to house it became the first home of the de Young Museum (see pages 118–121). The success of the museum encouraged Golden Gate Park's selection as the site of the California Academy of Sciences (pages 64–65), which opened across the Music Concourse from the de Young Museum in 1916.

Also created for the Expo, but perhaps more in keeping with the ethos of the park, the **Japanese Tea Garden▶▶▶** (tel: 415/752-1171; open: daily 8.30–6) is an elegant paradise of azaleas, cherry trees and a carp-filled pond, all linked by winding pathways. Laid out in traditional Japanese style with a bronze Buddha dating from 1790 at its center, the garden was the work of Makoto Hagiwara. A Japanese San Franciscan, Hagiwara remained in charge of the garden until he was interned following the Japanese attack on Pearl Harbor in 1941.

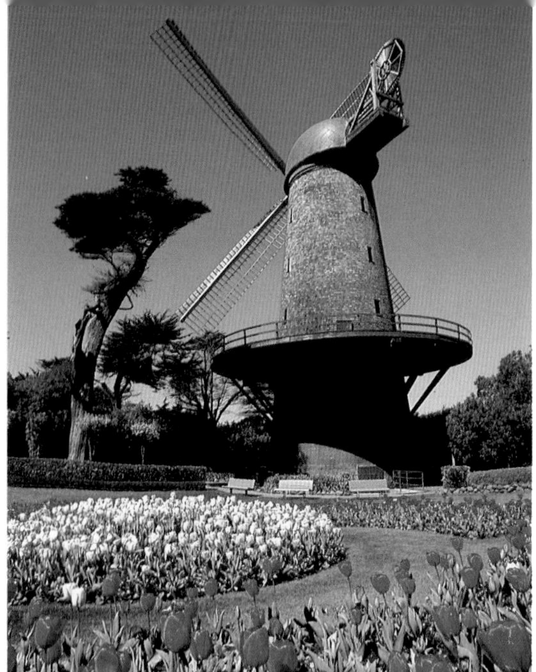

The park's restored Dutch Windmill

TOURING THE PARK
Golden Gate Park is far too big to be fully toured on foot, though determined pedestrians can visit its major points of interest by coupling their legwork with judicious use of buses along its perimeter. Another option, and one encouraged by the park's many miles of cycle trails, is to rent a bike from one of the outlets on Haight-Ashbury's Stanyan Street.

West of the Japanese Tea Garden, a road circles **Stow Lake▶**, and two bridges—or a boat rented from the boathouse—give access to tree-lined **Strawberry Hill▶** in the lake's center. Several steadily ascending footpaths wind up to the small reservoir and waterfall which mark the hill's 400ft (122m) summit.

Garden lovers should head south to the **Strybing Arboretum and Botanical Gardens▶▶** (tel: 415/661-1316; open: Mon–Fri 8–4.30, Sat–Sun 10–5) where 6,000 species of outdoor plants fill 70 carefully tended acres. The many volumes of the **Library of Horticulture** are devoted to all kinds of plant-related subjects, and visitors are welcome to browse at their leisure. Also here is the **Redwood Trail**, a pleasant walk beside some specimens of California's mighty redwood trees.

The traffic-bearing Cross Over Drive makes an unwelcome intrusion into the park, cutting north–south across it between the Richmond and Sunset districts. The 2 miles (3km) of park west of the drive contain recreational areas, such as the equestrian section, a dog-training field, four side-by-side soccer fields and Spreckels Lake, exclusively used by model sail- and motorboat enthusiasts.

Anyone drawn to San Francisco by its associations with 1960s Flower Power will want to gaze over the legendary **Polo Field▶**, scene of many later-mythologized rock concerts and communal LSD trips during the halcyon days of hippiedom.

A sewage treatment plant is the unappealing occupant of the park's southwest corner, but close by stands one of the two windmills originally used to pump water to Strawberry Hill's reservoir. This one, the **Murphy Windmill**, dates from 1905. Its slightly older partner, the **Dutch Windmill▶**, pleasingly restored in 1981, can be found in the park's northwest corner.

Enigmatic statuary—a park specialty

The great expanse of Golden Gate Park and the vast acreage of the Golden Gate National Recreation Area should be enough to satisfy the most ardent green-space enthusiast, but San Francisco also has a surprising number of small parks, some renowned throughout the city for their views or landscaping, others known only to neighborhood dog walkers.

PARK CHECKLIST
Other San Francisco parks worth a visit include the following, described elsewhere:
Buena Vista Park (page 62)
Golden Gate Park (pages 100–103)
Golden Gate National Recreation Area (page 99)
Ina Coolbrith Park (panel, page 157)
Sutro Heights Park (page 170)
Washington Square Park (page 137)

Washington Square Park: taking exercise seriously

Mission Dolores Park Walk south from Mission Dolores (see page 124) past several streets lined with elegant Victorian architecture, and you reach Mission Dolores Park. Once a Jewish cemetery, the large, palm-studded park rises to a summit where the views reach to the high-rise towers of the Financial District (note that the park has been tainted by drug dealing activity).

Huntington Park No better place for a breather after climbing Nob Hill (see pages 130–131), Huntington Park, opposite Grace Cathedral, is surrounded by historic hotels and expensive apartment buildings. Come here to pass a lazy Sunday morning watching the local Chinese doing Tai Chi exercises while a very affluent congregation goes to the cathedral for morning service. The park is on the site of the mansion of David Colson, a minor partner of the Big Four (see page 37), which was destroyed in the 1906 fire.

Lafayette Park The highest point in Pacific Heights (see pages 148–150), Lafayette Park is surrounded by mansions—indeed, until 1936, it had one in its center—with handsome trees, well-tended lawns and attractive flower beds, all struggling valiantly to wrest attention from a magnificent lookout over the city.

Alta Plaza Park Four blocks west of Lafayette Park and occupying a similarly impressive Pacific Heights vista point, Alta Plaza Park rises in stepped terraces from Clay Street.

South Park Oval-shaped South Park, in SoMa (see pages 166–169), was once a place of recreation for the wealthy occupants of the elegant homes which lined it, but as the area declined, so too did the park. Nowadays, despite the noisy elevated freeway which looms beside it, South Park's sycamores and weeping willows enjoyed a renaissance thanks to a steady influx of multimedia companies and cyberspace professionals who colonized the neighborhood from the mid-1980s. With the e-economy boom of the 1990s, the park and the restaurants surrounding it briefly became an informal recruitment center for the new industry.

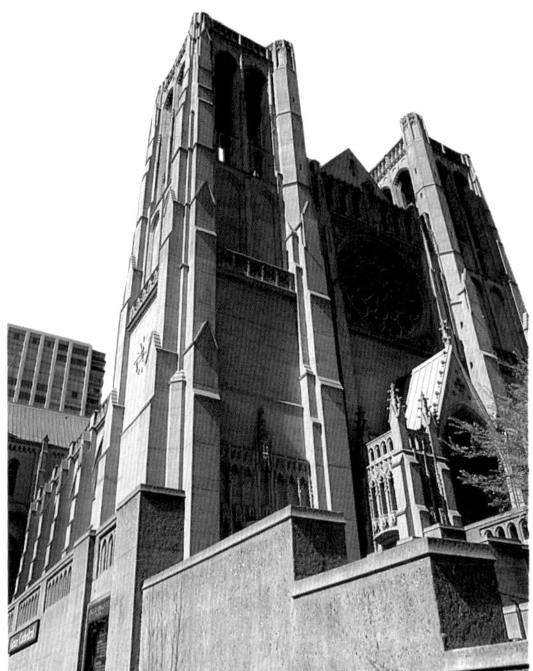

HAAS-LILIENTHAL TOUR TIMES
Tours of the Haas-Lilienthal House last 45 minutes and are conducted on Wednesday and Saturday (noon–3) and Sunday (11–4). Even if you do not have time for a tour, drop by the reception area for the entertaining Haas and Lilienthal pictorial family histories lining the walls and an excellent collection of books and pamphlets for sale, all relating to San Francisco history with special emphasis on the city's architecture.

The Episcopalian Grace Cathedral, which sits at the brow of Nob Hill, was finished in 1964. It took more than 50 years to build

►►► Grace Cathedral *IBCF5*

1051 Taylor Street (tel: 415/749-6300)
Tours: weekdays 1–3, Sat 11.30–1.30, Sun 12.30–2; tel: 415/749-6348 for tour information
Bus: 1

Grace Cathedral, consecrated in 1964, is a quietly stylish neo-Gothic structure modeled on Notre Dame in Paris. It sits confidently on top of Nob Hill, on the site of the Crocker Mansion (see pages 130–131). However, the position of the Cathedral House, on its southeastern corner, detracts from its most impressive exterior feature: a pair of gilded bronze doors from a Lorenzo Ghiberti cast used for the Baptistry in Florence.

Inside, a 15th-century French altarpiece and exquisite Flemish reredos can be seen in the Chapel of Grace (open only for services; otherwise view through a wrought-iron gate), while the stained-glass windows of the main building depict biblical scenes, and such diverse achievers as Albert Einstein, Henry Ford and Frank Lloyd Wright.

►► Haas-Lilienthal House *IBCE5*

2007 Franklin Street (tel: 415/441-3000)
Bus: 83

The Haas-Lilienthal House is the only fully period-furnished Victorian house in San Francisco open to the public. It also serves as a base for the Foundation for San Francisco's Architectural Heritage, devoted to spreading the word about the city's architectural legacy and, where possible, preserving choice examples of it.

Guided tours (see panel) tell the intriguing story of the Haas and Lilienthal families, who lived here over an 86-year period, enabling the house to survive as its neighborhood contemporaries were demolished. Countless details highlight changing tastes over the last 100 years.

A treasure trove of Victoriana: the Haas-Lilienthal House

One of many used clothing outlets on Haight Street, the effervescent commercial artery of Haight-Ashbury

UNIVERSITY OF SAN FRANCISCO
Not to be confused with San Francisco State University (see page 162), the University of San Francisco lies five blocks north of Haight Street on the borders of the Richmond District, easily spotted by the towering twin spires of the 1914 St. Ignatius Church (see panel, page 66), which sits in mock Italian Renaissance splendor amid the campus buildings. Other than the church, the university, founded by Jesuits in 1855, is unremarkable.

Haight-Ashbury's lampposts and road signs provide convenient billboards to publicize forthcoming events

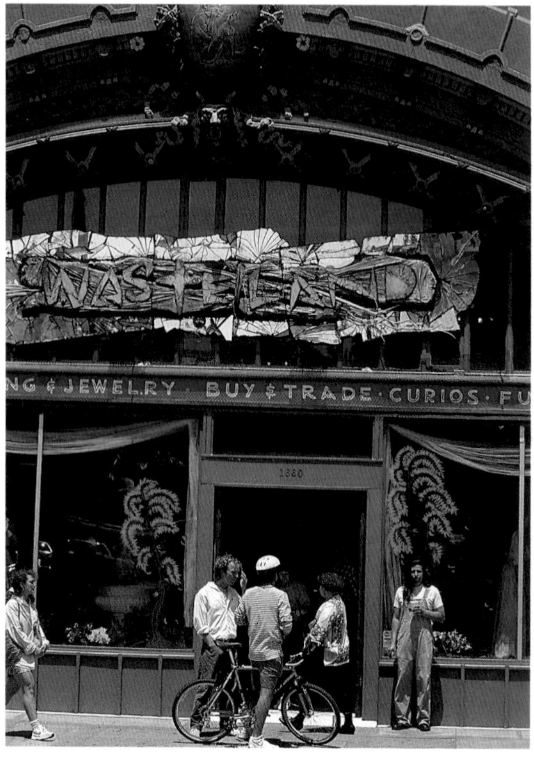

▶▶ Haight-Ashbury *IFCD4*

Buses: 6, 7, 66, 71

In 1967, Haight-Ashbury (between the Western Addition and Golden Gate Park) was described as "the vibrant epicenter of America's hippie movement." For the full story on Haight-Ashbury's role in the Flower Power era, see pages 110–111.

It was no accident that Haight-Ashbury became the home of hippies. Even by San Francisco's liberal standards, Haight-Ashbury has a long history of tolerance—a trait which continues into the present. Along Haight Street, the district's main artery, long-haired skateboarders in tie-dyed T-shirts skim along the sidewalks, the homeless panhandle, street musicians strum their guitar strings from a prone position and many shady characters offer dope *sotto voce*. Yet the street also boasts increasingly classy restaurants and exceptional used-book stores and vintage clothing outlets which draw shoppers from all over the city. Haight-Ashbury also has countless impressive examples of Victorian architecture (commonly known as "Victorians," see page 18).

What became Haight-Ashbury was dairy farmland dotted with squatters' camps when the grand plans for the creation of Golden Gate Park were unveiled in the 1870s. To carry visitors to the new park, a cable-car line was introduced along Market and Haight streets in 1883, and Haight-Ashbury (named for the intersection of two of its busier streets) became ripe for development.

(*continued on page 108*)

Walk

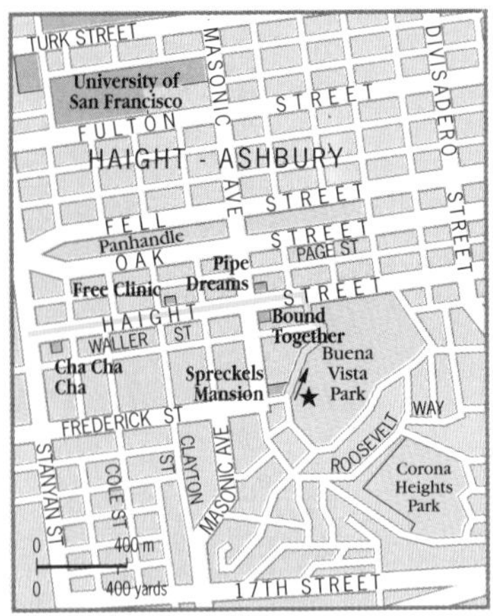

Haight-Ashbury

This walk is for visitors who are keen to capture the flavor of Haight-Ashbury. It begins beside Buena Vista Park and continues to the stores and restaurants that line Haight Street.

One of a series of fine Victorian houses overlooking Buena Vista Park, the **Spreckels Mansion** was completed in 1898 for the wealthy and powerful Adolph Spreckels and his wife.

Along Haight Street, retail outlets ranging from the wacky to the worthy sell vintage clothes, records, books and alternative-lifestyle paraphernalia. Some have the kind of price tags which indicate the area's increasing cachet and appeal to fashion-conscious consumers. Others, such as **Pipe Dreams**, with its 1960s posters, patchouli oil and king-size cigarette papers, along with **Bound Together**, a co-operatively run anarchist bookstore, are more redolent of the district's famous counterculture leanings.

Haight Street's cafés and restaurants, too, are steadily becoming upscale while still seeking to maintain their "alternative" appeal. Worthwhile simply for the food is **Cha Cha Cha** (1805 Haight Street), which offers interesting Cuban and Caribbean specialties.

Counterculture for sale—credit cards accepted

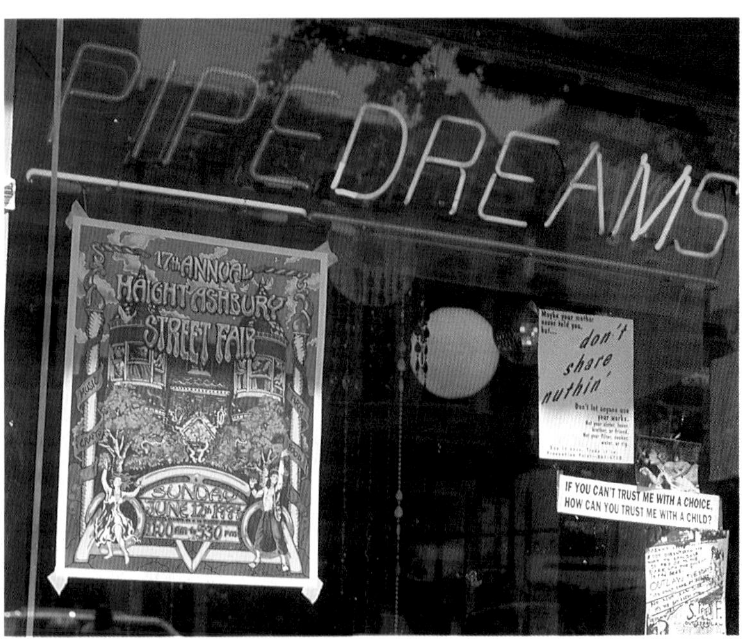

Haight-Ashbury's Spreckels Mansion, built for Richard Spreckels, part of the Spreckels sugar dynasty, in 1898. Once a bed-and-breakfast inn, the mansion is now a private home

(*continued from page 106*)

Though increasingly accessible, Haight-Ashbury was still considered to be some distance from the city. Its first opulent homes were intended as weekend retreats for wealthy families. Although Haight-Ashbury was untouched by the 1906 fire, many of its expansive homes were converted to multifamily dwellings to ease the subsequent housing shortage. The transient population caused Haight-Ashbury's social standing to fall, while the Depression saw the Victorian houses fall into disrepair.

Throughout World War II, many African-Americans, who had arrived in San Francisco to work in wartime

industries, spilled into Haight-Ashbury from the Western Addition, contributing to the ethnic diversity which the neighborhood still enjoys.

By the early 1960s, low rents lured students from the nearby University of San Francisco and would-be Beats escaping the upwardly mobile North Beach. Not since the Gold Rush had San Francisco received as many new arrivals as it did during the summer of 1967, all of them headed for Haight-Ashbury. While the events of the time passed into legend, the neighborhood was unable to cope with the 200,000 young people who arrived in pursuit of peace, love and a life without material possessions spent in a haze of pot smoke. By the early 1970s, Haight-Ashbury had degenerated into a seriously seedy area, filled with poverty and hard drug use.

In time, however, the falling prices of the Victorian houses encouraged the influx of a new and relatively affluent population. Eager to restore their homes and to foster Haight-Ashbury's unique sense of community, many new settlers became active in plans to aid the area's homeless and hungry, and to force drug dealers off its streets. While Haight-Ashbury is still far from problem free, Haight Street has become an offbeat addition to the city's shopping circuit, more and more Victorian houses are opening as bed-and-breakfast inns (such as the Red Victorian), and the many new bars and restaurants are targeting an upscale clientele. Exploring Haight-Ashbury means 1960s landmarks and architecturally interesting Victorian buildings—which in some instances are one and the same. Psychedelic rock music progenitors, The Grateful Dead, occupied various Haight-Ashbury addresses but are most closely associated with **710 Ashbury Street▶**, where they were busted for marijuana possession in October 1967. The house is one of a row of pretty Queen Anne-style residences built around 1890 by architect Robert Cranston.

Cranston's many contributions to Haight-Ashbury included a home for himself on **Page Street**. The owl-decorated number 1777 was Cranston's, but look too for the wedding cake Queen Anne at number 1901, a one-time home of 1920s novelist Kathleen Norris, and number 1899, which demonstrates the turn-of-the-20th-century shift in fashion from Queen Anne to Colonial Revival.

On the corner of Clayton and Haight streets, the **Haight-Ashbury Free Clinic▶** was founded in 1967 by an idealistic young doctor dismayed by the medical establishment's failure to respond to hippie health problems. The main workload of the volunteer doctors involved venereal disease, drug abuse and foot ailments (caused by going barefoot). The clinic still plays an important role in the community, offering free health care for Haight-Ashbury's poor, despite repeated efforts by the authorities to close it down.

The Diggers (see pages 110–111) opened their legendary Free Store at 1775 Haight Street, while number 1660 was the short-lived **Straight Theater**, where the management got around their lack of a music license by claiming that the concerts staged there were dancing lessons.

Reports of Haight-Ashbury's gentrification have been exaggerated, but the area is on the rise, set to receive an influx of residents as wealthy as those of the early 1900s.

A mannequin unmoved by Haight Street scenes

STRIKING STAIRWAYS
Sections of San Francisco's steepest streets are often traversed by stairways, and two of the most enjoyable—one for its lush foliage, the other for its views—are the Vulcan and Saturn stairways, on the hillsides dividing Haight-Ashbury from the Castro. The stairways can be accessed from Roosevelt Way, which runs between Buena Vista Park (see page 62) and Corona Heights Park.

LOWER HAIGHT
Leave Haight-Ashbury heading toward Market Street and you soon reach the loosely defined area called Lower Haight. Home to an alternative-minded community of artists, musicians and poets into the early 1990s, the area—its commercial center is on the 500 block of Haight Street—has steadily succumbed to the gentrification that has swept through Haight-Ashbury, many once rundown stores now housing trendy, pricey eateries and bars.

In 1967, when Scott McKenzie sang about going to San Francisco with flowers in your hair, Haight-Ashbury was in the incense-scented throes of what was to become known as the Summer of Love: the climax of the hippie movement. What had begun several years previously when a disparate assemblage of alternative-lifestyle seekers moved into the neighborhood and began developing an idealistic sense of community now seemed ready to unstitch the very fabric of American society.

PARK FROLICS
Journalist Ralph Gleason describing 1967's Human Be-In in Golden Gate Park: "A beautiful girl in an Indian headdress handed me a long stick of slow-burning incense and another handed out sprigs of bay leaves. Women and men alike carried flowers and wore ribbons in their hair. There were more clean long-haired males assembled in one place than at any time since the Crusades."

Top: In Haight-Ashbury today—the influence of the hippie movement lives on
Below: Strolling down Haight Street in 1967

Social ferment By the early 1960s, Haight-Ashbury was an ethnically mixed, low-rent neighborhood with shabby but spacious Victorian houses that made ideal shared homes for students from the nearby University of San Francisco and for anyone at odds with conventional society. For such people, the protest movement, radical campus politics and the previous decade's Beat generation were important influences.

Among the settlers were The Diggers, a revolutionary offshoot of an avant-garde theater group whose idealistic aims could be put into practice in the socially tolerant Haight-Ashbury. One project was the Free Store: a shop where everything was free—"customers" took what they needed and gave what they could spare.

The Grateful Dead and other local rock bands played music that veered from rhythm and blues to free-form improvization, and often did so for free "and for hours at a time" in the streets and parks. When indoor venues could be found, the concerts became multimedia experiences with light shows and body painting. Alcohol was seldom consumed, but fruit was provided for free.

Psychedelic drugs The hippies (derisively so-named by the Beats who regarded them as junior hipsters) also took a then-legal drug called LSD. The government had been testing the potent mind-altering drug on volunteers at Stanford University (one of whom, author Ken Kesey, began "borrowing" large amounts to enliven Haight-Ashbury's multimedia events and his own "acid tests"). In Berkeley, the unlikely named Augustus Owsley Stanley III manufactured LSD in a makeshift laboratory.

Revolution soon Many Haight-Ashbury hippies truly believed that a peaceful social revolution would occur just as soon as everyone discovered the joys of LSD. As the media discovered the strange activities in Haight-Ashbury, however, their sensationalist reporting encouraged a nationwide panic: LSD was made illegal in 1966, and the San Francisco police and other conservative elements missed no opportunity to harass the long-haired of Haight Street, where hippie-run businesses—dispensing head-bands, talismans, incense and other prerequisites of the lifestyle—were increasingly common.

A scene from daily life in a 1960s hippy commune

Summer of love By the summer of 1967, Haight-Ashbury was national news, and young people headed west for their share of the free love and drugs which they had heard about. Instead of earthly paradise, though, they found a neighborhood at bursting point: Haight-Ashbury's hippie population swelled from 7,000 to 75,000 in just six months.

Barefoot and beaded, the hippies of Haight Street quickly became a tourist attraction. The Gray Line bus company began running "Hippie tours" just as they had run "Beatnik tours" of North Beach a decade earlier.

While free concerts became regular events in the Panhandle, many of the original psychedelic bands—most spectacularly Jefferson Airplane—had become financially successful and were quickly sucked into the mainstream music business they professed to despise: Only the Grateful Dead remained fully true to their idealistic roots. By October 1967, the Diggers were sufficiently disenchanted to organize a Death of the Hippie march, complete with a replica hippie in a cardboard coffin.

Haight-Ashbury's decline As the original hippies left the increasingly unstable neighborhood for the rural peace of Northern California and beyond, Haight-Ashbury degenerated. Addictive hard drugs replaced LSD in popularity, and sinister figures such as Charles Manson—who recruited some of his "family" among the runaways of Haight-Ashbury—emerged. In 1969, the year of the most notorious Manson Family murders, a Rolling Stones concert at Altamont racetrack, in Alameda County, east of Oakland, culminated in a fatal stabbing, which for many symbolized the end of the American hippie dream.

HIPPIEDOM'S RIPPLES
However shortlived its heyday may have been, the impact of the hippie movement was profound. It encouraged many of the social freedoms now accepted as the norm and inadvertently created a mass market for rock music which was enjoyed and exploited by a new generation of musicians and music business entrepreneurs. Currently, as the hippie-influenced Baby Boom generation rises to positions of power, the movement's impact (albeit in diluted form) seems likely to continue far into the future.

WILLIS POLK
The groundbreaking Hallidie Building enhanced Willis Polk's already major reputation as one of San Francisco's most capable architects. His many contributions to the city include the Merchant Exchange Building (see page 87) and the remodeling of the Flood mansion into the Pacific Union Club (see page 131). Earlier, Polk—who as a young man had reveled in San Francisco's 1890s bohemia—built himself a characterful brown shingle home which still stands near the top of Russian Hill, at 1013–19 Vallejo Street.

▶ Hallidie Building *IBCJ8*

130–150 Sutter Street
Buses: 2, 3, 4

Many architects consider the Hallidie Building the most significant structure in San Francisco, as it was the first building in the world to utilize a "glass curtain" (actually a wall of glass and metal suspended in front of the concrete facade). Designed by the esteemed Willis Polk (see panel) and completed in 1917, the Hallidie Building—named for the inventor of the cable car—also features wrought-iron fire escapes to add to its esthetic appeal.

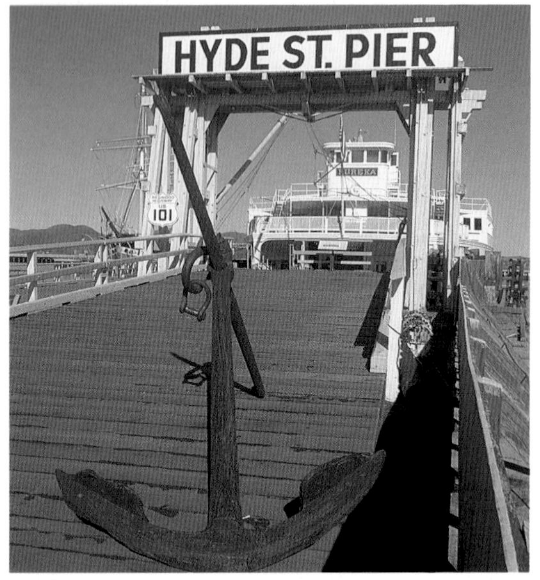

An anchor shows the way to Hyde Street Pier Historic Ships

▶▶ Hyde Street Pier Historic Ships *IBCF6*

Hyde Street Pier, Fisherman's Wharf (tel: 415/561-6662)
Open: daily 9.30–5, until 5.30 in summer; inexpensive
Bus: 32

In the days when Fisherman's Wharf was filled with fishermen rather than tourists, ferries to Berkeley and Sausalito sailed from the northern waterfront's Hyde Street Pier. One such ferry was the *Eureka*, built in 1890 and now one of several restored vessels moored here (part of San Francisco National Maritime Park, which includes the National Maritime Museum, see page 128).

The entertaining collection of vintage cars assembled around its lower decks gives only an inkling of the *Eureka*'s capabilities; in her day, she was the world's largest passenger ferry, able to haul more than 2,000 people and 100 vehicles across the bay in a single trip.

The most intriguing historic ship is the *Balclutha*, a steel-hulled, square-rigged sailing ship that was launched in Scotland in 1886. It rounded Cape Horn several times before ending its days transporting Alaskan salmon along the West Coast of the US. Clamber down the narrow ladders and around the claustrophobic decks to look at the restored cabins and scrutinize the informative explanatory texts.

The 19th-century Balclutha, a Cape Horn veteran built in Scotland

Among the other ships (over coming years; it is planned that many more will be added to the collection) are the *C. A. Thayer*, built in 1895 to move the lumber with which many early California cities were built, the *Alma*, a scow schooner whose flat bottom enabled her to navigate the shallow waters on the periphery of San Francisco Bay, and *Hercules*, a deepwater steam tug built in 1907.

▶ Jackson Square *IBCG5*

Buses: 41, 42

The 1850s brick buildings of Jackson Square (a district rather than an actual square, bordered by Washington, Pacific, Sansome and Columbus streets) saw all the wild excesses of the Barbary Coast (see page 35) before the 1906 earthquake and fire terminated such nefarious activities. As the fire razed neighboring streets, a mile-long (1.6km) hose brought water from Fisherman's Wharf and helped save Jackson Square, though lack of commercial interest in subsequent decades saw many of its distinctive buildings fall into disrepair.

Things changed in the 1950s when an inspired group of furniture wholesalers launched a restoration initiative, leading to Jackson Square becoming the city's first designated Historic District in 1971.

Ironically, rising rents drove the wholesalers out and in their place came law firms, architectural practices, advertising agencies—which have offices on the upper levels—and exclusive antique dealers, who display their expensive wares at street level.

▶ Japantown *IBCE5*

Buses: 38, 50

Concealed behind Japantown's unexciting exteriors are the stores, temples and social centers serving the city's Japanese community, only a small percentage of whom actually live here. In 1941, however, almost all of San Francisco's 7,000 Japanese-Americans had homes and businesses here, within the Western Addition.

America's entry into World War II following the Japanese attack on Pearl Harbor resulted in the mass

Nihonmachi Mall, above and below, was created as part of the renewal of Japantown in the mid-1970s. Ruth Asawa's street architecture uses traditional Japanese themes

JAPANESE-AMERICAN GENERATIONS

The Japanese population of San Francisco divides itself into distinct generations, each with a different name. The first wave of settlers who arrived in the early 1900s were the *issei*, and their American-born children were known as *nisei*. Subsequent generations have been *sansei*, *yonsei* and *shin issei*, respectively.

Fire-fighting relics

FIRE DEPARTMENT MUSEUM
(tel: 415/563-4630; open: Thu to Sun 1–4; free) Eight blocks west of Japantown at 655 Presidio Avenue, the Fire Department Museum fills a barn-like room with a colossal jumble of mementoes recording San Franciscan fire-fighting from its earliest days onward. The array includes helmets, badges, buckets, axes, a dainty 1810 fire truck imported from New York and photographs and press cuttings detailing the city's most famous fires and the men and horses who helped put them out.

Windsocks filling out in the breeze outside the Japan Center

internment of the US's Japanese citizens. After the war, while some reestablished their lives in the area, many moved on, and the Japanese-American population quickly became dispersed across the city and the entire Bay Area.

Visitors to contemporary Japantown are first struck by its smallness—a few blocks enclosed by Octavia and Fillmore streets, and Geary Boulevard and Pine Street—and secondly by the proliferation of concrete. The commercial core is **Japan Center▶**, a 3-acre (1.5-ha) indoor mall packed with good Japanese restaurants and mixed quality stores but entirely lacking in character. Immediately outside, a broad concrete plaza holds the 100ft (31m) **Peace Pagoda▶**, erected in 1968. More pleasing is the open-air **Nihonmachi Mall▶** (also called "Buchanan Mall"), a short pedestrian-only strip with street landscaping—benches, fountains and more—by the noted Japanese-American designer Ruth Asawa.

Away from the stores and restaurants, and the colorful **Cherry Blossom Festival**, which is celebrated with vigor each April, Japantown's main points of ethnic interest are religious.

The **Buddhist Church of San Francisco** (see page 62) warrants a look; others worthy of a visit are the **Konko-kyo Church of San Francisco▶** (1909 Bush Street; tel: 415/931-0453), built in the 1970s and employing traditional Shinto themes, and the **Soto Zen Mission Sokoji▶** (1691 Laguna Street), where the wood-beamed roof brings a traditional flavor to a recent building. A few remnants of pre-concrete Japantown can also be seen. Dating from 1910 and bearing a marked Japanese influence on its terracotta-tiled facade is the

Binet-Montessori School▶ (1715 Octavia Street). Meanwhile, number 1737 **Webster Street▶** is built in the Stick style popular in the 1880s.

Pre-dating the arrival of the Japanese, the **Atherton Mansion▶** (1900 California Street, on the corner with Laguna Avenue), was once occupied by Gertrude Atherton, whose novels caused a stir in early 20th-century California for their tales of strong women railing against inept men. Gertrude was perhaps inspired by her husband, George, a fellow described as "lacking the initiative even to tie his own shoelaces." When George embarked on a long sea journey and died en route of kidney failure, his body returned home preserved in a barrel of rum, arriving as Gertrude was hosting a dinner party. Whether by the spirits of George, his mother (who had the house built in 1881 and was described by her daughter-in-law as "a tyrannical old lady"), Gertrude, or by the fifty cats kept here by a subsequent occupant, the house is said to be the most haunted in San Francisco.

▶ Levi's Plaza *IBCF6*

Sansome and Battery streets, between Union and Greenwich streets
Buses: 42, 69, 83

The 1906 Levi Strauss factory in the Mission District (see panel, page 124) continues to manufacture the world-famous Levi jeans, but since 1982 the company's international headquarters has been within this creatively designed low-rise office complex. Utilizing a group of empty warehouses and a one-time ice house, Levi's Plaza is an admired example of modern corporate architecture and uses the sharp incline of Telegraph Hill, directly across Union Street, as a stunning scenic backdrop.

Pass by the fountains, stores and food stands around the plaza and enter the lobby of the main building to discover a modest historical display on Levi jeans, including some of the earliest pairs, which were colored brown and made for California's gold miners in the 1870s.

LEVI'S PLAZA'S BUILDINGS

Many of the buildings which make up Levi's Plaza are brick-built warehouses, which fell into disuse with the decline of the nearby Embarcadero. The Embarcadero once bustled with rows of ocean-going freighters which regularly unloaded their cargo here, filling the warehouses with coffee, coconuts, bananas, canned fish, clothing and other commodities carried across the high seas. In recent times, however, it was known for its ugly freeway, which was damaged in the 1989 Loma Prieta quake, and then mercifully demolished in 1992.

At the foot of Telegraph Hill, Levi's Plaza is modern corporate architecture with a human face

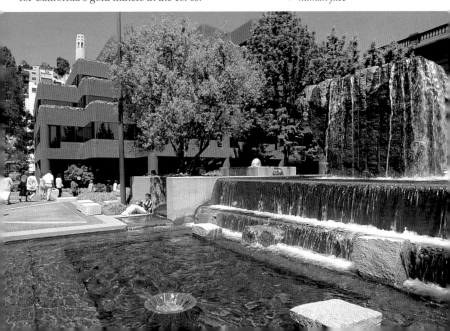

There's no mistaking Maiden Lane's Circle Gallery, designed by Frank Lloyd Wright

►► Maiden Lane *IBCF5*

Opposite Union Square, between Stockton and Kearny streets
Buses: 30, 45

Before it was gutted by the 1906 earthquake and fire, Maiden Lane was known as Morton Street and was the scene of some of the worst excesses of the Barbary Coast (see page 35). Along this two-block street, topless women would solicit passing males from behind open windows, and some of them claimed to service 100 customers per day. Present-day Maiden Lane is a complete contrast: a well-scrubbed alley entered through pretty white gates and lined by designer-clothes stores and upscale furniture outlets. Window-shop along the narrow thoroughfare and pause for a snack at one of the cafés which place their tables outside during the day, when Maiden Lane is closed to traffic. At number 140, admire the brickwork facade and arched entrance of Frank Lloyd Wright's **Circle Gallery**. Inside, the steadily ascending spiral ramp that carries browsers past the artworks (the building displays the paintings and graphics of three galleries) for sale was a prototype of Wright's Guggenheim Museum in New York.

► Marina District *IBCE6*

Buses: 22, 30

Dominated by comfortable family homes and spacious, tastefully designed low-rise apartments, the Marina District—occupying the waterfront directly north of Pacific Heights—has a personality closer to that of an affluent suburb than a city neighborhood. Its predominantly young and professional residents lead their well-groomed dogs on windy walks through Marina Green, take lone contemplative strolls through the wondrous Palace of Fine Arts (see page 152), which borders the district to the west, or rendezvous with their neighborhood friends in the chic restaurants lining Chestnut Street.

The area's abiding sense of stability is deceptive, however. Built on landfill, the homes of the Marina District are particularly vulnerable to earthquakes, and the area was one of the most seriously affected during the Loma Prieta quake which hit the city in 1989.

"MEXICANO" AND OTHER TERMS

The Mexican Museum defines the term "Mexicano" as describing Mexican, Mexican-American and Chicano people. The term "Chicano," derived from the Aztec word for Mexico, was adopted by US citizens of Mexican descent in a radical political movement of the 1970s. "Latino" is used to describe people of Latin American origin or descent, as is "Hispanic," meaning "descended from the Spanish." The latter term could be considered insulting if used to mistakenly describe a person of pure Latin American Indian stock.

THE FRENCH CHURCH

A short distance from Maiden Lane, two blocks north of Union Square at 566 Bush Street, the Church of Notre-Dame des Victoires (tel: 415/397-0113) was raised in 1913 by French architect Louis Brouchard to serve as a religious center and general meeting place for the city's French Catholic population (Mass is said in French each Sunday morning). It occupies the site of the city's earliest French church, built in 1856 and destroyed by the 1906 earthquake.

▶▶ Mexican Museum *IBCE6*

Building D, Fort Mason Center (due to move during 2006)
Tel: 415/441-0404
Opening times to be announced

Founded in the predominantly Latino Mission District (see page 124) in 1975, the Mexican Museum evolved into Fort Mason Center's most successful museum. Its fast-growing collections and critical acclaim resulted in a new $20-million facility on SoMa's Mission Street facing the Yerba Buena Center for the Arts due to open at some future date. Designed by Ricardo Legorreta, the new building is clad in dark red Mexican lava rock, and has 63,000sq ft (19,203sq m) of exhibition space. This will provide a tremendous increase in the space available at Fort Mason and allow much more from the museum's permanent collection of 12,000 objects to be shown.

It is with short-term shows, however, that the Mexican Museum has forged a unique niche. Many Mexican and Chicano artists who would otherwise not be represented in a museum are exhibited, encouraging more conservative establishments to take an interest in them. At the same time, the museum is able to present known Mexican and Latin American art and artists in a sympathetic setting: An exhibition of works by Frida Kahlo, for example, drew 20,000 people here in 1987.

Among past exhibitions has been a retrospective of two decades of work by Gronk, a category-defying performance artist who emerged from Latino East Los Angeles in the early 1970s. His early "pieces" included an "erasure" of the US–Mexico border, and the No Movie Awards, a comment on Hollywood back-slapping that presented an awards ceremony for movies shot with no film in the camera. By contrast, Visiones del Pueblo presented folk-art objects from 17 Latin American countries, while Chicano Codices offered contemporary Latino artists' interpretations of the Spanish Conquest of Mexico. Large-scale portraits of residents of the Mission District and the city's East Bay area, commissioned by San Francisco's Galeria de la Reza, formed another exhibition.

A piece of Mexican folk art on display in the Mexican Museum

The yacht moorings in the foreground help give the Marina District its name

A NEW DE YOUNG
When the new-look de Young Museum opened in October 2005, it brought a striking copper-coloured addition to Golden Gate Park that will steadily fade to a greener hue to remain in keeping with its wooded surrounds. While the museum's reduced foot print returns 2 acres (1ha) to the park, the interior has expanded, the collections spread over three floors connected by a series of courtyards. Ribbon windows provide glimpses of the park, reinforcing the sense of integration between the museum and its setting.

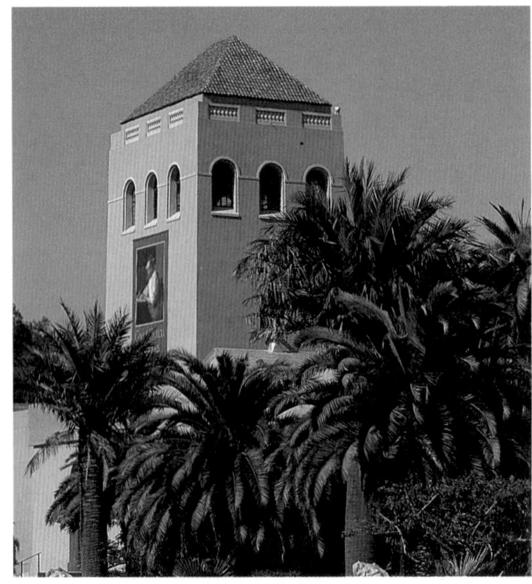

Above right, and below: The de Young Museum, set in Golden Gate Park and housing major works of art

▶▶▶ M. H. de Young Museum *IFCC4*

Golden Gate Park (tel: 415/863-3330)
Open: daily 10–4.45; free
Buses: 28, 29, 44

Containing San Francisco's major collection of American art, the de Young Museum enjoys a picturesque setting in Golden Gate Park (see pages 100–103).

Anyone who has experienced San Francisco in midwinter knows that the California idyll of year-round sunshine and palm trees applies only to the south of the state. Despite this, in 1894 the publisher of the *San Francisco Chronicle*, Michael de Young, organized the California Midwinter International Exposition on a 200-acre (81ha) site in Golden Gate Park. He intended to convince the world that the city had a balmy climate while raising some much-needed revenue after a year of economic depression.

To the chagrin of the park's creator, John McLaren (see panel, page 100), the idea of a permanent museum in the park to remember the successful Expo gained popularity. The Egyptian-style Fine Arts Building, which had drawn more than its share of Expo visitors, had been intended as a temporary structure but was reopened in 1895 as the Memorial Museum. Although unskilled as a collector, de Young began avidly acquiring pieces for the new museum, and art-starved San Franciscans visited in the thousands. Within a few years, however, the collections had outgrown the building, and de Young commissioned Louis Christian Mulgardt—an architect involved in the city's 1915 Panama–Pacific Exposition—to design a new home for them. Mulgardt's rather undistinguished Spanish-style structure was completed in 1919, and the expanded museum was renamed following de Young's death in 1925. With the re-locating of the Asian Art Museum (see pages 122–123), which had shared the de Young's home for decades, the museum took the opportunity for a complete rebuild (see panel, facing page).

The de Young Museum's collection of European paintings and sculpture was moved to the California Palace of the Legion of Honor (see pages 67–68) when the museums were formally merged in the 1970s. The de Young's collection of American paintings begins with the work of John Singleton Copley and his 18th-century contemporaries such as John Smibert. A self-taught artist who emerged as the country's foremost painter with his finely executed society portraits, Copley's 1763 *Mrs. Daniel Sargent* highlights his many skills.

One of the museum's earliest acquisitions and still among its most striking works, John Vanderlyn's *Marius Amidst the Ruins of Carthage* was painted in 1807 and won a gold medal at the following year's Paris Salon. Through its mighty scale and scope and its successful tackling of a historical subject, the painting came to epitomize the growing self-confidence of American artists of the time. Refusing offers for the work in France, Vanderlyn returned the painting to the US for exhibition, but it failed to excite collectors in the way he anticipated.

In fact, by the first half of the 19th century, as many American painters were beginning to combine assuredness in their own abilities with the young nation's sense of self-discovery, the interest in European-influenced American art was steadily declining. In the early 1800s, Thomas Cole's landscapes—spearheading the Hudson River School, the nation's first homegrown art movement—highlighted American painters' turning away from European traditions and toward the untamed North American continent.

Some minor examples of Cole's work can be seen here, although much more imposing is a canvas by one of his former pupils: Frederic Church's 1866 *Rainy Season in the Tropics*. Like many of Church's paintings, this piece offers

TEXTILES

It may play second fiddle to the fine arts, but the museum's textile collection has many devoted admirers. From Anatolian prayer rugs and Polish chasubles to Amish quilts and the dresses of Yves Saint-Laurent, the textiles displayed are diverse and intriguing. The selections can be viewed in the Caroline & H. McCoy Jones galleries.

AFRICAN ART

African art is often overlooked by visitors to the de Young Museum; it contains the unsettling *Nail and Blade Oath Making* image from 19th-century Zaire, a fearsome figure used in settling legal disputes.

Snacking among the statues in the museum café garden

Federal-period furniture decorated the nation's finest homes at a time when San Francisco was still a tiny settlement

ANCIENT ART
The museum collection also has ancient art from Egypt, Rome and the Near East. You might spend time contemplating the 2nd-century Roman *Torso of Hermes*, or the group of 8th-century BC Nimrud plaques, but you may find the oldest exhibit to be the most absorbing: a Cycladic figure from 2500BC.

MODERN ART
The museum's 20th-century holdings are generally less impressive than the older material. Take a look, though, at George Bellows' paintings and cast an eye over the two rooms devoted to mixed-media works by Bay Area artists.

a detailed study of nature's handiwork, and is crowned by a double rainbow. Curiously, Church's paintings of far-off, exotic lands were sometimes exhibited in galleries decorated with appropriate vegetation. In this painting, however, the far-off, exotic land seems to be an imagined combination of the Andes and the Caribbean.

High-intensity natural drama is also evident in the landscapes of Albert Bierstadt, who focused his attention on the American West. Among Bierstadt's pieces are *Sunlight and Shadow, California Spring* and the colossal *Storm in the Rocky Mountains*. Interestingly, a Bierstadt painting of the early 1870s, *View of Donner Lake, California*, was commissioned by railroad baron Collis P. Huntington to mark the building of the highest and most difficult section of the transcontinental railroad. While the painting shows the railroad's taming of nature and the conquering of Donner Pass—infamous as the spot where the Donner Party met its doom in the 1840s (see page 188)—it also depicts a romantically charged Sierra Nevada landscape, typical of the artist's mythologizing of Western scenes.

Another painting by Bierstadt, *Indian Hunting Buffalo*, gives a misleading impression of Native American life and contributed to the inaccurate opinions formed of Native Americans on the East Coast. It was a natural progression, nevertheless, for American art to celebrate the colonization of the American West. The most significant figure to do so was Frederick Remington; many of his sculptured tributes to the cowboy are collected here.

As Western images proliferated during the 19th century, a small band of artists took the increasing industrialization of society as their main subject. Several works of Thomas Anshutz are powerful examples of this school; they are displayed in the same room as a number of studies by his former teacher, Thomas Eakins, noted for his carefully observed portraits and sporting scenes.

Other emerging talents still sought inspiration in Europe. Among them was John Singer Sargent, who produced the subtle and distinguished *A Dinner Table at Night* in England in the 1880s. Finally, among its 19th-century paintings, the museum offers an entertaining selection of trompe-l'œil. But the center of attention tends to be William Michael Harnett's *After the Hunt*, a canvas turned into a door hung with slaughtered birds and a rabbit.

If you have concentrated on the paintings, you will need to retrace your steps through the galleries to admire the many impressive examples of American decorative art, from the Colonial period onward, which share many of the rooms. Among the earliest exhibits are New England armchairs from English and Dutch settlements of 1670, and two rooms re-created with original furnishings: an Adam-style George III dining room and a Federal parlor from 1805 Massachusetts. California was still a thinly populated outpost of Mexico when these furnishings were used by the most refined East Coast society. Among the silver knives, forks, spoons, teapots and kneebuckles in the display cases, look for the work of Paul Revere. Although more famous for his midnight rides to warn American revolutionaries of approaching British troops, he followed in his father's footsteps and made a mark as a silversmith.

In furniture, the flowing curves of the Queen Anne style were popular during the Colonial period, but by the time of the Revolution, American craftsmen had acquired the skill to evolve a new and distinctive look, using recognizable Queen Anne features but adding unique rococo touches. Philadelphia emerged above Boston and New York as the center of the craft, and a grand 1780 Philadelphia High Chest serves as an excellent example.

By contrast, a room is devoted to ten murals by Gottardo Piazzoni, a Swiss-born artist who was captivated by California's landscapes as a boy and became a prominent San Francisco artist and teacher over the turn of the 20th century.

The elegant dining room typical of an early upper-class American family (above) contrasts with the simple furniture made by the religious sect known as the Shakers (below)

Be it Chinese jade, Thai ceramics, Japanese netsuke *or a Tibetan thigh-bone trumpet, the Asian Art Museum of San Francisco has the largest collection of its kind in the US and is certain to have something among its wealth of treasures from the East to catch your eye.*

NEW HOME
The home of the Asian Art Museum is the Beaux Arts former main library at 200 Larkin Street (tel: 415/581/3500; www.asianart.org), completed in 1917 as part of the Civic Center complex which reshaped the heart of San Francisco after the 1906 earthquake (open: Tue–Sun 10–5, Thu until 9; moderate; bus: any Market Street; BART: Civic Center

Avery Brundage Remembered by most people only as a long-serving president of the International Olympic Committee, Avery Brundage amassed a fortune as an engineering company mogul and sank some of his millions into a world-class collection of Asian art. By the late 1950s, Brundage was ready to donate this incredible treasure trove and looked around for a suitable home. On account of its long-standing social links with Asia, San Francisco was chosen as the beneficiary, with the proviso that the city erect a suitable home for the collection.

The Asian Art Museum of San Francisco—built alongside the de Young Museum in Golden Gate Park—opened in 1966. As its collections increased, the museum outgrew its home and moved into the elegant former main library in Civic Center.

Touring the galleries The collection spans 6,000 years of inspiration from diverse cultures and religions, and taking it all in is not easy. There is a lot to be said for simply wandering through the galleries pausing at whatever catches your attention.

Chinese collections The scale and scope of the Chinese collections reflect the fact that China was Brundage's main interest. Among the treasures is the oldest dated example of Chinese Buddhist art (AD338) and elegant ceramics from the 10th to the 14th centuries, a period when Chinese craftsmen scaled new heights in the balancing of form and glaze: Look for the flower-shaped dishes bearing impossibly delicate outlines of dragons, and the leaf-shaped cup stands.

There are numerous examples, too, of blue-and-white porcelain of the Xuande Era (1426–1435), regarded as the finest period for this particular craft, intriguing and important examples of Ming Dynasty calligraphy and fan painting (1368–1644), and the amazing scroll paintings, including some breathtaking landscapes, housed in the Tang Family Gallery. Save the Magnin Jade Gallery for last; its stunning jewelry and decorations span several thousand years.

Japanese collections Taking up a large portion of the upper floor, the Japanese collections include many excellent Edo-period screen paintings (1615–1868). Marked by its isolationist policies

and prolonged peace, the Edo period saw a great flourishing of arts and culture as artists began exploring new directions. The Japanese galleries culminate in a tremendous display of *netsuke* (exquisitely carved wooden, bone, or ivory toggles used to fasten purses and pouches) fashionable during the 18th and 19th centuries, and of *inro*, lacquer boxes used to carry medicines.

Tibet and the Himalayas A thigh-bone trumpet, bone aprons and a human skull ewer from Tibet are among the museum's more curious artifacts. More significant, however, are the 13th- to 15th-century religious paintings, or *thangkas*, from the country's leading monasteries. Do not miss the three-headed Bon figure, a symbol of Tibet's indigenous religion which coexisted alongside Buddhism. Take the trouble, too, to scrutinize the modest assemblage of Bhutanese wood carvings, silverwork and textiles, which offer a rare insight into this obscure country.

Southeast Asia Among the relatively small Southeast Asia collections are several worthwhile examples of Thai sculpture from the former capitals, Sukhothai and Ayutthaya. As Buddhism arrived from India, these centers produced the earliest Buddha images bearing the curving eyelids and arched eyebrows which came to define the Thai Buddha image. The Connell Collection offers a major ceramics collection (2000BC to the 17th century) from Thailand.

Asian Art spans centuries, nations and religions

INDIAN COLLECTIONS
A large gallery is devoted to the museum's extensive Indian holdings. Useful maps aid comprehension of this vast land. They show the geographical spread of its three main religions—Buddhism, Hinduism and Jainism—and the incredible range and richness of the art which they have inspired.

Overlooked by Bernal Heights, the Mission District is the main home of San Francisco's Latino population

THE LEVI STRAUSS FACTORY

Arriving in San Francisco in 1853, Levi Strauss created what he called a "waist-high overall" for the miners of the Gold Rush, a garment which later became much better-known as a pair of "jeans." Following the earthquake of 1906, Strauss built a new factory in the Mission District at 250 Valencia Street. The building still stands, and its workers still produce the world-famous jeans.

►► Mission District *IBCF4*

Buses: 14, 26, 49
BART: 24th Street

Mission Dolores is what brings most visitors to the Mission District, slotted between the Castro, SoMa and Potrero Hill, and extending southward. Surprisingly few, however, take the time to explore more of San Francisco's most vibrant ethnic enclave, the home of a Spanish-speaking population drawn from all over Central and South America. Founded by the colonizing Spanish in 1776 and originally named for San Francisco de Asís, **Mission Dolores►►** (320 Dolores Street; tel: 415/621-8203; open: daily 8–12, 1–4; inexpensive) was completed in 1791 and still retains the thick adobe walls which enabled it to survive earthquakes and become the city's oldest building.

The mission's fresco-decorated chapel contains numerous artifacts carried by mule from Mexico at the time of construction; a modest assortment of other historic pieces is gathered in a small museum: In the mission's cemetery, a few Spanish- and Mexican-era pioneers are buried alongside the remains of an estimated 5,000 Native Americans. While the chapel is used for special services, the **Basilica**—built next door in 1913—serves the everyday spiritual needs of the Mission District's current Catholic population.

The quiet streets around the mission give little indication of the hustle and bustle which more accurately characterizes the Mission District. To find the local pulse, head for **Mission Street** and its crowded Mexican bakeries, secondhand furniture outlets and grocery stores. At the corner of 24th Street you will see a few of the district's many **murals**, described on page 126.

Through the 1980s, the Mission District's earthiness and low rents attracted avant-garde writers and artists, and galleries and cafés opened in Valencia and 16th streets. **Valencia Street** was also the unofficial base of the city's lesbian population. An influx of upwardly mobile young professionals saw rents rise in the 1990s, and chic restaurants and bars replaced the former community hangouts.

Mission District

This walks starts at Mission Dolores and highlights the history and social diversity of the Mission District, before it concludes at the original mission site.

The oldest building in San Francisco, **Mission Dolores** (see page 124) was completed in 1791. The tiny adobe chapel, small museum and its graveyard are all reminders of the city's early Spanish settlement.

The relaxing greenery of **Mission Dolores Park** rises steadily upward, culminating in a spectacular outlook across the city. The south side of Mission Dolores Park is fringed by splendidly restored Victorian houses, and more of these can be seen along **Liberty Street**.

Fashionable bars and restaurants are a feature of **Valencia Street** (see page 124), while **Mission Street** has the bakeries, cafés and businesses serving a largely Latino community.

An unmarked spot near the corner of Albion and Camp streets was chosen by the 18th-century Spanish settlers as the original site of what was later

to become Mission Dolores.

After erecting a chapel here, however, the settlers then found that the ground was unsuitable for construction.

Mission Dolores: the reredos (above) and, in its cemetery (below), the oldest tombs in the city

Unlike Los Angeles, which has a large and long-established Mexican community, San Francisco began acquiring a significant and visible Latino population from the 1950s, when Central American immigrants were attracted northward by the factory and shipyard jobs created during World War II and the boom that occurred in the postwar years. For geographical convenience and to save money, they settled in the low-rent Mission District.

MURAL TOURS
A free guided walking tour of some of the Mission District's murals begins at 11am on the first and third Saturdays of each month, led by City Guides (tel: 415/557-4266). The BART Mural Tour is one of several arranged by the Precita Eyes Mural Arts Center, 2981 24th Street (tel: 415/285-2287). It is a 90-minute walking tour through the Mission District at 1.30pm on Saturdays and Sundays, and costs $12 for adults, $5 for senior citizens, $8 for students and $2 for under-18s.

Latino influx The Mission's Latino population doubled each decade between 1950 and 1970, and by the time another major influx came—to escape the Central American turmoil and strife of the 1980s—they were easily the area's dominant ethnic group, as the former Irish and Italian Mission District dwellers had moved on. The community includes Mexicans, Guatemalans, Costa Ricans, Nicaraguans and Salvadorians, with lesser numbers from Bolivia, Colombia, Peru and Chile.

With radical Central American political groups and support centers for refugees, the Mission is a self-supportive and politically aware community. While some Latinos have risen to the city's professional ranks, the traditional white American perception of the Spanish speaker as an undereducated manual worker is hard to break. The effects of economic recession have been strongly felt in the Mission, where gang violence and drug abuse have become increasingly prevalent.

Mission murals Bold and colorful murals adorning public spaces and buildings are often seen in the Mission, and continue the muralist tradition established in Latin America. Some murals are simple pieces of street art, others are far more complex affairs involving several artists, and some are funded by the city in recognition of their artistic and cultural value.

A Latin American tradition, street murals bring color, fun and comment to Mission District streets

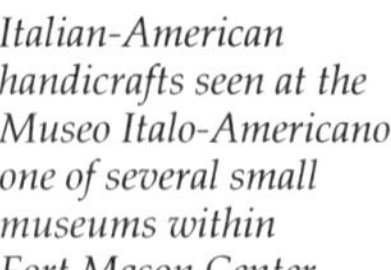

Italian-American handicrafts seen at the Museo Italo-Americano, one of several small museums within Fort Mason Center

▶ Museo Italo-Americano
IBCE6

Building C, Fort Mason Center (tel: 415/673-2200)
Open: Wed–Sun 12–4; free
Bus: 28

After beginning, appropriately perhaps, in a room above a North Beach café in 1978, the Museo Italo-Americano has evolved into a respected showplace for the work of Italian and Italian-American artists. There are a few permanent exhibits of painting, sculpture and photography, but the core of the gallery space is devoted to temporary shows mostly drawn from new artists living in the Bay Area. Besides the galleries, a library and gift store stock items relating to past and present Italian-Americans.

▶▶ Museum of Money of the American West
IBCJ8

Union Bank of California, 400 California Street
Open: Mon–Fri 9–5; free
Cable car: California Street line

Housed in a vault in the Bank of California's basement, this one-room museum holds a small but surprisingly interesting collection, ranging from chunks of gold and silver to the various coins and bank notes which changed hands before the advent of a unified currency across the United States. Among many enjoyable single exhibits are $20 coins minted in gold, as well as several special coins produced to commemorate the Panama–Pacific Exposition of 1915.

Also here are the dueling pistols used in 1859 in a celebrated dispute between the Chief Justice of the California Supreme Court, David S. Terry and a US Senator, David Broderick. The duel, the result of an alleged slander, ended in the death of Broderick after his pistol fired prematurely. It was claimed that Terry knew one pistol had a sensitive trigger, and he chose the other.

The Bank of California was one of the first to become established in the state, and the city's Financial District grew up around the original bank, which was built on this site in 1866.

WILLIAM C. RALSTON

Through shrewd investment in silver mines, Ohio-born William C. Ralston made the Bank of California the American West's most respected financial institution by the 1860s, and became one of San Francisco's most prominent figures. In August 1875, however, with the silver mines exhausted, the bank was forced to close its doors, which plunged the city into economic uncertainty. On the day the bank failed, Ralston took his usual daily swim in the bay—and was later found drowned.

On board the SS Jeremiah O'Brien, the National Liberty Ship Memorial

USS *PAMPANITO*
(tel: 415/775-1943)
After touring the National Liberty Ship Memorial, the World War II maritime theme can be continued by exploring the claustrophobic innards of the USS *Pampanito*, moored at Pier 45. Launched in 1943, the submarine saw action in the Pacific and sank 27,000 tons of enemy shipping. The cramped crew's and officers' quarters, the engine rooms and the torpedo room are included on the self-guided tour. The only thing missing is a chance to peer through the periscope.

▶ National Liberty Ship Memorial *IBCE6*

Pier 32, opposite Brannan Street (tel: 415/544-0100)
Open: daily 10–4; inexpensive
Bus: 42

Preserved as the National Liberty Ship Memorial, the *Jeremiah O'Brien* is the sole floating survivor of the 2,751 "Liberty Ships" launched between 1941 and 1945, part of the merchant fleet designed to carry wartime supplies and troops across the Atlantic.

Antiaircraft guns provide some interest on deck, but the absorbing matter lies below. Weave around the mazelike corridors and you will find the entire ship maintained in its 1940s appearance: the crew's quarters, the radio operator's room, the bridge and much more.

Descend to the lower level of the vessel to find the boiler room and the enormous engines in working order: The *Jeremiah O'Brien* makes regular runs in the bay and in 1994 crossed the Atlantic to participate in the 50th anniversary of the D-Day landings.

One fact worth pondering as you tour the craft is that this huge vessel took just 57 days to build.

▶ National Maritime Museum *IBCF6*

Aquatic Park, north end of Polk Street (tel: 415/561-6662)
Open: daily 10–5; free
Bus: 19

The development of San Francisco has been dominated by its links with the sea, and the National Maritime Museum sets out to chronicle the city's remarkable seafaring history.

Unfortunately, compared to the preserved vessels of Hyde Street Pier Historic Ships (see page 112), the USS *Pampanito* (see panel) or the National Liberty Ship Memorial (see above), the exhibits in this museum seem somewhat commonplace. The countless model ships are unlikely to appeal to anyone other than the saltiest of sea dogs. Do come here, though, if only to admire the building itself: an impressive ship-shaped slab of 1930s art deco with a great many of its original features intact.

Few inhabitants of San Francisco are aware of the San Francisco Columbarium, tucked away in a tidy residential neighborhood on the fringes of the Richmond District. And this is despite the fact that the cremated remains of many of the city's most illustrious early citizens lie within its walls—and also that the Columbarium is an outstanding example of Victorian architecture.

An elegant rotunda decorated with stained glass, the Columbarium was designed by British architect Bernard Cahill and opened in 1898. By 1937, it stood at the heart of a 3-acre (1.5ha) cemetery in which an estimated 10,000 people were buried. That year, however, cemeteries were made illegal in San Francisco following concerns about public health. The graves were exhumed and their contents moved to Colma (a now cemetery-filled town on the San Francisco Peninsula), while the cemetery's walls, and allegedly some of its tombstones, were used in the sea wall at Aquatic Park, near Fisherman's Wharf. Homes were built over the vacated lot, and few property developers informed prospective buyers that a shortage of funds meant that many of the graves had not been moved at all—the houses had simply been built on top of them.

Officially declared a memorial, the Columbarium was spared demolition, but as cremations were banned, it soon found itself without a purpose and was left to decay by its successive owners. Not until 1980, when the Neptune Society acquired the Columbarium, did restoration work on the handsome structure begin and its niches (where urns are placed) again put on sale.

In the three-story interior, you will find the final family resting places of the Eddys, the Turks and others who gave their names to city streets, and more recent arrivals such as the man who shares his niche with dolls based on TV's Munster family, and another placed here with a miniature set of golf clubs.

WHERE AND WHEN
Located at 1 Loraine Court (tel: 415/221-1838; open daily 10–1), intriguing and sometimes spooky tours of the Columbarium take place every morning subject to demand. The tours are free but a reservation should be made in advance.

A PRICEY NICHE
Only 20,000 of the Columbarium's 30,000 niches are occupied and, if a visit encourages you to consider a long-term stay, you might ask at the adjacent office for the latest niche price list. Currently the cheapest niches, unelaborate affairs which resemble mailboxes, cost $700. The choicest spot, however, will set you back $56,000.

A well-kept secret: San Francisco Columbarium (above) and (below) its interior—the higher the niche, the higher the price

THE CROCKER "SPITE FENCE"
Determined to call a whole block of Nob Hill his own, Charles Crocker bought up all the homes which stood on his desired plot except one: a German-born undertaker called Nicholas Yung refused to sell. The enraged Crocker promptly erected a 40ft (12m) high "spite fence" around three sides of Yung's home, blocking out the sunlight. Yung still refused to sell, however, and only after his death did the Crocker family purchase the house.

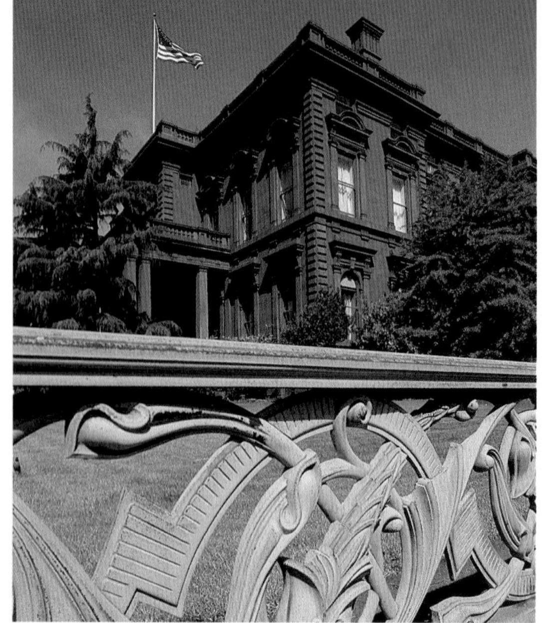

The sole Nob Hill survivor of the 1906 fire, the Flood Mansion now houses the exclusive Pacific Union Club

The Fairmont Hotel's luxurious lobby, partly designed by architect Julia Morgan, responsible for much of William Randolph Hearst's San Simeon mansion. The Fairmont is one of a group of top-class hotels on Nob Hill

▶▶▶ Nob Hill *IBCF5*

Buses: 1, 27
Cable car: California Street line

Rising steeply above Chinatown and the Financial District, Nob Hill became the city's most prestigious address in the late 1800s, when the Big Four—railroad magnates Charles Crocker, Mark Hopkins, Collis P. Huntington and Leland Stanford (see page 37)—and several Comstock Lode silver barons, chose it as the site of the most expensive homes California had ever seen.

Previously known as California Street Hill and dotted with the plain houses of modest city merchants, Nob Hill acquired its lasting title (derived from "nabob," a term used in colonial India to denote a man of wealth or importance) following the moneyed invasion inspired by the creation of the cable car in 1873. As this new mode of transportation made the city's steep slopes negotiable, Leland Stanford helped finance a new cable-car line along California Street, linking the sandy hilltop site to the Financial District.

As Nob Hill's existing homes were bought and razed to make room for new construction, each incoming millionaire vied to outspend his neighbor. Charles Crocker's home cost $2.3 million and was decorated with a million-dollar art collection; William Sharon's mansion boasted the first hydraulic elevator in the western US; Mark Hopkins topped them all with a $3-million home designed, in a bizarre hodgepodge of styles, by his wife.

Although their cost was stunning, the Nob Hill mansions were seldom esthetically satisfying. Architect Willis Polk (see panel, page 112) described the Crocker Mansion as "wood carver's delirium," while a newspaper of the day derided them as "gingerbread, ignorance and bad taste." Meanwhile, such blatant displays of wealth and privilege, from the men whose fortunes enabled them to control the city, bred resentment among ordinary San Franciscans.

Few tears were shed when all but one of the Nob Hill homes—sandstone walls saved the James Flood Mansion—were destroyed by the fire which followed the 1906 earthquake. Apartment buildings now cover much of Nob Hill and lend it an air of dignified wealth. Nevertheless, evidence of its more flamboyant past is plentiful.

Grace Cathedral (see page 105) sits on the plot of land formerly occupied by the Crocker Mansion, while the neighboring **Huntington Park▶**, often filled with Chinese-Americans going through the routines of Tai Chi, marks the site of the home of David Colton, a junior partner of the Big Four. In a sensational late-1800s court case, Colton's widow used her late husband's correspondence with Collis Huntington to expose the railroad barons' corrupt business practices. Across Cushman Street, the sturdy brownstone Flood Mansion, paid for with $1.5 million of silver-mining profits (see page 37), was greatly remodeled by Willis Polk following the 1906 fire and has been occupied since 1911 by the **Pacific Union Club**, an exclusive all-male social club for the rich and prominent.

Nob Hill's luxury hotels also have their share of history. The **Fairmont Hotel▶▶** (950 Mason Street) was founded in 1902 by the daughter of silver-mine beneficiary James G. Fair (see page 37). During the 1906 fire, the decision to dynamite parts of the city to stop the spread of the flames was made in the unfinished hotel's ballroom. Architect Julia Morgan contributed many of the beaux-arts features which still grace the hotel's lobby; a valuable art collection lines the corridors. Opened in 1926, the **Mark Hopkins Hotel▶▶** occupies the corner of California and Mason streets, former site of the Hopkins Mansion. At the summit of the 20-story tower, the Top of the Mark offers stunning views for the price of a cocktail. The quiet and elegant **Huntington Hotel▶** (905 California Street) sits on the site of Leland Stanford's mansion. With the Big Four restaurant, the hotel boasts one of the city's most illustrious establishment dining rooms.

NOB HILL'S FIRST SETTLER

The first house on what became Nob Hill is believed to have been that of Arthur Hayne, whom history records as hacking his way through the chaparral hillside to erect a wood-and-clay home for himself and his bride in 1856. The Hayne house stood on the site of the present Fairmont Hotel.

A doorman pays little attention to the everyday sight of a Rolls Royce approaching Nob Hill's Mark Hopkins Hotel

Increasingly in San Francisco, everything stops for tea. Growing numbers of deals are now sealed over cucumber sandwiches and scones—intended as a health-conscious alternative to the alcohol-soaked business lunch—thus enabling high-class hotels to fill the idle hours between lunch and dinner.

TEA WITH A VIEW
During afternoon tea, your attention should be devoted to the table and your companion seated across it. However, from a window seat in the Rotunda restaurant of Neiman Marcus (150 Stockton Street), where afternoon tea revives jaded shoppers, a bird's-eye view of Union Square vies for your gaze.

ANOTHER AFTERNOON-TEA HOT SPOT
Mandarin Oriental, 222 Sansome Street.

For visitors, afternoon tea (typically served from 2.30 to 5) offers a relaxing hour or two's break from sightseeing and a chance to observe San Francisco's high society, some of whom have adopted teatime as part of their daily routine.

Teatime etiquette Social inepts who normally drink tea by the large, steaming mugful should tread carefully through the ultracivilized environs of the afternoon tea lounge. Even at the most elegant location you are unlikely to be expelled for not holding your cup correctly, but upsetting the calm atmosphere or showing yourself bereft of manners is considered the mark of a barbarian.

The full tea The first task is to select the actual tea. Most establishments offer a choice which includes some or all of the following: Earl Grey, orange pekoe, darjeeling, jasmine, lapsang souchong, oolong, peppermint, Russian caravan and camomile. The tea will arrive in individual teapots and a strainer will be provided.

Shortly after the tea arrives, a waiter or waitress will arrive at your table with a large, split-level tray holding any or all of the following: delicate sandwiches (filled with bacon, cucumber, smoked salmon, ham, egg and parsley or English cheddar cheese), scones and assorted fancy pastries. You might also find a bowl of seasonal berries. Imported Devonshire cream and a selection of fine jams await your scone—but the first item to be eaten should be the palate-cleansing cucumber sandwiches.

Tea, gossip…

...*and music*

Select locations The choice of tea and nibbles aside, the most important aspect of afternoon tea is simply where you have it: The event puts some of the most luxurious public rooms in the city at your disposal, and the ambience on offer and surroundings can be surprisingly varied.

San Francisco interiors seldom come any finer than the **Garden Court** of the Palace Hotel (2 New Montgomery at Market Street) which, with its high glass ceiling, palm trees and ornate chandeliers, successfully recaptures the aura of unbridled opulence which the hotel, built in 1873, epitomized during San Francisco's early years. Gunpowder green is one of the teas on offer and the price includes a glass of champagne.

At the marginally less elegant but no less venerable Laurel Court (950 Mason Street) housed in the Fairmont Hotel atop Nob Hill, you'll dine under three ornate domes. After the scones with lemon curd, Devonshire cream and preserves, you'll be presented with a selection of finger sandwiches, French pastries and a glass of champagne.

The top-notch hotels of Nob Hill all provide afternoon tea, but while the farmhouse fruitcake served on Wedgwood china in the **Lobby Terrace** at the Mark Hopkins (999 California Street) has many admirers, the setting lacks atmosphere. The cognoscenti's choice for Nob Hill afternoon tea is the **Ritz-Carlton** (see panel) or the **Stanford Court Hotel** (905 California Street), where the goodies are served in the hushed surroundings of the lobby lounge and include smoked salmon with crème fraîche on pumpernickel. Round things off with a glass of fine port (though purists would disapprove of such a suggestion).

Finally, if the thought of having tea surrounded by San Francisco high society gives you the shivers, you might seek solace at the **Windsor Tearoom** of the King George Hotel (334 Mason Street), where the mood is egalitarian and a pianist tinkles gently as you munch the à la carte pasties, pastries and cakes.

TEA AT THE RITZ-CARLTON

The deep-carpeted lobby lounge, complete with harpist, of the Ritz-Carlton (600 Stockton Street) is the setting for one of San Francisco's best teas. Brews include delicate delights such as Japanese Cherry and China Rose Petals. For vegetarians, there is a tea that offers such treats as eggplant pesto on rye bread and roasted pepper mousse on brioche. Reserve a window table for a view of the gardens.

CHURCH OF ST. FRANCIS OF ASSISI
The well-scrubbed facade of North Beach's Church of St. Francis of Assisi (610 Vallejo Street) does little to advertise the fact that this was the first Catholic church founded in California since the time of the Spanish missions. None of the original 1856 church remains, but part of its 1860s successor is incorporated into the present structure, which dates from 1913.

▶▶▶ North Beach *IBCF6*

Buses: 15, 30, 41

The spiritual home of San Francisco's Italian population, North Beach—between Chinatown and Fisherman's Wharf—has dozens of community landmarks and is packed with highly regarded Italian restaurants. It was North Beach, too, that helped cafés and coffee become part of San Francisco life. Whether to gorge on melt-in-your-mouth pastries or sip a cappuccino while watching the world go by, a North Beach café is the place to be.

There was a time when North Beach really did have a beach, but the stretch of sand disappeared when 1860s landfill extended the city's northern shoreline to what is now Fisherman's Wharf.

North Beach had long been home to an ethnically diverse, working-class population, but gained its first substantial influx of Italians during the 1890s. Many arrived from Italy's depressed south and sought a living from fishing. The Italian-American community quickly thrived and, by the 1930s, five Italian-language newspapers were operating in North Beach and 60,000 Italian-Americans were calling the district home. Meanwhile, San Franciscans of all ethnic backgrounds were discovering the pleasures of pasta and pesto.

Although the Italian businesses stayed, the neighborhood began losing its established population during the 1950s as immigration from Italy fell and many established North Beach families became wealthy enough to move to quieter, more comfortable parts.

Attracted by affordably low rents, cheap wine, the wild and radical sounds of bebop jazz emanating from its numerous jazz clubs and the prospect of caffeine-fueled conversation in the cafés, 1950s North Beach became a stamping ground for the seminal figures of the Beat generation, whose followers were (*continued on page 136*)

Molinari's Deli

Walk

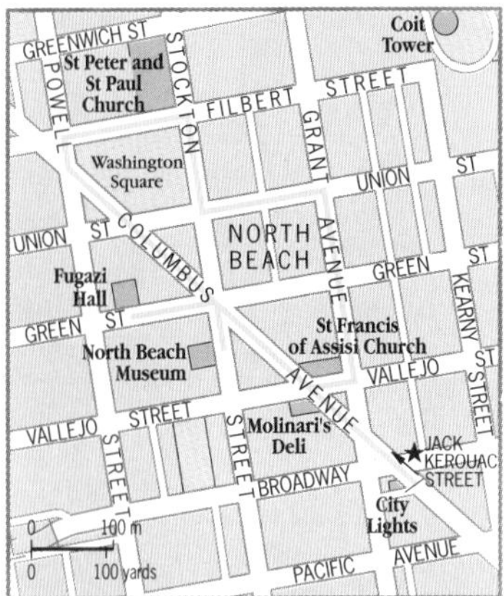

North Beach

Starting at the famous City Lights bookstore, this walk traces the Italian roots and the Beat-era associations of North Beach, and includes Washington Square and the funky stores of Grant Avenue before concluding at the Church of St. Francis of Assisi, built on the site of one of California's oldest churches.

City Lights was the country's first paperback bookstore, which opened in 1953 (see pages 136–137) and has taken its place in the city's literary history. **Molinari's Deli** has been popular among North Beach's Italian population since the store opened its doors in 1896 (see page 137).

On the mezzanine level of the US Bank, the **North Beach Museum** does an excellent job of preserving neighborhood history (see page 137). Around the corner from the Museum, **Fugazi Hall** was donated to North Beach Italians in 1912 by John Fugazi (see page 137).

The building of the twin-spired **St. Peter and St. Paul Church** was started in 1922 and took 15 years to complete (see page 137). The church, which is gracefully illuminated at night, overlooks **Washington Square** (see pages 137 and 138).

As Grant Avenue leads back toward Broadway, it is lined by offbeat stores and cafés, such as **Caffè Trieste** (see page 137).

Built in 1913, the **Church of St. Francis of Assisi** occupies the site of an 1856 church (see panel, page 134), the first Catholic church in California since the Spanish missions.

North Beach street scene

GRANT AVENUE
Aim to spend at least part of your time in North Beach taking a leisurely walk along the section of Grant Avenue which climbs gently north from Broadway toward Telegraph Hill. Once lined by family-run Italian stores, the street became synonymous by the early 1990s with one-of-a-kind art and bric-à-brac outlets. Today, rising rents and gentrification have brought an influx of pricier stores such as Martini Mercantile (number 1453) with choice vintage clothing, and the decadent footwear of Insolent (number 1418).

Opened in the 1940s, Beat-era landmark Vesuvio still has its bohemian atmosphere—and its original graffiti

THE HOME OF "*HOWL*"
Allen Ginsberg's epic poem, *Howl*, not only brought what became known as the Beats to national prominence, but also helped establish the author as the world's foremost counterculture poet during the 1960s. The long, breathless poem, its cadences reminiscent of jazz rhythms, was written when Ginsberg was living at 1010 Montgomery Street, between North Beach and Telegraph Hill. Not a San Francisco native, Ginsberg had arrived in the city from New York ostensibly to work in advertising.

(*continued from page 134*) derisively dubbed "beatniks" by San Francisco newspaper columnist Herb Caen (see page 42). By the late 1950s, North Beach had garnered national headlines as the center of a counterculture explosion and literary renaissance that rocked the establishment and paved the way for the mass protest movements, and the psychedelia, of the 1960s.

The busy intersection of Broadway, Grant and Columbus avenues blurs the boundaries of North Beach and Chinatown, and carries the traffic that helped make North Beach into a major nightlife area.

By the late 1950s, North Beach comedy clubs were hosting cutting-edge comics such as Lenny Bruce and Mort Sahl, while jazz clubs in shabby cellars would periodically be taken over for riotous nights of poetry and bebop by the key players in what became the Beat movement.

Another cultural pioneer was Carol Doda, who starred in the nation's first topless show, staged at the Condor Club in 1964. The club is now the lackluster Condor Bistro (300 Columbus Avenue); a plaque on an outside wall commemorates its historical contribution.

Testament to the creativity and long-lasting influence of the Beats is provided by **City Lights▶▶▶** (261 Columbus Avenue). Cofounded by North Beach-based artist and poet Lawrence Ferlinghetti in 1953, this was the first all-paperback bookstore in the US and its profits were intended to finance a literary magazine. City Lights gained nationwide notoriety in 1957 when US Customs officials seized copies of *Howl*, an Allen Ginsberg poem branded obscene, which City Lights was intending to publish and which was destined to become the defining verse of the Beat generation. The ensuing controversy alerted the world to North Beach's underground cultural scene, and the neighborhood soon filled with goateed youths and beatnik-seeking tourists.

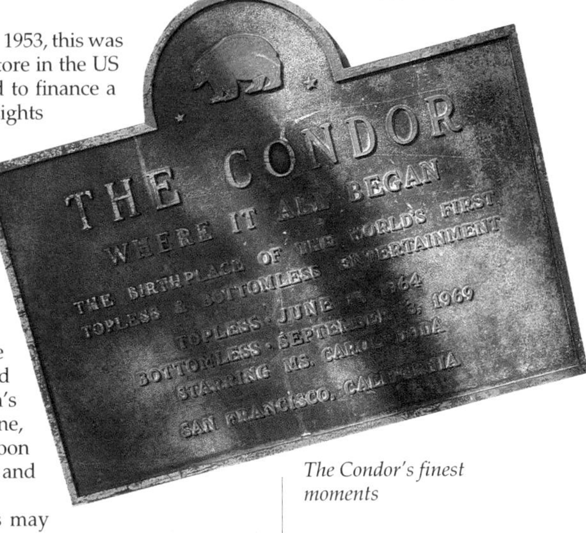

The Condor's finest moments

As a movement, the Beats may be long gone, but City Lights bookstore survives and thrives with writings by and about the Beats, and much more, filling its tightly packed shelves.

Facing City Lights across Jack Kerouac Street, **Vesuvio▶** was a popular Beat rendezvous and still draws a faintly bohemian crowd. Another Beat-era favorite was **Caffè Trieste▶** (601 Vallejo Street), which is still a great place for coffee, cakes and live opera on Saturday afternoons (see page 138).

The 1950s literary associations may have brought North Beach fame, but on its streets the Italian influence is much more in evidence. On the corner of Columbus Avenue and Vallejo Street, the arty window display of **Molinari's Deli▶**—purveyor of fine cheeses, meats and pastas—attracts many photographers. Equally mouthwatering is the **Victoria Pastry Company▶** (1362 Stockton Street), with its array of Italian cakes and pastries.

Also on Stockton Street, the changing displays at the **North Beach Museum▶▶** (tel: 415/391-6210; free), on the mezzanine level of the Bay View Bank (number 1435), make an absorbing social history of the area. Part of that history is the 1912 **Fugazi Hall▶** (678 Green Street), an Italian community hall donated by John Fugazi, a locally born banker and founder of what became the Transamerica Corporation. The first floor houses the long-running revue *Beach Blanket Babylon* (see page 234). Upstairs are memorabilia and photographs from North Beach's past.

With a statue of Benjamin Franklin in its grassy center and the twin-spired Church of St. Peter and St. Paul on its northern side, **Washington Square▶▶** brings some much-needed open space to North Beach. Each morning, one side is filled with Chinese-Americans practicing Tai Chi. On weekends, Bay Area artists and sculptors converge on the square to display and sell their work. The square's benches are inviting, but it is hard to resist the allure of the **Church of St. Peter and St. Paul▶▶** (tel: 415/421-5219). Although construction began in 1922, this engaging Romanesque edifice took 15 years to finish.

TAI CHI
A common sight on any morning is scores of Chinese-Americans going through the slow, graceful exercises of Tai Chi Ch'uan. This 1,000-year-old form of callisthenics is based on carefully balanced rhythmic movements which use all the body's joints, ligaments and muscles, and help to regulate blood flow.

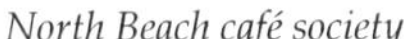

North Beach café society

For many residents, copious consumption of high-quality coffee in a public place is what being a San Franciscan is all about. Every neighborhood has its fair share of cafés, and each one differs a little from the next. Some offer newspapers and magazines for perusal by their never-in-a-rush customers, some are bohemian settings with poetry readings and chess matches, others are favored for their post-jog fruit juices or for the fancy cakes which provide an incentive for walking the dog. Every one of them has its devoted group of regulars.

COFFEE TYPES
San Francisco's coffee devotees place great stock on the type of coffee bean used by a particular café, but most casual drinkers—and city visitors—are more intrigued by the varieties of coffee offered. Besides espresso (coffee brewed at high pressure) and cappuccino (espresso topped by a creamy milk head), most San Francisco cafés also dispense *caffè latte* (espresso with steamed milk) and *caffè mocha* (espresso with chocolate). Many also offer house specialties.

The connoisseurs' dream: a North Beach coffee shop (below) and (top) the Caffè Roma

North Beach Italian cafés Probably the first Italian café in the city was **Tosca Café**, opened in 1917 and moved to its current location (242 Columbus Avenue) in 1947. Allegedly serving the first espresso in California, Tosca is still worth a visit, but—despite the opera reverberating from its jukebox—it lacks a gregarious atmosphere, not least because its customers are often well-heeled, or would-be well-heeled, socialites.

Much more in keeping with North Beach bohemia, **Caffè Trieste** (601 Vallejo Street) opened in 1956 and quickly became a hangout for the seminal figures of what developed into the Beat generation. Still a great place for entertaining eavesdropping, the Trieste's family owners stage a free operatic performance on Saturday afternoons. Other North Beach notables are **Caffè Puccini** (411 Columbus Avenue), where the window tables make for North Beach's best people-watching, and **Mario's Bohemian Cigar Store** (566 Columbus Avenue), one of the better spots for snacks and light meals.

Very serious coffee drinkers on the loose in North Beach might prefer to treat their tastebuds—and their noses—to a cup at **Caffè Roma Coffee Roasting Company** (526 Columbus Avenue), which roasts its own beans on the premises.

MORE CAFÉS

The cafés mentioned here are just a few selected from a very large number and are chosen for being distinguished in some way, by their history, clientele, decor or mood. Sampling a few of them will give you a good introduction to what San Francisco-style café society is all about. To assist with further investigation, more are described in the Restaurant listings (pages 274–281).

Relaxing at Caffè Trieste: a place for coffee, cakes and opera

Contemporary bohemia Located right in the vibrant heart of the strongly Latino Mission District (see page 124), **Café La Bohème**, at 3318 24th Street, has epitomized the spirit of the bohemian café since it was first opened in the 1970s.

Also in the Mission near Bernal Heights, **Café Commons** (3161 Mission Street) attracts a similar crowd. Rub elbows on the sunny deck, where patrons sip coffee and nibble on sandwiches and bagels. Also worth a look in the Mission District are **Muddy Waters** (521 Valencia Street, also in the Castro at 262 Church Street), and **Dolores Park Café** (501 Dolores Street), with sandwiches, salads, soups and more, plus large windows and sidewalk tables facing Dolores Park.

Window seats are prized commodities: diners at this Italian restaurant have a perfect view of North Beach street scenes

Classy cafés If you prefer sophistication to shabby bohemia, try **Tosca Café** (see page 138); **Café Bastille** (22 Belden Alley), where the staff and many customers like to pretend they are in a stylish Parisian bistro rather than a Financial District alley; or the Castro District's **Just Desserts** (248 Church Street and several other locations), where you can sip hot coffee, listen to classical music, and munch decadent cakes and pastries.

Curious cafés With cafés being a popular feature of the city, it should be no surprise to find inspired variations on the standard format. In Haight-Ashbury, **Kan Zaman** (1793 Haight Street) is an exotic Arabian-style coffee spot complete with hookahs and pillow-adorned sunken seating. A bit off the beaten track, **Farley's** (1315 18th Street) offers a relaxed, neighborhood feel, with 23 kinds of coffee, blank books to doodle in, board games and a diverse crowd of friendly locals.

OAKLAND HARBOR TOURS
A close inspection of one of the world's largest container docks may not strike everybody as a wildly enthralling prospect, but Port of Oakland Tours (tel: 510/627-1188) offers exactly that, plus an informative historical commentary on the waterfront area, on free boat tours operating throughout most of the year.

OAKLAND TEMPLE
A striking sight in the hills above Oakland, the Oakland Temple (4770 Lincoln Avenue) was erected by the Mormon Church both as a place of worship and as a visitor center to relate the story of Joseph Smith, the religion's founder, and the Mormons' epic cross-country journey to Salt Lake City. The attendants make every effort to interest you in Mormonism, but the temple is worth a visit, if only for its great views across Oakland and far beyond.

►► Oakland 45D2

BART: 12th Street or Lake Merritt
Ferry: from Ferry Building

Famously derided by author Gertrude Stein's comment "There is no *there*, there," and still notorious to some as the birthplace of the Black Panthers, Oakland is actually a pleasing mix of old and new, with a strollable waterfront and a lively Chinatown district—plus the wonderful Oakland Museum of California (see pages 142–143).

Ferries from San Francisco berth at what is now **Jack London Square**, an uninspiring conglomeration of souvenir shops and seafood-with-views restaurants (on Sundays between 10 and 2, a **Farmer's Market** of fruit and vegetables adds to the atmosphere) loosely themed around the writer. He spent some of his formative years doing odd jobs in the warehouses and canneries built for the goods carried by the freighters that once docked here.

London would be unlikely to recognize the area as it is today, though he might remember the turf-roofed log cabin which he occupied during his winter in Alaska's Yukon Territory during the Klondike gold rush of 1897. The reassembled cabin sits a stone's throw from **Heinhold's First & Last Chance Saloon►**, where London was known to enjoy a drink or two. The bar's interior is worth a look, as are the photos lining its walls. More stores occupy the deliberately ramshackle **Jack London Village**, immediately south. The USS *Potomac*, President Delano Roosevelt's "Floating White House," has less direct connection with Oakland. It is now open for tours at 540 Water Street (tel: 510/627-1215), close to Jack London Square.

Between the waterfront and the elevated I-880 freeway, an energetic **produce market** lines Third Street, but

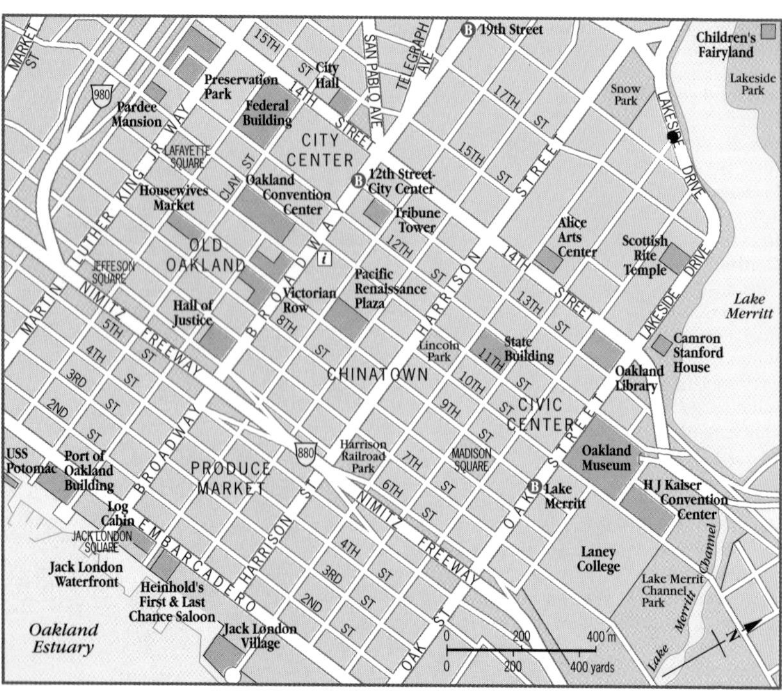

otherwise there is little reason to linger at the waterfront. You should make your way to Chinatown and Old Oakland, which lie on either side of Broadway.

Though it lacks the claustrophobic atmosphere and historical resonance of its San Francisco equivalent, Oakland's **Chinatown▶▶**, with its markets and inexpensive Asian restaurants in the streets south of Broadway, deserves exploration. Besides many Chinese-American-run businesses, the district's numerous ethnic groups include Thais, Vietnamese, Koreans and Burmese.

Cross north of Broadway onto Ninth Street and you will discover the restored Victorian buildings of the **Old Oakland Historical District▶▶**. These handsome structures were at the center of local commercial life a century ago, and most now earn their keep as offices, stores and food outlets, though one or two house good art galleries.

A block ahead, mouthwatering smells waft across the intersection with Clay Street from the food stands of the **Housewives Market▶**.

A symbol of Oakland's booming economy and of the late-1980s regeneration of its downtown area, **City Center▶** is an imaginative integration of office space, plazas and a sculpture garden.

Directly across 14th Street, the well-proportioned **City Hall** was considered a breathtakingly high skyscraper when it was completed in 1914. City Hall's construction came on the heels of another boom: the 1906 earthquake, which devastated San Francisco and did wonders for Oakland's economy. Superior in design, the adjacent **Tribune Tower▶** became the home of Oakland's daily newspaper in 1923.

Further contrast to City Center is provided two blocks north by the group of vintage Oakland homes that comprise **Preservation Park▶**. Most of the houses, the majority dating from the late 1800s, were moved here when the I-980 freeway cut through the neighborhood. Kept in good order, these old homes are reached by walking along spotlessly clean pathways.

(Continued on page 144)

Above, and below: A few blocks north of the waterfront, Oakland's Chinatown is packed with restaurants, bakeries and other Asian-owned businesses

OAKLAND'S TWIN CITIES
Fukuoka, Japan
Nakahoda, Russia
Takoradi, Ghana
Dalian, China
Ocho Rios, Jamaica
Santiago de Cuba, Cuba

The best museum in the Bay Area, and probably the best anywhere devoted to California, the Oakland Museum explores California's natural surroundings, history and art. On three levels, it provides hours of informative and entertaining insights into the Golden State's past, present and future.

California ecology Few regions have a more diverse ecology than California. The state encompasses high mountains, low deserts and a 1,200-mile (1,935km) coastline. Spread across a 38,000sq ft (3,530sq m) gallery, the **Hall of Ecology** uses dioramas to reveal the broad sweep of plant and animal life which makes its home in these vastly different habitats. The **Aquatic California Gallery** does a similar job for underwater life, illustrating the strange goings-on in California's rivers, bays and hot springs, and deep beneath its ocean waves.

A visitor is intrigued by one of the Cowell Hall of History exhibits at the Oakland Museum of California

California history Even seasoned California visitors would be hard pressed to find a better or more user-friendly historical record of the state than the **Cowell Hall of History**. Every episode in the region's action-packed past is remembered, and the collections are enhanced by interactive computer programs offering more detailed information on particular exhibits, recorded commentaries from experts and oral folk histories.

The conflicts between the indigenous people and the Spanish settlers who came in the wake of the missions, and the subsequent transformation of California by the discovery of gold, are thoughtfully explored and copiously documented, whether with Native American basketry or a re-created assay office from gold-rich Nevada City.

Equally impressive are the collections illustrating more recent California: the internment of the Japanese during World War II, the rise of Disneyland and the subcultures of the 1950s and 1960s highlighted with surfboards, a mock-up beatnik coffee house and assorted hippie-era peace-and-love paraphernalia.

The gallery comes up to date with the invention of the mountain bike and an outline of the state's changing ethnic composition, and poses questions about the economic impact of the end of the Cold War—which has greatly affected the state's defense industries.

California art On the museum's top floor, an imaginative gathering of art and artists with California connections skillfully demonstrates how the art of the Golden State has developed over the decades.

ADMISSION AND GUIDED TOURS

In 1993, the Oakland Museum broke with a 25-year tradition of free admission and began requesting a $4 donation. Admission is now $6 and the sum is well worth paying. Closed on Mondays and Tuesdays, the museum opens Wednesday to Saturday 10–5, Sunday 12–5. Regular talks, tours and other events complement the collections; information is available from the reception desk (tel: 510/ 238-2200) or website.

Landscape artists Throughout the 19th century, landscape painting was the rage in American art, and the artists of the day were inspired by the exploration of the American West, where undeveloped territories teemed with scenes of natural beauty.

Albert Bierstadt was among the main figures to emerge during the mid-1800s, infusing his canvases with a feeling of nature as a spiritual force: *Yosemite Valley* provides a good example. Working from a studio in the Sierras, another devotee of wild California was Thomas Hill, who is impressively represented here, notably with *Yosemite Valley.*

Historical records Besides being quality works of art, Hill's paintings also contributed to the protection of Yosemite as a national park. Several other pieces here carry a significance beyond their esthetic appeal. Henry Raschen's *California Miner with Packhorse* is an important documentation of the Gold Rush era, as is George Henry Davis' *San Francisco, July 1849,* a panoramic view of the embryonic city complete with ships abandoned in the bay as their crews headed for the gold mines.

Though painted in the last decades of the 19th century, Davis' painting was acknowledged as accurate and provides an important historical record. Similarly, the same artist's picture *Fort Ross* captures the Russian settlement on the Northern California coast prior to its 1840s abandonment.

Twentieth-century art The changing social and artistic mood of California becomes apparent in later periods. Several works by Arthur Mathews, such as *Youth,* which puts classical figures into a California setting, are examples of the 1910s California Decorative style spearheaded by Mathews and his wife.

More recent works illustrate the growing self-confidence of California artists. Among many bold paintings, ceramics and collages are contemporary works by Richard Diebenkorn, Bruce Conner and others.

PHOTOGRAPHY
Among the Gallery of California Art's photographic collection is Dorothea Lange's 1936 *Migrant Mother,* which provided the abiding visual image of the Depression and its effect on ordinary Americans. Lange moved to California in 1918 and established a studio in San Francisco. At one time she was married to Maynard Dixon, who is represented here with some of his emotion-packed studies of the people of New Mexico and Arizona.

BIKE TOURS
Usually twice a month during the summer, docent-led two-hour cycling tours of historic Oakland begin at the museum at 10am (tel: 510/238-3514). Participants should bring their own bikes and equipment; the route is 5 miles (8km) long and flat.

California's days of speed and shiny chrome remembered at the Oakland Museum

Completed in 1931, the Paramount Theater was the crowning glory of Oakland's short-lived art deco building boom and underwent a successful restoration in 1976

SAMUEL MERRITT
A wealthy landowner and civic leader, Samuel Merritt became mayor of Oakland in 1867 and instigated the damming project creating the lake which now bears his name. In 1888, Merritt loaned his schooner to Robert Louis Stevenson and it was used by the Scottish writer for his voyage to the South Pacific.

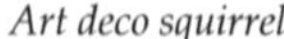
Art deco squirrel

(*Continued from page 141*)
Dotted with sailboats and paddleboats and picturesquely fringed by greenery, **Lake Merritt▶** occupies 150 acres (61ha) of southwest Oakland and provides a popular weekend recreation spot. The sole survivor of the extravagant homes which surrounded the tidal saltwater lake at the turn of the 20th century is the **Camron Stanford House▶▶** (1418 Lakeside Drive; tel: 510/444-1876; tours: 2nd and 3rd Wed at 11 and 4, 3rd Sun 1–5). Completed in 1876, the house was in private hands until 1910, when it became the site of the Oakland Museum, a role it retained for a remarkable 57 years. The house has been partly restored to illustrate the lifestyles of some of its former occupants. Guided tours begin with a slide show on the history of Oakland. From here, the present-day **Oakland Museum of California** (see pages 142–143) is a short walk away.

► Ocean Beach *IFCA4*

Stretching for several miles between the Cliff House (see page 80) and Fort Funston (see page 99), Ocean Beach is where San Franciscans might head if, for a few crazed minutes, they ever wanted to pretend that they lived in Southern California. Diminishing the appeal of the pebble-strewn strand, however, are the strong winds which frequently blow in off the ocean and a treacherous undertow, making swimming dangerous.

► Octagon House *IBCE5*

2645 Gough Street (tel: 415/441-7512)
Open: 2nd Sun and 2nd and 4th Thu of the month 12–3, except Jan; donation requested
Bus: 45

The Octagon House was completed in 1861, one of five eight-sided houses built in San Francisco. The National Society of Colonial Dames (an organization founded in 1891 to preserve the heritage of America's colonial period) acquired the house in 1951, organized its restoration and now uses it to display decorative arts of the Colonial and Federal periods. (See also page 157.)

►► Old US Mint *IBCF5*

Corner of Fifth and Mission streets
Buses: 14, 26, 27

Constructed in neoclassical style in 1874, the granite and sandstone Old Mint survived the earthquake and fire of 1906, and won a place in local hearts by honoring the certificates issued by the city's destroyed banks, allowing cash to reach the stricken population. Minting ceased in 1937, and various government departments used the building until 1968. After serving as a numismatic museum for several years, the mint closed its doors 1995, unable to meet new earthquake safety codes. Nonetheless, the mighty structure retains its imposing presence and may become the home of the San Francisco Historicl Society.

A NEW MINT'S TROUBLES

In 1937, a new mint opened on a hilltop site in Duboce Street. The mint's fortress-like appearance did little to dampen the eagerness of some of its workers to shortchange the US government. During a succession of scandals in the 1960s, tales abounded of mint employees walking out with money taped to their legs and tossing bags of loot out of windows to collect later. In 1966, the mint announced a discrepancy for the year of $15,000—all of it in quarters.

With its eight sides, believed to bring good luck and good health to its occupants, the Octagon House, below, dates from 1857 and originally stood on the other side of Gough Street

Since the days of the Gold Rush, San Francisco has attracted writers, and every neighborhood has at least a few literary landmarks to call its own. The sites mentioned below are some of the most interesting, most accessible or simply the most curious among a very large number.

THE BOHEMIAN CLUB
Founded in 1872 by city newspapermen, the Bohemian Club included among its members Ambrose Bierce, Jack London and influential poet George Sterling. As its genuinely bohemian members were replaced by lawyers and financiers, the club steadily became (and remains) a preserve of wealthy—and exclusively male—power brokers. A plaque reading "Weaving Spiders Come Not Here" marks the club's present site at 624 Taylor Street.

Top: The plaque marking the birthplace of novelist Jack London. Below: Haight-Ashbury's Spreckels Mansion—a lodging for Bierce and London?

North Beach and Telegraph Hill Thanks to what became the Beat generation, North Beach's literary links are plentiful. **City Lights** (261 Columbus Avenue) was the country's first paperback bookstore but, more importantly, it published the earliest of the Beat poets in the 1950s, beginning with Allen Ginsberg's controversial *Howl*.

Ginsberg and poet/artist Lawrence Ferlinghetti, City Lights' owner, as well as other seminal figures, patronized North Beach cafés such as **Trieste** (601 Vallejo Street), while another Beat character, Jack Kerouac, became well known to the bartenders at **Vesuvio** (255 Columbus Avenue, just across what is now Jack Kerouac Street).

Ginsberg wrote *Howl* while living at **1010 Montgomery Street** on the edge of Telegraph Hill, a neighborhood which appealed to many writers until gentrification took hold. Fans of Armistead Maupin's Tales of the City series, however, might pay respects to **60–62 Alta Street**, Maupin's first home in the city and where the first tales were written in the early 1970s.

Pacific Heights and Russian Hill Best-selling romance writer Danielle Steele purchased a 42-room mansion in Pacific Heights, a neighborhood with literary associations stretching way back. Gertrude Atherton, a pre-feminism feminist and one of California's most important early 1900s novelists, rented an apartment at **2101 California Street** in 1929 and presided over many literary gatherings there. On Russian Hill, Jack Kerouac occupied an attic room at **29 Russel Street** during 1952, revising the drafts of what would become the classic Beat novel, *On the Road.* Three years later, Allen Ginsberg read *Howl* for the first time in public at what was then the Six Galleries (**3119 Fillmore Street**).

Nob Hill Dashiell Hammett perfected the hard-boiled private-eye genre in the 1920s, and after several Tenderloin addresses refined *The Maltese Falcon* at **1155 Leavenworth Street** on Nob Hill. Hammett's creation, Sam Spade, left many fictional footprints around the city and often dined at **John's Grill**. The restaurant actually exists (two blocks south of Union Square at 63 Ellis Street) and keeps a replica Maltese Falcon in its second-floor dining room.

SoMa In his writings, Jack Kerouac eulogized the inexpensive hotels, cargo docks and railroad freight yards of 1950s SoMa. In the same district six decades earlier, Jack London, one of the few internationally known writers to be born in San Francisco, entered the world at a site at

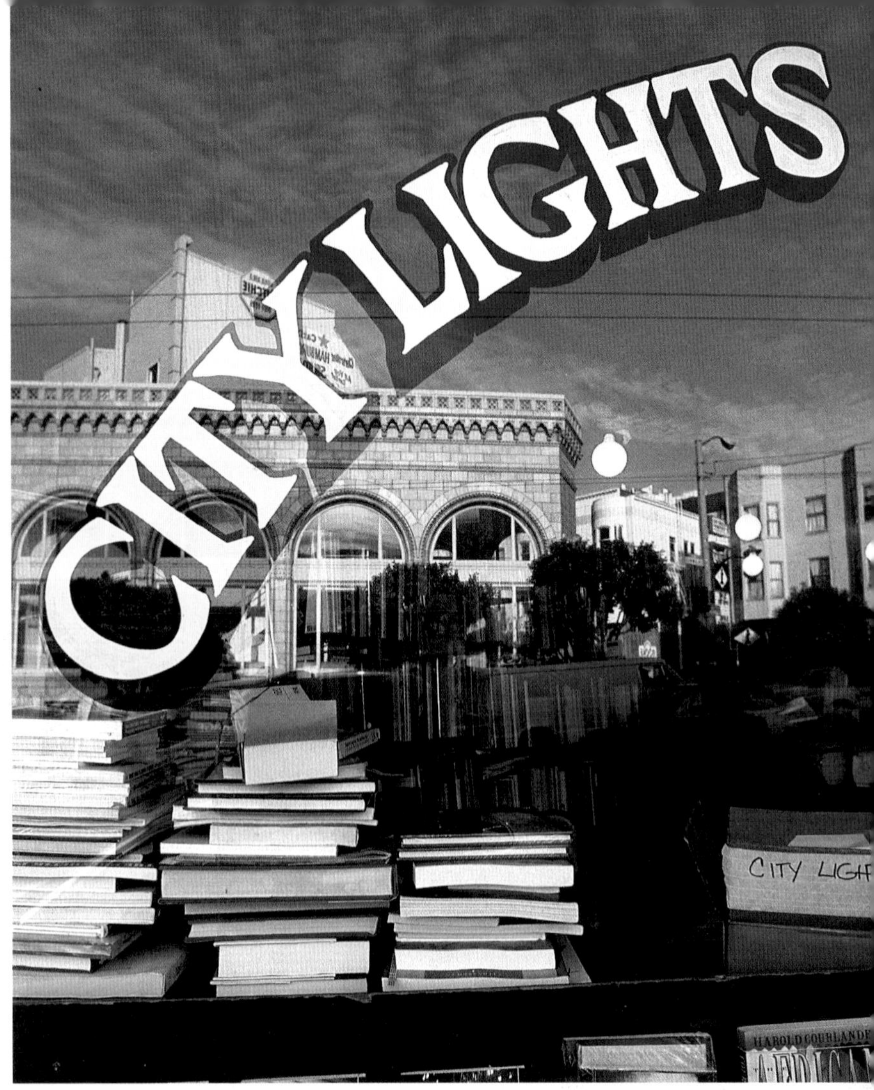

A literary landmark since the 1950s

601 Third Street now marked by a plaque (see page 169). His enduring reputation is also acknowledged by **Jack London Street**, which runs through SoMa's South Park.

Haight-Ashbury Although Jack London moved across the bay to Oakland when still a child, he returned to the city as an adult and for a time (it is claimed) occupied an attic room of Haight-Ashbury's **Spreckels Mansion** (737 Buena Vista Avenue West). The same room (it is also claimed) was once occupied by Ambrose Bierce (see page 37). A leading literary figure in late-1880s California, Bierce was an acclaimed columnist and wrote the darkly witty *Devil's Dictionary* before he mysteriously disappeared in Mexico.

The influential Kenneth Rexroth lived at **250 Scott Street** before Haight-Ashbury's mid-1960s hippie boom, which was underway when maverick journalist Hunter S. Thompson occupied **318 Parnassus Avenue** while conducting the "research" (mostly drunken parties) leading to his name-making *Hell's Angels*.

CHINATOWN

Chinatown can also claim literary associations. An impoverished Robert Louis Stevenson first passed the time in Portsmouth Square in 1879 (he is remembered by a granite plinth, see page 75). A riotous atmosphere helped make tiny Sam Wo's (813 Washington Street) a favorite of the Beats in the 1950s. More recently, Amy Tan captured the flavor of the neighborhood in her 1989 novel, *The Joy Luck Club*.

PACIFIC HEIGHTS' VICTORIAN HOMES
From Lafayette Park (see page 104), not only does every street lead invitingly downhill, but most also hold examples of the playful Victorian architecture that took the fancy of affluent San Franciscans at the turn of the 20th century. Today, in immaculately renovated form, many of these homes are the prized possessions of the city's wealthiest people.

Pacific Heights' Union Street is a popular shopping area, with live fashion shows (right) and retail outlets occupying carefully restored 19th-century cottages (below)

▶ Pacific Heights *IFCD5*

Buses: 3, 22, 41, 45

West of Van Ness Avenue between Nob Hill and the Marina District, Pacific Heights is among the city's most affluent neighborhoods. Two main reasons prompt a visit. One is the collection of upscale stores and restaurants. The other is Pacific Heights' impressive diversity of residential architecture, from 19th-century Queen Anne mansions to streamlined 1930s art deco apartment buildings.

On the 1700–2000 blocks of Union Street are the antique stores, boutiques and chic restaurants where Pacific Heights' well-to-do and fashion-conscious residents like to buy expensive ornaments, select European designer clothes off the rack and dine on expensive French and Italian food. There is a similar scene along Fillmore Street north of Pine Street. For the price of a coffee, a sidewalk table at one of the local cafés can easily provide a relaxing hour of people-watching.

In the late 1800s, as opulent homes first began appearing on the slopes of Pacific Heights, the valley through which present-day Union Street runs was known as Cow Hollow because of its numerous dairy farms, which supplied the city's fresh milk and cheese. As a result of pressure from the wealthy inhabitants to rid their chosen neighborhood of nasty smells, the farms—and the slaughterhouses which had grown up around them—were closed down in the 1890s, though not all the clapboard farm buildings disappeared. One of them, at 2040 Union Street, now occupied by stores and a restaurant, was the home of dairy farmer James Cudworth. At number 1980 are the so-called "twin houses," identical one-story homes joined by a common wall, which Cudworth built in the 1870s as wedding presents to his two daughters. Many of the other farm buildings remain along Union Street, expensively restored, decorated by imitation gas lamps and fronted by neat wrought-iron fences.

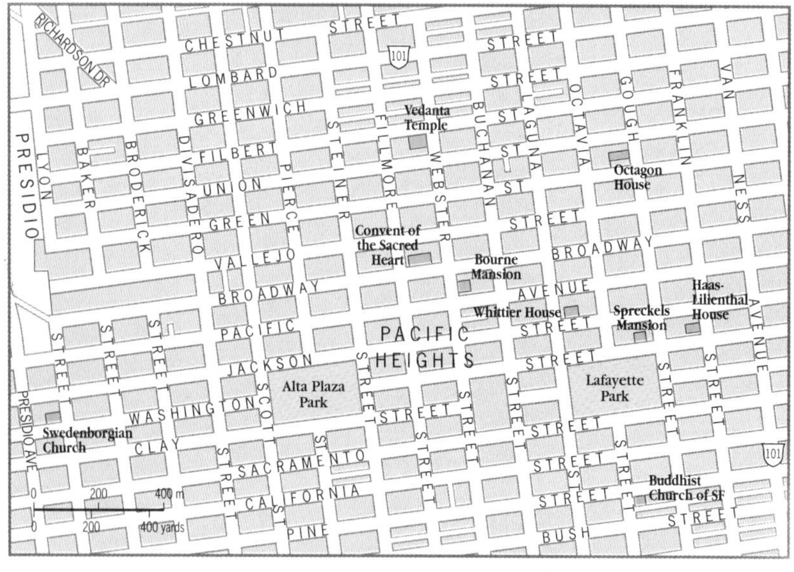

A few blocks south of Union Street rise the slopes which give Pacific Heights its name. As you climb, look back to see the impressive views across the Golden Gate which encouraged the rich to settle the district during the 1880s. Gaze ahead of you, and you will see many of their architecturally adventurous homes. Among them, two of the most intriguing specimens are the **Octagon House▶** (2645 Gough Street; tel: 415/441-7512, see page 145) and the **Haas-Lilienthal House▶▶** (2007 Franklin Street, see page 105).

Union Street's "twin houses," a wedding gift from the builder to his two daughters

Convent of the Sacred Heart

ARCHITECTURAL CRITICISM
Critic Ernest Peixotto was unimpressed by Pacific Heights' architecture. Commenting on the area in 1893, he described its homes as "nightmares of an architect's brain piled up without rhyme or reason—restless, turreted, loaded with meaningless detail, defaced with fantastic windows and hideous chimneys."

PERRY MASON'S BIRTHPLACE
Fans of lawyer-sleuth Perry Mason may care to pay their respects to 1700 Octavia Street, on the corner of Bush Street, the house where prolific writer Erle Stanley Gardner created the character during 1933.

Many interesting clusters of Victorian and early 20th-century homes can be discovered in a leisurely stroll through the neighborhood. Faced with the steep slopes, however, you might prefer to focus your attention on a few properties.

The 1896 **Bourn Mansion▶** (2550 Webster Street) was designed by Willis Polk (see panel, page 112) for William B. Bourn II, who ran gas and water companies and inherited a gold-mining fortune. Polk also designed Bourn's country home, Filoli (see panel, page 203).

The **Convent of the Sacred Heart▶▶** (2222 Broadway) occupies a trim granite mansion erected for bartender-turned-silver-baron James Flood in 1912. An earlier Flood mansion, successfully modified in the mid-1960s, stands close by, housing the very select and academically renowned **Hamlin School for Girls** (2120 Broadway).

Modeled by architects Swain & Tharp on the brownstone town houses of New York, the **Whittier House▶** (2090 Jackson Street) was completed in 1896 for paint manufacturer William Whittier. The mansion's red sandstone walls enabled it to survive the 1906 earthquake and fire. This was one of the first homes in the city with electric lights and central heating.

Overlooking Lafayette Park (see page 104), the **Spreckels Mansion▶▶** (2080 Washington Street) was built for sugar mogul Adolph Spreckels and his wife Alma, largely, or so it seems from the features, in deference to Mrs. Spreckels' French ancestry.

▶ Pacific Heritage Museum *IBCJ8*

608 Commercial Street (tel: 415/399-1124)
Open: Tue–Sat 10–4; free
Buses: 1, 15, 69

The Bank of Canton on the edge of Chinatown is an appropriate setting for the changing exhibitions that explore the links between the countries of the Pacific Rim. Anyone who regards San Francisco as having more in common with New York than Hong Kong should find plenty of food for thought here.

The Bank occupies the site of the city's first US Branch Mint which, in 1875, was replaced by a new US Subtreasury (itself superseded by what is now the Old US Mint). The story of both is told within the brick-walled vault: Exhibits include coins, bullion bags and the sturdy carts required to move large consignments of gold.

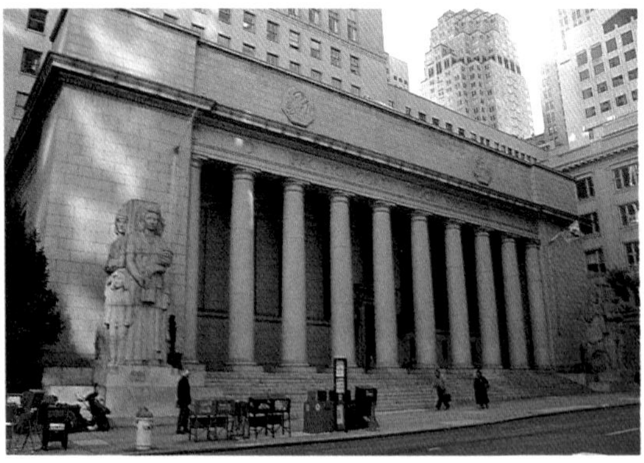

▶ Pacific Stock Exchange *IBCJ8*

301 Pine Street
Bus: 12 (weekdays only)

A row of neoclassical columns greets brokers as they climb the steps of the Pacific Stock Exchange, presumably intended to instill a serious mood as people enter what has been a citadel of West Coast finance since 1915. The building, formerly a US Treasury, underwent an architectural overhaul in 1930 (see panel), which explains why the more recent features, and the large and arresting sculptures by Ralph Stackpole on either side of the steps, are in the art deco *moderne* style. Tightened security in the early 1990s resulted in the closure of the public gallery, but you can see the Stock Exchange's impressive Diego Rivera mural by making an appointment through the Mexican Museum (see page 117; tel: 415/202-9700).

THE STOCK EXCHANGE'S ARCHITECTURE

"One of the major sources of modernism in the Bay Area" is how the Foundation for San Francisco's Architectural Heritage describes the city's Stock Exchange, which, ironically, acquired its form as a result of the 1920s economic crash. The firm of Miller and Pfleuger had been commissioned to build a new stock exchange on a different site, but financial constraints led instead to their radical conversion—employing an inspired blend of classical and *moderne* styles—of the recently vacated US Treasury.

Left: The neoclassical exterior of the Pacific Stock Exchange. In the decades following the Gold Rush, San Francisco was unchallenged as the US's major west-coast financial center. Despite the introduction of screen-based trading, below, the city now lags well behind Los Angeles as the hub of Pacific Coast commerce

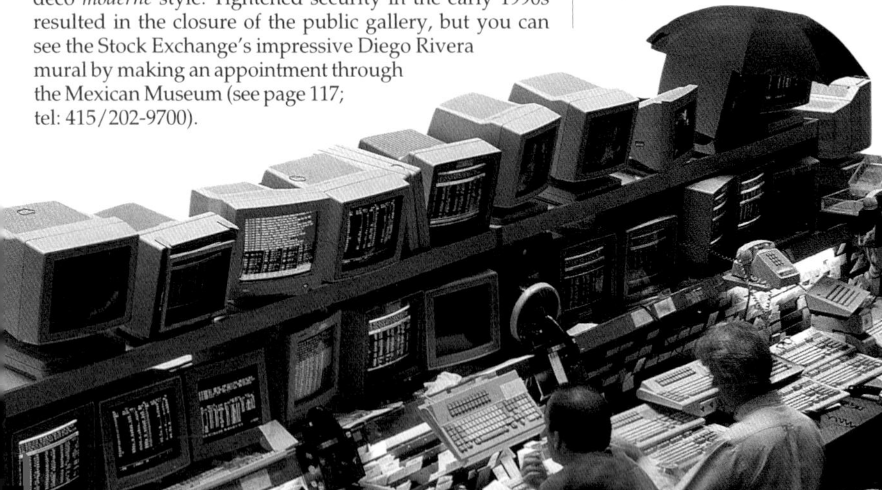

▶▶▶ Palace of Fine Arts *IFCD6*

West end of Lyon Street
Buses: 28, 30

In 1915, using the opening of the Panama Canal as an excuse, San Francisco announced its recovery from the devastation of the earthquake and fire of nine years earlier by staging the Panama–Pacific International Exposition (see page 40). On land created with sand dredged up from the bay (the birth of the Marina District), a group of noted architects was commissioned to erect temporary structures to house the Expo.

As their theme, the architects adopted the beaux-arts style that had graced similar fairs around the country. One of the architects was Bernard Maybeck, and it was his dream-like Palace of Fine Arts which, more than any other building, captured the imagination of the Expo's 20 million visitors.

Designed as a Roman ruin, Maybeck's inspired work used a classical domed rotunda as its centerpiece and flanked this with a fragmented colonnade, each group of columns topped by weeping maidens and decorated with aimless stairways and funeral urns. The intention was to instill a sense of "moderated sadness" to prepare visitors for the classical art exhibited in the Expo's Great Hall (now housing the Exploratorium, see page 82).

As the other Expo buildings were razed, public admiration, and the fact that the army owned the land (rather than private speculators, who quickly developed what became the Marina District) saved the Palace of Fine Arts. By the late 1950s, however, the structure was becoming a genuine ruin rather than a symbolic one, and a campaign was launched to save it.

At a cost of $7.5 million, the restored Palace—its features replicated in concrete—was unveiled in 1967. Though longer-lasting than Maybeck ever intended, the Palace has lost none of its mysterious enchantment. Take a stroll through the archways and stand beneath the 132ft (40m) high rotunda, and pause to ponder the structure's haunting reflection among the birdlife of the adjacent lagoon.

BERNARD MAYBECK
Born in New York in 1862, Bernard Maybeck studied architecture at the École des Beaux-Arts in Paris and settled in Berkeley in 1889. He assisted Phoebe Hearst in organizing the competition for Berkeley's university campus, but soon began designing buildings of his own around the Bay Area. His creations were distinguished by their inspired fusing of diverse architectural ideas, such as the Swedenborgian Church (see page 172).

From the ground, some of the features of Maybeck's Palace of Fine Arts are hard to spot, such as weeping maidens (above) and the details of the frieze ringing the rotunda (right)

▶ Performing Arts Library & Museum *IBCF4*

399 Grove Street (tel: 415/255-4800)
Open: Tue–Sat 11–5, Wed until 7; free
Bus: 21

It may have been regarded as the wild capital of the Wild West, but settlers in Gold Rush-era San Francisco were quick to display a taste for the performing arts. No fewer than 5,000 operatic performances took place in the city between 1849 and the 1906 earthquake, and during this time all the celebrated performers of the day—be they populist vaudeville entertainers like Lola Montez, adored actresses such as Sarah Bernhardt, or opera stars of the caliber of Enrico Caruso—included San Francisco on their US tours. It was also here that America saw its first full-length *Swan Lake* and its first complete *Nutcracker*.

Proof of the city's long-thriving cultural scene is to be found among the million or more individual items—posters, programs, costumes, rare footage of early shows on lithograph and more recent ones on video—stored and cataloged by the Performing Arts Library & Museum.

Not surprisingly, not all of the material can be displayed at any one time. The museum does, however, mount stimulating temporary exhibitions, and the library is a great resource for anyone wishing to delve deeper into the city's performing arts past.

The ins and outs of Lola Montez's provocative Spider Dance, which wowed San Franciscan audiences in the mid-1800s, are among the minutiae of the city's cultural life archived at the Performing Arts Library & Museum

▶ Potrero Hill *IBCF3*

Bus: 15

Between the Mission District and the docks of the eastern waterfront, primarily residential Potrero Hill is off the beaten tourist track. Nonetheless, the **Anchor Steam Brewery▶** (1705 Mariposa Street), home of the beer synonymous with the city and offering hour-long tours followed by tastings (for an appointment tel: 415/863-8350), provides one reason to visit the area. Another is **Vermont Street**, claimed to be even more crooked than Russian Hill's prettier and more famous (and more crowded) Lombard Street. Tackle the Vermont Steps (between 20th and 22nd streets) for great views.

THE POTRERO HILL RUSSIANS

One of San Francisco's more curious ethnic footnotes concerns the Potrero Hill Russians. The first Russians to live in San Francisco colonized this area from the 1850s and, half a century later during the Russo-Japanese War, many more arrived to avoid conscription into the Tsarist army. Many of them were dissenters from the Orthodox Church and members of pietistic sects. The chickens and goats kept by these resolutely nonurban Russians were a feature of Potrero Hill until the 1950s.

For the latest intrigue at City Hall or simply to find out which restaurants are worth going to, San Franciscans are avid readers—and what they like to read about most is San Francisco. When not reading, they turn to the radio or TV for more Bay Area news and views.

SAN FRANCISCO ON LINE
Explore San Francisco via the Internet for everything from the San Francisco Symphony (www.sfsymphony.org) to local bars and cafés operating their own websites. Daily and free newspapers can all be read online (www.sfgate.com; www.examiner.com; www.sfbg.com; www.sfweekly.com), and large general sites for entertainment, eating, drinking and museum information include www.sfstation.com; and the Convention and Visitors Bureau site at www.sfvisitor.org

SPORTS FINAL **San Francisco Chronicle**
NORTHERN CALIFORNIA'S LARGEST NEWSPAPER

Daily newspapers The city's major daily newspaper is the *San Francisco Chronicle*, which appears every morning. A long-time rival, the *San Francisco Examiner*, used to appear every evening but ailed steadily until 2001, when it acquired a new proprietor, subsequently becoming a free weekday tabloid. Both papers spent decades under the same ownership but the Chronicle's morning appearance helped make it the more popular.

San Francisco Examiner

Free weekly newspapers The former rivalry between the *Chronicle* and *Examiner* exists now between the city's major free weekly newspapers, the *San Francisco Bay Guardian* and *SF Weekly*. Both take a left-of-center stance in their reports on city news and the arts, and carry extensive listings. The *Bay Guardian* was founded in the 1960s; *SF Weekly* started in 1989, and at first demonstrated its youthfulness with sharp writing and better coverage of contemporary culture. The *Guardian*, though, is more likely to expose corruption in high places with well-researched investigative journalism.

Top, and above: San Francisco newspaper vendors await customers

Radio Aided by several college stations and the diverse interests of the local population, San Francisco and the Bay Area have an abundance of radio stations, offering everything from Top 40 hits to classical music and analysis of international affairs.

Television A number of local and foreign-language cable channels add to the usual network fare. Most hotel room TVs carry a selection of cable and pay-TV channels, and/or in-house movie rental channels. The main San Francisco TV channels are 2 (KTVU/FOX), 4 (KRON/NBC), 5 (KPIX/CBS), 7 (KGO/ABC) and 9 (KQED/PBS); only PBS differs from the rest, with no commercials and predominantly serious programs.

GAY PUBLICATIONS
Published biweekly, the free *Bay Times* is an excellent source of news and information for gays, lesbians and bisexuals. Also free and worth reading is the politically oriented weekly *Bay Area Reporter*.

▶ The Presidio *IFCC5*

Main Gate at the corner of Lombard and Lyon streets (Presidio Information Visitor Center; tel: 415/561-4323)
Bus: 29

Across the more than 1,500 acres (607ha) of hills and woodlands that cover the northwest corner of the city, the earliest Spanish settlers founded a *presidio* (or garrison) in 1776 to guard San Francisco Bay—though its limited armory and poor location made the Presidio a token defense—and protect Mission Dolores, then being established in what is now the Mission District (see page 124).

As Mexico sought and eventually achieved independence from Spain, keeping the settlement supplied became more trouble than it was worth; the Presidio, along with its adobe buildings, was abandoned. After the US acquisition of California in 1846, the Presidio again became a military installation, spending many years as the base of the Sixth Army. It was decommissioned in the early 1990s, when its land became part of the National Parks Service in 1998.

The Presidio is now partly administered by the Presidio Trust with the intention of becoming an financially self-sufficient entity by 2013. A boost to the Presidio economy came with the announcement in 2005 of a $350-million base to be erected across 23 of its acres (9ha) by film-maker George Lucas as a home for his digital arts empire.

Longer-serving elements of the Presidio include the Officers Club (50 Malaga Avenue; tel: 415/561-4323), currently operating as a temporary visitor center, which can still boast a section of the original Spanish adobe wall, and the former Post Hospital, around which stand ageing artillery pieces and a couple of "earthquake cottages," two of the many that provided shelter to those rendered homeless by the 1906 earthquake and fire. A newer site of appeal is Immigration Point Overlook (Washington Boulevard), which offers a stupendous vista over the Golden Gate.

Presidio pet cemetery

A SPANISH VIEW

In 1776, contemplating the outlook from the hill which would later hold the Presidio, Franciscan missionary and expedition cartographer Pedro Font recorded in his diary: "This mesa affords a most delightful view, for from it one sees a large part of the port and its islands...the mouth of the harbor, and all of the sea that the eye can take in."

Emergency earthquake housing, 1906

THE RUSSIANS OF RUSSIAN HILL
Russian Hill is believed to have been named after a group of Russians who were working for a fur-trapping company on the Northern California coast in the early 1800s, when they perished during an expedition and were buried on the southeast crest of what became Russian Hill. The story is given credence by historical records.

TEMPLE EMANU-EL
The bulbous Byzantine-style dome that looms above the northern section of the Richmond District belongs to Temple Emanu-El, a 2,000-seat synagogue serving the oldest Jewish congregation in California. It was founded in 1850 and was completed in 1926 at a cost of $3 million. One of the temple's architects was Arthur Brown, of City Hall fame (see page 78).

In the commercial maelstrom of the Richmond District's Clement Street are some of the best Asian restaurants in the city

▶ Richmond District *IFCB5*

Buses: 1, 2, 5, 28, 31, 38

What might otherwise be a fairly bland residential district filling the space between Golden Gate Park and the Presidio, the Richmond District has been enlivened since the mid-1970s by a major influx of Asian-Americans, including particularly large numbers of Chinese. Thirty-five percent of San Francisco's substantial Chinese population now resides here.

The Chinese influence, with Thai and Vietnamese also well established, is most apparent along the district's main commercial artery, Clement Street, which is lined with Asian restaurants, bakeries and supermarkets.

Also found on Clement Street, and along nearby Geary Boulevard, are the longer-established German, Russian and East European cafés and stores reflecting the ethnic origins of earlier generations of Richmond District settlers. Further indication of the Russian presence is provided by the **Cathedral of the Holy Virgin** (6210 Geary Boulevard; tel 415/221-3255), seat of the Russian Orthodox religion in the western US and dating from 1961.

▶ Rincon Center *IBCK8*

Mission Street between Spear and Steuart streets
Buses: 1, 32

Enter the spacious atrium of the Rincon Center at lunchtime and you are liable to find snack-munching office workers being entertained by a dinner-suited pianist, the sound underscored by the splashes of a fountain tumbling 90ft (27m) down a wall.

Opened in 1988, the modern structure was cleverly grafted onto the rear of the 1939 **Rincon Annex Post Office▶**. This delectable art deco building is heightened by Anton Refregier's hard-hitting **murals▶▶**, showing scenes ranging from the Spanish conquering of Native Americans to the violent industrial disputes of the 1930s. Financed by a WPA grant (see page 175), they caused controversy on their unveiling, and are still compelling.

Above: Famously crooked Lombard Street. Left: the Rincon Center, inspired modern architecture

▶▶ Russian Hill *IBCF6*

Buses: 15, 30, 41, 45

Most visitors stay on Russian Hill only long enough to point their cameras at the section of **Lombard Street▶▶** famously hailed as "the crookedest street in San Francisco"; its descent between Hyde and Leavenworth streets is landscaped into a series of curves decorated by herbaceous plants and shrubs. The steepness of the grade made the street impassable for vehicles until the gardens were added in the 1920s, enabling traffic to make the downward journey in a zigzag fashion.

Take a look at Lombard Street, but while on Russian Hill also seize the opportunity to visit the **San Francisco Art Institute**, the oldest art school on the West Coast, described fully on page 159.

Russian Hill also boasts many notable examples of the architectural styles that have shaped San Francisco. Several interesting places on the 1000 block of Green Street include the **Feusier Octagon House▶** (number 1067), one of the city's two remaining eight-sided dwellings, partially hidden by shrubbery (see also Octagon House, page 145).

INA COOLBRITH PARK

A much-admired poet, Ina Coolbrith was a Russian Hill resident and became California's first poet laureate in 1919. She did much to nurture aspiring writers—Jack London and Ambrose Bierce among them—from the time of her arrival in San Francisco in 1862 until her death in 1928. Ina Coolbrith Park (corner of Vallejo and Taylor streets) is the city's only park named in honor of a writer.

MACONDRAY LANE

Steep slopes notwithstanding, much of Russian Hill makes pleasant strolling territory. The slender Macondray Lane is a charming tree-lined street that stretches for two pedestrian-only blocks between Union and Green streets. It can be reached from a wooden staircase which rises sharply above Taylor Street, a block and a half north of Ina Coolbrith Park.

St. Mary's Cathedral, which seems even bigger on the inside than the imposing exterior suggests

THE HAUNTED BELL TOWER
Reports of odd happenings in the bell tower of San Francisco Art Institute began in 1947 when a student claimed to have heard unexplained footsteps. Later stories involved a vanishing woman in a blue dress and strange electrical malfunctions. In the late 1960s, building work on the tower was interrupted by unusual sounds and a series of bizarre accidents. After a seance in 1976, some mediums suggested the emotions of frustrated artists were responsible for the peculiar events, while another pointed out the possible relevance of the tower's setting, on a former cemetery.

►► St. Mary's Cathedral *IBCE5*

Geary Boulevard at Gough Street (tel: 415/567-2020)
Entrance by donation
Buses: 19, 38

Four hyperbolic paraboloids rising 190ft (58m) into the air and forming the shape of a Greek cross help make St. Mary's Cathedral (formally known as St. Mary's Catholic Cathedral of the Assumption) the most striking and original piece of modern religious architecture in the whole of San Francisco.

Built at a cost of $7 million, the cathedral opened in 1971 and replaced a previous St. Mary's, which had been destroyed by fire in 1962 after serving the city's Catholic community for 71 years.

Inside, the overwhelming feeling is one of space. The open-plan cathedral can seat 2,400 people (with a further 1,300 standing), and its design is intended to eliminate the traditional divisions between the different areas of a cathedral.

Here, the apse, nave, transepts, baptistry and narthex are undivided beneath the towering ceiling, in the center of which is a skylight in the shape of the Cross. The four stained-glass windows which rise from floor to ceiling height are each 139ft (42m) tall and just 6ft (2m) wide. The windows are positioned in each main wall and represent the four elements.

Anyone visiting Chinatown after touring St. Mary's Cathedral might like to contrast its striking size and modernity with the compact interior of Old St. Mary's Church (see page 72), which served as the city's Catholic cathedral until 1891. From 1891, the role was taken on by a new St. Mary's built in impressively proportioned red-brick style at the corner of Van Ness Avenue and O'Farrell Street, until it was razed by fire in 1962.

►► San Francisco Art Institute *IBCF6*

800 Chestnut Street (tel: 415/749-4564)
Bus: 30

Founded in 1871 (see panel) and moved to its current premises in 1926, the San Francisco Art Institute is the oldest art school on the West Coast, and still one of the region's most respected bases of artistic learning and creativity. Just as appealing as the student art which hangs in the corridors and galleries, however, is the building itself, styled after a Mediterranean monastery. It includes a cozy courtyard which is often enlivened by avant-garde student sculpture.

Acclaimed Mexican muralist Diego Rivera taught at the institute for a brief period in the 1930s, and a work of his—an intriguing mural of a mural-in-progress which includes a self-portrait—covers one wall of the **Diego Rivera Gallery►** (open: daily 9–9; see also page 151). A 1970 addition is a **café** with inexpensive food, where you might mingle with the students, or just enjoy the views of Fisherman's Wharf. Before leaving, be sure to glance at the bell tower, said to be haunted by the spirits of frustrated artists (see panel, page 158).

The allegedly haunted bell tower of San Francisco Art Institute

► San Francisco Craft & Folk Art Museum *IBCE6*

Building A, Fort Mason (tel: 415/775-0991)
Open: Tue–Fri and Sun 11–5, Sat 10–5; free
Bus: 28

It may be a tough job to predict what might be on display at the San Francisco Craft & Folk Art Museum, but few of the shows mounted here fail to be informative and entertaining. Previous exhibitions have explored the strange world of the decoy duck, native American glassworks, and traditions in puppetry from around the globe.

The mission of the museum is threefold: to exhibit fine examples of handicrafts; to highlight the folk art of untrained artists that would otherwise be ignored by museums; and to use traditional ethnic art to promote understanding between the diverse cultures which exist among the population of San Francisco and the Bay Area. A visit here can be a delight: be sure to include it on your itinerary. The museum is planning to move to the Yerba Buena Gardens area in the future.

ART INSTITUTE ORIGINS
What became the San Francisco Art Institute was originally the San Francisco Art Association, set up in 1871 and the first art school west of the Mississippi.

Mural of a mural-in-progress by Diego Rivera, at the San Francisco Art Institute

THE MUSEUM SHOP
The retail outlet of the Museum of Modern Art, MuseumStore, already established as the city's best source of art books, has unveiled a new line of merchandise. The design cue comes from museum holdings or from the architecture of the building, and the goods range from stationery to pieces of furniture all created by a team of West Coast artists headed by Bay Area designer Michael Cronan.

San Francisco Museum of Modern Art, housed in a magnificent structure

▶▶▶ San Francisco Museum of Modern Art *IBCG5*

151 Third Street (tel: 415/357-4000)
Open: Fri–Tue 11–6, Thu until 9
Buses: 14, 15, 26, 30, 45

During the 1940s, the decade-old San Francisco Museum of Modern Art established its forward-thinking credentials by presenting the first solo exhibitions by the pioneering artists of abstract expressionism—Arshile Gorky, Jackson Pollock, Robert Motherwell and Mark Rothko—but its continued emergence as a major showplace of modern art was restricted by lack of space. With its new custom-built five-story premises formally opened in January 1995, however, the museum finally looks set to become one of the country's leading art centers, with the room and facilities to mount challenging exhibitions in the new fields of video, computer and interactive art.

The core of the permanent collections is shown in the second-floor galleries, which highlight painting and

sculpture from 1900 to 1970. Here you will find significant contributions from Europeans, including Pablo Picasso's *Head in Three-quarter View* and *The Coffee Pot*, and what might be the zenith of analytical cubism: Georges Braque's *Violin and Candlestick*.

Be sure not to miss the museum's most prized possession: Matisse's seminal *Woman with the Hat* (1905), a work which made a crucial contribution to what became Fauvism, the century's first radical art movement.

There is also a formidable and engaging stock of German Expressionism and over 100 works by Paul Klee, often arranged into special exhibitions. Surrealism also features, with secondary offerings from primary figures such as Salvador Dali and Max Ernst.

Screaming more loudly for attention, however, is a striking complement of abstract expressionist canvases. Jackson Pollock's *Guardians of the Secret* is foremost among them, but there are notable contributions from fellow gesturist Willem de Kooning, and the last completed work by leading color-field painter Barnett Newman.

Sharing the floor are architecture and design exhibitions, ranging from drawings by early San Francisco-shaper Willis Polk (see panel, page 112) to a full set of office furniture by L.A.-based modernist designers Charles and Ray Eames.

The third floor holds some fine 20th-century photography from international greats such as Man Ray and Moholy-Nagy, and equally well-acclaimed local practitioners such as Ansel Adams and Edward Weston. There is a unique collection of 1920s and 1930s experimental photography from eastern and central Europe. On the fourth floor, the museum keeps its video, audio and interactive installations.

It is hard to visit the new Museum of Modern Art without forming some impression of the $60-million building which contains it. The museum was the first project in the U.S. by award-winning Mario Botta, a Swiss architect who worked with major figures such as Le Corbusier and Louis Kahn during his formative years. Aiming for a modernist boldness without severity, the museum has a set-back brick-and-stone facade with a truncated cylinder rising through its center, decorated in bands of black and white brick. Inside, the cylinder keeps natural light flooding into a full-height atrium.

The Museum of Modern Art reflected in a building opposite

MEXICAN MODERNISM
While many of the major names of North American and European art are represented in the museum, there are also several welcome examples of modern Mexican painting. Look for Diego Rivera's *Flower Carrier* and *Kneeling Child on Yellow Background*, Frida Kahlo's *Frida and Diego Rivera* and Joaquin Torres-Garcia's *Constructivist Painting No. 8.*

The museum from Yerba Buena Gardens

As the San Francisco Zoo is several miles from the city center, visiting the animals requires a special trip. Once there, don't expect the peacocks to show any gratitude

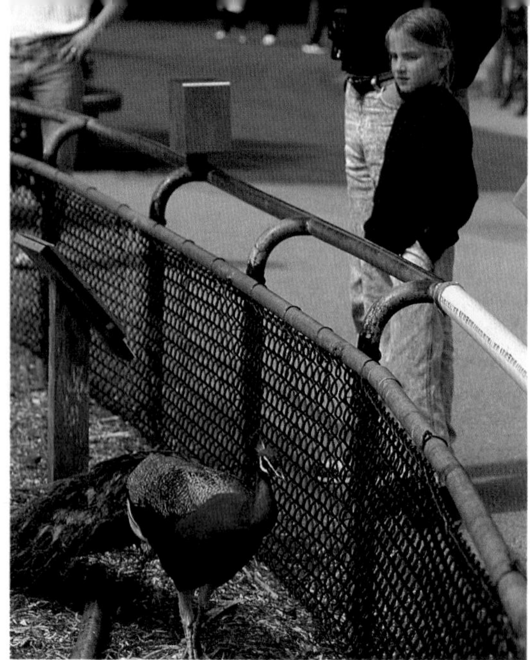

SAMUEL I HAYAKAWA
After he was appointed to run San Francisco State University (then San Francisco State College) in 1968, Samuel (S.I.) Hayakawa astonished the media by turning somersaults in his office, evidently enjoying an otherwise tense period of campus confrontation between students and authority. Canadian-born and of Japanese descent, Hayakawa took an individualistic stance on many issues, and the resultant publicity helped him run successfully for the US Senate in 1976, aged 70. In Washington DC, he captivated the press by falling asleep in session and tap-dancing in the corridors.

SUTRO'S LIBRARY
Adolph Sutro roamed Europe in the 1880s seeking material for what would become the world's largest private library. Among the treasures with which he returned was the world's largest collection of pre-1500 printed books (termed *incunabula*), Lutheran pamphlets including 15 by Martin Luther himself, ancient Hebrew scrolls, and the first four folios of Shakespeare. Sadly, around half of the collection was destroyed in San Francisco's 1906 fire. Much of what remains is devoted to genealogy and American and Mexican history. Although geared to the serious researcher, the library (tel: 415/731-4477) is open to the public and has several cases of objects relating to San Francisco history.

▶ San Francisco State University *IFCB2*

1600 Holloway Avenue
Buses: 17, 28, 29

Fans of singer Johnny Mathis, once a student here, may enjoy strolling around San Francisco State University, but for anyone else the unprepossessing campus holds little of interest. It does provide a home, however, for the **American Poetry Archives▶** (tel: 415/338-2227), holding works by and about American writers as diverse as Walt Whitman and Amy Tan, and interviews with many recent American authors are available on audio and video tape.

Books also feature just off campus at 480 Winston Drive, where the **Sutro Library** (see panel) maintains the vast collection of books bequeathed to the city by wealthy philanthropist Adolph Sutro (see page 171).

▶ San Francisco Zoo *IFCA2*

Sloat Boulevard and 45th Avenue (tel: 415/753-7080)
Open: daily 10–5; moderate
Buses: 18, 23

A grizzly bear called Monarch, captured by the *San Francisco Examiner* as a publicity stunt in 1899, is remembered as its first inmate, but the San Francisco Zoo only really began in the 1920s when it acquired a 60-acre (24ha) plot of land at its present site. While the zoo has greatly improved over recent years, replacing many cages with natural and psychological barriers to keep animals and humans separate, it is not one of San Francisco's top attractions.

The zoo's most successful section is **Gorilla World▶**, costing $2 million in the 1980s and probably one of the most luxurious places for a captive gorilla to be. Elsewhere, the zoo has the usual complement of koalas, tigers, lions and rhinos, insect and reptile houses, and a **Children's Zoo▶** with plenty of furry four-legged creatures waiting to be petted.

▶▶ Sausalito *44A3*

Buses: Golden Gate Transit
Ferries: from the Ferry Building or Fisherman's Wharf

A 19th-century whaling port and rail terminal, Sausalito also acquired a significant shipbuilding industry during the 1940s and became a stamping ground of artists, bohemians and misfits from the 1950s. Few of these things are immediately evident in today's Sausalito: The bayside community has evolved into an affluent—if still nonconformist—San Francisco suburb.

With many of its homes set across a steep hill and linked by winding, tree-lined streets and pathways, the small and picturesque town has also become a major day-trip destination. Try to visit in midweek and arrive on an early ferry, thereby ensuring at least a few hours of peaceful exploration before the midday crowds arrive.

Besides its scenic appeal and a number of raffish bars located along Bridgeway, the main thoroughfare, Sausalito initially appears to have little other than souvenir shops, ice-cream outlets and a few noted restaurants.

But climb up any near-vertical street (some have stairs) for a taste of local living and a memorable view of San Francisco across the bay, and then continue for half a mile north along Bridgeway—leaving the commercial area behind—to discover two of Sausalito's best-kept secrets.

Built by the Army Corps of Engineers, the **Bay Model▶▶** (tel: 415/332-3871) is a scale re-creation of San Francisco Bay covering a 2-acre (1ha) indoor site. Enabling the study of water flow and tidal patterns in the bay, the model has gangways lined with informative texts on Bay Area ecology; an introductory film describes the features of the model in detail.

Further along Bridgeway is a community of brightly painted **houseboats**. These floating homes have been decorated with individual flair by their owners, who have resisted attempts to be moved.

WILLIAM RICHARDSON

Sausalito's name derives from the Spanish word *saucelito*, or "little willow," which was given to the 20,000-acre (8,097ha) ranch granted in 1838 by California's Mexican governor to English-born William Richardson. Previously a whaler, Richardson had settled in Yerba Buena (as San Francisco was then known) in 1822 and married the daughter of the Presidio's commander. Responsible for enforcing Mexican trade bans and collecting taxes from vessels using the bay, Richardson allegedly also led a smuggling operation from Sausalito's sheltered coves.

Escape from the pressures of freeway driving: Live on a Sausalito houseboat and commute to work by yacht

The US is a nation of sport lovers. Where San Franciscans differ noticeably from the residents of many other cities, however, is in their wholehearted personal embrace of active sports. Their passion for getting outside and keeping fit is perhaps induced by an extraordinarily high level of health awareness, and by living among some of the finest surroundings for outdoor pursuits to be found anywhere in the country.

GOLF
San Francisco not only has affordable public golf courses, but it also has some of the most dramatic landscapes in which to birdie, bogey or just lose your ball. There is an 18-hole course at Lincoln Park (entrance at 34th and Clement streets; tel: 415/750-GOLF) and a pitch-and-putt 9-hole course in Golden Gate Park (tel: 415/751-8987). Greens fees are slightly more expensive at Lincoln Park than at Golden Gate Park.

Radio station KNBR supports the Giants!

CANDLESTICK BECOMES 3COM
In 1996, Candlestick Park officially became known as 3Com Park following the sponsorship of the stadium by a Silicon Valley-based computer company. The new name fell uneasily from the lips of most San Francisco sports fans, and few were disappointed when the deal ended in 2001, with a new sponsor being sought.

Baseball During the April-to-October baseball season, the **San Francisco Giants** draw large crowds to SBC Park, at China Basin in SoMa. Buses 15, 30 and 45 stop close by, and Metro line N runs directly to the stadium. Tickets are available through agencies such as www.ticketsolutions.com (tel: 1-800/477-5285), from the stadium box office and from Giants Dugout stores, including one at Four Embarcadero Center, and online at sfgiants.com.

Across the bay, the **Oakland Athletics** (or **"A's"**) play in a different league from the Giants and have the ultra-modern 50,000-seat McAfee Coliseum to call home. Tickets are available through ticketsolutions.com mentioned above, and from the Coliseum box office (tel: 510/638-0500). BART trains (see page 252) link San Francisco to Oakland, where the Coliseum has its own stop.

Football The five-times Superbowl-winning **San Francisco 49ers** are also based at Monster (formerly Candlestick) Park. Their season runs from August to December with most games played on Sundays, kicking off at 1pm. For ticket details, tel: 415/656-4900. In 1995, Oakland regained the **Raiders**, who returned north from Los Angeles and who now play at the McAfee Coliseum (tel: 510/569-2121). Be warned, however, that most seats are usually sold months in advance. Some tickets may be available at marked-up prices (the face value is upward of $25) through agencies such as ticketsolutions.com (see above).

Avid football fans unable to obtain a ticket for the 49ers might cross the bay to the Berkeley campus, where the professionals of tomorrow play for the university's **Golden Bears** at the campus's Memorial Stadium. Tickets (usually $17–32) are sold on campus at the Athletic Ticket Office; for details, tel: 1-800/GO BEARS.

Basketball Basketball fans residing in San Francisco must travel to Oakland to see the Bay Area's sole professional basketball team—the **Golden State Warriors**—in Western Conference action at the McAfee Coliseum Arena (see above). The basketball season runs from October to April, and most games are played on weekday evenings from 7.30pm. Tickets are available through agencies and at the Coliseum box office. For more details tel: 1-888-GSW-HOOP.

Baseball fills 3Com Park to capacity

Participant sports No visitor to San Francisco who arrives with jogging clothes and energy to burn will find themselves running alone. The city has innumerable popular **jogging** places: Golden Gate Park, Marina Green, Golden Gate Promenade (between Fisherman's Wharf and Fort Point) and Lake Merced (near Fort Funston, part of the Golden Gate National Recreation Area) are just four of the many popular locations. Hills notwithstanding, the simplest and most enjoyable sport for visitors is **cycling**. The city has two excellent posted scenic bike routes. One stretches from Golden Gate Park to Lake Merced, the other winds south to north across the city and crosses Golden Gate Bridge into Marin County. Depending on the model, bike rentals run at around $6 an hour (or $30 a day). Rental outlets are plentiful along Stanyan Street, on the east side of Golden Gate Park; many others are listed in the Yellow Pages. More daringly, **City Kayak** (tel:415/357-1010) offer a variety of kayak trips on and around San Francisco Bay; the gentlest lasts four hours, costs $40, and brings fish-eye views of the Ferry Building and the Bay Bridge.

SAN FRANCISCO MARATHON
On a Sunday in mid-July, several thousand runners compete in the San Francisco Marathon (regarded by San Franciscans with less affection than the Bay to Breakers race), which includes a crossing of Golden Gate Bridge en route to the finish line in Golden Gate Park.

Below: View from the Lincoln Golf Course

SOUTH OF THE SLOT
In the days when cable cars ran along Market Street, SoMa was known as "South of the Slot," a reference to the cable-car slot in the middle of the road. A ballad of the day ran:

"Whether you know your location or not,
The heart of the city is South o' the slot!
That is the spot,
True to the dot,
The heart of the city is south o' the slot"!

The media attention focused on SoMa over the last few years has brought about a revival of interest in some of the neighborhood's architecturally distinguished older structures, such as the US Post Office and Court of Appeals Building, shown below, dating from 1902

▶ SoMa *IBCF5*

Buses: 15, 30, 45

No part of San Francisco has changed as quickly or as dramatically during the last 15 years as SoMa (an abbreviation of its location, South of Market Street). Traditionally industrial, downtrodden and sometimes dangerous, it is now a showplace of art and architecture, and site of some of the city's most rapid and controversial gentrification.

In the late 1800s, while the city's rich were outspending each other building palatial homes on Nob Hill or in Pacific Heights, the flatlands south of Market Street were exclusively the domain of the laboring classes. Unloading cargo ships and toiling in rail freight yards were the main occupations, and many of the city's militant labor leaders of the 1930s emerged from the neighborhood.

As shifting economic and transportation patterns caused SoMa's warehouses and factories to be abandoned during the 1970s, a small group of artists—eager for light-filled loft apartments—moved into some of them, and avant-garde galleries opened at ground level to display the artists' output.

Simultaneously, a section of Folsom Street suddenly found itself at the center of the city's newest nightlife scene, with a host of clubs and restaurants opening up to take advantage of SoMa's rising profile and its still comparatively low rents.

When the vast Moscone Convention Center opened in 1981, it triggered more development, including high-rise hotels—such as the distinctive Marriott—bringing more money and people (many employed in multimedia and internet companies that operated in converted warehouses) into the district. The influx of new companies and people drove up rents throughout SoMa and also affected the adjacent Mission District, forcing many low-income residents out of the city.

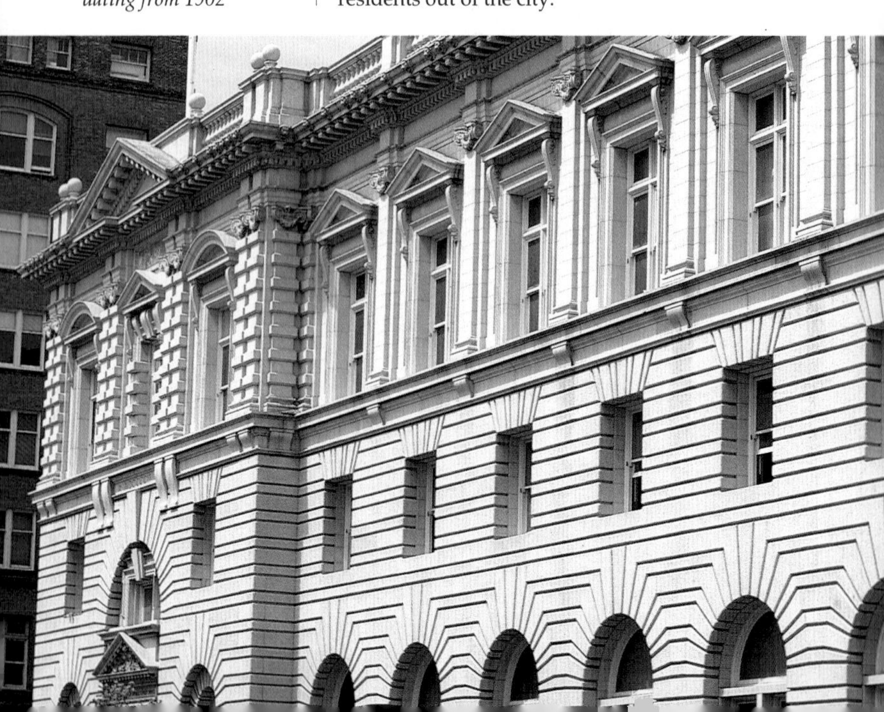

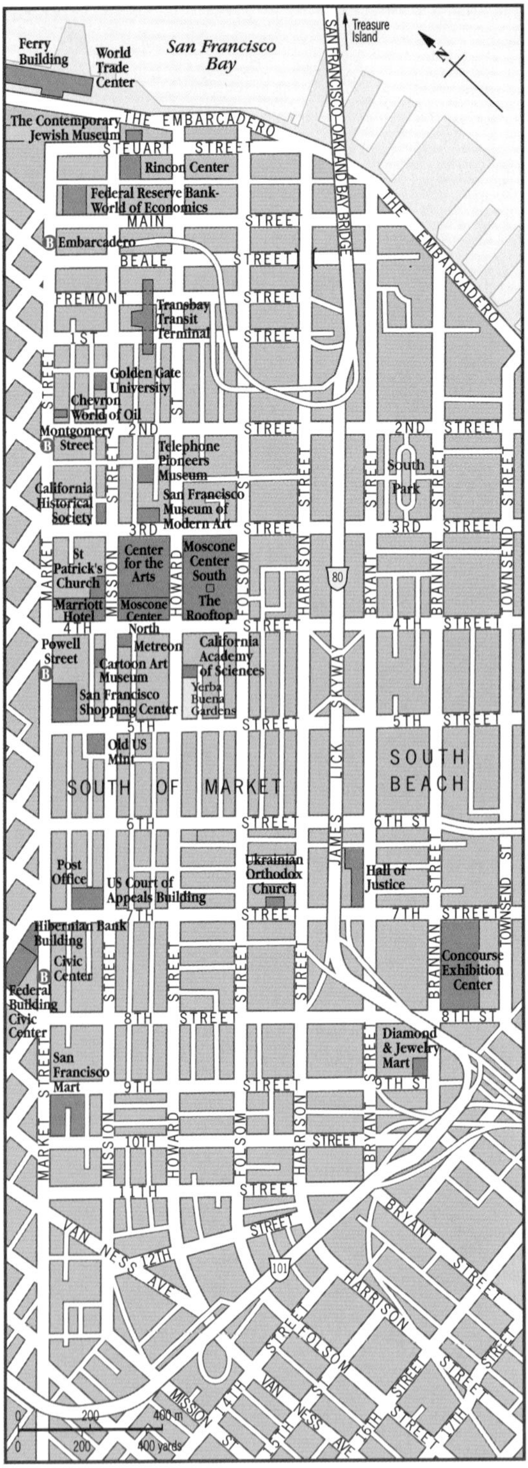

Close up: the US Post Office and Court of Appeals Building

SOMA'S STREETS OF SIN
Three of SoMa's side streets—Jessie, Clementina and Minna—are said to be named for a trio of the city's best-known 19th-century prostitutes.

EMERGENCY PLUMBING
After the 1906 earthquake and fire devastated the city, the authorities were determined that San Francisco would never again be left without an emergency supply of water if the city's mains were ruptured. An innovative system of water pumps was subsequently devised, and the San Francisco Fire Department Pumping Station, 698 Second Street, was unveiled in 1920 to house it. The pumping station is an attractive example of restrained neoclassical architecture. Peer through the large windows for a glimpse of the workings.

The 1920s Pacific Telephone Building, which houses the Telephone Communications Museum

METREON
Another major addition to the Yerba Buena Gardens area is Metreon, a shopping and entertainment complex at 101 Fourth Street which opened in spring 1999. It includes 15 movie theaters, an IMAX theater, restaurants and interactive attractions.

Yerba Buena Gardens—new territory for SoMa joggers

By far the most ambitious project, however, is **Yerba Buena Gardens▶▶**, a 12-block area enclosed by Market, Harrison, Second and Fifth streets.

Encompassing a landscaped garden complete with waterfall (enclosing a monument to Martin Luther King) and walkways, Yerba Buena Gardens also holds the expansive **Center For the Arts▶▶**. Completed in the mid-1990s, the center boasts a 775-seat indoor theater, an outdoor auditorium, several galleries (tel: 415/978-ARTS; open: Thu–Sat 12–8, Sun–Tue 12–5; inexpensive, free first Tue of month) with exhibitions of contemporary art, sculpture and multi-media work, and the Media Screening Room for contemporary film and video.

The Rooftop▶▶ (Moscone Convention Center) is aimed at youngsters and includes an indoor ice-rink, a 12-lane bowling alley, a carousel and **Zeum▶▶** (Wed–Sun 11–5, sometimes open on weekdays; moderate), a high-tech media center with an emphasis on creative learning.

Along with the nearby Museum of Modern Art (see pages 160–161), Yerba Buena Gardens gives the city a modern cultural heart. Several other institutions, such as the California Historical Society (see page 66) and the Cartoon Art Museum (see page 68) have already moved to new premises here, and others, including the Jewish Museum (see page 115), the Mexican Museum (see page 117) and the San Francisco Craft & Folk Art Museum, will arrive in the vicinity as soon as time and money allow.

The dark-glass peak of the **Marriott Hotel▶** (on Mission Street) can be seen across much of San Francisco and generally wins more favor among visitors than locals. Derided as the "jukebox Marriott," the building seems set to follow the fate of the Transamerica Pyramid two decades earlier—loathed at first but eventually acclaimed as a distinctive addition to the city skyline.

Quaint and anachronistic it may appear in the Marriott's shadow, but the Gothic-style **St. Patrick's Church▶** (756 Mission Street; tel: 415/421-3730) is a sturdy survivor. Still bearing the scars of the 1906 earthquake, the church is decorated with the Irish national colors of green, white and orange, ancient Celtic patterns are embroidered on the priests' vestments, and its stained-glass windows depict scenes from the life of Saint Patrick. Even so, St. Patrick's original Irish congregation has long since departed, and its regular worshippers—and its staff—are now mostly Filipino. This is one of the few places in the city where you will hear Mass celebrated in Tagalog.

Another survivor is the elegant, set-back skyscraper completed in 1925 for the Pacific Telephone Company (140 New Montgomery Street). The building's architect was Thomas Pflueger, who took his design cue from Eliel Saarinen's influential (though never built) plan for the Tribune Tower in Chicago. Pflueger also created the contrasting form of the Castro Theater (see page 69) and oversaw the design of the Pacific Stock Exchange (see page 151).

A few blocks south of Yerba Buena Gardens, the elevated I-80 cuts above SoMa transporting traffic to and from the Bay Bridge. Just beyond the freeway between Second and Third streets, **Jack London Street** is named for the writer born in the district in 1876. Although the site is disputed, a plaque on the wall of the Wells Fargo Bank (601 Third Street), near the corner of Brannan Street, claims to mark the precise location of **Jack London's birthplace**.

▶ Sunset District *IFCB3*

Buses: 66, 71

In most US cities, a home overlooking the ocean is the stuff dreams are made of. This is rarely the case in San Francisco, where fog regularly renders invisible what might be a stunning ocean vista, and causes local temperatures to drop while other parts of the city bask in sunshine.

Known as the Great Sand Waste before the creation of Golden Gate Park (immediately north) stimulated its settlement, the Sunset District, at the city's western edge, sometimes has the spectacular sunsets that its name suggests, but to enjoy them locals must leave their homes, make their way across the Great Highway to Ocean Beach (see page 145), and hope the fog stays away.

SOMA'S UKRAINIAN ORTHODOX CHURCH

St. Patrick's is not the only SoMa church to have seen its original congregation move on. The 1906 Ukrainian Orthodox Church of St. Michael (345 Seventh Street; tel: 415/861-4066), a striking twin-towered affair approached by a double stairway flanked by palm trees, no longer sits at the heart of a sizeable Ukrainian community. It does, however, retain an important cultural significance for the city's Ukrainian émigrés and their descendants.

Seen from Yerba Buena Gardens, the controversial Marriott Hotel towers above St. Patrick's Church

This photograph captures the size and splendor of the Sutro Baths in their heyday. Opened in 1896, the baths could accommodate 20,000 people either in the seven separate pools or as onlookers in the spectator galleries, beneath a roof holding 100,000 panes of glass

A Sutro Park lion

▶ Sutro Heights Park *IFCA5*

Buses: 18, 38

Part of the 1,000-acre (405ha) plot purchased and developed by the remarkable Adolph Sutro (see page 171) in the 1880s, and what is now Sutro Heights Park, was formerly the site of Sutro's mansion home. A pair of stone lions and a statue of Venus are the main remnants of the house, occupied by Sutro's daughter, Emma, until her death in 1938.

Take an invigorating stroll across the breezy, tree-studded park and then wind your way across Point Lobos Avenue to the site of the Sutro Baths. Again, only ruins remain of what was Sutro's most cherished contribution to San Francisco: a saltwater bathhouse spread across a 3-acre (1ha) indoor site that opened in 1896.

A devout capitalist, but one with socialist leanings, Sutro never worried about recouping the $600,000 he spent on the Baths and undermined the profit-crazed Southern Pacific Railroad Company by laying his own streetcar line to bring people to the Baths from the city for a fare of just 5¢.

A 40-piece orchestra playing from a floating platform celebrated the Baths' opening, and subsequent entertainment included circus acts—one was a man credited with "eating, drinking and smoking" underwater—and competitions for the public, such as underwater walking races.

The Baths used an ingenious engineering system to pipe 1.8 million gallons of salt water from the ocean into seven separate pools, each one maintained at a particular temperature. Meanwhile, three levels of galleries displayed some of the objects—medieval armor, Aztec pottery, stuffed animals and more—which Sutro had acquired on his world travels and which he hoped would inspire and educate the citizenry.

The Baths remained enormously popular into the 1920s, but as his heirs did not share Sutro's altruistic leanings, they fell steadily into decline and were destroyed by fire in 1966.

Rarely in the history of American cities has a mayor been as popular or as altruistic as Adolph Sutro, a millionaire philanthropist elected to San Francisco's highest public office in 1894 but, curiously enough, still best remembered for his saltwater bathhouse.

Born in Prussia in 1830, Adolph Sutro arrived in San Francisco at age 21, eager to claim his share of the Gold Rush. In fact, he ran a tobacco shop before heading for the mining regions, and it was fortuitous shares in a silver rather than a gold mine that brought him his first taste of serious money.

A man of the people, Adolph Sutro (below) also had friends in high places, such as President Harrison, with whom Sutro is pictured (above)

Sutro's major venture was a new system of tunneling, using improved methods of drainage and ventilation to allow miners better access to the lucrative seams. Although the silver barons of the time attempted to outwit him, Sutro went ahead with his plans, raising $6.5 million and winning federal approval for a 3-mile (5km) tunnel with 2 miles (3km) of lateral branches through Nevada's silver-rich Comstock Lode.

Recognizing that the silver bonanza was about to end, Sutro sold the tunnel in 1879 and moved what was by now a substantial personal fortune into San Francisco property, eventually owning a twelfth of the city and creating the 1,000-acre (405ha) area still known as Sutro Heights.

Sutro's battles against the Big Four—the merchants turned corrupt railroad barons who used their wealth and power to dominate California politics (see page 37)—earned him grassroots respect and helped him become the city's mayor in 1894, running as a Populist candidate. Occupying this political hot seat did not suit Sutro, however: the stubbornness which contributed to his success in business did not help him at City Hall, and his inability to delegate wrecked his eagerly awaited anticorruption program. Sutro described the end of his two-year term as a "perfect blessing."

Before his death in 1898, Sutro financed two Cliff Houses (see page 80), founded what quickly grew into a major collection of rare books (see panel, page 162), donated land to the University of California, and, most famously of all, built the Sutro Baths (see page 170), putting the healthy pleasures of indoor saltwater swimming within reach of every San Franciscan.

SUTRO AND EUCALYPTUS

In the late 1800s Sutro played a part in the import of millions of eucalyptus seedlings for use as windbreaks and ground cover. This, however, has left California with an environmental headache: The fast-spreading eucalyptus has damaged other plant life and, when dead, is a major fire hazard.

▶ Swedenborgian Church — IFCD5

2107 Lyon Street (tel: 415/346-6466)
Buses: 3, 43

Few San Franciscans would be able to pinpoint the whereabouts of the city's Swedenborgian Church, though if you are in the area it would be a shame to miss visiting this relatively minor but extremely intriguing example of religious architecture. In keeping with the Swedenborgian philosophy, which regards nature as the symbol of the human soul, the church is designed along the lines of a simple log cabin, complete with fireplace and rough-hewn wood beams, and its doorway is reached by passing through a lushly planted garden.

Completed in 1895, the church is also a fine specimen of the late 19th-century Arts and Crafts movement, which the original pastor, Joseph Worcestor, helped to establish in the Bay Area, partly by means of the brown shingle homes which he himself designed.

The main architect of the church was Arthur Page Brown, a seminal figure of the time who was also responsible for the Ferry Building (see page 83). Brown worked from plans drawn up by, among others, Bernard Maybeck, better remembered for the Palace of Fine Arts (see panel, page 152), and the mystically inclined Bruce Porter, who designed the church's stained-glass windows. Gustav Stickley's furniture, handcrafted from California lumber, continues the church's prevailing themes, as do William Keith's landscape paintings.

Nature and architecture fuse at the intriguing Swedenborgian Church

SWEDENBORGIANISM
San Francisco's Swedenborgian Church is one of 45 in the US, the first of them founded in the early 1800s as the works of Swedish scientist/mystic Emanuel Swedenborg spread from Europe. The Church teaches that "the church is within man, and not without him," values personal development and tolerance, and encourages involvement in social issues.

▶ Tattoo Art Museum — IBCF6

841 Columbus Avenue (tel: 415/775-4991)
Open afternoons and evenings only; free
Bus: 30

Getting a tattoo may not be top of your list of things to do in San Francisco, but if you have ever considered indulging in this form of body decoration, look inside this working tattoo parlor—lined by photos of extravagantly tattooed people.

Tattoo art inside North Beach's Tattoo Art Museum

Filbert Steps; walking down is easier than walking up

▶ Telegraph Hill *IBCF6*

Bus: 39

Telegraph Hill, rising with formidable steepness between North Beach and San Francisco Bay, once housed a bevy of impoverished writers and artists but is now one of the city's most coveted residential addresses, graced by million-dollar homes offering stunning views. Standing on top of Telegraph Hill is the unmistakable Coit Tower (tel: 415/362-0808; open: daily in summer 10–6.30, rest of year 9–4.30), a memorial to the city's volunteer firemen erected in 1933 (see pages 174–175).

The slopes of Filbert and Greenwich streets as they lead from the tower down toward the bayfront Embarcadero are so steep that sections of each are traversed by stairways: the Filbert and Greenwich steps.

A wooden walkway comprises the uppermost portions of the **Filbert Steps▶▶** and is lined with greenery; the lush vegetation is the fruit of a 30-year labor of love by local resident Grace Marchant. It was the late Marchant who turned what was—believe it or not—a garbage dump into the welcome array of plants and shrubbery that you see today.

Carefully maintained Victorian cottages, far more expensive than their diminutive size might suggest, and said to have been saved from the 1906 fire by being doused in red wine, can be seen from the steps. The oldest among them, number 224, dates from 1863. Along the impossibly slender **Napier Lane▶**, just a few feet wide and accessed only from the steps, are more tiny cottages—though, understandably, their residents do not appreciate casual visitors lingering longer than they need to.

The **Greenwich Steps▶** are also wooden for part of their course and cross Montgomery Street close to the Julius Castle. Built in 1923, this haphazardly assembled wood-framed restaurant vaguely resembles a Moorish castle.

From a slightly more recent period, take a look at the nautical motifs adorning the 1936 art deco apartment building at 1360 Montgomery Street. It was here that Humphrey Bogart took a glass-sided elevator to Lauren Bacall's apartment in the 1947 film *Dark Passage*.

TELEGRAPH HILL'S NAME

What is now Telegraph Hill has had a number of earlier names. During the 1840s, it was known as Windmill Hill but became Signal Hill following the installation of a semaphore on its summit, intended to notify city dwellers of ships entering the bay. The present name stems, simply enough, from the West Coast's first telegraph station, built on the hill in 1853.

Uncharitably said to resemble a fire hose, Coit Tower sits at the top of Telegraph Hill and—strange but true—owes its existence to a young girl's fixation with San Francisco's firefighters. Much more than a city landmark, Coit Tower also holds a remarkable collection of 1930s murals, the political content of which put the tower at the center of a bitter controversy at the time of their completion.

FIRES AND LILLIE COIT
Various explanations have been put forward for Lillie Coit's obsession with fires and the men who put them out. One suggestion is that the young girl's fancy was really taken by the horses which then pulled the fire trucks. Perhaps more likely is the tale that as a child Lillie lost two of her friends when a fire broke out at the empty house in which they were playing, and Lillie, after raising the alarm, tried to extinguish the flames herself.

Above and below: Coit Tower's murals. The detail shown below is from the City Life mural

Lillie Coit When seven-year-old Lillie Hitchcock arrived in San Francisco in 1851, she began what would become a lifelong obsession with fires and firefighters—and ferocious blazes were a regular feature of life in the fast-growing city.

Although groomed to take her place in high society (she was once presented to Napoleon III in Paris), Lillie became better known for her eccentric behavior. Even in San Francisco, it was considered unusual for women to wear men's clothes, play poker with longshoremen and smoke cigars, but Lillie (who married Howard Coit in 1868) did all three, and also relished her honorary membership in one of the city's fire crews.

When she died in 1929, Lillie left $100,000 for the beautification of the city, and it was decided to use these funds to erect a memorial to the city's volunteer firefighters. Volunteer companies were private firefighting organizations which existed prior to the creation of a municipally run Fire Department.

Arthur Brown, better known for City Hall, was chosen as the project's architect, and the tower—actually a 210ft (64m) high reinforced concrete column—was completed in 1933.

Coit Tower looks its best in the early dusk, silhouetted against the sunset sky

Coit Tower's murals The long-running debate over whether or not it resembles a fire hose (the architect insisted that this was not part of the design), the tower's form and the views from its observation level play second fiddle to its interior decoration, a superb collection of Depression-era murals which covers the first-floor walls.

As economic gloom gripped the country, 25 artists were each paid $94 a month by the Works Project Administration (the WPA, which created work during the Depression) to cover the tower's interior walls with frescoes depicting life in California (see also page 156).

Controversy ensues In the tradition of muralists such as Diego Rivera, many of the Coit Tower artists depicted the ordinary working people of California—the steelworkers and farm laborers—and reflected the radical political ideas percolating through the financially stricken state.

When the murals were due to be unveiled in 1934, one of the bloodiest episodes in San Francisco's labor history was in progress—a longshoremen's strike during which battles between strikers and police left two people dead.

Against this background, a hammer and sickle, a copy of Karl Marx's *Das Kapital,* and a scene showing copies of the *Daily Worker* on sale at newsstands, all depicted in the murals, proved too much for the city authorities, and the opening was canceled. Following a picket by the Artists' Union, the tower and its murals were eventually opened in October 1934—but not until the offending hammer-and-sickle image had been removed.

Viewing the murals While the murals vary greatly in style and quality, they collectively comprise one of the state's most important examples of public art and can be viewed for free (open: daily in summer 10–5, rest of the year 9–4.30; tel: 415/362-0808).

Look in particular for the idealized farm workers in Maxine Albro's *California*, for John Langley Howard's *California Industrial Scenes* and its contrasting of migrants' camps with wealthy capitalists, and for Bernard Zakheim's *Library* and its controversial image of a worker's hand reaching for *Das Kapital*.

Another mural worth studying is Victor Arnautoff's *City Life*, depicting the intersection of Montgomery and Washington streets in San Francisco's Financial District. In the human maelstrom, a man is robbed at gunpoint as the unconcerned crowd flows by.

WPA ART IN SAN FRANCISCO

The WPA's arts project was extremely active in San Francisco. In addition to the Coit Tower works, its money financed murals at the San Francisco Zoo and at the Rincon Annex Post Office (see page 156), as well as Lucien Labaudt's depictions of recreational pursuits in 1930s San Francisco. Labaudt's murals adorn the walls of the Beach Chalet, a Willis Polk-designed building beside the Great Highway on the western edge of Golden Gate Park. The first floor serves as a visitor center for Golden Gate Park, while the upper level holds the Beach Chalet restaurant and bar.

PAPER SONS AND DAUGHTERS
The loss of official records in the 1906 fire stimulated a boom in "paper" sons and daughters from China claiming kinship with a US resident. Officials at Angel Island devised intimidating questions for would-be immigrants, who could be held for weeks before being granted or denied entry. In the 30 years to 1940, 175,000 passed through successfully; some carved despairing poems on the walls, later published by the Chinese Cultural Foundation.

▶ The Tenderloin IBCF5

Buses: any Civic Center bus

The area bordered by the Civic Center and Mason Street, known as the Tenderloin, is commonly regarded as San Francisco's most depressing quarter. The rising property values and creeping gentrification that have affected so much of the city have yet to make an obvious impact on streets where San Francisco's large homeless population tend to gather and where drug use and petty street crime is apparent. However, others regard the Tenderloin as one of the city's most determinedly self-sufficient neighborhoods, and one that is determined to improve is image and its character without losing its distinctive sense of community.

Because the area still has low rents, dozens of good Asian diners have been encouraged to open alongside independently run shops, while trendy bars and music venues have put the Tenderloin on the city's nightlife map

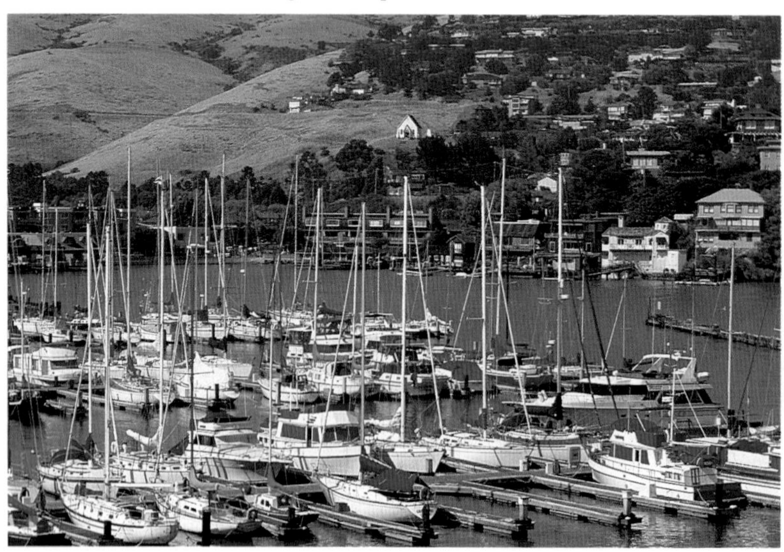

Tiburon, an easy ferry ride from the city

ANGEL ISLAND
The largest island in San Francisco Bay, Angel Island lies close to Tiburon and can be reached by Blue & Gold Fleet ferries from Fisherman's Wharf, and by a summer service from Tiburon. Crisscrossed by cycle and foot trails, the island also contains buildings from its time as a military prison and immigration processing center.

▶ Tiburon 44B3

Ferry: from Ferry Building or Fisherman's Wharf

While Sausalito (see page 163) is the major destination for tourists venturing across San Francisco Bay, discerning travelers opt instead for the quieter and smaller community of Tiburon, a few miles east of Sausalito and occupying a bucolic bayside niche.

Once ashore, you will find that Tiburon proper comprises little beyond Main Street and the shops and galleries which make up **Ark Row▶**, occupying dainty wood-framed buildings and, in some cases, one-time houseboats. To discover more, head for **Lyford House▶** (tel: 510/388-2524), the home of a 19th-century doctor who tried to lure San Franciscans across the bay with the promise that Tiburon was better for their health and free of "vices and vampires." The house now serves as headquarters for the **Tiburon Audubon Center** (tel: 510/388-2524), which administers a 900-acre (364ha) wildlife refuge.

▶ Transamerica Pyramid *IBCG5*

600 Montgomery Street
Buses: 15, 42,9 69

Since it was unveiled in 1972, the Transamerica Pyramid has had no rivals as the dominant feature on the San Francisco skyline. Emerging from the Financial District's forest of even-sided high-rise buildings, the 853ft (260m) Pyramid has an unforgettable profile: a slowly tapering spire flanked by windowless wings, and a tower continuing for 212ft (65m) above the 48th floor. The building's design has even won over the majority of the San Franciscan people, in spite of widespread antipathy to the structure to begin with.

The best view of the Transamerica Pyramid is from a distance. The struts that support it at ground level offer improved earthquake safety, but do nothing to enhance Montgomery Street. Further protection is provided by the panels that form the exterior. These can move laterally to absorb stress caused by movements below ground.

TRANSAMERICA REDWOOD PARK
On the eastern side of the Transamerica Pyramid, Tom Galli's half-acre Transamerica Redwood Park—a fountain and concrete plaza fringed by genuine redwood trees—offers a chance to escape the Financial District hub-bub. On Friday lunchtimes during the summer months, the park hosts free concerts.

The Financial District by moonlight with the Transamerica Pyramid looming large

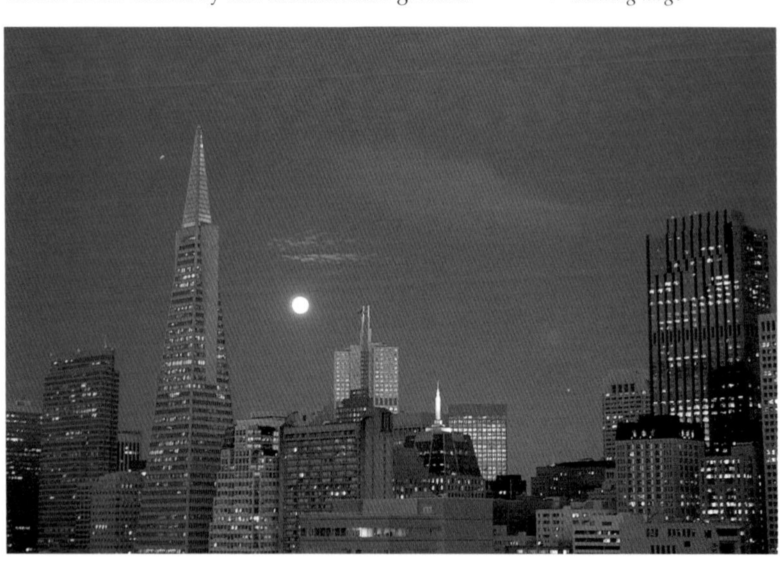

▶ Treasure Island *IBCH6*

Bus: 108

A man-made island in San Francisco Bay, Treasure Island was created with the aid of a $3-million grant from the WPA (a federal body administering funds to create jobs during the Depression) as the site of the 1939 Golden Gate International Exposition. Deemed unsuitable for its proposed post-Expo role as the city's airport, the island was used as a US naval base from 1941 to 1997. Treasure Island, covering some 400 acres (162ha), is dotted with remnants from the 1939 Expo and, until the navy left, boasted a fine museum with mementoes of 1930s travel and exhibits on the Marine Corps and Coast Guard services. It is now owned by the Mayor's office and its future is under discussion.

Treasure Island resident

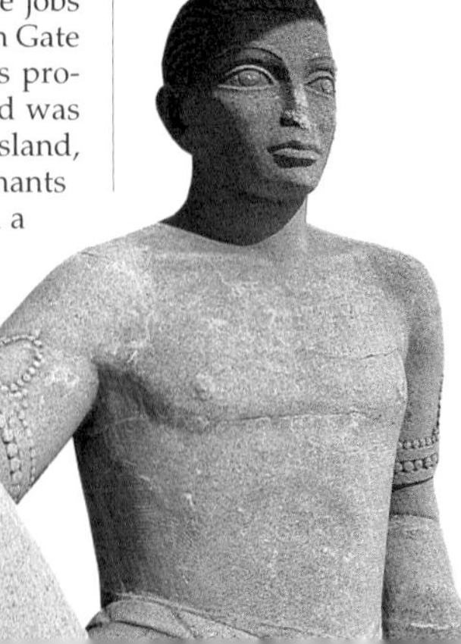

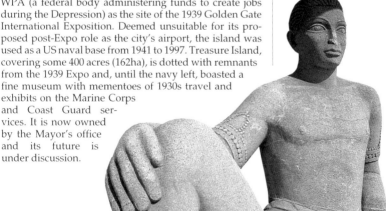

▶ Union Square *IBCF5*

Buses: 30, 45

With a $25-million facelift completed in late 2002, Union Square acquired a granite platform for hosting concerts, a café with outdoor seating, new sculptures, more palm trees, and something of the grandeur that might be expected of a patch of greenery occupying a prime location in the heart of the city. Intended to bring to the square something of the pedestrian-friendliness of an Italian piazza, the full impact of the re-shaping remains to be seen, but certainly provides shoppers, office workers and anyone else with a good excuse to linger within its confines.

The square is enclosed by big-name department stores, high-fashion retail outlets and luxury hotels such as the esteemed St. Francis Hotel (see panel) and for many years was used mostly by people taking a short cut between these establishments or looking to retrieve their vehicles from the multilevel parking lot built beneath the square in the 1940s; this was the first parking lot of its kind and one which, in the war years, served the city as a potential bomb shelter.

San Francisco's first mayor, John W. Geary, allocated a plot of what was then rough scrubland for development as a grassy public space in 1850, but not until large-scale pro-Union rallies were staged there prior to the Civil War did Union Square acquire its lasting name. In 1903, the square also acquired the 97ft (26m) granite column topped by a figure of Victory to mark Admiral George Dewey's triumph over the Spanish fleet at Manila during the Spanish-American War.

Surviving the 1906 earthquake intact, Victory has since gazed down upon countless soapbox orators, as well as on numerous organized protests—from 1960s anti-Vietnam War marches to the 1990s gay political street theater of the Sisters of Perpetual Indulgence—which have exploited Union Square's central position.

Weekend art shows bring more people to the square, as do annual events such as April's Rhododendron Festival and July's Cable Car Bell-Ringing Contest (see page 26).

MONEY LAUNDERING

The St. Francis (now the Westin St. Francis) Hotel overlooking Union Square is the site of a major money-laundering operation. In the 1930s, seeing the white gloves of society ladies becoming soiled by grimy coins, the hotel began to clean all the coins that came into its possession. The practice continues today.

Union Square (below) and (above) its Dewey Monument

With wagons as rickety as the one pictured here, the Wells Fargo Company blazed a trail across the Wild West in the 1860s

▶ Wells Fargo History Museum *IBCJ8*

420 Montgomery Street (tel: 415/396-2619)
Open: Mon–Fri 9–5; free
Buses: 15, 42, 69

After establishing an express mail service in the eastern US by the 1840s, Henry Wells and William G. Fargo began viewing the opportunities offered by gold-crazed California with relish and opened an office in San Francisco in 1852. Whether buying, selling, or transporting gold, transferring funds, or delivering mail, the company earned a reputation for trustworthiness in an era dominated by rogues.

By 1861, Wells Fargo provided the main line of communication between California's gold-mining towns and, by the late 1860s, the company monopolized the movement of mail and people across the entire western US.

A few steps from the site of the 1852 office, the Wells Fargo Museum records the rise of the company, now one of the country's major financial institutions. Sitting inside an 1860s stagecoach provides the highlight for some visitors, but there is much more to see amid the clutter of a re-created Gold Rush-era Wells Fargo office: among the debris are gold-weighing scales, bulky mining tools and numerous aging letters which miraculously survived their trip across the Wild West.

▶ Western Addition *IBCE5*

Buses: 5, 31

Squeezed between Haight-Ashbury, Japantown and the Tenderloin, the Western Addition derived its name from being a "western addition" to the 1858 city, whose western edge was defined by Van Ness Avenue. Long one of the city's less revered areas and home to a largely African-American population, the area changed in the mid-1990s when gentrification and preservation of old homes was spreading through neighboring Lower Haight (see page 109) and Alamo Square (see page 54). A section is being transformed into the **Fillmore Jazz District**, with markers to many noted musicians who appeared at the neighborhood's music venues, a massive mural outside the Boom Boom Room, a John Lee Hooker-founded blues club at 1601 Fillmore Street and outdoor concerts on Friday evenings during August and September.

CHURCH OF JOHN COLTRANE

On the edge of the Western Addition, the St. John's African Orthodox Church (temporarily at 930 Gough Street; tel: 415/673-3572) is popularly known as the Church of John Coltrane. Each Sunday, a 4-hour service is presided over by the sax-playing bishop who founded the church after undergoing a religious experience when hearing the late jazz musician John Coltrane play live in the 1960s. All are welcome at the services, and those who bring instruments are encouraged to play them.

The discovery of gold in California underpinned the emergence of the state and also brought the Wells Fargo company to prominence, as these exhibits show

▶▶▶ **HIGHLIGHTS**

Gold Country and Lake Tahoe *pages 184–189*

The Monterey Peninsula *pages 192–195*

The northern coast *pages 196–199*

San Francisco may be a captivating city, but it is also a surprisingly small one, and visitors are liable to feel they have exhausted it after a week of energetic sightseeing.

Fortunately, the city is ideally placed for traveling farther afield, be it a simple day trip to the rugged hills and picturesque coastal towns of Marin County, a two- to three-day tour around the old towns of the Gold Country or through the wild vistas of the northern coast, or a few days spent sampling the pastoral surroundings and highly rated produce of the Wine Country.

In fact, so wide-ranging are the possibilities within easy reach of the city that some San Franciscans, who may take several short vacations each year, seldom consider it necessary to venture out of Northern California at all.

A landscape for lovers: Lake Tahoe's Emerald Bay

Empire Mine State Historic Park, Grass Valley

Gold Country and Lake Tahoe Like San Francisco, Sacramento, about 95 miles (153km) northeast, grew rich and powerful following the 19th-century discovery of gold. Sacramento has matured into a likeable, modestly sized state capital and is an excellent place for gaining an understanding of California's unique history. Several defining moments in the state's development occurred here and they are well documented in a number of interesting museums.

Scores of Gold Rush towns—some immaculately preserved, others a pile of ruins beside the road—are found along the routes east of Sacramento and recall the boom-and-bust days of old. Some of the most engrossing and prosperous of the towns are found in the grassy, tree-studded slopes of the Sierra Nevada foothills and can make atmospheric overnight stops.

The same foothills, their greenery giving way to exposed granite and (even in summer) snowcapped peaks, provide a breathtaking setting for Lake Tahoe, a massive cobalt-blue body of water which straddles the California–Nevada border.

Besieged by skiers in winter, and by gamblers year-round (massive casinos lie immediately across the state line), the idyllic alpine surroundings of Lake Tahoe are also perfect for walking, hiking or simply relaxing beside the enormous pine-bordered lake—and perhaps taking a sightseeing cruise across it.

Marin County Just a few minutes' drive from the hurly-burly of the city, the untamed hills and canyons of Marin County give a glimpse of how coastal California once looked. Here the wild landscapes and seascapes of Point Reyes National Seashore will stay in your mind

WHEN TO GO

Geography and geology conspire to give Northern California a number of microclimates; the weather is likely to vary considerably over a short distance. Overall, however, you can expect conditions not to vary too much from those described on page 250. Exceptions are the Lake Tahoe area and parts of the Gold Country, which are almost certain to see snow between late October and early April, and the northern coast, which has considerable rainfall between November and February.

The coastal landscapes at Point Reyes National Seashore are the work of the San Andreas Fault

for years, and also offer a close-up look at how earthquakes, in particular the rumblings of the infamous San Andreas Fault, have rumpled California's surface over the centuries.

Marin County can serve as a prelude to the longer northern coast excursion. Alternatively, treat it as a day trip and take the inland route back to San Francisco, passing a famous piece of modern architecture on the way.

The Monterey Peninsula The peninsula, named for California's first capital, 120 miles (193km) south of San Francisco, has a rich history displayed in a wealth of 19th-century buildings. Monterey's modern sights, such as the excellent Monterey Bay Aquarium and the shops of Cannery Row, are also worthwhile and have greatly contributed to the area's recent upsurge in popularity.

Nonetheless, Monterey is still far from overcommercialized and the Peninsula's other communities—Carmel with its whimsical architecture and beautiful mission, and Pacific Grove, which faces the windy ocean from a granite headland and is seasonally invaded by colorful butterflies—offer plenty of opportunity for unhurried exploration and lots of possibilities for spending the night within earshot of crashing surf.

The northern coast The northern coast should be a compulsory excursion for anyone who thinks that the California coast means sun, sand and surfers. Beyond Marin County (see above), the vista quickly becomes one of wave-battered headlands, a restless ocean far too dangerous for swimming in, and far-flung communities set in sheltered coves and populated by a few hundred hardy souls.

The dipping and winding Highway 1 follows a scenic route through the region, revealing some of the state's

CAR RENTAL
All the larger towns described on the excursions can be reached by public transportation, but it is far more convenient, and sometimes cheaper, to rent a car in San Francisco. If you are sure of your plans, you may save money by arranging car rental in advance. Otherwise, all the best-known firms have desks at the airport, offices in the city, and are reachable on the toll-free numbers given on pages 254–255.

most spectacular landscapes and passing the restored site of a 19th-century Russian settlement before reaching the time-locked village of Mendocino and the comparative metropolis of Fort Bragg, a town built on the lumber trade.

The San Francisco Pensinsula Travel in a southerly direction from the city along I-280 or SR1 and you will quickly be rewarded with fine views of mountainous coastline and undulating valleys. The Peninsula is also home to major points of interest such as Stanford University, its immense campus the scene of many a scientific breakthrough.

Computer buffs scouring the map for Silicon Valley—a nickname often applied to the Santa Clara Valley—will be relieved to find San Jose, the self-proclaimed capital of the region whose futuristic downtown symbolizes its place at the heart of the state's electronics industries. Sizeable chunks of the valley resemble Southern California-style suburbia, but a cluster of offbeat attractions adds spice to a navigation of the area's web of freeways.

The Wine Country Wineries exist all over California, but the most successful lie in the Sonoma and Napa valleys, 50 miles (81km) northeast of San Francisco. It was the Napa Valley which finally brought international recognition to the state's wine industry in the 1970s, although commercial wine production in California actually dates back to the 1850s.

Almost all wineries, be they multimillion-dollar concerns with well-equipped visitor centers or family-run operations where the vintner might personally greet you, offer free tours and tastings which are intended to delight beginners and seasoned oenologists alike.

Neat rows of vines off the Silverado Trail in the Napa Valley

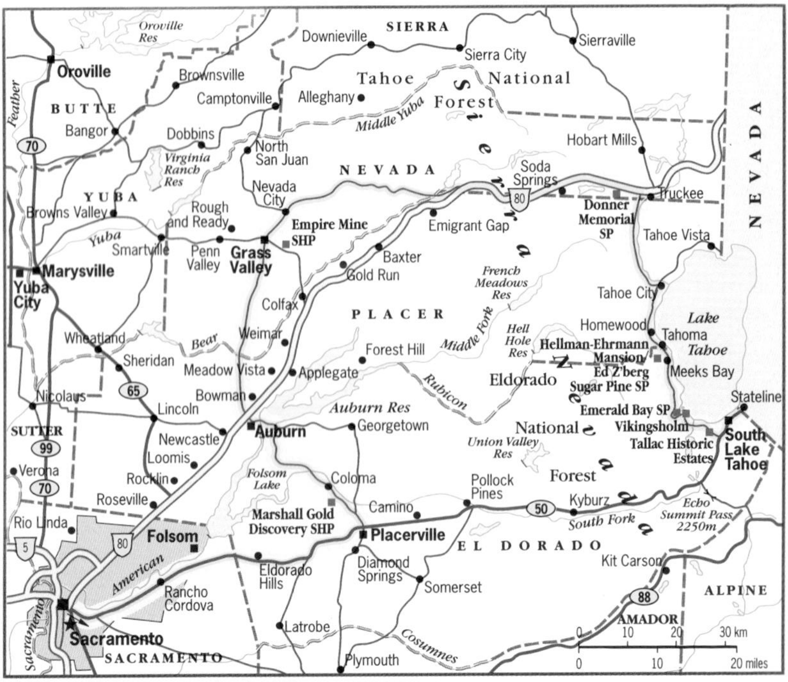

Drive

Gold Country and Lake Tahoe

Heading west from the state capital of Sacramento toward the Sierra Nevada Mountains, this drive passes through some of the more noteworthy of California's 19th-century gold-mining towns, which do much to evoke the flavor of bygone days. Farther on, the route swings south and makes a spectacular approach to Lake Tahoe, an immense expanse of water surrounded by snow-capped granite peaks and intensely green swaths of pine forest.

Places of interest in the Gold Country and Lake Tahoe are fully described on pages 185–189.

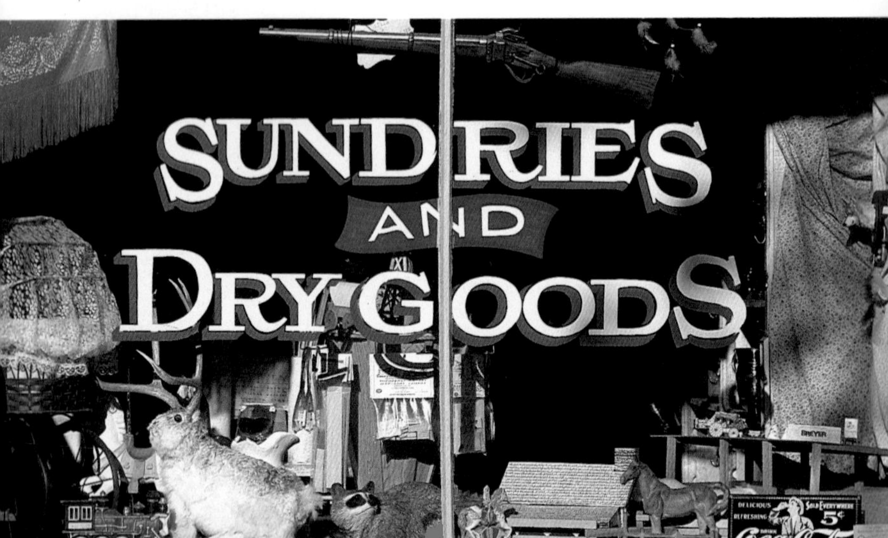

Gold Country bric-a-brac

▶▶▶ Gold Country and Lake Tahoe

California's attractive state capital, Sacramento, provides the gateway to the Gold Country, where some of the key communities of 19th-century California remain in lovingly preserved form. Within easy reach, too, is Lake Tahoe, the world's second largest alpine lake, whose surroundings provide some of the state's most memorable landscapes.

As big and as imposing as the national Capitol Building in Washington DC, California's State Capitol (above) was intended to demonstrate to the world at large that the gold-rich state was a force to be reckoned with

Sacramento Small, sedate and filled with trees, **Sacramento▶▶▶** might seem an unlikely place to be California's capital, but during the mid-19th century the men and machinery destined for the state's thriving gold mines arrived here on the Sacramento River (deep enough to carry the ocean-going vessels of the time) and helped turn a thinly populated farming settlement into a thriving commercial center.

In 1874, 20 years after it became the state capital, Sacramento's leaders unveiled the $2.5-million **State Capitol Building▶▶▶** (tel: 916/324-0333), symbolizing California's enormous independent wealth and sending an unmistakable signal to the federal government, still recovering from the Civil War, that California was not to be pushed around.

Inevitably, the power and grandeur suggested by the sheer size of the State Capitol a century ago have diminished, but it remains as a majestic advertisement of the state's riches, and is the perfect place to begin a visit to Sacramento.

From 9 to 5, free guided tours depart hourly from the lobby, or you can wander around on your own viewing the restored period rooms, the portraits of former governors (look out in particular for the semi-abstract portrayal of Jerry "Governor Moonbeam" Brown) or, when it is in session, watch the state legislature in action. Outside, the 40-acre (16-ha) Capitol Park merits a stroll.

THE GOVERNOR'S MANSION

Erected in 1897 as one of Sacramento's most luxurious residences, the elegant wooden house at the corner of 16th and H streets was the official residence of 13 California state governors until 1967, when newly elected Ronald Reagan decided to live elsewhere. Stuffed with Victoriana and items reflecting gubernatorial taste, and inspiring a lively anecdote at every turn, the house can be explored on hourly guided tours (daily 10am–5pm; last tour at 4pm).

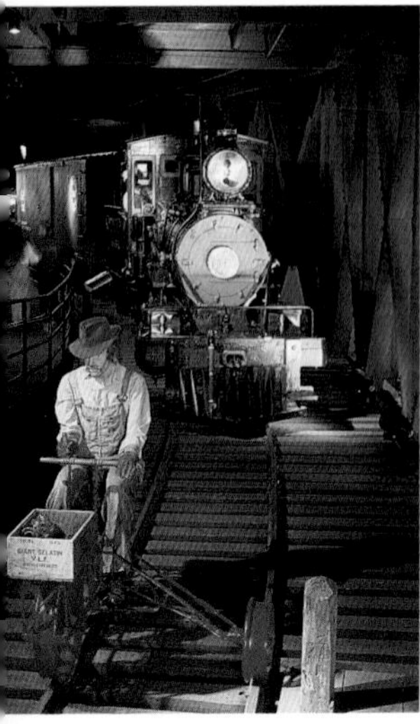

Old Sacramento: railroad maintenance…

PLACERVILLE'S HANGTOWN FRY
Drop into almost any restaurant in Placerville and you are liable to be offered "hangtown fry." This local specialty comprises eggs, bacon and fried oysters, and is a dish allegedly consumed by Placerville miners to mark special occasions.

…and auto preservation

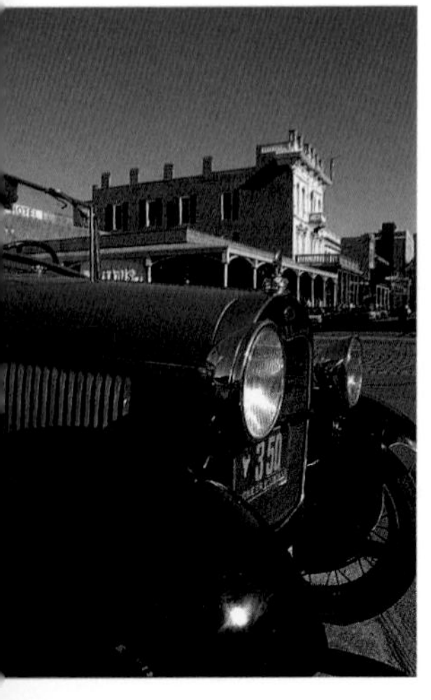

Old Sacramento For a clearer impression of the incongruous size of the State Capitol at the time of its completion, make the short walk to **Old Sacramento▶▶**, where souvenir stores, restaurants and several historical collections fill dozens of two-story wooden buildings dating from the mid-1800s.

The Gold Rush enabled Sacramento's merchants—many based in what is now Old Sacramento—to amass fortunes without ever going near a mine. Among those to thrive were the so-called Big Four—Charles Crocker, Mark Hopkins, Leland Stanford and Collis P. Huntington (see page 37)—who not only became millionaires but also wielded considerable political power, largely through their Pacific Railroad Company. This company oversaw the construction of the transcontinental railroad, California's first fixed link with the rest of the US.

The story of the Big Four and the transcontinental railroad is told in Old Sacramento's **California State Railroad Museum▶▶▶** (tel: 916/323-9280), which also finds space for locomotives and carriages from the great days of American train travel. More general state history fills the **Sacramento Discovery Museum** (see panel, page 187).

Whatever the advantages of traveling by train, there are few Americans who would opt for it when they can be at the wheel of a car. On the periphery of Old Sacramento, the **Towe Ford Museum▶** (tel: 916/442-6802) displays an enormous number of (predominantly Ford) vehicles from Model T's to Thunderbirds.

If art and local history hold more appeal, head instead for the **Crocker Art Museum▶▶** (tel: 916/264-5423). This is the oldest art museum in the western US, although the exhibits are actually less impressive than the building itself: an enormous Italianate villa completed in 1873 for Edwin Bryant Crocker, brother of Charles Crocker.

Sutter's Fort Sacramento's oldest structure, **Sutter's Fort▶▶** (tel: 916/445-4422), stood at the center of the 48,000 acres (19,433ha) acquired by German-born John Sutter in 1839. It was on Sutter's land that gold was discovered, although the find was to result in Sutter's bankruptcy and eventually his impoverished death. Within the adobe-walled fort, several workshops have been reconstructed and are staffed by volunteers in period dress.

Already decimated by European diseases carried by the colonizing Spanish, California's Native Americans were caused further harm by the Gold Rush. Next door to Sutter's Fort, the small but engaging **State Indian Museum▶▶** (tel: 916/324-0971) chronicles what little is known about the region's indigenous peoples.

Folsom and Placerville East of Sacramento on Highway 50, **Folsom** makes a pleasant base for state capital commuters and is steadily re-discovering its 19th-century roots in a developing **Historic District**, maps of which can be found at the Visitor Center (tel: 916/985-2698. Entertaining relics from its Gold Rush origins displayed in the **Folsom Museum▶** (tel: 530/985-2707). Most Californians, however, know the community for **Folsom Prison**, the oldest section of which dates from 1880 and is concealed behind a surprisingly picturesque granite gatehouse.

Left: A period-attired guide awaits visitors to Sutter's Fort
Below: A monument to the man on whose land California gold was discovered

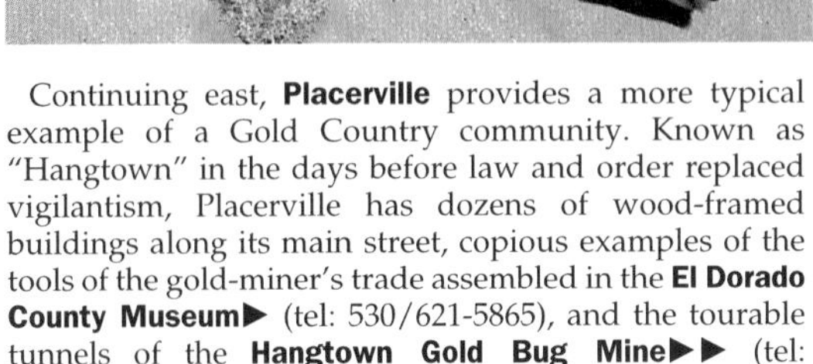

Continuing east, **Placerville** provides a more typical example of a Gold Country community. Known as "Hangtown" in the days before law and order replaced vigilantism, Placerville has dozens of wood-framed buildings along its main street, copious examples of the tools of the gold-miner's trade assembled in the **El Dorado County Museum▶** (tel: 530/621-5865), and the tourable tunnels of the **Hangtown Gold Bug Mine▶▶** (tel: 530/642-5207).

North on Highway 49 A few miles north of Placerville on Highway 49, **Marshall Gold Discovery State Historic Park▶▶▶** (tel: 530/622-3470) preserves the spot where, on January 24, 1848, James Marshall, an employee of landowner John Sutter, spotted flakes of gold in the American River. This chance discovery, and its profound impact on California, is documented in the park's museum. Follow the foot trails and you will also find a replica of Sutter's sawmill and the cabin where Marshall died, broke and dispirited, in 1879, never having benefited from his find.

First impressions of **Auburn▶**, 20 miles (32km) farther north, are uninspiring, but a closer look reveals the cobbled streets of the **Old Town▶▶**, where many of Auburn's 19th-century structures are impressively preserved. The **Gold Country Museum▶▶**(tel: 530/889-6500) traces the affluence which Auburn enjoyed during the days of the Gold Rush, with mining implements and explanatory displays, plus some informative artifacts from the Chinese community which settled here.

SACRAMENTO DISCOVERY MUSEUM
Through five galleries of permanent and changing exhibits, the Sacramento Discovery Museum, in Old Sacramento at 101 1st Street (tel: 916/264-7057), documents major aspects of the state's past, from the cultivation of the land to the expansion of its cities, and explains the rudiments and quirks of science in entertaining, interactive displays aimed chiefly at kids.

DOWNIEVILLE
On Highway 49 north of Nevada City, Downieville retains the gallows that brought the town the dubious distinction of being the one mining community ever to hang a woman.

ROUGH AND READY
Four miles (6km) west of Grass Valley, Rough and Ready, once a thriving Gold Rush community, is the only town ever to secede from the US. Angry over a new federal miners' tax, its citizens elected to leave the Union on April 7, 1850. Denied supplies of alcohol, however, they rejoined on July 4.

Grass Valley Two more significant Gold Rush communities lie in close proximity north of Auburn. The first, **Grass Valley▶▶**, prospered from the fruits of California's most technologically advanced mine: The Empire Mine produced an annual yield of $5 million in its peak years. The **Empire Mine State Historic Park▶▶▶** (tel: 530/273-8522) offers a chance to explore some of the mine's buildings and penetrate a modest section of its 367 miles (592km) of tunnel. The mine's success was partly due to the know-how of miners from Cornwall, England; a by-product of their arrival was the Cornish pasties which are now a specialty of many local restaurants. One Grass Valley settler who never ventured beneath ground was Lola Montez, a European dancer of great flamboyance and notorious in America for her sensual "spider dance." A replica of her home in the 1850s now houses the local tourist office and displays remnants from her eventful life.

Nevada City Grass Valley may have enjoyed its 19th-century affluence, but 5 miles (8km) farther along Highway 49, **Nevada City▶▶▶** was at that time California's third-largest city, growing rich as the seat of Nevada County, a region which produced at least half of the state's total output of gold. Throughout the town, markers to the great days of the past are numerous. The 1865 **Nevada Theater▶** is believed to be the oldest continuously operating theater in the western US; Mark Twain gave his first public lecture here. The **National Hotel▶▶** opened in 1856 claims to be the West's oldest hostelry, which is easy to believe after viewing its renovated lobby and bar area. More organized historical artifacts fill the 1861 **Firehouse Museum▶** (tel: 530/265-5468), while exhibitions of arts and crafts occupy the former workshops of the **Miners Foundry Cultural Center▶** (tel: 530/265-5040).

Nevada City's carefully preserved wooden buildings

The Sierra Nevada foothills West of Nevada City, Highway 20 and then I-80 carry you farther into the conifer-covered foothills of the Sierra Nevada Mountains. For 19th-century pioneers at the mercy of the elements, the sierras were a potentially fatal obstacle on the overland journey to California. In 1846, the **Donner Party**—a wagon train of 89 men, women and children hoping to reach Sutter's Fort—became trapped by winter snow at what is now Donner Pass, through which I-80 travels. As food supplies were exhausted, 40 of the travelers died and the survivors resorted to cannibalism to stay alive. At **Donner Memorial State Park▶▶** (tel: 530/582-7892), a museum recounts the party's doomed journey.

The Lake Tahoe shoreline Traveling south from **Truckee**, Highway 89

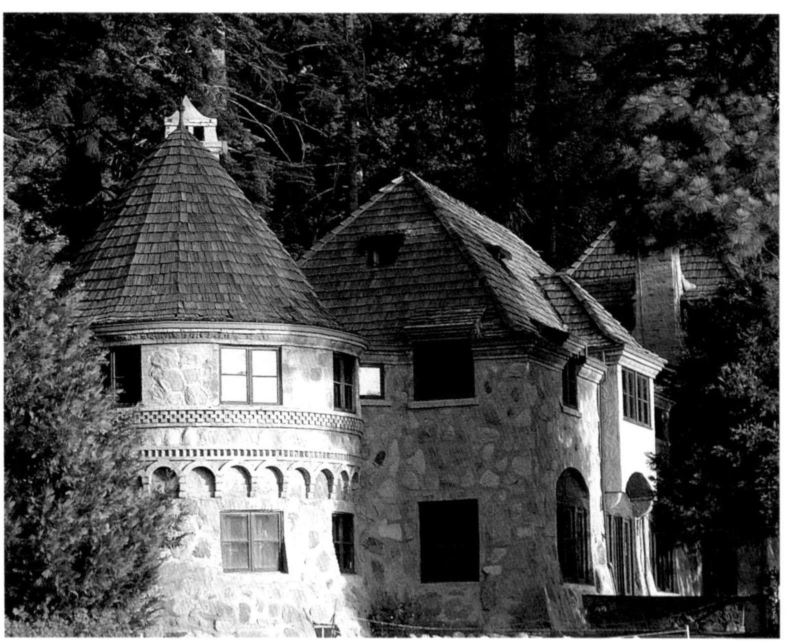

reaches Lake Tahoe at **Tahoe City**. Despite its name, Tahoe City has just 5,000 inhabitants and the **Gatekeepers Cabin and Marion Steinbach Indian Basket Museum▶** (tel: 530/583-1762), which keeps the dust off local historical artifacts and native handicrafts. Far more alluring are the lakeside landscapes which proliferate on the southbound route—green hillsides studded with grey granite boulders rising above the glacier-sculpted shoreline of the vibrantly blue lake. Such views were savored in the 1920s by the cream of San Francisco society staying at the Hellman-**Ehrmann Mansion▶▶**, built two decades earlier for a wealthy banker (guided tours). The stone and wood structure also serves as a visitor center for **Ed Z'berg Sugar Pine Point State Park▶** (tel: 530/525-7982) and its 2,000 acres (810ha) of hillside trails.

Continuing south through **Emerald Bay State Park▶** (tel: 530/541-3030), Highway 89 rises above a tree-lined inlet holding Lake Tahoe's sole island, **Fanette Island**. A mile-long (1.6km) trail descends from the highway to the **Vikingsholm▶▶▶**, a 38-room mansion built in the 1920s by a Swedish architect in the style of a 9th-century Nordic castle as a retreat for heiress Lora Josephine Knight.

South Lake Tahoe Scenery gives way to commerce at **South Lake Tahoe**, the largest lakeside community and one that offers accommodations but little else. Of chief appeal are the casinos of **Stateline▶**, adjoining South Lake Tahoe but over the border in Nevada (where, unlike California, gambling is legal). On the California side, **Lake Tahoe Historical Society Museum▶▶** (tel: 530/541-5458) focuses on the lake's geology and human history. At **Tallac Historic Estates▶▶** (tel: 530/542-4975), buildings have been recreated on the site of the legendary "Lucky" Baldwin's Tallac Hotel and Casino (1898), scene of much high living.

Vikingsholm, in Emerald Bay Park

LAKE TAHOE CRUISES
The *Tahoe Queen* makes an enjoyable voyage between South Lake Tahoe and Emerald Bay several times daily (in summer), and at night hosts a dinner-dance cruise. The MS *Dixie* plies between Zephyr Cove (on the Nevada side of the lake, a few miles north of Stateline) and Emerald Bay (tel: 1/800-238-2463).

CALIFORNIA'S GOLD
No precise records were kept of the value of the gold mined in California during the peak years of the Gold Rush. Nonetheless, the following statistics are considered reliable:
1848 $245,301
1849 $10,151,360
1850 $41,273,106
1851 $75,938,232
1852 $81,294,700
1853 $67,613,487
1855 $55,485,163
1860 $44,095,858
1865 $17,930,858

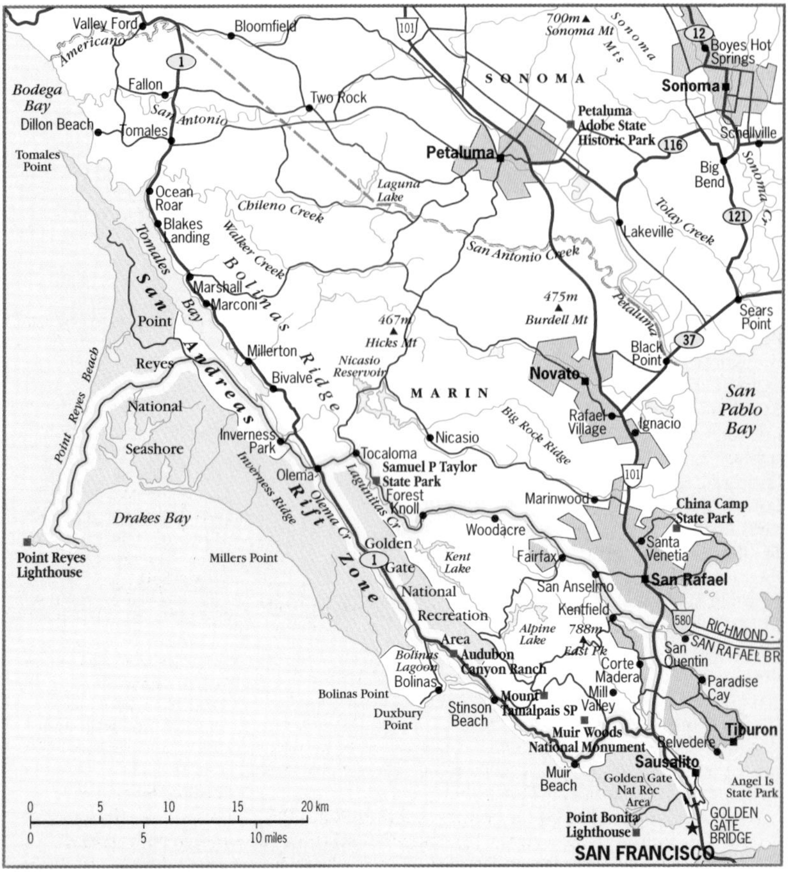

Drive

Marin County

A day's outing from San Francisco, this drive reveals many impressive natural features of coastal California. Once over Golden Gate Bridge, the route navigates the undeveloped landscapes of the Marin Headlands, part of the Golden Gate National Recreation Area (see page 99) and continues along the San Andreas Fault to Point Reyes National Seashore and its isolated lighthouse. Returning, the drive explores forested inland hillsides and several attractive towns before returning to the city. Marin County is described in more detail on pages 190–191.

►► Marin County

Marin County begins as soon as you cross Golden Gate Bridge, arriving at the hills of the Marin Headlands.

Along Highway 1 Branch off Highway 101 to join Highway 1 and after a winding 20-minute drive you pass the small town of Muir Beach. Here the **Pelican Inn** does a fair imitation of a 16th-century British hostelry.

A few miles north, the 3-mile (1.5km) long **Stinson Beach►** is a favorite haunt of San Franciscans, but although the ocean is free of the riptides that limit swimming elsewhere along the coast, its waters are very cold.

Immediately beyond, Highway 1 skirts the edge of **Bolinas Lagoon▶▶** and passes a side road leading to the **Audubon Canyon Ranch▶**. A wildlife sanctuary and research center, the ranch welcomes amateur ornithologists to its canyon trails from mid-March to mid-July.

Anyone interested in observing people rather than wildlife should detour off Highway 1 along Horseshoe Hill Road, which hugs the western side of the lagoon and eventually reaches the tiny town of **Bolinas▶**. This close-knit community discourages commercial tourism by sabotaging street signs so that it cannot be found.

Point Reyes Heading north, Highway 1 follows the line of the San Andreas Fault. The fault is responsible for the extraordinary landscapes of **Point Reyes National Seashore▶▶▶** (tel: 415/461-5000). Outside the park's informative **Bear Valley Visitors Center▶**, the **Earthquake Trail▶▶** reveals evidence of the 1906 quake (epicentered locally), and a second path leads to **Kule Loklo▶▶**, a re-created Native American settlement of the kind used by the Miwok people, the original inhabitants of what became Marin County.

Heading back To return to San Francisco, take Sir Francis Drake Boulevard. This inland route passes the hillside towns of **Fairfax**, birthplace of the mountain bike, and the antique-store-filled **San Anselmo▶▶**. Above San Anselmo, two 19th-century stone buildings form part of the **San Francisco Theological Seminary▶** (tel: 1-800/447-8820), where future ministers of the Presbyterian Church are trained. The public is welcome to share the stupendous views from the seminary's 21-acre (9ha) grounds.

Your final stop should be the county seat, **San Rafael▶**, where the replica of the town's 1817 Spanish **mission** is less significant than the **Marin County Civic Center▶▶**, the last work of the influential architect Frank Lloyd Wright, completed beside the highway in 1969.

ENGLISH CALIFORNIA
Perhaps the first British visitor to California was Sir Francis Drake, who landed here in 1579. Drake spent 36 days ashore while his ship, the *Golden Hind*, was repaired. During this time, he declared California a possession of Queen Elizabeth I and named it Nova Albion, or "New England."

MUIR WOODS NATIONAL MONUMENT
Head inland from Muir Beach along the Panoramic Highway to Muir Woods National Monument (tel: 415/388-2595) and you will find a modestly sized grove of California redwood trees. The world's tallest living things, redwoods can reach 350ft (107m) high, and most of the world's specimens are found along a narrow stretch of the Northern California and Oregon coast. While in the area, you should also visit Mount Tamalpais State Park (tel: 415/388-2070).

For the Bay Area's best views, choose a fog-free day, pack a picnic lunch, and climb Marin County's Mount Tamalpais

Drive

The Monterey Peninsula

From the historic heart of Monterey, this short but spectacular drive weaves along the Peninsula's northern side to reach Pacific Grove and reveal stunning coastal vistas of crashing waves and wind-tormented cypress trees.

Turning south, the drive continues through some exclusive residential areas and alongside lushly landscaped golf courses before reaching the pretty community of Carmel and ending at the beautiful Carmel Mission. Places to visit on the Monterey Peninsula are fully described on pages 192–195.

THE OLD MONTEREY JAIL

Among the more curious of Monterey's many historic structures is the Old Monterey Jail, its entrance behind Colton Hall. Incarcerating its first unfortunate in 1854 and its last a century later, each of the jail's gloomy cells is arranged to re-create an episode from the past—such as the short, unhappy stay of Anastacio Garcia, described as "the very beau ideal of a brigand" and murdered in his cell in 1857.

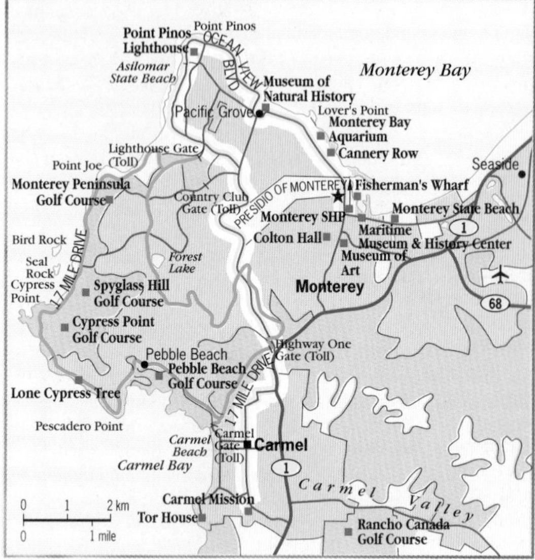

Among the features of the Monterey Bay Aquarium is the million-gallon "indoor ocean," where creatures feeding from kelp can be seen close up

▶▶▶ The Monterey Peninsula

Between them, the three distinctive communities of the Monterey Peninsula offer substantial insights into California's history, some memorable ocean vistas and an example of town planning at its most bizarre and insular.

Monterey A fine natural harbor encouraged the Spanish to land and settle at what they named Monterey in 1770. The town became California's administrative base during the mission-building period, retaining this role through the region's Mexican era and during the early years of statehood.

The well-preserved buildings which make up **Monterey State Historical Park** (tel: 831/649-7118)—ranging from Spanish adobes with their elaborate decorative tilework intact to the neoclassical Colton Hall, the seat of California's first state legislature—are among the ordinary offices and stores which comprise the compact core of present-day Monterey. To locate the old buildings, use the widely available *Path of History* map. Not all of them are open to the public, but each merits at least a quick look.

Three places of historical interest you should be certain to see are the **Old Customs House▶**, stuffed with the intriguing mix of essentials and exotica typical of an 1830s cargo ship; **California's First Theater▶▶**, scene of dramatic productions since 1846; and the **Robert Louis Stevenson House▶▶**, where the Scottish writer spent part of 1879 and which now holds mementoes from his stay, his literary career and his South Seas travels.

Stevenson was just one of a number of writers drawn to Monterey in its heyday. But the town ceased to be the seat of California's legislature in 1849 and, by the 1920s, had acquired a less glamorous position as the world's largest sardine-canning center. As its fortunes waned, another writer, John Steinbeck, penned the novels *Tortilla Flat* and *Cannery Row*, which described life on the Monterey waterfront. This rough-and-ready area, defined by fish guts, low-paid workers and prostitutes as described by Steinbeck, is now the spick-and-span tourist magnet of **Cannery Row▶**, the old warehouses having evolved into souvenir stores, seafood restaurants and **A Taste of Monterey**, a chance to sample the produce of more than 35 area wineries.

Better places to spend a few hours are the **Monterey Bay Aquarium▶▶▶** (tel: 831/648-4800), a state-of-the-art facility exploring and explaining the intricacies of life beneath the local Pacific waves, and the $6-million **Maritime Museum of Monterey** (tel: 831/372-2608), charting Monterey's role as a seaport with a multitude of maps, model ships and nautical knickknacks.

Pacific Grove Joined to Monterey and extending to the northern tip of the Peninsula, **Pacific Grove** acquired its first visitors in 1875 when a band of vacationing Methodists pitched tents on the then-uninhabited headland and founded a summertime religious retreat.

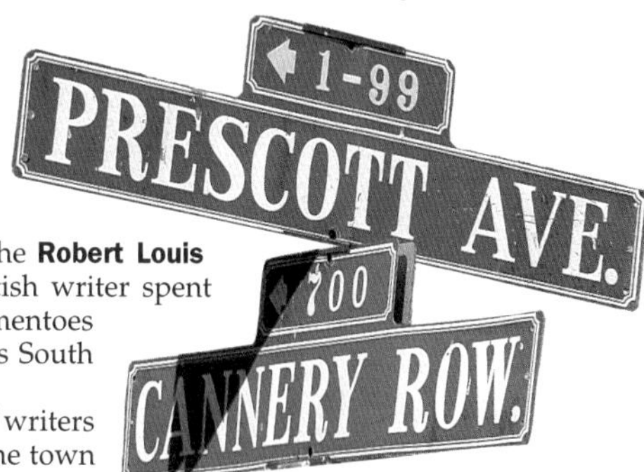

Getting lost is hard in Monterey

THE SHORELINE BIKE PATH

Many miles of scenic bike paths can be found in California, but few can surpass the Monterey Peninsula's Shoreline Bike Path for easily enjoyed coastal views. The flat, 3-mile (5km) route runs between Monterey's Fisherman's Wharf and Lover's Point, beside Ocean View Boulevard in Pacific Grove. Bikes can be rented from Bay Bikes (640 Wave Street; tel: 831/655-BIKE).

Cyclists admire Pacific Grove

Pacific Grove lodgings

Today, Pacific Grove is a pleasant place to live. Its main thoroughfare, Lighthouse Avenue, is lined with intriguing stores and cozy cafés and is also where you will find many impressive examples of wood-and-shingle Victorian architecture.

Pine trees are another common sight. Between November and March, many of the trees' branches appear to be hung with yellow and black flags. In fact, these are the wings of **monarch butterflies**, thousands of which migrate to Pacific Grove from Alaska and Canada. The small **Pacific Grove Museum of Natural History▶** (tel: 831/648-5716) has a display on the butterflies, and highlights other aspects of local history and ecology.

Do not leave Pacific Grove without taking a drive along **Ocean View Boulevard▶▶▶**. Beginning just west of the Monterey Bay Aquarium, the road follows a scenic coastal route and eventually swings south past the tiny **Point Piños Lighthouse▶▶** (tel: 831/648-5716), which has cast its beam into the distance since 1855. The lighthouse's 19th-century furnishings and historical displays are open to visitors on weekend afternoons.

THE 17-MILE DRIVE
Snaking between Pacific Grove and Carmel, the 17-Mile Drive is a marked toll route with views of craggy headlands and the famous Lone Cypress Tree, growing in defiance of ocean winds from an inaccessible outcrop. Maps of the drive are issued at the entry gates on Sunset Drive (in Pacific Grove) and San Antonio Avenue (Carmel).

Carmel Literary notables George Sterling and Mary Austin led a band of artists, writers and academics to **Carmel▶▶▶** in the early 1900s, dreaming of an idyllic bohemian existence on this then-isolated and thinly populated coastal bluff.

Their presence turned out to be temporary, however, and by the 1920s an ambitious architect was busy creating half-timbered cottages which, combined with the oceanside setting, attracted wealthy San Franciscans. The town's Tudor-style buildings have been rigorously preserved by its residents, the zoning regulations at times banning fast-food outlets, neon lighting and live entertainment in bars and restaurants, to keep Carmel's charm intact.

The town center, with its boutiques, art galleries and restaurants, justifies an hour's stroll.

A few minutes' walk away at the foot of Ocean Avenue, **Carmel Beach▶▶** comprises several miles of white sand

Point Lobos, near Carmel

Carmel Beach

framed by cypress groves. Bring your own picnic supplies and you can enjoy a barbecue using one of the beach's fire pits.

One writer who arrived in Carmel on the heels of the would-be bohemians, and not only stayed but also built a strange and imposing home for himself and his family, was poet Robinson Jeffers. Completed in 1919, Jeffers' **Tor House**▶▶ (tel: 831/624-1813) was constructed from granite stones hauled up by horses from the cove beneath. The building was intended to resemble a Tudor barn which the poet had seen in England, and it provided a home for Jeffers until his death in 1962. There are guided tours on Fridays and Saturdays by reservation.

Carmel Mission Perhaps Carmel's greatest day came in 1771 when it acquired the mission established a year earlier in Monterey, the second link in the California mission chain. The **Carmel Mission**▶▶▶ (tel: 831/624-1271) served as the main base of Junipero Serra, the leader of Spain's Sacred Expedition to establish the missions, convert Native Americans to the Catholic faith, and co-opt their labor for the colonial cause. Largely due to a comprehensive rebuilding program carried out during the 1930s, the Carmel Mission has become one of the best restored and most evocative of all the state's missions. The centerpiece is an eye-catching sandstone **church** with twin Moorish towers; completed in 1879, the church replaced the simple adobe chapel of Serra's time. Behind the church, a **museum** stores remnants from the mission's earliest days, the reconstructed living quarters of Father Serra, a few of his 600 books and the sarcophagus which holds his remains: Serra died here in 1784, aged 71.

As you stroll around the bougainvillea-lined pathways and fountains of the mission's extremely well-maintained **gardens**, you might contemplate the controversy surrounding Serra's beatification in 1988. With California's native population dying from European diseases, and their cultures suppressed and eventually destroyed by the mission system, many believe that the Spanish impact on the native people amounted to genocide, and that Serra's beatification was wrong.

CARMEL'S BACH FESTIVAL

For two weeks each July, Carmel's Bach Festival celebrates not only the German composer but also his 18th-century musical contemporaries. Concerts, opera and ballet are staged at the town's Sunset Cultural Center, but the climax of the festival is a special candlelit performance at the Carmel Mission. For details, write to Carmel Bach Festival, PO Box 575, Carmel, C.A. 93921 or tel: 831/624-2046.

Carmel Mission

Drive

The northern coast

This drive follows Highway 1, a route which winds along the entire California coast and in this section holds some of the most dramatic oceanside landscapes to be found anywhere in America. From the fishing hamlet of Bodega Bay north to the logging town of Fort Bragg, the two-lane highway makes endless twists and turns, and navigates sharp grades to reach dizzying clifftops revealing fabulous views of the Pacific. The northern coast is fully described on pages 196–199.

ALFRED HITCHCOCK'S BODEGA BAY
Much of Alfred Hitchcock's 1963 movie *The Birds* was shot in Bodega Bay. While some landscapes may be recognizable, the schoolhouse and the boarding house which appear in the film are actually located in the town of Bodega, 5 miles (8km) inland (on Bodega Highway, off Highway 1). The Tides restaurant, where locals sought refuge as the birds attacked, still exists in Bodega Bay, but in a different location from that of Hitchcock's time.

Bodega Bay birds

►►► The northern coast

To Bodega Bay Beyond Marin County (see pages 190–191), Highway 1 spans 200 miles (323km) of spectacular coastline and links some of California's most distinctive seaside communities. The first town on the route, **Bodega Bay►**, sits beside a sheltered lagoon. Although the fishing fleet is much depleted since its commercial heyday, it is still one of the largest in the area. The main appeal, however, is

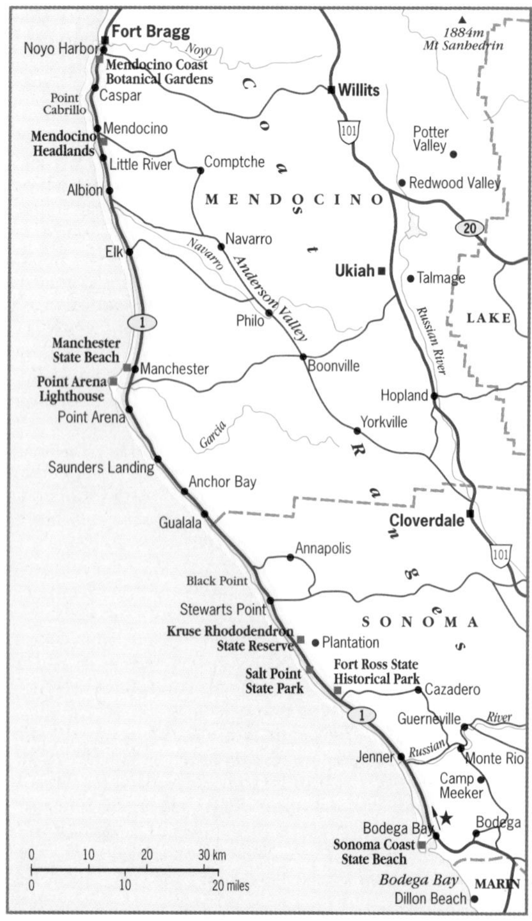

simply the setting, the relaxed ambience, and the discernible community spirit. Never is this more apparent than during April's **Fishermen's Festival**, which, among other things, includes a Blessing of the Fleet and the hilarious Bathtub Race.

North from Bodega Bay, Highway 1 passes a succession of coastal towns and a 13-mile (21km) string of sands which collectively comprise **Sonoma County State Beach▶**. Strong currents render the beaches unsuitable for swimming, but beachcombers, fishermen and anyone who enjoys peering into tidepools will find much to their liking.

Toward Fort Ross After crossing the Russian River (look for seals basking on its banks), Highway 1 spends the next 11 miles (18km) making steep and twisting ascents—bringing tantalizing glimpses of ocean surf pounding against the granite outcrops many feet below—before dropping sharply downward.

This stretch of coast still looks much as it did in the early 19th century, when Russian fur trappers purchased a 125-mile (202km) strip from Native Americans and founded a colony at Fort Ross, now remembered by **Fort Ross State Historical Park▶▶▶** (tel: 707/847-3286).

With their crops failing and sea otters (who were pursued for their pelts) hunted to near extinction, the colony was abandoned in 1841. Weather and earthquakes subsequently took their toll on the fort's traditional-style wooden buildings, but restoration has turned the living quarters, warehouses and Orthodox chapel into an absorbing reminder of the Russian presence in California.

A few miles north, **Salt Point State Park▶** (tel: 707/847-3221) covers 6,000 wild coastal acres and has an underwater portion allowing divers to explore the marine life of Gerstle Cove. On dry land, hiking trails reach sites of Native American habitation, and the neighboring **Kruse Rhododendron State Reserve▶▶** is an essential stop in springtime. For information on the Park and Reserve, tel: 707/847-3221.

Bodega Church

CALIFORNIA CRAFTS IN RUSSIA

The Russians at Fort Ross enjoyed good relations with the local Native American community and frequently traded with them. Often the Russians exchanged otter fur for feathered baskets, important symbols of native cultural identity and the specialty of the Pomo Indians who lived here. As a consequence, the world's largest collection of Kashaya Pomo basketry is held in St. Petersburg, Russia.

Russian-built Fort Ross is now a state park with exhibits that bring a rare insight into pre-Gold Rush California

NORTHERN COAST WHALE WATCHING
From mid-December to the end of March, the much-loved California gray whales may be spotted on their annual migration between the Arctic Ocean and the warmer waters off Baja California in Mexico. Marked whale-watching points are a feature of the northern coast, and most have texts and maps describing the whales and their migration. Mendocino and Fort Bragg demonstrate their admiration for California's state mammal by staging a Whale Celebration Week each March.

Gualala Less spectacular views predominate for the next 30 miles (48km), until the small town of **Gualala** appears. Take a stroll around the town's art galleries—showcases for the work of the area's many painters and sculptors.

North from Gualala Leaving Gualala and approaching **Saunders Landing**, the hills retreat inland, allowing Highway 1 to follow an unusually level section of the coast. This occurs largely because the San Andreas Fault, a rift of geological instability, moves westward and continues beneath the ocean. **Manchester State Beach**, a desolate and windswept area of dunes and driftwood, covers 760 acres (308ha) here, and on its southern edge stands the 1908 **Point Arena Lighthouse▶▶** (tel: 707/882-2777). Reached by Lighthouse Road, off Highway 1, the present lighthouse replaced a wooden original which was destroyed in California's 1906 earthquake. A museum recounts the story of the lighthouse.

Mendocino If mist is swirling across the highway as you reach **Mendocino▶▶▶**, 30 miles (48km) from Point Arena, this town of 1,000 souls nestling on a coastal bluff could well be mistaken for a ghostly apparition.

Founded by New England lumbermen a century ago, Mendocino retains much of the wooden Yankee architecture of their time. The isolated location deterred property developers from razing the town, and strict building codes have recently been enforced to preserve the mid-1800s look.

As the logging industry declined, Mendocino fell upon hard times until a colony of get-away-from-it-all artists and writers began arriving in the 1950s and 1960s. Today, many of Mendocino's old homes are bed-and-breakfast inns, and numerous art galleries are aimed at visitors.

Despite the commercial trappings, Mendocino is enormously appealing and has much to be enjoyed on a half-hour stroll. Drop into the 1854 **Ford House▶** (tel: 707/937-5804), which now serves as a visitor center, for background on the town and local wildlife, and into the

Worldwide, California is synonymous with golden beaches, but on the state's northern coast, rocky headlands and bluffs lashed by waves, such as these close to Mendocino, are far more prevalent than sandy expanses

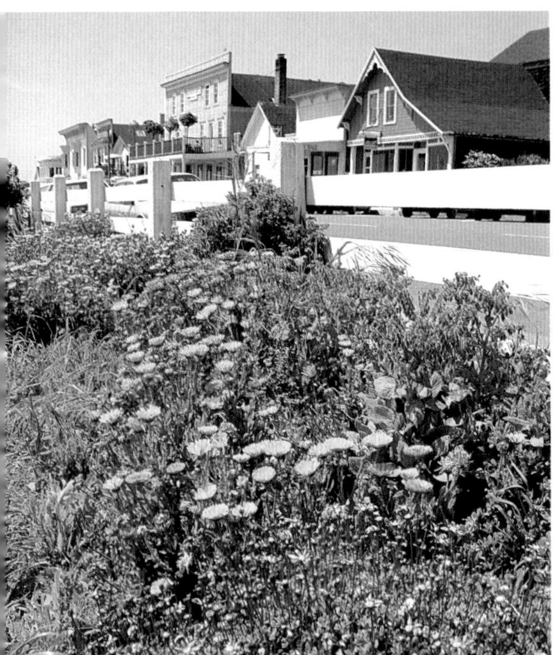

Mendocino Headlands is rich in wildflowers

NORTHERN COAST WINERIES
Though less celebrated than their counterparts in the Wine Country (see pages 204–209), the wineries dotted along Highway 128, which cuts inland from Highway 1 south of Mendocino and runs through the handsomely wooded Anderson Valley, are well worth investigating. The free Anderson Valley Winegrowers leaflet (from local chambers of commerce) lists them and their creations. This route can also be used to return to San Francisco, by continuing to Boonville and heading south on Highway 101.

Kelley House Museum▶▶ (tel: 707/937-5791) for a more personalized insight into local history through archive photographs, original Mendocino furnishings and temporary exhibitions. When it all seems too much of a metropolis, Mendocino residents put on their windbreakers and take contemplative walks across the **Mendocino Headlands▶▶**, a protected area of striking wildness and beauty adjacent to the town.

Fort Bragg Just 10 miles (16km) north, **Fort Bragg** could hardly provide a greater contrast. The gas stations and fast-food franchises which are banned in Mendocino are legion in what is by far the largest town in a 200-mile (323km) stretch of coast.

An army fort in the 1850s intended to subdue Native American opposition to white settlement, it quickly came under the thumb of the Union Lumber Company, which was succeeded in recent times by Georgia-Pacific (or G-P).

As Highway 1 enters the town, you will see G-P's sprawling sawmill, eradicating an otherwise rewarding ocean view. Tours of the sawmill are periodically available, but more valuable background information on the local logging industry lies within the **Guest House Museum▶** (tel: 707/961-2840), occupying the elegant former home of a 19th-century Fort Bragg resident.

Two places on the town's southern periphery merit a call. **The Mendocino Coast Botanical Gardens▶** (tel: 707/964-4352) offer winding walkways through 47 acres (19ha) of impressively landscaped headland. **Noyo Harbor**, meanwhile, located off Highway 1, is where locals head when they want fresh seafood. The catch is unloaded from the small fishing vessels which fill the harbor and is then served in no-frills restaurants.

The Skunk Train: linking Fort Bragg and Willits

THE SKUNK TRAIN
Fort Bragg's Skunk Train, which once transported lumber and was nicknamed for the smell of its engine, makes a 40-mile (65km) inland run to and from Willits, a scenic trip above rivers and redwood groves. Visitors can enjoy the ride as a half- or full-day trip. For details, tel: 1-866/45-SKUNK.

The San Francisco Peninsula

On either side of its hilly spine, the San Francisco Peninsula splits into distinct sections. On the Pacific side, secluded coves and pocket-sized communities are separated by wind-swept farmlands. The bay side, by contrast, is a ribbon of commercial and residential development.

This loop drive explores both sides. Facing the Pacific, picturesque Half Moon Bay is a scenic starting point from which the route moves south, passing unspoiled beaches, before swinging inland to cross the Peninsula to Palo Alto and Stanford University. From there, the drive explores San Jose and its environs, a thickly populated area but one with some surprising finds. The Peninsula is fully described on pages 201–203.

A young visitor surveys a Half Moon Bay pumpkin farm

►► The San Francisco Peninsula

Along the coast Skimming the coastline as it threads south from San Francisco, Highway 1 passes several beaches—among them Gray Whale Cove, a popular spot for nudists—before reaching the town of **Half Moon Bay►►**, its dainty proportions doing little to suggest that this is the Peninsula's largest coastal community. Antiques and craft stores, cafés, bakeries and numerous 19th-century homes converted into bed-and-breakfast inns line Half Moon Bay's handful of streets. Locals who know their pumpkins head for Half Moon Bay just before Halloween: The fields around the town grow the state's plumpest pumpkins, which can be admired at October's Art and Pumpkin Festival.

Highway 1 continues along more sparsely populated coast, passing the handful of homes which constitute **Pescadero**, founded by Spaniards in 1856, the photogenic Pigeon Lighthouse and the Año Nuevo State Reserve (see panel), a protected breeding ground for thousands of elephant seals (males weigh up to 3 tons).

Heading inland As it cuts inland from Half Moon Bay, Highway 92 takes you past the commendable **Obester Winery►** (tel: 650/726-9463), open for tastings of its sauvignon blanc, riesling and chardonnay—sip from your glass while overlooking acres of pumpkins.

The highway continues east between the Montara and Santa Cruz mountains, crossing Crystal Springs Reservoir, which was created by the San Andreas Fault.

Highway 92 reaches San Francisco Bay at San Mateo, grown large and uninteresting partly through its proximity to San Francisco International Airport. Just north of **San Mateo**, however, the interactive computers, dioramas, and general exhibits of the **Coyote Point Museum►►** (tel: 650/342-7755) provide cogent insights into the wildlife habitats of the San Francisco Peninsula and Bay and the problems they are facing.

AÑO NUEVO STATE ELEPHANT SEAL RESERVE

Thousands of elephant seals come ashore here between December and March to mate. The males spend several months battling for supremacy before the victors copulate noisily with 50 or so females. This spectacle can be seen in the company of a park ranger (reservations essential, tel: 800/444-4445; for recorded information tel: 650/879-0227).

Pigeon Point Light

Stanford University's fine sandstone architecture

THE PENINSULA RAILROAD
Fittingly perhaps, one way to reach Silicon Valley is with the state-of-the-art CalTrain rail link which connects San Francisco with Palo Alto (trip time 58 minutes) and San Jose (93 minutes). Services are most frequent during rush hours. For more information, tel: 800/660-4287.

SAN JOSÉ DE GUADALUPE
San Jose, which discarded its accent long ago, takes its name from Mission San José de Guadalupe, located 15 miles (24km) northeast. Founded in 1797, the mission was the 14th built in California and was treated to a much-needed $5-million restoration in the 1980s. The mission's chapel and small museum are both worth visiting, not least because the latter includes some of the musical instruments played by the only orchestra of neophytes (Native Americans converted to Christianity) in California.

Stanford University Unrelenting sprawl and heavy rush-hour traffic are the prime features of Highway 101 as you travel south from San Mateo, quickly reaching **Palo Alto** where you should watch for the University Avenue exit. This leads to **Stanford University**, an academic institution which brings 13,000 students to the otherwise bland and lifeless town. Founded by railroad magnate Leland Stanford and his wife in 1885 in memory of their son, Stanford University remains a privately run institution and a relatively conservative counterpart to the University of California at Berkeley (see pages 58–61). Stanford students pay approximately $20,000 tuition per year, and the university reputedly earns $5 million annually in royalties derived from patents on research departments' inventions. The older part of the campus was designed by Frederick Law Olmstead, fresh from laying out New York City's Central Park, and its centerpiece is the Main Quad, framed by sandstone buildings.

The mural-decorated **Memorial Church▶** is particularly eye-catching, but the Main Quad is dominated by **Hoover Tower▶**. With a good view across the campus and far beyond from its 285ft (87m) peak, the tower is named after Herbert Hoover, a member of Stanford's first class of 1891, who was elected US President in 1929. Elsewhere, the **Stanford Museum of Art** and **Iris & B. Gerald Cantor Center for Visual Arts▶** display items collected by the Stanford family, including the shovel used to begin the building of the transcontinental railroad, and an art collection which is less impressive than the works by Rodin in the neighboring **Cantor Sculpture Garden▶▶**.

Easily the most memorable part of a Stanford University tour is the **Stanford Linear Accelerator Center▶▶▶**, stretching for 2 miles (3km) into the hills immediately northwest of the campus. Explaining the basics of particle physics to scientific beginners, the two-hour guided tours are highly recommended. Reservations online only.

Silicon Valley The breakthroughs achieved at Stanford helped the Peninsula area gain a reputation as a center of innovative electronics from the 1940s. Four decades later, the development of the (locally invented) silicon chip and the personal computer revolution earned the region—the Santa Clara Valley—the nickname "Silicon Valley."

South of Palo Alto, **San Jose** became the de-facto capital of Silicon Valley, expanding at lightning speed as highly paid computer company employees flooded in, stimulating an economic boom but creating some of the worst smog in California as they commuted to and from work. The **Tech Museum of Innovation▶▶** (tel: 408/294-TECH) highlights the region's scientific achievements with impressive interactive exhibits.

Egyptian artifacts It would be hard to find a greater contrast to the town's high-tech ambience than the intriguing assemblage of amulets, mummies, textiles, scrolls and other antiquities from the cultures of Assyria, Babylon and Egypt, which are displayed inside the **Rosicrucian Egyptian Museum▶▶** (tel: 650/947-3636). The entryway to the museum is modeled on the Egyptian town of Thebes, and its gardens are planted with

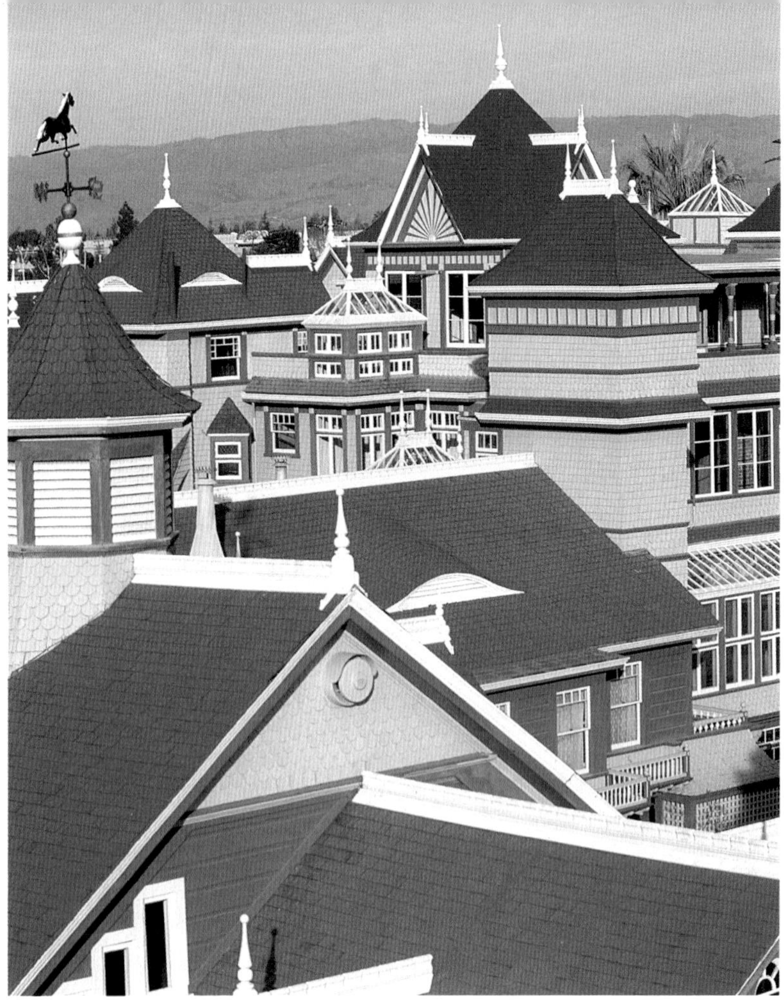

Egyptian trees and plants and decorated with sphinxes and obelisks.

A mystery house Just as unlikely is the **Winchester Mystery House▶** (525 S. Winchester Boulevard; tel: 408/247-2001). Sarah Winchester, heir to the rifle fortunes, believed she was haunted by the spirits of those killed by Winchester weapons and was certain to die if the house was ever completed. At her insistence, construction work continued day and night for 38 years, until her death in 1921. Inside, stairways lead nowhere, corridors narrow to a width of a few inches, and some of the 2,000 doors and 10,000 windows open on to blank walls.

Villa Montalvo Hugging the foothills west of San Jose, **Saratoga** is a snug and affluent community and one which, with **Villa Montalvo▶** (tel: 408/961-5800), makes a pleasant conclusion to a Peninsula excursion. James D. Phelan, US Senator, local mayor and patron of the arts, built and lived in the 19-room villa. Later it provided a home for the writers, painters, and musicians chosen as recipients of a Phelan endowment.

The 160-room Winchester Mystery House sprawls across 9 acres (4ha)

FILOLI

Designed by Willis Polk (see panel, page 112), Filoli is an exquisite 43-room mansion completed in 1919 for William B. Bourn II, inheritor of a Gold Rush fortune. The house may be familiar from the opening sequence of the TV serial *Dynasty*. At least as memorable are the gorgeous gardens, certain to have something in bloom at any time of year. Filoli is close to Woodside, off I-280 just inland from Palo Alto (tel: 650/364-8300).

Drive

The Wine Country

These drives explore Sonoma Valley (pages 204–207) and Napa Valley (pages 208–209). Although less famous than neighboring Napa Valley, Sonoma Valley holds several of the state's best wineries and is less congested than Napa. The route runs from the history-laden town of Sonoma—with the most northern of California's Spanish missions—to the very modern Santa Rosa. The second excursion, from Napa, travels past more wineries, including the oldest in Napa Valley, and two literary shrines before reaching the health resort of Calistoga, with nearby geysers, a petrified forest and an (extinct) volcano. (*See map opposite.*)

Hotels, restaurants and stores line Sonoma Plaza, the heart of the town founded in 1823 as the site of California's northernmost Spanish mission

CALIFORNIA WELCOME CENTER
Just off Highway 101 between Santa Rosa and the dairy town of Petaluma, the computers of the California Welcome Center hold information on the many wineries of Sonoma County and will even print out an itinerary listing details of those you would like to visit (tel: 800/404-7673).

►► The Wine Country

Sonoma Valley Quieter and less commercialized than better-known Napa Valley immediately east, Sonoma Valley nevertheless boasts some of the state's finest—and oldest—wineries, and has historical and literary associations worth savoring as much as the produce of its vines.

At the southern end of the valley, the town of **Sonoma**►► grew around the site of California's last and most northern Spanish mission. By the time the mission was completed, control of California had passed to Mexico and General Mariano Vallejo was developing Sonoma as a base for his enormous agricultural estate.

Apart from the impressive chapel funded by Vallejo, the **Sonoma Mission**► (open: daily 10–5; admission charge, includes Sonoma Barracks and Lachry Montis; tel: 707/938-1560) itself is not particularly interesting, but it does sit neatly among the 19th-century adobe and wood buildings which form the perimeter of the 8-acre (3ha) plaza at Sonoma's center.

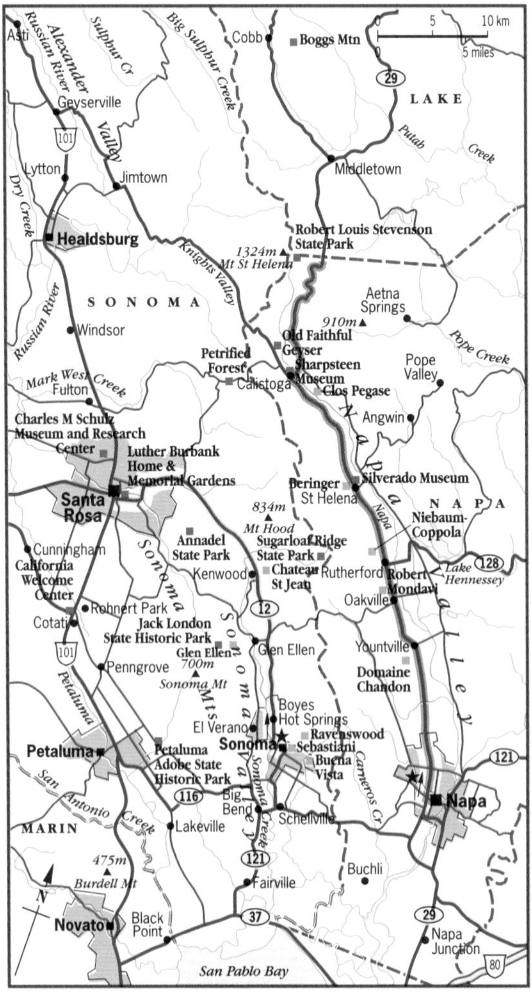

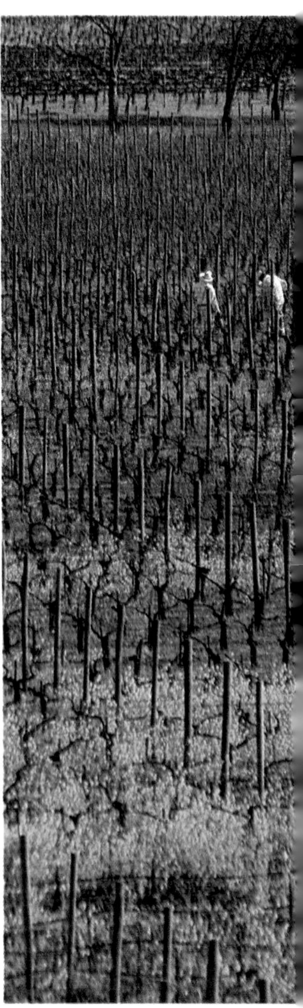

Springtime vineyards

Many of these buildings now have stores, hotels and restaurants, although several on the northern side have been restored and contain historical displays and exhibits.

The most substantial collection is inside the **Sonoma Barracks▶▶** and focuses on the 1846 Bear Flag Revolt, when a group of American fur trappers descended on the town, captured Vallejo and Sonoma's small Mexican garrison and declared California an independent republic (a few weeks later came the declaration of full US rule).

Although his enormous *rancho* was broken up, Vallejo accepted the change in government and became a member of the new state's first senate, moving in 1851 into a pretty wooden house named **Lachryma Montis▶▶**, a short walk from the plaza. Today, the house holds mementoes of Vallejo's occupancy and a small museum which makes clear his deep influence on the Sonoma region.

First wines It was Vallejo's vineyards which encouraged a visiting Hungarian, Agoston Haraszthy, to import

ZINFANDEL: MYSTERY GRAPE

While most California grapes are clearly of European origin, the roots of zinfandel are shrouded in mystery. A black zinfandel wine appeared on America's East Coast in 1838, and zinfandel grapes were first grown in California 20 years later, but where the grapes actually come from is uncertain. Experts have cited southern Italy, Slovenia, and even California itself, as the true home of zinfandel.

Loved and loathed...

European vine cuttings and start a winery just outside Sonoma. Haraszthy's wines triggered the growth of the California wine industry during the 1880s, earning him the sobriquet "the father of California wines." Haraszthy died in Nicaragua in the 1860s, and his abandoned winery was severely damaged by the 1906 earthquake, but the **Buena Vista Winery▶▶** (tel: 1-800/926-1266) was restored and resumed wine production in the 1940s. It can now claim to be the oldest premium winery in the state.

Lacking such historical resonance but winning plenty of acclaim for its wines, the **Sebastiani Vineyard▶▶** (tel: 707/933-3200), within walking distance of Sonoma's plaza, is another promising visit; so too is **Ravenswood▶** (tel: 707/933-2332), which specializes in zinfandel (see panel, page 205).

Glen Ellen North from Sonoma, Highway 12 runs the 17-mile (27km) length of the valley, but opting instead for the less congested Arnold Drive will carry you 6 miles (10km) into the town of **Glen Ellen**, where you should veer off along London Ranch Road and climb up into the hills.

... the Napa Valley Wine Train serves food and wine to its passengers, amid the polished brass of a restored 1917 Pullman carriage

Jack London After several rapidly ascending miles, the route takes you to the entrance of **Jack London State Historic Park▶▶▶** (tel: 707/938-5216). This covers roughly half of the 1,400 acres (567ha) of meadows and woodlands which the San Francisco-born writer bought in the early 1900s with the intention of building a home—the 26-room Wolf House—and running a farm. He named the area the Beauty Ranch. Tragically, the Wolf House, three years in construction and costing $80,000, was destroyed by an unexplained fire just days after its completion in 1913. London died here in 1916.

Near the park's entrance, the **House of Happy Walls▶▶**, lived in by London's widow until her death in 1955, now serves as the park's visitor center. It holds two floors of engrossing London-related material, spanning his writings and travels, and also displays some of the custom-built furniture intended for the Wolf House.

Outside, a short footpath leads to the stone walls of the **Wolf House▶▶**, which reveal the building's layout and incredible size.

A side trail leads to London's **grave site**, where his ashes were buried beside the graves of two pioneer-era children. Another trail loops back to the parking lot and continues to the remains of London's farm and the wooden cottage where he and his wife briefly lived.

Kenwood Continuing north from Glen Ellen, you will come to **Kenwood,** another friendly town and one with several worthwhile wineries. The best known among them is **Château St. Jean▶▶** (tel: 707/833-4134), as appealing for its beautifully landscaped grounds and stone buildings as for its award-winning white wines.

North from Kenwood, **Sugarloaf Ridge▶** (tel: 707/833-5712) and **Annadel▶** (tel: 707/539-3911) state parks protect wide areas of hillside; both offer a chance to shake off wine-induced lethargy and strike out across many miles of hiking trails.

Santa Rosa Impossible to miss from a high vantage point in either park is the urban sprawl which consumes the northern end of the valley, where Highway 12 swings westward to reach **Santa Rosa**. This is the route you should take to return to San Francisco (joining Highway 101 from Santa Rosa). If you have time to spare, drop into **Luther Burbank Home and Memorial Gardens▶▶** (415 Steele Lane; tel: 707/524-5445), the home and experimental garden of a now-legendary horticulturalist.
Creator of the cartoon strip Peanuts, Charles Schulz gained a worldwide following from his home in Santa Rosa and is celebrated by the **Charles M.Schulz Museum and Research Center** (2301 Hardies Lane; tel: 707/579-4452), recording the development of Schulz's work and staging exhibitions of aspects of cartoonery, often with a canine angle. Outside is the intriguing Snoopy Labyrinth.

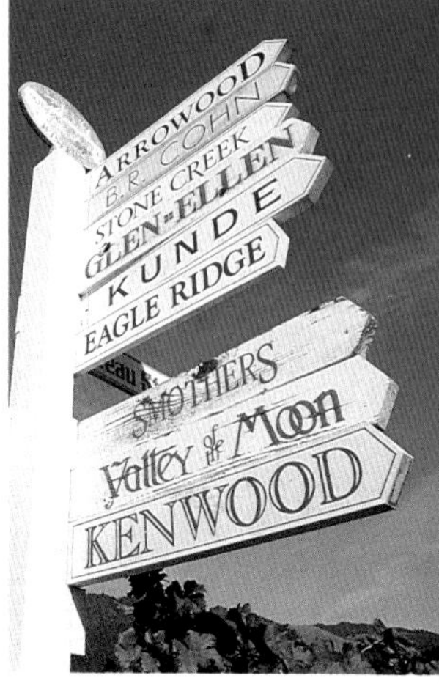

Wineries in all directions

VALLEY OF THE MOON
Sonoma Valley was the setting for Jack London's 1913 novel, *Valley of the Moon*, which bestowed a lasting nickname on the area. In fact, the title originated from a mistaken translation of the Native American name for the valley.

The imposing facade of Sonoma City Hall, built from local rock in 1906, is hard to mistake

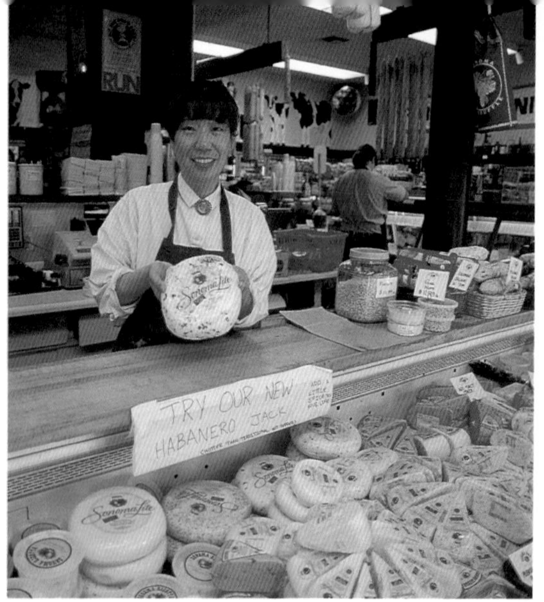

A popular stop for Sonoma visitors, the Cheese Factory's stock includes many varieties of jack cheese

NAPA VALLEY BY TRAIN
The 1915 Pullman cars of the Napa Valley Wine Train—locally dubbed the "swine train" for its noise, diesel fumes and gung-ho tourists—run between Napa and St. Helena, serving expensive gourmet-standard food and a selection of Napa Valley wines for lunch or dinner (or weekend brunch). The round trip generally costs $60 to $90, including food. Early reservations are strongly advised (tel: 800/427-4124).

NAPA VALLEY BY BIKE
Napa Valley's Silverado Trail, a route running parallel to busy Highway 29, makes for trouble-free bicycle touring, provided you do not overdo the wine tasting on the way. Bikes can be rented for around $15–$25 a day from a number of outlets, including St. Helena Cyclery, 1156 Main Street, St. Helena (tel: 707/963-7736).

NAPA VALLEY BY BALLOON
Soaring above it in a helium-filled balloon is one way to tour the Napa Valley, and several companies offer a few hours aloft for around $150. A light meal and a few glasses of champagne are usually included in the price. Reserve early and keep your fingers crossed for a wind-free day (strong gusts may cause the ride to be canceled). Among the many operators are Above The Valley (tel: 800/464-6824), and Adventures Aloft (tel: 800/944-4408).

Napa Valley An hour's drive from San Francisco and marking the southern end of Napa Valley, the town of **Napa** grew rich as a transit center for the produce of Napa Valley's wineries in the mid-19th century and has many Victorian buildings in its historic riverside area.

The town has few wineries, however, and a better first stop in the valley is **Yountville▶**, a few miles north on Highway 29 (which runs the length of the valley), where champagne devotees will be in seventh heaven sampling the fare of **Domaine Chandon▶** (tel: 707/944-2892), owned by the first-rate French company, Moët.

Oakville and Rutherford Many of the valley's best wineries are scattered along Highway 29 near the neighboring towns of **Oakville** and **Rutherford**. Here, the one-hour complimentary tours and tastings offered by the **Robert Mondavi Winery▶▶** (tel: 1-888/766-6328) are recommended for learning something about the intricacies of California wines and the wine-making process.

At the **Neibaum-Coppola** winery, housed in an ivy-covered chateau (1991 St. Helena Highway; tel: 1-800/782-4266), tastings can be followed by a tour of a museum stocking exhibits on wine- and film-making (the winery owner is movie-director Francis Ford Coppola).

St. Helena A favorite weekend destination for San Franciscans, St. Helena has numerous gourmet restaurants and bed-and-breakfast inns. Wood-framed buildings of the late 1800s line pretty Main Street.

Historically, the California wine industry has endured two major setbacks. A plant louse destroyed almost all the valley's vines in the 1870s, while during Prohibition the only wineries able to continue production were those manufacturing sacramental wine—among them St. Helena's **Beringer Vineyards▶** (tel: 707/963-8989), the valley's oldest continuously operating winery.

Scottish writer Robert Louis Stevenson passed through St. Helena in 1880 and based his novel *The Silverado Squatters* on the area's silver-miners. He is remembered

with a collection of memorabilia at the **Silverado Museum▶▶** (tel: 707/963-3753). A lesser-known writer's shrine is the **Ambrose Bierce House▶** (tel: 707/963-3003), a compact bed-and-breakfast inn dating from 1872, now containing an intriguing collection devoted to Bierce, a journalist and novelist of the late 1800s (see page 37).

A few miles north of St. Helena, what **Clos Pegase▶▶** (tel: 707/942-4981) lacks in historical pedigree—the winery opened in 1986—is more than compensated for by its design. The complex has an imposing Greco-Roman look.

In Sonoma County, Petaluma Adobe State Park holds the 19th-century buildings and implements of the ranch of General Vallejo, a prominent Californian under both Mexican and US rule

Calistoga Strange as it may seem, water and mud do more to bring visitors to **Calistoga▶▶** than wine. With its mineral-rich springs and volcanic mud baths, Calistoga was developed as a health resort in the 1860s by Sam Brannan, a flamboyant California pioneer and millionaire (see page 37). The dioramas of the **Sharpsteen Museum▶▶** (tel: 707/942-5911) illustrate the town's growth, and the museum keeps one of Brannan's original resort cottages furnished in 1860s style.

Geysers and volcanoes Any doubts about the area's geothermal activity will be dispelled by **Old Faithful Geyser▶** (tel: 707/942-6463), a mile (1.6km) north of Calistoga, which propels a jet of boiling water 60ft (18m) high about every 40 minutes. A less dramatic but more impressive manifestation of the area's seismic rumblings is the **Petrified Forest▶▶** (tel: 707/942-6667), 5 miles (8km) west of Calistoga off Petrified Forest Road. A grove of redwood trees which stood on this site 6 million years ago was uprooted by an eruption of nearby (and now extinct) Mount St. Helena. Chemicals in the volcanic ash reacted with the wood, and the trees were turned to stone.

Mount St. Helena 3,000 acres (1,215ha) of desolate mountain slopes form **Robert Louis Stevenson State Park▶▶** (tel: 707/942-4575), where the writer and his Oakland bride, Fanny Osbourne, enjoyed a two-month honeymoon, in the bunkhouse of an abandoned silver mine.

The psychic palm reader may be a recent addition, but the spa treatments and mineral pools advertised on this Calistoga street have been a feature of the town since its founding in the 19th century

The Red Victorian, a landmark inn on Haight Street

ACCOMMODATIONS INFORMATION
San Francisco Visitors and Convention Bureau publishes a free lodgings guide, packed with listings and room rates, which can be picked up from the Visitor Information Center on Hallidie Plaza. At the same place, you can help yourself to countless leaflets and brochures.

Accommodations

From fax-equipped suites in marble towers to four-poster beds in wood-framed Victorian mansions, places to stay in San Francisco are as abundant as the hills and as varied as the views. The choices appeal to all tastes and budgets and even better is the fact accommodations is a fiercely contested business here, with an overabundance of hotels, motels and inns all vying for your valuable patronage.

Price ranges A few hotels are able to offer very inexpensive accommodations, as low as $55 per night, by providing small rooms without private bathroom, TV and phone (though frequently such establishments do offer rooms with these items for $10–$15 extra). Spend anything from about $75, however, and you can expect a pleasantly appointed private bathroom, color TV (usually with cable channels) and a direct-dial phone as standard features.

Not surprisingly, room prices rise with room size and also reflect the quality. As the price rises above about $150 a night, your expectations should include a well-stocked mini-bar, a video library from which movies can be rented and, in the bathroom, a hair dryer and a fine array of soaps, shampoos and lotions.

Spend $250 or more and you really start tasting the good life, with private Jacuzzi, stunning view, perhaps a CD player, fluffy bathrobes, around-the-clock room service and complimentary morning newspapers.

Special levels Many top hotels have a particular floor where the rooms may be no different from those on other floors but are priced (from about $300) to include the use of meeting areas and a communal room, where complimentary newspapers, magazines, snacks and drinks are replenished throughout the day, and where staff is on hand to attend to your every whim. More often than not, guests reach this exclusive level with a special elevator key.

City areas San Francisco is small and easy to get around with few unpleasant areas; therefore, choosing where you stay is a much less critical consideration than it is in some cities. The densest concentrations of hotels are in and

The hostel at Fort Mason

Expensive lodgings: the Westin St. Francis and Tower, overlooking Union Square

around tourist-dominated Fisherman's Wharf and the geographically convenient Union Square.

Increasingly, however, adventurous visitors are discovering the smaller and less impersonal hotels and bed-and-breakfast inns which are scattered throughout colorful residential neighborhoods such as Pacific Heights and Haight-Ashbury. By contrast, the area around the intersection of Van Ness Avenue and Lombard Street has been dubbed "motel row" with dozens of motels offering clean if uninspired rooms ($70–$125).

Obviously, there is no need to spend all your San Francisco nights in one location, and a night or two outside the city (see panel) is also worth considering.

Hotel types San Francisco hotels come in all shapes and sizes. Many of the major chains such as Hyatt and Marriott have built properties in the Fisherman's Wharf area. There are few bargains to be found in this neighborhood (prices are generally $90–$200), but these hotels provide dependable bases and are where many tour groups find themselves staying.

Around Union Square, the heart of the city as far as most visitors are concerned, many mid-priced ($100–$199), medium-sized hotels benefit from their closeness to the city's transportation centers, as well as having much of interest (Chinatown, North Beach, Nob Hill and more) within walking distance.

OUTSIDE THE CITY

Spending a night across the bay provides an enjoyable change of pace and scenery. Sausalito has several hotels perched on its hillsides; none are cheap and all are fully reserved on weekends, but they offer a chance to stroll in the quaint village after the day-trippers have departed. A stopover in Berkeley encourages a long and leisurely gourmet meal in one of the town's award-winning restaurants without the prospect of indigestion induced by a dash back to the city.

ACCOMMODATIONS AGENCIES
San Francisco accommodations can be reserved through most travel agents or by contacting a particular property directly. In addition, San Francisco Reservations (tel: 800/677-1500; www.hotelres.com), provides a free reservation service for its 300 member hotels, and B&B accommodations can be arranged through Bed & Breakfast San Francisco, PO Box 42009, San Francisco, CA 94142 (tel: 1-800/452-8249 or 415/899-0060; www.bbsf.com). Hotellocators.com, 9 Sumner Street, San Francisco, CA 94103 (tel: 800/576-0003 or 800/423-7846), claims to offer discounted rooms at 800 properties in the city and throughout the California area.

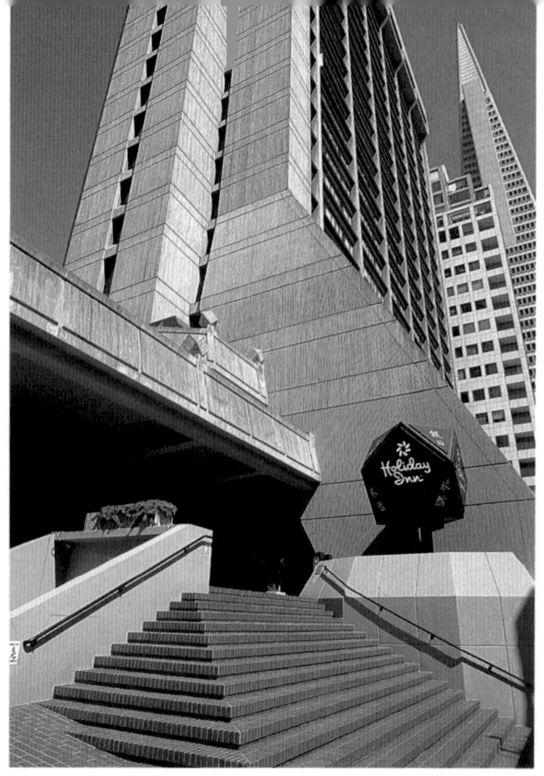

The concrete blocks of Chinatown's Hilton Financial District (right) contrast with the Japanese architectural esthetic displayed by the Radisson Miyako, across the city in Japantown (below)

Also close to Union Square, the Financial District and its environs are dotted with high-rise hotels (from $200) targeted at expense-account guests. While the facilities—such as in-room fax machines and a complimentary *Wall Street Journal* each day—may be the stuff of business travelers' dreams, the vacationer may be tempted instead by attractive weekend discounts liable to bring prices down quite considerably.

Boutique hotels Mostly scattered between Union Square and Nob Hill, a growing number of "boutique hotels" (typically $110–$240) has turned what might once have been an affluent family home into a small, elegantly furnished hotel with as few as 20 rooms. Boutique hotels pride themselves on fostering a close, informal relationship with their guests. Breakfast is normally included, and complimentary wine or sherry will often be served in the early evening.

Bed and breakfast Many rambling Victorian homes throughout the city have been refurbished and converted into bed-and-breakfast inns. Widely fluctuating prices ($80–$200) reflect the fact that both the individual properties and the rooms within them can vary greatly. Some rooms may be small with a shared bathroom, others might be fully equipped suites with Jacuzzi and ultra-modern CD sound systems.

B&Bs commonly serve complimentary wine and sherry in the afternoon or evening, sometimes with nuts, fruit and an array of home-baked cakes. Breakfast is included and, in most cases, is far more delicious and nutritious than a trip to the local diner. Some B&B rooms do not have

TVs or phones as standard features (and some B&Bs boast of offering an escape from such things), but these can be provided if required.

The popularity of B&Bs means that you should make a reservation early, especially if arriving during the summer or staying over a weekend. Besides contacting the B&B directly, reservations can be made through the specialist agencies listed in the panel on page 212.

Gay accommodations Wherever they stay in this tolerant and liberal city, gay and lesbian travelers are unlikely to encounter unpleasantness or hostility from hotel staff. A number of hotels and bed-and-breakfast inns, particularly in the Castro District, are staffed by, and cater specifically to, gays and lesbians.

Budget accommodations While hotel rooms typically cost at least $100 a night, San Francisco is still good news for travelers on tight budgets, with a number of official AYH and privately run hostels, plus a YMCA, offering beds in small dormitories for around $22 a night and single and double rooms for $55–$70. The hostels include the 170-room San Francisco International Hostel at Fort Mason, the largest youth hostel in the country. Others are found all across the city, giving a wide range of location options. Many hostels impose a three-night maximum stay during the busy summer season, and some employ an evening curfew.

Seasonal considerations
Most visitors to San Francisco arrive from June through August, when it is wise to reserve accommodations well in advance. Prices are $10–$30 higher throughout this period than during the rest of the year (when advance reservations are still advisable, though not absolutely essential). Do remember, however, that the city enjoys its best weather from late September through to early November, when sunshine is common and unhindered by the famous San Francisco fog, which cools many summer days.

Except for hotels especially geared for business travelers, weekend prices are always higher than weekday prices. Be warned that accommodations can sometimes be at a premium when the city hosts a major convention, though this chiefly applies to Financial District and Union Square hotels and those in SoMa near the Moscone Convention Center.

Hidden extras The prices quoted are average rates for double rooms but—like most advertised rates—do not include a total tax surcharge of 14 percent which, once added to bills, can provide a shock for unsuspecting guests when they check out. If your room has a mini-bar, be sure to scrutinize the price list before helping yourself: prices can be three or four times higher than normal.

CHILDREN AND EXTRA GUESTS
Most hotels welcome children and allow them to share their parents' room at no charge, though the age limit for this ranges from 12 to 18 years. Many double rooms in hotels can also accommodate one or two extra guests for an additional charge of $15–$20 per person.

Ecclesiastical bed-and-breakfast: Alamo Square's Archbishop's Mansion

DEPOSITS AND PAYMENTS
Most rooms can be reserved with a deposit equivalent to the nightly rate. Rooms can be reserved without a deposit, though they may not be held after 6pm unless you inform the hotel that you will be checking in at a later time. Charges are usually settled by presenting your credit card on arrival and signing for the total owed when checking out. Travelers' checks can also be used as payment when checking in.

San Franciscans are enthusiastic eaters

Food and drink

Eating and drinking are major preoccupations in San Francisco. Here, everything is on offer, from down-home American diner fare to cuisines culled from every corner of the globe—Laotian, Peruvian, Mongolian, whatever your taste. For Californians with cultured palates—or just big appetites—San Francisco is much less about bay views, cable cars and Golden Gate Bridge, than it is about putting the latest restaurant to the test and keeping up with the comings and goings of the city's top chefs.

Prices Fierce competition helps keep prices to levels which many well-traveled Americans will find impressively low. All but the most exclusive restaurants are well within the range of the majority of travelers and it is fairly easy to eat well wherever you are in the city.

As a general rule, budget for at least $6–$8 per person for breakfast, around $10 for lunch and $15–$20 for dinner. Expect all of these figures to rise sharply as the quality of the setting improves, and for a special dinner with liberal amounts of wine, expect to spend between $60 and $80 per person.

Wherever you dine, a tip of at least 15 percent is expected; reward extremely good service with a tip closer to 20 percent.

Breakfast fare Breakfast is the only dish of the San Francisco day which differs little from what is found all across the country. A three-egg omelet with a choice of fillings likely to include various cheeses, vegetables, ham and even fruit, accompanied by hash browns and toast (or a muffin), is the staple offering in most coffee shops, where the breakfast menu will also include waffles and generous stacks of pancakes.

Classier places, and the on-site restaurants of many upscale hotels, can provide a more varied breakfast, offering any combination of the above plus cereals, fresh-baked breads and muffins, fruit and fresh juices.

EATING WITH CHILDREN
All but the most exclusive San Francisco restaurants welcome children. Young diners will often be handed toys and coloring books as soon as they sit down and those who are old enough to read will find they have their own section of the menu, where child-sized portions and perennial kids' favorites such as burgers, french fries, onion rings and ice cream feature prominently.

Culinary neighborhoods Like the local climate, food in San Francisco can change considerably within the space of a few blocks, and some neighborhoods are synonymous with a particular ethnic fare. North Beach (American-Italian food) and Chinatown (Chinese) are the obvious examples, and both are worth exploring.

There is much more to stimulate the touring gastronome elsewhere, be it the new influx of Asian restaurants taking root in the Tenderloin, the Salvadorean bakeries of the Mission District, the high-class French restaurants of Nob Hill or the nouveau hippie hangouts of Haight-Ashbury.

Eating Italian The streets of North Beach are jammed with American-Italian restaurants offering first-rate cuisine. Almost all of them provide excellent value: A simple fresh pasta dish is unlikely to be more than $10, and a six-course dinner for less than $20 is not unknown.

North Beach dining is no secret, however, and for evening meals you should plan to dine early (before 7pm) to avoid the worst of the crowds, especially on Fridays and Saturdays. The more upscale North Beach restaurants will accept reservations, but many of the more intimate and enjoyable places do not.

Earlier in the day, you should have no difficulty finding a cozy niche inside one of the neighborhood's many cafés, where you can linger over a cappuccino and a wide choice of light Italian lunches and dessert delicacies to your heart's (and your stomach's) content.

North Beach may be the spiritual home of Italian cuisine in San Francisco (and Italian food is available across the city), but not every restaurant located there is guaranteed to delight.

Over the last two decades, the increasing commercialism of the area has caused many locals to remain true to the tried and tested haunts (and some restaurants are almost as old as the city) and give a wide berth to some of North Beach's newer and brasher dining places.

A SPECIAL CRAB

During its mid-November to June season, look out for Dungeness crab, which many Italian restaurants serve as the centerpiece of an Italian-San Francisco seafood dish called *cioppino*, a throw-everything-in type of fish stew which, the story goes, was first concocted by the wives of the city's late-1800s Sicilian settlers. Dungeness crab also claws its way onto menus elsewhere—in Chinatown, look for it deliciously prepared with ginger and garlic.

Italian delis offer plenty of picnic choice

Chinatown fare Chinese food has long been a feature of San Francisco, and Chinatown its culinary hot spot, despite the fact that many of the top Chinese chefs have departed for other areas, notably the Richmond District, where Clement Street has many renowned Chinese and other Asian (mainly Vietnamese) restaurants.

Within Chinatown, prices are low ($8 buys a good lunch, $13–$15 a filling dinner), and cooking styles, which reflect every region of China, have been expanded by the diverse ethnic backgrounds of recent immigrants. Besides the subtly seasoned fare of Canton, the northern style of Peking, the more esoteric cuisine of Hakka and Chao Chow and the hot and spicy cooking of Hunan and Szechuan, some unusual Vietnamese-Chinese and even Peruvian-Chinese dishes can also be found enlivening local menus.

DIM SUM DELIGHTS
Popular dim sum dishes include *cha sil bow*—steamed pork bun; *gai bow*—steamed chicken bun; *chern goon* —egg rolls; *sil mi*—steamed pork and shrimp dumpling. Less popular ones among Westerners include *gai guerk*—braised chicken feet, and *op guerk*—braised duck's feet.

Only in Hong Kong are you likely to encounter a greater variety of dim sum—a selection of pastries and dumplings filled with seafood, meat or vegetables—than in Chinatown. The most popular dim sum restaurants (locally called "tea houses") are large and lively, and predominantly cater to a neighborhood Chinese clientele. Dim sum is usually served from 10am to 3pm, though the best dishes have often been consumed by 1pm. Many tea houses serve regular Chinese dinners during the evening.

Dim sum is not ordered from a menu but is served from carts which are wheeled around the tables, pausing at each one long enough for diners to make their selections before returning to the kitchen to be restocked. Westerners unfamiliar with this system will do well to look interested but puzzled, and hope that the waiter or waitress will offer a description of what is offered in English. If they do not, just point to whatever looks good—but remember that one of the carts will be carrying dessert dishes.

When you have eaten your fill, which may take some time (dim sum is intended to be a leisurely experience), the

A North Beach garlic specialist

American classics—around the clock

cost is determined by the number of empty dishes or baskets on your table.

Thai and Indian Many Thai, and a lesser number of Indian, restaurants are well established all over San Francisco, and are much like their counterparts in any other Western country—most Indian and Thai dishes are served in milder forms. Hotter dishes are usually indicated on the menu. Few are budget-priced, but most offer good value: You can expect to pay $10–$15 for the average lunch and $15–$20 for dinner.

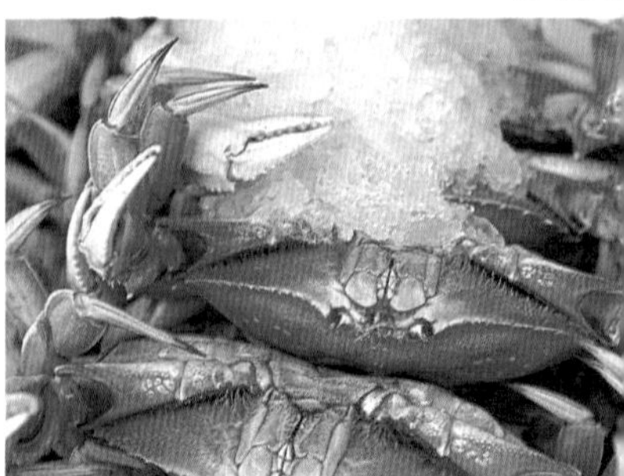

Seafood at its freshest

More Asian More appealing to the gastronomically adventurous—and the budget-minded—are the batch of Vietnamese, Laotian and Cambodian restaurants which have appeared on the city's culinary scene in recent years. Many of them are located in the seedy Tenderloin area, which deters some would-be diners, while their bare tables and spartan furnishings come as a shock to San Franciscans weaned on luxurious decor and fancy tablecloths.

Within these unpretentious surroundings, however, you can feast on barbecued shrimp on sugarcane or spicy chicken in coconut milk and still emerge with plenty of change from $20.

Look out, also, for *phó,* a delicious Vietnamese noodle soup usually containing beef and vegetables.

Mexican The relative lack of variety and sophistication in the usual American version of south-of-the-border fare tends to deter San Francisco's spoiled diners from raving about Mexican food, although there are a number of reliable restaurants throughout the city.

Most of these offer a meat-free alternative, such as fish tacos and the cheese-filled *quesadilla,* to the staple beef, pork and chicken main dishes (served with a variety of corn or flour tortillas), together with margaritas delivered by the glass or pitcher in a variety of frozen and fruit flavors.

JAPANESE FOOD
In San Francisco, aim for Japantown's Japan Center and you will discover several dozen restaurants and sushi bars providing a treat for the tastebuds for under $8 (lunch) and $14 (dinner).

The cuisines of Asian countries are easy to come by in San Francisco

SOURDOUGH BREAD
Slightly bitter and chewy, sourdough bread has been around for thousands of years in many countries but first appeared here during the Gold Rush, when yeast and baking powder were in short supply and settlers made bread using a sour starter, a fermented mixture of flour and water which enabled the dough to rise (see also panel, page 93).

VEGETARIAN DINING
Most vegetarians need never go hungry in San Francisco, where every restaurant—except possibly the most red-blooded steak house—will offer at least one, usually several, vegetarian dishes. There is also a generous sprinkling of exclusively vegetarian eating places, from the gourmet-standard Greens at Fort Mason Center, to innumerable small, inexpensive ethnic hole-in-the-wall diners.

The festive atmosphere of such places contrasts with the simple Mexican restaurants of the strongly Hispanic Mission District, which concentrate much less on atmosphere—bare tables and peeling paint on the walls are the order of the day—than on presenting a large, wholesome meal at a price rarely reaching $8.

Latin American Mexican may be the Mission District's dominant cuisine, but the area also holds dozens of restaurants and bakeries representing many of the countries of Latin America. Here you can sample a Puerto Rican seafood stew, try goat curry or wrestle with an authentic Cuban sandwich—all for just a few dollars. Salvadoran cuisine may be new to some, and is certainly worth trying out. Even if you find the rough-and-ready atmosphere of the restaurants—and the staff's lack of English—intimidating, stick around long enough to try a few gluttonous snacks from the bakeries lining Mission and 24th streets.

Bohemian eats For a meal in the company of the city's cutting-edge artists, writers, lesser media celebrities and full-time nightclubbers, try any of the restaurants and cafés that drift in and out of fashion along Haight-Ashbury's Haight Street or SoMa's Folsom Street. Many of these serve no more than basic, filling American food—such as enormous omelets, huge sandwiches and all types of burgers—but do so surrounded by bizarre decor and a carefully cultivated bohemian atmosphere. Prices are rarely much higher than run-of-the-mill coffee shops, though some turn out food of a standard high enough for food snobs in suits to be found dining next to embryonic poets in thrift-store rags.

Tourist grub Few San Franciscans would dream of eating in tourist-packed Fisherman's Wharf. Despite claims to the contrary, comparatively little of the seafood offered actually comes from local waters, and most dishes can be found in better and less expensive forms elsewhere. Visitors with hunger pangs are well advised to limit their eating to snacks from seafood stalls on the street. Clam chowder in a bowl of sourdough bread (a chewy, slightly tangy bread otherwise best eaten toasted—see panel) is one tasty if expensive option (over $3). But try to preserve your appetite for more inspiring surroundings. If this proves impossible, forego the seafood for the costly but usually excellent ethnic restaurants found at Ghirardelli Square.

California cuisine In the late 1970s, the upscale restaurants on Berkeley's Shattuck Avenue pioneered what became known as California cuisine. A handful of inventive chefs like Alice Waters took the abundant supplies of fresh meat, vegetables and fruit raised or grown on the state's farms, and the produce of its fish-stocked rivers and ocean, and began crisscrossing the borders of international cuisine, juxtaposing traditional methods of preparation, flavoring and styling.

The masterminds of California cuisine selected ingredients for their nutritional balance, appealing to the digestive tract as much as the tastebuds. In some cases, animals were reared and vegetables grown to the exact specifications of a restaurant, and some chefs bought seafood only from known and trusted fishermen. To satisfy the true gourmet's esthetic sense, color coordination was also important, aiding the artful presentation of food on the plate.

The individuality of each chef prevented any single dish, which might be anything from grilled pigeon breasts to red snapper in peanut sauce, from becoming uniquely associated with California cuisine, although the techniques from the period have since been widely adopted—and almost taken for granted—among San Francisco's latest influx of first-rate chefs. The best of a number of San Francisco restaurants continue the themes of California cuisine. On any particular day, the menu will feature whatever ingredients are in season, and preparation will span a diverse assortment of cooking styles. Often a California wine will be recommended to enhance the experience. Do not expect platefuls of red meat, but do expect a small portion of food to cost upward of $30.

SUNDAY BRUNCH
This combination of late breakfast and early lunch is a Sunday fixture for many San Franciscans. With the cost depending on the chicness of the restaurant, and the types of food and alcohol included in the price, it usually lasts from 10am to 2pm. The restaurant sections of local newspapers and magazines have plenty of suggestions as to the best brunch spots—but be sure to make a reservation before heading out.

The Massawa restaurant on Haight Street, the main commercial strip of Haight-Ashbury, is a survivor in a neighborhood steadily filling with newer, trendier places to eat and drink. It serves Eritrean cuisine from East Africa

Luxury Chinese dining at the Parac Hong Kong Restaurant in the Richmond District

A more egalitarian offshoot of California cuisine has been the exotically topped pizzas—goat's cheese, duck and lobster are among the favorites—baked in traditional wood-fired brick ovens and delivered to the masses (or anyone who does not mind spending $10–$15) by a number of establishments, including Vicolo (201 Ivy Street), Pauline's (260 Valencia Street), Tommaso's (1042 Kearny) and the ever-expanding California Pizza Kitchen chain.

US regional As their tastebuds steadily exhaust the cuisines of the world, many San Franciscans—like their counterparts in other major American cities—are greatly enjoying rediscovering the regional cuisines of their own country.

Many of San Francisco's "contemporary American" restaurants are nestled among the ritzy boutiques of the city's more expensive residential areas, particularly Pacific Heights. Here, top-rated chefs present gourmet variations on regional themes which bear the nutritional and esthetic imprint of California cuisine and often use regional inspiration in the preparation, spices and sauces, rather than in the dish itself.

Be it jambalaya with duck or grilled quail pie, regional American fare can be full of surprises, though many restaurants distanced from the frontiers of gastronomy simply include mesquite-grilled seafood (swordfish is a favorite) and steaks as their token regional dishes. Places worth trying include Biscuits and Blues (401 Mason Street), Chow (215 Church Street), Elite Café (2049 Fillmore Street), Fly Trap (606 Folsom Street) and Farallon (450 Post Street).

LEGAL DRINKING AGE
To legally buy or consume alcohol, you must be aged 21 or older. In many places, be it bar, nightclub or restaurant, customers with the slightest hint of youthfulness about them will be asked to show identification bearing their date of birth.

French Legend has it that the French chefs who traveled west from New York with their wealthy, financier bosses in the late 19th century and opted to open restaurants here rather than return, were the root of San Franciscans' obsession with good eating.

The more affordable of the city's present-day French restaurants are the cozy imitation Paris bistros which usually offer well-priced lunchtime fare (around $15).

In the evening, candlelight and lingering romantic dinners are the rule (expect to pay around $25 per person plus wine).

When they feel like dressing for dinner, however, San Franciscans head for one of the city's expensive French restaurants where the napkin creases are razor sharp, the staff is as smartly attired as the customers, and full-length gold-framed mirrors reflect the city's great and glamorous wining, dining and not batting an eyelid at spending over $100 each. French eateries include Anjou (44 Compton Place), Bizou (598 Fourth Street), Café Claude (7 Claude Lane), Gary Danko (800 North Point Street), Masa's (648 Bush Street) and Rubicon (558 Sacramento).

Coffee-drinkers' paradise The aroma of freshly roasted beans may waft across North Beach's streets less frequently than in the past, but San Francisco is still a coffee-drinkers' town. Like their counterparts all over the country, every diner in town serves steaming mugs of fresh-brewed coffee ($1–$2) to patrons with the usual choice between regular and decaffeinated and supplies free refills as often as desired.

For its many coffee aficionados, however, the city has hundreds of cafés which earn customer loyalty through the brand of bean they use, and the taste and appearance of the cappuccino or espresso they serve.

Italian cafés are intrinsic to North Beach culture, but many more—be they refined or bohemian in ambience—are found in every neighborhood (see pages 138–139). In a café, expect to pay between $1 and $2 per cup, more for an exotic brew.

Tea-drinkers' alternatives The freshness and quality of San Francisco's coffee may encourage devoted tea drinkers to change their habits, at least for the duration of their visit.

BUYING ALCOHOL
Antisocial drinkers, or anyone who wants to make their hotel room a more convivial place, will find plenty of choice (provided they are 21 or over) in supermarkets and in most grocery stores between 6am and 2am. California wines can be exceptionally good value, often costing as little as $4 a bottle. Imported beers and lagers are generally $6–$7 per six-pack, domestic beers around $4 per six-pack. Hard liquor is predictably pricier and cannot be sold between 2am and 6pm.

Eating al fresco is easy

Above: Early evening wine and snacks are a bonus at many hotels
Below: For Italian fare try North Beach

Tea in San Francisco can mean selecting between high-grade leaves such as oolong or Earl Grey, which are liable to be offered in the more upwardly mobile cafés and in upscale hotel lounges.

Top-rate tea can also be sipped in the company of cucumber sandwiches and scones as part of afternoon tea, an increasingly popular activity among the city's more affluent residents (see pages 132–133).

Irish coffee If a North Beach espresso fails to get the blood flowing, you might try Irish coffee, which allegedly made its first US appearance when served at the Buena Vista Café (2765 Hyde Street) in 1952. The late San Francisco columnist Stan Delaplane is credited with importing the Gaelic concotion. Whatever the truth in this tale, Irish coffee—a mix of coffee, Irish whiskey, sugar and whipped cream—turns up in many bars, cafés and restaurants, and a warming glassful will undoubtedly help you face the city's bracing sea breezes.

Alcohol Most restaurants have a liquor license, and many cafés also serve a limited range of beer, wine and liquor. The city's many bars are seldom intimidating affairs, and an unaccompanied woman is by no means a rare sight. Most bars are also refreshingly free (or almost free) from cigarette smoke.

Domestic beers such as Budweiser and Miller are sold on draft and in bottles in virtually every bar, and many establishments also carry a small selection of more expensive bottled European lagers (occasionally found on tap) and Mexican beers. Fans of these imported brews claim they are far higher in quality, and strength, than their American counterparts.

Most bars also stock Anchor Steam Beer, which is brewed in San Francisco (and has been since the Gold Rush) and has many local fans. If the bar stocks them, the adventurous beer drinker should also investigate the output of California's microbreweries, increasingly prevalent

OPENING HOURS

Legally, bars can be open at any time between 6 and 2am, though most choose to open their doors around 11am and close them around midnight (later on Fridays and Saturdays). Provided they are licensed, restaurants can serve alcohol throughout their hours of business except between 2am and 6am.

across the state and often making excellent beers. At least two San Francisco bars brew their beer on the premises (see pages 84–85). Other California beers of distinction are Sierra Nevada Ale and Red Tail Ale.

California wine Many wine drinkers are drawn to San Francisco by its proximity to the Wine Country (see pages 204–209), the country's major wine-producing region. Indeed, a number of the city's restaurants have access to many of the best Californian wines unavailable elsewhere (some of the wineries' productions are so small that they never leave the state).

California wines may cost between $10 and $500 a bottle, and many are among the best in the world. While the wineries of the Napa and Sonoma valleys (the heart of the Wine Country) undoubtedly lead the field, skilled vintners are found all across the state and often produce wines of impressive quality.

The classier a restaurant is, the lengthier its wine list will be (and it may also carry selected European vintages). Asking the waiter for advice is regarded not as a sign of oenological ignorance, but as an indication of genuine interest and enthusiasm.

Wines ordered in a restaurant will usually cost $5–$9 a glass, or proportionately less if ordered by the bottle or half bottle. Most bars stock a reasonable selection of wines. California wines are usually labeled and categorized by the grape varietal rather than by regional or proprietary names.

Juice power Caffeine- and sugar-laden soft drinks, such as the ubiquitous Coke and Pepsi (but not yet Diet Coke), have tended to fall from favor among health-conscious San Franciscans, for whom fresh fruit juices are often a preferred soft drink.

Special protein-packed juice blends—varieties of orange, grapefruit and carrot juice, combined with parsley, ginger, spinach and other root vegetables—which are sold in juice bars and at some gyms, are enjoying a surge in popularity. You should expect to spend $2–$4 for an energizing glassful.

Hot-dog lovers will find health-conscious San Francisco has relatively few sidewalk food stands, but liquid refreshment is always available

 Saks…Union Square

COMPUTER SOFTWARE
With Silicon Valley less than an hour's drive away, it should be no surprise that San Francisco is a good place to buy computer equipment. Centrally located suppliers include **CompUSA** (750 Market Street; tel: 415/391-9778) and **Apple Store San Francisco** (1 Stockton Street; tel: 415/392-0202).

Shopping

From the sleek and sophisticated department stores of Union Square to the sometimes wacky stores of Haight-Ashbury, San Francisco has plenty to offer the discerning and adventurous shopper. Partly because San Franciscans like to cultivate a close relationship with their favorite retailer and partly because the tight-packed city has no spare room, the vast impersonal shopping malls common elsewhere around the country are rarely found here.

Union Square shopping While one-of-a-kind stores may be very much in keeping with its character, San Francisco also has its share of those mid-20th-century shrines to consumerism, department stores. Four of the leading names have outlets within a well-filled wallet's throw of Union Square.

An enormous branch of **Macy's** takes up the entire length of one block, imposing itself along the south side of Union Square and stocking virtually everything you can think of. There are seven floors of women's fashions, perfumes and cosmetics, as well as myriad home furnishings and kitchen items. Across Stockton Street is a menswear department, children's clothing and the latest electronic appliances, gadgets and gizmos, plus an extensive range of luggage for all those who prefer to travel heavy.

Macy's built a formidable reputation by putting dependable, good-quality merchandise within the budget of middle-income Americans. By contrast, it is expensive evening wear for those with important functions to attend that fills the racks of **Neiman Marcus** (150 Stockton Street), where several other sections are devoted to fine china and dazzling (and dazzlingly expensive) jewelry.

Department store aficionados will need no encouragement to continue round the corner to **Saks Fifth Avenue** (384 Post Street). Compared to its neighborhood rivals, the casual browser might find Sak's rather short on flair and imagination.

Near Union Square Any money left over after scouring the Union Square department stores will quickly be gobbled up along nearby Maiden Lane. This cobbled street is lined with stylish boutiques, such as **Chanel** (number 155), where three floors are filled with the French company's finest products, and **Candelier** (number 33), with a remarkable stock of candles and candelabras in weird and wonderful forms. Seekers after ethnic art should venture inside the architecturally striking (see page 116) **Folk Art International** (number 140).

Close by, **Gump's** (135 Post Street) has forged an unassailable reputation as a home of fine china, crystal and world-class pearls—all sold at world-class prices—and, by San Francisco standards, has been in business forever (since 1861). A more recent arrival equally well thought of by those who are financially secure and have traditional taste, is **Polo-Ralph Lauren** (90 Post Street).

If the stores in and around Union Square only whet your appetite for even more shopping, gather up all your credit cards and head for **Nordstrom** in the San Francisco Shopping Centre (865 Market Street). After riding the spiraling escalators, you will find yourself amid a colossal assortment of men's and women's fashions. If you cannot find shoes to your liking here, you probably never will—Nordstrom's stocks more than 100,000 pairs.

Fisherman's Wharf San Francisco's tackiest array of tourist trinkets—garish T-shirts, souvenir mugs, toy cable cars and worse—fills the stores lining Jefferson Street in Fisherman's Wharf. In the same area, however, are four shopping complexes which may not promise bargains, but do offer a varied selection of merchandise a cut above the usual neighborhood junk: Pier 39, The Cannery, Ghirardelli Square (see page 226) and The Anchorage (see panel, page 226).

Lining **Pier 39**'s wooden walkways is a large complex of intriguing specialty stores. Among them, **Krazy Kaps**, with a wide variety of hats, and the **Marine Mammal Center**, with clothing, toys and books relating to marine mammals. If its movie memorabilia you're craving,

Completed in 1982, the three-level Crocker Galleria is a stylish shopping mall squeezed into the heart of the busy Financial District. Its vaulted glass roof allows sunlight to reach the popular first-floor plaza and provides views of surrounding high-rises

A PIECE OF JAPAN
Less than a mile from boisterous Haight Street are the far quieter environs of Japantown. As you would expect, the local stores are well stocked with everything from kimonos to rice cookers. There are also a number of outlets for quality Japanese arts and crafts: To find them, cruise the shops of Japan Center (on Post Street) and continue to Nihonmachi Mall, across Post Street.

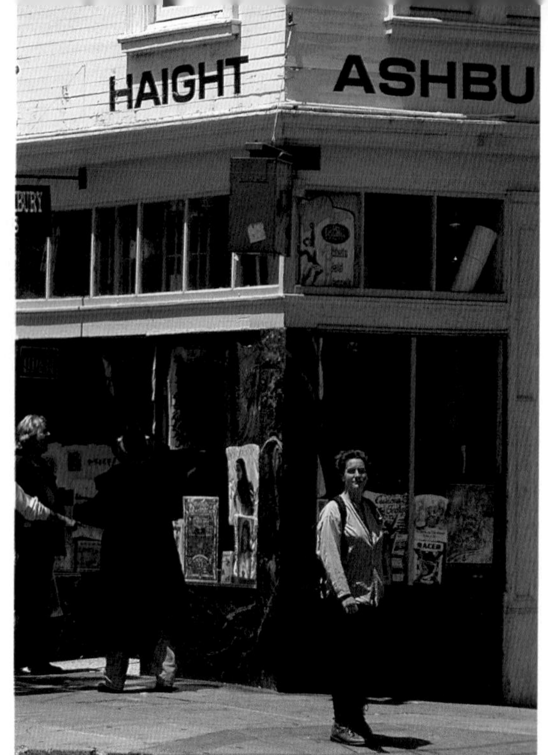

San Francisco T-shirts come in many forms, from the typical tourist versions of Fisherman's Wharf to the neo-psychedelic specialties of Haight Street

Hollywood USA will oblige, while **Only In San Francisco** carries plenty of local mainstream souvenirs.

The Cannery (2801 Leavenworth Street) offers everything from the well-made Native American crafts and eye-catching jewelry of the **Kachina Gallery** to the Slavic curiosities of **Russian Treasure**, a store piled high with intricate lacquerwork boxes, woolen shawls and scores of the inevitable stacking dolls from East Europe.

In what was once a chocolate factory, **Ghirardelli Square** (900 Northpoint) provides more outlets for artistic creations from near and far. **Beastro by the Bay**, in business for almost a decade, is worth a peek for pet-lovers. Meanwhile, **Operetta** boasts original gift items from Italy.

THE ANCHORAGE
With a bright, nautical theme and 50 stores, The Anchorage in Fisherman's Wharf's is located directly across Leavenworth Street from The Cannery. The fire-eaters, jugglers and clowns who regularly perform in its courtyard are likely to have at least as much appeal as the stores, but if you want to get your Christmas paraphernalia early, the Incredible Christmas Store has just what you might need and is open all year round.

Financial District deals The brokers of the Financial District put their platinum cards to the test in the expensive stores found around the elegant **Crocker Galleria** (bordered by Sutter, Post, Kearny and Montgomery streets). The Galleria's three tiers of walkways, lined with tables and benches, wind up to a pleasant rooftop garden. On the way, **The Polo Store** is the city's second outlet for Ralph Lauren's elegant clothing; quality menswear also fills **Fil à Fil**.

For women, **Gianni Versace** offers first-class Italian fashions, while **Aricie Lingerie De Marque**, **Versus Gianni Versace**, **Lìolà** and **Nicole Miller** stock other tempting threads. For jewelry and timepieces, there is **Conway Jewelers** and **Ravits Watches and Clocks**, and unusual stationery and greeting cards can be found at **Cardology** and **Paper-Mania**. For accessories and sunglasses, head to **AMA Accessori**.

Purchasing opportunities are more varied and less expense-account oriented at **The Embarcadero Center**, on the Financial District's eastern edge (see page 81). Look for **Bare Escentuals,** which sells divinely decadent bath oils and lotions, and popular chain stores like **Ann Taylor**, **Banana Republic** and **Williams Sonoma**.

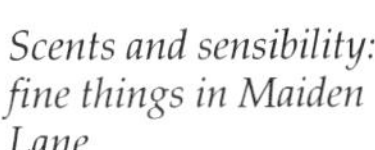

Scents and sensibility: fine things in Maiden Lane

Discount shopping If serious shopping threatens to burn a hole through your budget, remember that numerous factory-outlet stores can be found in SoMa. Many leading design companies discount their damaged or discontinued lines here, and retail operations pass on some of the savings from the area's low rents. Prices are usually 20–50 percent less than in regular stores. **Esprit** (499 Illinois Street) features brightly colored California casualwear; ladies on the look-out for simple but stylish clothing should investigate **ISDA & Co**. (29 South Park), the discount outlet of a nationally known designer. For designer labels like Armani and Calvin Klein at delightful prices, visit nearby **Jeremy's** (2 South Park). If you run short of shopping ideas, a cruise around the multistore outlet **Yerba Buena Square** (899 Howard Street) might provide inspiration. Here, the **Burlington Coat Factory** sells coats and lots more clothing for men, women and children over three floors. At the Six Sixty Center (660 Third Street), **Tower Records** offers discounted CDs, records and books. For sports gear relating to every sport you can think of, from running to snowboarding, stop by the hard-to-find **Sports Basement** (1301 Sixth Street; tel: 415/437-1011), a vast warehouse of discounted merchandise.

THRIFT-STORE SHOPPING
Dedicated rummagers will pass many happy hours sorting through the odds and ends—from clothes, books and ornaments to 1950s boomerang coffee tables and tube-filled TVs—which can be found gathering dust in the city's many thrift stores. Every neighborhood has at least a few, their profits usually benefiting charities or the local church. To find the nearest thrift store, consult the Yellow Pages.

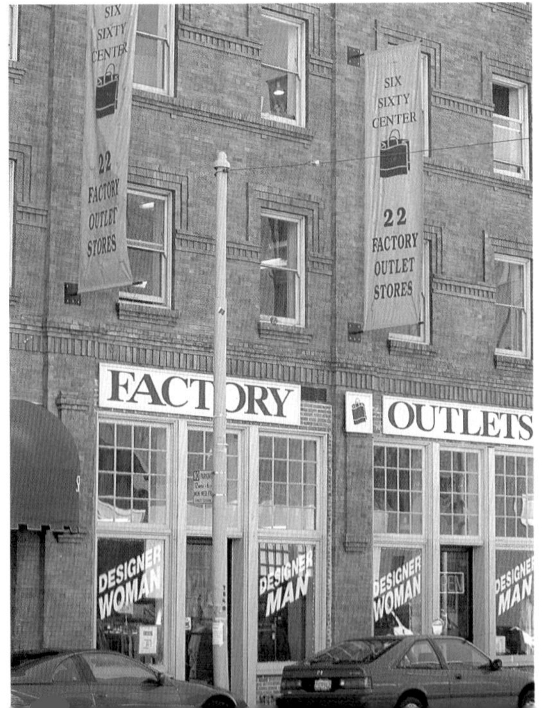

Discount shopping: a factory outlet store

FILLMORE STREET SHOPPING
The upscale stores lining Fillmore Street between Sutter and Washington streets are good for browsing, even if the prices are often prohibitive. Most sell items for the home, such as **Nest** (number 2300) promising "rustic adornments for homes of taste," **Cedanna** (number 1919) with creative and inventive ornaments and **Zinc Details** (number 1905) with sharply contemporary furnishings. By contrast, **Nile Trading Co.** (number 1856) carries African ethnographic art, textiles and basketry and **Cottage Industry** (number 2326) is packed with comparatively inexpensive decorative oddments.

Haight Street With its eccentric used-clothing stores, book and record outlets, funky cafés and restaurants and skateboarding neo-hippies, Haight-Ashbury's Haight Street is rapidly becoming one of the city's most entertaining and innovative shopping strips. Bellbottom pants, felt hats, lacy dresses and evening dresses last worn in earnest during the 1920s are all liable to appear among the racks of vintage, bizarre or just inexpensive apparel in the never-boring used-clothing stores.

These start up and close down with alarming frequency, but the most firmly established include **Aardvark's** (number 1501), which has a very large stock; **Held Over** (number 1543), strong on 1950s sartorial favorites; **Dharma** (number 1600), specializing in Third World clothing; **Buffalo Exchange** (number 1555) with a glorious jumble of ageless threads; and **Happy Trails American Vintage** (number 1615) has 1950s and 1960s clothing alongside household accessories from the same period.

Also on or close to Haight Street, **Revival of the Fittest** (1701 Haight Street) recycles and re-creates crazy American household knickknacks of the 1940s and 1950s; **Piedmont Boutique** (1452 Haight Street) stocks wigs, fetish wear, costumes and accessories; **Gargoyle** (1310 Haight Street) sells an array of beads from around the globe; and the giant-sized rolling papers and water-pipes of **Pipe Dreams** (1376 Haight Street) recall local enthusiasms during Haight-Ashbury's hippie times.

Music fans in pursuit of vinyl and CDs are also well served by Haight Street. Hours of fun can be had

Shop till you drop at the countless establishments gathered under one roof at the San Francisco Shopping Centre

rummaging through the used discs of **Amoeba Music** (number 1855). For jazz and soul sounds, old and new, head for **Groove Merchant** (687 Haight Street).

Union Street In contrast to the wild wares of Haight Street, the 1700–2100 blocks of Pacific Heights' Union Street provide a happy hunting ground for fine—and often very expensive—antiques and curios and for chic clothing.

Eye-catching decorative glasswork is the stock-in-trade of **The Enchanted Crystal** (number 1895), and that long search for a Sino-Tibetan gilt-wood Buddha figure might be ended by a peek inside **A Touch of Asia** (number 1784). Meanwhile, Chinese silk paintings and Japanese *netsuke* (wooden, bone or ivory carved toggles) are among the exquisite merchandise of **Fumuki Fine Asian Arts** (number 2001).

For women's clothing, swing by **Girlfriends** (number 1824), a boutique that's designed to feel like a friend's cozy studio apartment. You'll find casual designer clothes, plus plenty of T-shirts and mugs with the playful store logo. If you're willing to spend as much on your kids as you spend on yourself, drop into **Mudpie** (number 1694) and peruse the selection of adorable clothes and toys.

Accessory-seekers won't pass up **Stuart Moore** (number 1898), a gallery of European-style designer jewelry. Simple, minimalist pieces are in platinum and 18-karat gold only. In the same block, **Jest Jewels** (number 1869) has toe rings, earrings, hats and other accessories that are far less damaging to the pocketbook.

More antiques In the unlikely event of antique-seekers' thirst not being quenched on Union Street, a trip to the historic brick buildings near Jackson Square is in order. In close proximity to the corner of Montgomery and Jackson streets, a score of upscale antique galleries are packed to the rafters with 18th- and 19th-century European dressing tables, armchairs, chests of drawers, Turkish rugs and fine Asian tapestries and decorative pieces. Little of this will fit comfortably into a traveler's suitcase, but most items can be shipped anywhere in the world.

Chinatown enterprise Be it bird's-nest soup or colorful kites, Chinatown thrives on buying and selling, and more shops than you can shake a chopstick at line the neighborhood's frenetic streets.

Local Chinese buy their essential supplies along Stockton Street and the district's many alleyways. Visitor attention focuses on Grant Avenue and bustling emporiums that stock anything and everything Asian—from sofa-sized hunks of pottery to intricate wood-carved ornaments. Silks, jade and porcelain are for sale at competitive prices all along Grant Avenue; *netsuke* (if far from great quality) are another bargain buy.

Chinatown is one of the few places in San Francisco where tea is more highly revered than coffee. Many of the fine teas imported by **Natural Tea Shop** (1199 Stockton Street) can be sampled at the counter before your selection is purchased—you could even buy a complete Chinese tea service.

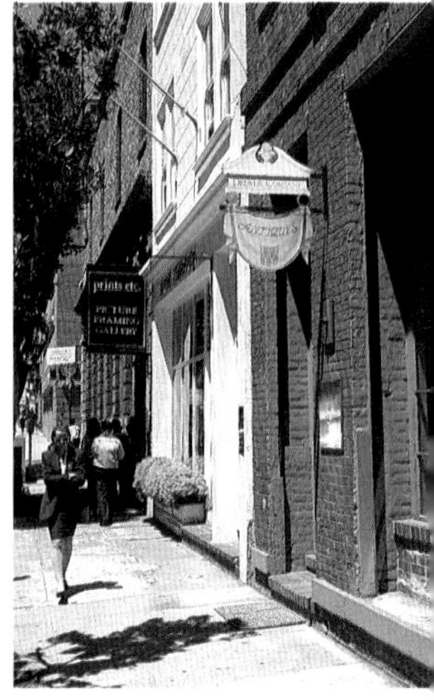

Jackson Square has some of the city's oldest buildings, many of them now housing antique stores

CHINATOWN SIDE STREETS

The reward for venturing along Chinatown's side streets is a plethora of unusual and less tourist-oriented stores. For example, at **Clarion Music** (entrance on Waverly Place, off Sacramento Street) is a wondrous gathering of Asian musical instruments ranging from Burmese temple bells to Chinese egg rattles.

Chinatown shops

BOOKS ACROSS THE BAY
Insatiable bibliophiles will find plenty of stimulation along Berkeley's Telegraph Avenue, where wide-ranging new titles are found at **Cody's Books** (number 2454), and vast numbers of used volumes fill the shelves of **Moe's** (number 2476) and **Shakespeare & Co.** (number 2499). A ferry to Oakland's Jack London waterfront leaves you just steps from a huge link in the Barnes & Noble chain.

Should something stranger and stronger be required, drop into one of the area's many herbalists, such as **Chung Chou City** (900 Stockton Street) or **Fun Yun Wah** (868 Jackson Street), where the cure for what ails you is certain to be in stock.

For shoppers looking for nothing more exotic than postcards, Chinatown is still the place to be; many street stalls offer ten cards for $1.

Bookstores San Francisco is a city of bookworms and has plenty of welcoming bookstores in which to browse, buy, and even hear acclaimed authors reading their work. Chain stores such as **Borders** and **Barnes & Noble** are always stocked with the latest titles, often at reduced prices, but specialty bookstores are where the city excels. Many of these also carry a wide range of overseas newspapers and magazines.

Almost every neighborhood has at least one excellent bookstore. Those worth going out of your way to visit include **The Booksmith** (1644 Haight Street) and **A Clean Well-Lighted Place for Books** (601 Van Ness Avenue), both with a broad range of recently published fiction and nonfiction; **City Lights** (261 Columbus Avenue), which features writings by and about the Beat generation, as well as a wide range of general titles; **William Stout Books** (804 Montgomery Street) packed with books on architecture and design; and **A Different Light** (489 Castro Street), the premier spot for books of gay and lesbian interest.

Anyone stopping in San Francisco on the way to California's great outdoors will find plenty to inform and inspire them at the **Sierra Club Bookstore** (tel: 415/977-5600), where the publications of the state's long-serving environmental protection organization describe the Far West's wildest areas with informative texts and stunning photographs.

Should you be stumped for what to read about next, weave through the many miles of shelving inside **McDonald's Bookshop** (48 Turk Street), cluttered with everything from vintage *TV Guides* to esoteric occult tomes. Another tremendous stock of used volumes awaits your gaze at **Forever After** (1475 Haight Street), while some of the best used-book bargains turn up at the **Friends of San Francisco Library** outlet at Fort Mason Center (see page 96).

Browsing on Clement Street

Dizzying neon on North Beach, for many years a center for city nightlife at the junction of Broadway and Columbus Avenue

Nightlife

Be it ballet or the blues, San Francisco's nightlife has something to satisfy all tastes and suit all pocketbooks. Even more impressively, the city's diverse range of evening entertainment is on a surprisingly small and friendly scale. Visitors looking for after-hours enjoyment are more likely to be welcomed than treated like gate-crashers at someone else's party (as is often the case in many other major American cities).

Everything from comedy clubs to avant-garde dance is included in the nightlife listings carried by the free weekly papers, the *San Francisco Bay Guardian* and *SF Weekly*. The pink Datebook section of Sunday's *San Francisco Chronicle* also has comprehensive nightlife information for the upcoming week.

Boasting the earliest municipally run opera company in the US and the world's first (and possibly only) lesbian and gay chorus, a vibrant and varied cultural diet is an integral part of San Francisco's nightlife. The major events—socially, none are more spectacular than the opening night of the opera season in September—take place in the buildings of the Civic Center's Performing Arts Complex. More esoteric presentations—such as avant-garde music and dance shows—can be found in small and medium venues dotted about the city.

TICKETS
The major ticket agency, Tickets.com, has numerous outlets including Supermail, at Four Embarcadero Center and 24 Willie Mays Plaza (Pacific Bell Park). For a credit-card booking or recorded information, tel: 510/762-2277. TIX offers half-price day-of-performance tickets (cash only) for Bay Area arts events from a booth on the Stockton Street side of Union Square (tel: 415/433-7827).

Classical music The San Francisco Symphony performs at the Louise M. Davies Symphony Hall (201 Van Ness Avenue; tel: 415/864-6000), frequently joined in its main September-to-May season by internationally acclaimed guest conductors and soloists. The summertime program includes a Beethoven Festival and a Pops series. The symphony's more unusual activities have included a collaboration with rock band Mettalica, featuring songs from the band's album *Kill 'Em All*. Tickets start at around $20, and quickly sell out for top-name appearances.

The Civic Center's **Herbst Theater** (the auditorium of the Veterans Building, 401 Van Ness Avenue; box office,

Conducting the symphony

The San Francisco Symphony, rehearsing at the Louise M. Davies Symphony Hall, a venue that opened in 1980 at a cost of $33 million and underwent a $10-million acoustic refit in 1992

(tel: 415/392-4400) enjoys an annual season of chamber music, recitals, dance and jazz, organized by **San Francisco Performances** (tel: 415/398-6449), and often starring internationally recognized performers. Other events under the same umbrella take place at the Center For The Arts and Louise M. Davies Symphony Hall.

From September to April, the Herbst Theater also hosts the **Philharmonia Baroque Orchestra** (tel: 415/252-1288), performing works by the great composers of the 17th and 18th centuries. Under the name of **Cal Performances**, the University of California at Berkeley organizes music, dance and performance art events throughout the academic year. Nearly all the events take place across the bay in Berkeley, the main venue for these concerts being Zellerbach Hall, on Bancroft Avenue (tel: 510/642-9988).

Away from the mainstream Those in search of new auditory experiences should try **Audium** (1616 Bush Street; tel: 415/771-1616), a music installation where pulsating tones from 136 speakers are experienced in total darkness over a period of 75 minutes. Meanwhile, the **Gay Men's Chorus of San Francisco** (tel: 415/865-3650; www.sfgmc.org) can be found at various venues around the city, most often giving concerts over holiday periods.

Opera The highly regarded **San Francisco Opera** has a star-studded season of performances that runs from September to December at the War Memorial Opera House (301 Van Ness Avenue; tel: 415/864-3330). Tickets, which may cost anything between $25 and $150, are snapped up by eager fans by mail order months in advance. However, there are usually a limited number of low-price standing tickets which go on sale at the box office of the Opera House two hours before a

The San Francisco Opera, founded in 1919, strengthened San Francisco's reputation as the opera capital of the American West. In 1932, it became the first company in the US to have a municipally run Opera House

Home of the hits: Geary Street theater district

STERN GROVE SUNDAYS
On Sunday afternoons from June through August, a eucalyptus-shrouded natural amphitheater at Stern Grove (off Sloat Boulevard at 19th Avenue; tel: 415/252-6252; www.sterngrove.org) offers a luxuriant setting for free concerts and performances. These vary from classical music and opera to jazz and modern dance; all performances start at 2pm.

performance begins. Even for these, there is strong demand; arrive early to be sure of a place in line.

Any opera buffs visiting out of season might well be content with the enjoyable **Pocket Opera** (tel: 415/972-8930), a small professional company which, from February to June, stages informal interpretations of comic operas in one of the city's smaller theaters (the specific venue varies from year to year).

A dress rehearsal of the San Francisco Ballet's Sleeping Beauty

Dance The **San Francisco Ballet** (tel: 415/865-2000) enjoys a reputation as one of the country's most accomplished and exciting companies, regularly adding striking new works to the repertoire of favorites which fills its February-to-May season. Performances take place at the War Memorial Opera House, and tickets are priced from $10 to $120. The company returns for Christmas performances of the *Nutcracker*, each presentation promising to be more spectacular than the previous year's.

Unfairly in the shadow of the better-known company just across the bay, the **Oakland Ballet** (tel: 510/452-9288) regularly presents a program of innovative modern works—as well as established classics—at the Paramount Theater (2025 Broadway).

Many small modern-dance companies are based in the city and they, and other touring dance companies, can frequently be found at one of the following venues: **Center for the Arts** (Yerba Buena Gardens;

Will it never end? Beach Blanket Babylon

BEACH BLANKET BABYLON

Now the longest-running theatrical show in US history, *Beach Blanket Babylon* began in 1971 and, in various forms, this witty and raucous high-camp revue—tracing the unlikely adventures of Snow White—has been packing them in ever since. Plays nightly except Monday and Tuesdays at Club Fugazi, 678 Green Street (tel: 415/421-4222); reservations essential. Ticket prices $25–$75; patrons must be over 21 for nighttime performances.

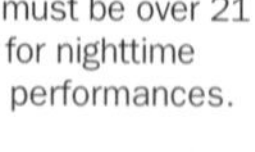

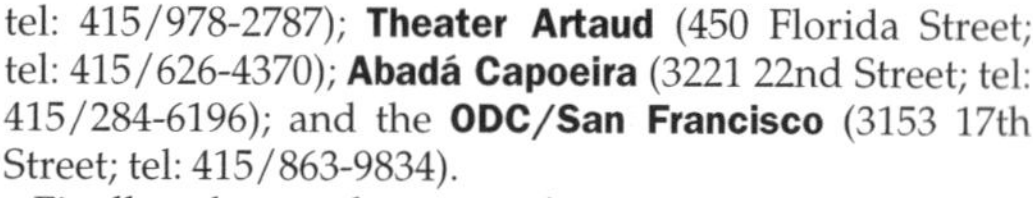

tel: 415/978-2787); **Theater Artaud** (450 Florida Street; tel: 415/626-4370); **Abadá Capoeira** (3221 22nd Street; tel: 415/284-6196); and the **ODC/San Francisco** (3153 17th Street; tel: 415/863-9834).

Finally, the students at the **San Francisco State University Department of Dance** periodically demonstrate their skills on the university campus (1600 Holloway Avenue; tel: 415/338-2062).

Theater Many visitors are perfectly happy to explore no more of San Francisco's nightlife than the commercial theaters grouped together just west of Union Square. Several of these were erected during the 1920s as homes for vaudeville, and the best of them have retained—and maintained—their lavish fixtures and fittings. The best seats at a blockbusting show can be around $80 or more, but most seats are $20–$50. For smaller theaters, expect to spend less.

A trio of 1920s stalwarts, able to seat audiences of up to 2,000, are also the first West Coast stops for the hottest plays and musicals arriving from New York's Broadway. On any particular night (or the Wednesday and weekend matinees), the **Curran Theater** (445 Geary Street; tel: 415/551-2000); the **Golden Gate Theater** (1 Taylor Street; tel: 415/551-2000); and **The Orpheum** (1192 Market Street; tel: 415/551-2000) are all likely to be staging hit plays and musicals.

For theater-goers for whom the *oeuvre* of Andrew Lloyd Webber holds less appeal than that of Molière or George Bernard Shaw, the much respected **American Conservatory Theater** (or ACT; tel: 415/749-2228) can be relied upon to please. ACT's main base is the **Geary Theater** (415 Geary Street; tel: 415/749-2228). Across the bay, the **Berkeley Repertory Theater** (2025 Addison Street; tel: 510/647-2949) has a reputation for classy drama, be it modern plays or old chestnuts.

A mix of mainstream and experimental drama is the staple fare of the medium-sized **Marines**

Memorial Theater (609 Sutter Street; tel: 415/771-6900); **Theater on the Square** (450 Post Street; tel: 415/433-9500); **Lorraine Hansberry Theater** (620 Sutter Street; tel: 415/474-8800); and the **New Conservatory Theater Center** (25 Van Ness Avenue; tel: 415/861-8972). Premieres—ranging from children's plays to political satire—are the forte of the intimate **Magic Theatre** (Building D, Fort Mason Center; tel: 415/441-8822).

Venues for innovative and challenging—and sometimes just pretentious—drama include the **Exit Theater** (156 Eddy Street; tel: 415/673-3847); **Venue 9** (252 Ninth Street; tel: 415/920-2223); **Noh Space** (2840 Mariposa Street; tel: 415/621-7978); and **The Marsh** (1062 Valencia Street; tel: 415/826-5750). Student productions of standard and experimental drama take place at the **Studio Theater** (Creative Arts Building, SFSU Campus, 1600 Holloway Avenue; tel: 415/338-2467).

The city also serves as the base for America's first gay and lesbian company, **Theater Rhinoceros** (2926 16th Street; tel: 415/861-5079), which presents a diverse program, often exploring social attitudes and behavior.

Comedy In the early 1960s, Mort Sahl and Lenny Bruce were among the stand-up comics who, appearing at San Francisco comedy clubs and encouraged by the city's liberal and appreciative audiences, began to change the face of American comedy. Even today, the San Francisco audience is one which appeals to new talents and established names alike, both being fairly easy to find in several dozen comedy clubs.

Most clubs have a cover charge of around $10 (sometimes with a minimum charge of two drinks) depending on the night of the week and on the stature of the evening's star performer.

The major venue is the plush and comfortable **Cobb's** (915 Columbus Avenue; tel: 415/928-4320), which regularly features major names, though its

SHAKESPEARE IN THE PARK
During weekends in September, the Shakespeare in the Park Festival stages open-air performances of several of the Bard's plays for free, close to the site of the Conservatory of Flowers in Golden Gate Park. For details, tel: 415/865-4434.

Always good for a laugh: San Francisco comedy clubs

Stand-up comedy

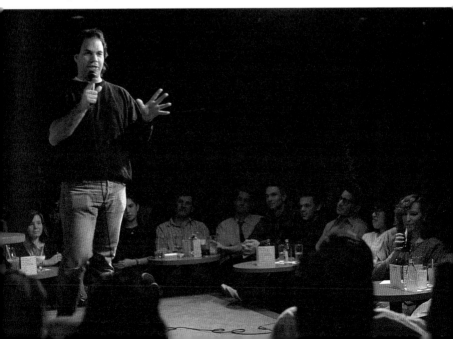

FILM FESTIVALS
The biggest of dozens of film festivals which take place in the city each year, the San Francisco International Film Festival brings new and innovative works from international directors to selected movie theaters each spring. Another major movie event is the International Lesbian and Gay Film Festival, featuring new films of gay and lesbian interest from around the world each June; main screenings take place at the Castro Theater.

strongly tourist crowd can render it short on atmosphere. A better bet might be the **Punch Line** (444 Battery Street; tel: 415/397-7573) or the occasional comedy nights (call for details—not on a regular schedule) at **Café Du Nord** (2170 Market Street; tel: 415/861-5016).

Movies On any given day, San Francisco's movie theaters sport a tempting mix of first-run, cult and even a few foreign-language films in venues ranging from multiscreen complexes to tiny arthouse theaters. The pick of the multiscreen complexes include the **AMC Kabuki 8** (corner of Post and Fillmore streets; tel: 415/931-9800); **AMC** (1000 Van Ness Avenue tel: 415/922-4262); and the **Metreon** (corner of Fourth and Mission streets; tel: 415/369-6000) where the latest offerings from Hollywood tend to make their first local appearance.

When quality of setting matters, however, the discerning movie buff watches first-run fare at one of the following: the **Clay** (2261 Fillmore Street; tel: 415/267-4893), built in 1910; or the Th**e Balboa** (3630 Balboa Street; tel: 415/221-8184), the city's only surviving 1920s art deco movie theater.

Cult classics, foreign-language and arthouse films—often featured in mini-seasons—are the viewing pleasure at the **Castro Theatre** (429 Castro Street; tel: 415/621-6120); the **Roxie** (3117 16th Street; tel: 415/863-1087); and the **Red Vic** (1727 Haight Street; tel: 415/668-3994). For new and revived movies, go to the **Landmark Embarcadero** (in the Embarcadero Center shopping complex; tel: 415/267-4893; the **Lumiere** (on the corner of California and Polk streets; tel: 415/352-0810) and

Specialist seasons and cult movies prevail at the Castro Theatre

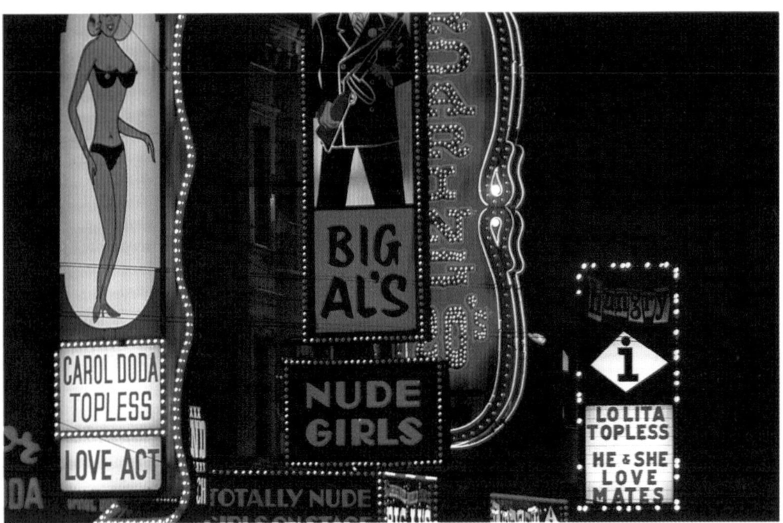

Opera Plaza (on the corner of Van Ness and Golden Gate avenues).

Nightclubs Unlike their ultraglamorous counterparts in New York or Los Angeles, San Francisco's nightclubs are rarely places where you will find major celebrities dodging *paparazzi* as they sprint between limo and club entrance. The city does have a few chic and sophisticated discotheques where the rich and the beautiful glide across the dance floor with consummate ease, but much more in keeping with its character are the dozens of clubs pulsating to contemporary sounds, often found in the converted warehouses of SoMa.

As in cities the world over, the nightclub scene is constantly changing. The suggestions below are simply the most interesting of those most likely to be still in operation at the time of your visit.

To sample the nightlife adventurous San Franciscans head to the China Basin area and **Sno-Drift**, a ski lodge meets swank atmosphere with a lively dance floor and live DJs (1830 Third Street; tel: 415/431-4766); the discerning San Francisco sophisticate-about-town stops for a drink at the **Redwood Room** (495 Geary, inside Clift; tel: 415/775-4700) where the venerable redwood paneling is now dotted with slowly morphing digital video "paintings."

Other likely spots for the well-heeled night-owl are **Rosewood** (732 Broadway; tel: 415/951-4886); **Matrix Fillmore** (3138 Fillmore Street; tel: 415/563-4180); the **Redwood Room** and **Harry Denton's Starlite Room** (see page 84). Should you be more intent on simply dancing your legs off, try the highly energetic and spacious dance floor at **Ruby Skye** (420 Mason Street; tel: 415/693-0777).

A more recent addition to the fast-changing alternative club circuit is **111 Minna Gallery** (111 Minna Street; tel: 415/974-1719), a gallery by day and bar and dance club by night. Other firmly established favorites are the **DNA Lounge** (375 Eleventh Street; tel: 415/626-1409), where dressed-in-black twentysomethings show up for

North Beach's gaudy signs give a misleading impression of the neighborhood, which most San Franciscans visit at night for its excellent Italian restaurants and cafés

GUIDED NIGHTCLUBBING

If deciding where to strut your stuff in the San Francisco night proves impossible, you might relish the assistance of Three Babes and a Bus (tel: 800/414-0158), a company which will carry you—and a busload of similarly indecisive individuals—on a four-hour tour of some of the city's hottest nightspots (Saturdays only). For around $35 you get admission and special ID allowing you to walk right in, even when people are lined up outside.

BRAINWASH
If only for the novelty, show up at one of the early evening rock music shows at Brainwash (1122 Folsom Street; tel: 415/861-FOOD). This combined bar and laundromat offers the chance to drink, eat, and tap your foot to live sounds as your dirtiest duds are regaining their whiteness. Bringing a sackful of dirty laundry is not compulsory, however.

early-evening live bands and dance till dawn to goth, indie and industrial sounds, with occasional House, reggae and 1970s nights.

Other clubs with diverse nights include **26 Mix** (3024 Mission Street; tel: 415/826-7378); **Justice League** (628 Divisadero Street; tel: 415/289-2038); **330 Ritch Street** (330 Ritch Street between 3rd and 4th streets; tel: 415/541-9574); and **Sound Factory** (525 Harrison Street; tel: 415/339-8686).

More daring fare is provided by the **Paradise Lounge** (1501 Folsom Street; tel: 415/621-1912), usually featuring live bands first and then following them with a hit-or-miss conglomeration of multimedia happenings—poetry readings, body painting and tattooing, throbbing disco—liable to be found as you make your way through its three floors.

With many gay and lesbian residents enjoying open and assertive lifestyles, visitors might expect San Francisco's gay and lesbian nightclubs to be wild, no-holds-barred affairs. In fact, perhaps because the need to get together and let off steam is less great than in more oppressive urban centers, the city's gay and lesbian nightlife is often surprisingly restrained—which is not to say there is not a lot to please hedonistic gay and lesbian travelers.

Of the predominantly gay male bars and clubs, **The Stud** (399 Ninth Street; tel: 415/252-7883) has long been a favored watering hole, both to mellow out with a drink on a quiet weeknight, and to start an evening of urgent clubbing on the much busier Fridays and Saturdays. The **Metro** (3600 Sixteenth Street; tel: 415/703-9750) has a beckoning balcony bar and famed margaritas.

Twin Peaks Tavern (also known as the Glass Coffin, at 401 Castro Street; tel: 415/864-9470) has an older clientele, and was the first gay bar in the US with windows.

One of the casinos at Stateline: gambling is not legal in California, but San Franciscans who cannot resist the lure only need to cross over the border into Nevada

The historic Italian-American Club Fugazi makes an unlikely home for the wacky Beach Blanket Babylon

SAN FRANCISCO JAZZ FESTIVAL

For two to three weeks beginning in late October, the annual San Francisco Jazz Festival finds the top local names and many overseas guests appearing at venues the length and breadth of the city. Tickets for the biggest shows are snapped up early, but many are available for other nights during the festival through the usual agencies; for details tel: 415/398-5655. For tickets, tel: 415/788-7353.

Country & Western fans might be more at home amid the plaid shirts and cowboy boots of **Rawhide** (280 Seventh Street; tel: 415/621-1197), which not only spins C&W discs but provides free country-dancing lessons.

Many of the city's nightclubs have a gay or lesbian night once a week, but the top gay and lesbian nightclubs are **End-Up** (401 Sixth Street; tel: 415/357-0827) and **El Rio** (3158 Mission Street; tel: 415/282-3325), an often riotous disco hosting differently themed nights through the week.

Another place for lesbians to socialize is **The Café** (2367 Market Street; tel: 415/861-3846), with two large bars, pool tables, a smoking dance floor and a patio.

Jazz In the 1940s and 1950s, San Francisco was one of the hottest spots for live jazz in the country, and the sweaty North Beach cellar clubs became particularly revered by bebop enthusiasts. These days, a jazz venue can be anything from a hotel lounge where guests are serenaded by a pianist tickling the ivories in a vaguely jazzlike manner, to tiny bars where knowledgeable jazz buffs and scruffily dressed art students flip out to the latest uneasily defined jazz genres such as jazz-rap, acid-jazz and hip-bop.

The majority of jazz venues, however, are the well-equipped backrooms of restaurants, where a bite to eat often (but not necessarily) precedes an evening

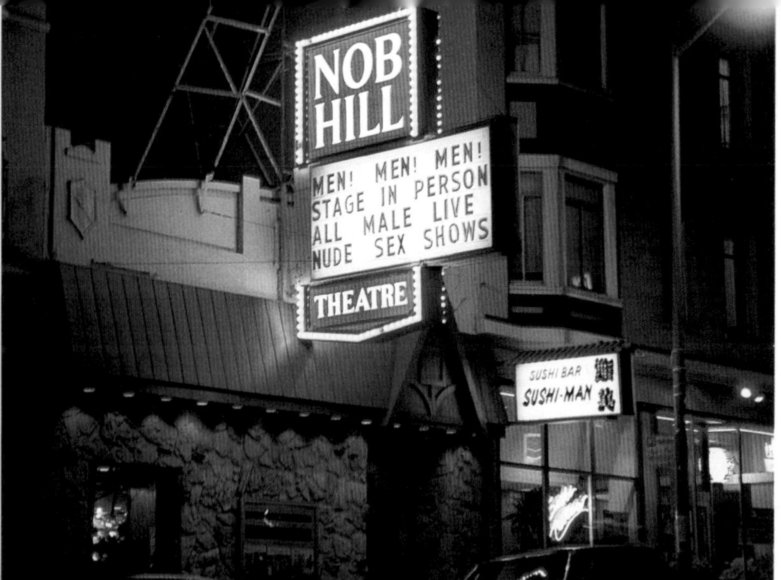

Baring all…

listening to accomplished mainstream jazz. At any of the following, expect a cover charge of $5–$15 depending on the night of the week and the status of the performer; on occasion there may also be a minimum drink charge.

The more enjoyable and dependable of the medium-sized jazz venues are **Pier 23 Café** (Pier 23, Embarcadero; tel: 415/362-5125), an upbeat waterside eatery which also features mambo and reggae bands several times a week; **Slim's** (333 Eleventh Street; tel: 415/255-0333), a small and pricey club which mixes jazz acts with rock and R&B; **Up & Down Club** (1151 Folsom Street; tel: 415/626-2388), a great spot for catching the best of the up-and-coming acts; **Rasselas** (1534 Fillmore Street; tel: 415/567-5010), a jazz and supper club serving Ethiopian food and presenting some of the better local combos; **Jazz at Pearl's** (256 Columbus Avenue; tel: 415/291-8255), showcasing many of the city's top-rated performers; and **Café Du Nord** (2170 Market Street; tel: 415/861-5016), probably the likeliest venue to catch the hottest fresh talents.

Among the smaller venues which give an airing to jazz and blues, try **Boom Boom Room** (1601 Fillmore Street; tel: 415/673-8000) and **Elbo Room** (647 Valencia Street; tel: 415/552-7788). The East Bay is home to **Yoshi's** (510 Embarcadero West, at Jack London Square; tel: 510/238-9200), one of the top-notch jazz spots in the country.

SAN FRANCISCO BLUES FESTIVAL

Over a weekend each September, the San Francisco Blues Festival brings some of the genre's leading exponents to day-long open-air concerts at Great Meadow, near Fort Mason Center (see page 96), with a Friday afternoon curtain-raising concert taking place at Justin Herman Plaza, next to the Embarcadero Center (see page 81). For ticket details, tel: 415/979-5588.

Rock music San Francisco gets its share of national and international rock acts, with many of the big names playing south of the city at the **Cow Palace** or across the bay at the **Oakland Coliseum**, with tickets available through the major agencies. The largest rock venues in the city are **The Warfield** (982 Market Street; tel: 415/775-7722) and **The Fillmore** (1805 Geary Street; tel: 415/346-6000).

More intimate than the major venues, and better places for putting your finger on the pulse of the local rock scene, are the many neighborhood clubs where exotically named unknown, semi-known and a few almost well-known bands do their thing, sometimes to packed houses, sometimes to an audience of friends. Admission typically ranges from free to $10. The likeliest venues are **Makeout Room** (3225 22nd Street; tel: 415/647-2888); **Bottom of the Hill** (1233 17th Street; tel: 415/621-4455); **DNA Lounge** and **Paradise Lounge**, the last two doubling as lively nightclubs (see pages 237–238) after the bands conclude.

You are more likely to discover no-frills R&B and garage bands at spit-and-sawdust venues such as **The Saloon** (1232 Grant Street; tel: 415/989-7666); **Last Day Saloon** (406 Clement Street; tel: 415/387-6343); and **Grant and Green** (1371 Grant Street; tel: 415/693-9565).

By contrast, some of the area's best blues players can be found in the relatively swanky confines of **Lou's Pier 47** (300 Jefferson Street; tel: 415/771-5687), one of the few reasons locals brave the Fisherman's Wharf tourist crowds.

Poetry It might be the legacy of the Beats or the inspirational qualities of the landscape, but sometimes it seems that everyone in San Francisco is a poet—a feeling compounded by the poetry readings taking place around the city every night.

Poetry Above Paradise (1501 Folsom Street; tel: 415/621-1912) is a poets' reading room operating weekly above the Paradise Lounge nightclub. Other venues with at least a once-weekly poetry night include **Café Du Nord** (see page 240); **Café International** (508 Haight Street; tel: 415/552-7390).

San Francisco's numerous bookstores, particularly **City Lights** (261 Columbus Avenue; tel: 415/362-8193) and **A Clean Well-Lighted Place For Books** (601 Van Ness Avenue; tel: 415/441-6670), frequently offer published poets the opportunity to give public readings from their latest works.

BERKELEY POETRY

Poetry addicts not satisfied by what is on offer in the city might cross the bay to Berkeley, where regular poetry-reading venues include **Black Oak Books** (1491 Shattuck Avenue; tel: 510/486-0698) and the **La Peña Cultural Center** (3105 Shattuck Avenue; tel: 510/849-2568). A likely location to find established poets and prose authors giving readings is **Cody's Books** (2454 Telegraph Avenue; tel: 510/845-7852).

Streamlined sculptures match the contours of the Louise M. Davies Symphony Hall to the rear, a stylish addition to the Civic Center complex

Not an average place

Children's San Francisco

A generous helping of child-friendly museums, wide open spaces and exotic neighborhoods makes San Francisco an enjoyable and rewarding place to explore with children.

The **Metreon** (see panel, page 168), opened in 1999, bills itself as an "entertainment and technology marketplace." This four-story complex, on the corner of Fourth and Mission streets right next to Yerba Buena Gardens, has 15 movie theaters, an IMAX screen and futuristic play zones where you can try activities such as virtual bowling or interactive dancing, as well as shops and restaurants.

With **Zeum** (see page 168), mixing technology with creativity, and **Exploratorium** (see page 82), the city has two of the finest places for discovering and learning about science anywhere in the world.

Interactive computers, which the Exploratorium has by the dozen, are also a feature of the **California Academy of Sciences** (see pages 64–65). Here, though, it is likely to be the huge aquarium, the dolphins and the prehistory exhibits which steal the show for younger children; older ones are more likely to be enthralled by the re-creation of San Francisco earthquakes and the planetarium shows.

Across the bay on the Berkeley campus, the **Lawrence Hall of Science** (see page 61) is smaller and less well-equipped than the Exploratorium but nonetheless has much to inform and entertain among its science-based exhibits and computer quizzes.

Other museums not specifically targeted at children but likely to be much appreciated include the **Cable Car Museum** (page 63), the **Fire Department Museum** (see panel, page 114), the **Wells Fargo History Museum** (page 179), the **Hyde Street Pier Historic Ships** (page 112), the **National Liberty Ship Memorial** and **USS *Pampanito*** (see panel, page 128) of Fisherman's Wharf.

The Exploratorium

Fisherman's Wharf's more commercial attractions,

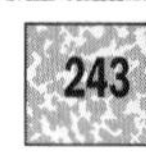

particularly **Ripley's Believe It or Not!** (see page 93), are proven child pleasers, as are the street entertainers who perform along Jefferson Street and the daytime open-air shows at **Ghirardelli Square** (page 93) and **The Cannery** (page 93). While at Fisherman's Wharf, remember to take a look at the colony of sea lions which have taken up residence close to **Pier 39** (see panel, page 92). More sea lions can be seen frolicking around Seal Rocks, at the city's western extremity, just beyond the **Cliff House** (see page 80).

Another promising stop is **Fort Point** (page 96), with its Civil War-uniformed guides and proximity to **Golden Gate Bridge** (page 98), which older children will be itching to walk across. Toddlers may find the ferry ride to **Alcatraz** more enjoyable than exploring the former prison—but young teens developing a taste for the macabre will relish it.

The city may not have the greatest zoo in the world, but young charges are still likely to enjoy a trip to **San Francisco Zoo** (page 162). The biggest and best open space, however, is **Golden Gate Park** (pages 100–103), which has plenty to thrill kids. After a few hours at the **California Academy of Sciences** (pages 64–65), younger children can be introduced to the residents of the buffalo paddock, watch remote-controlled model boats zipping over Spreckels Lake, sit on a purple dragon or ride a restored 1912 carousel. Older ones might prefer a bike ride through the park, or a paddle-boat cruise around Stow Lake.

The **Golden Gate National Recreation Area** (page 99) is ideal territory for a breezy nature walk, which might conclude with a picnic at China or Baker Beach. **Fort Funston** has hang-gliders launching off from its tall cliffs every weekend.

Killer whales perform at Africa USA/Marine World, near Vallejo

BABYSITTING

The majority of hotels can arrange babysitting or can recommend a company providing this service. Among those with established reputations are the American Childcare Service (tel: 415/285-2300), whose sitters can entertain your offspring in a hotel room or escort those over seven on museum visits; and SF Magic Home Services (tel: 415/640-7259), tending tots since 1978.

ALWAYS FREE MUSEUMS
Cable Car Museum (page 63)
Chinese Cultural Center (page 75)
Chinese Historical Society (page 74)
Fire Department Museum (panel, page 114)
Fort Point National Historic Site (page 96)
Museum of Money of the American West (page 127)
National Maritime Museum (page 128)
North Beach Museum (page 137)
Presidio Museum (page 155)
Wells Fargo History Museum (page 179)

San Francisco for free

Whether you are a hard-up culture vulture or just a person who likes to get something for nothing, San Francisco offers plenty of enjoyable ways to fill your day without spending a cent. Museum enthusiasts strapped for cash will do well to be in the city on the first Wednesday of the month, when a number of museums, such as the **Asian Art Museum** (pages 122–123), waive their usual admission charges. A visit to one or both can easily be combined with an exploration of **Golden Gate Park** (pages 100–103), where the parkland and the Strybing Arboretum are free. The **Yerba Buena Center for the Arts** (701 Mission Street; tel: 415/978-2787) is free on the first Tuesday of every month.

Budget-minded parents should note that the city's two most popular child-friendly attractions—the **California Academy of Sciences** (pages 64–65) and the **Exploratorium** (page 82)—waive their admission fees on the first Wednesday of the month, as does the **San Francisco Zoo** (page 162).

The **San Francisco Museum of Modern Art** (pages 160–161) goes against the normal grain by allowing free entry on the first Tuesday of the month.

Impecunious art lovers who miss the free museum days have plenty more to content themselves with. Besides a large collection of galleries, such as the **Folk Art International** (140 Maiden Lane), Frank Lloyd's Wright's model for the Guggenheim Museum in New York (see page 116), several hotels seek to cement their top-class status by lining their public rooms with top-class art.

A stroll through the corridors of the **Ritz-Carlton** (600 Stockton Street) reveals 18th- and 19th-century landscapes, seascapes and portraits by English and

A stroll through Golden Gate Park can be full of surprises; these jugglers use the park's ample green spaces to practice their art

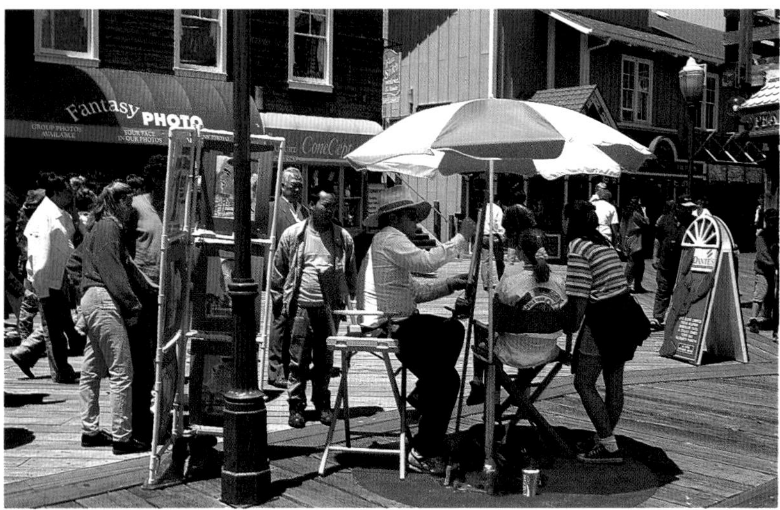

Pier 39, where there is always something to look at

American painters. At the **Stanford Court** (905 California Street) the treasures include a diverting collection of Far Eastern pieces, among them some 240 theme paintings by Kan Wing Lin, and beautiful 18th-century hand-painted screens.

The **Palace Hotel** (2 New Montgomery Street) not only boasts the Garden Court, one of the city's most elegant interiors, but also several stunning murals, including one by Maxfield Parrish valued at $2.5 million.

Lining the corridors of the **St. Francis** (Union Square) are several signed photographs by San Francisco-born Ansel Adams.

Some of the finest 1930s public artworks in California can be seen for free in San Francisco, at **Coit Tower** (pages 174–175) and the **Beach Chalet** (see panel, page 175). Among the more interesting of many museum/galleries is the **Cartoon Art Museum** (655 Mission Street), featuring vintage and contemporary cartoons ranging from comic book superheroes to political cartoons.

The musicians, magicians, clowns and comedians of **Fisherman's Wharf** regularly give their services for free (though a donation is appreciated). Free events often enliven lunchtimes on **Justin Herman Plaza** at the Embarcadero Center (see page 81), and the slightly seedy **Hallidie Plaza** also features free amusements on some weekday afternoons.

Walking around this pedestrian-friendly city's many distinctive neighborhoods obviously costs nothing—though you might spend more energy than you would like on scaling some of the hills. For Victorian mansions, head for Pacific Heights or Haight-Ashbury. For modern architecture, pace the Financial District, and cross Market Street into SoMa for the Rincon Annex and the Yerba Buena Gardens complex.

Wherever you go, remember that neighborhood churches may be among the city's most intriguing landmarks, be it the soaring post-modern **St. Mary's Cathedral** (page 158) or the log cabin-like **Swedenborgian Church** (page 172).

FREE WALKS

Almost every day, the City Guides (tel: 415/557-4266) offer free guided walking tours of many of the city's neighborhoods and historical and architectural points of interest. From May through October, the San Francisco Parks Trust (tel: 415/750-5105) conduct free walks around various sections of Golden Gate Park. Hotline for free walks; tel: 415/263-0991.

SCENIC ELEVATORS

If you want to get a loftier perspective on the city, there are several glass-sided elevators that offer a refreshingly vertical (and free) ride. A the Westin St. Francis hotel (Union Square), the high-speed elevators seem to burst through the roof, zooming skyward as Union Square recedes into the distance below and panoramic vistas open up. Across town at the Hyatt Regency (Market and California streets) circular cars whiz up through a dramatic lobby to reach the city's only revolving rooftop restaurant.

THE PERILS OF PARTYING

Guests booking into the St. Francis to celebrate a business success will be eager to avoid the fate which befell silent-screen comedian Fatty Arbuckle in 1921. Arriving for a weekend party to mark the signing of a new $800,000 contract, Arbuckle booked a suite overlooking Union Square. The subsequent death of actress Virginia Rappe ended Arbuckle's career, despite the fact that he was eventually exonerated of any wrong-doing.

San Francisco for the rich

San Francisco may not be the rich persons' playground that New York or Los Angeles can claim to be, and money certainly is not a prerequisite for enjoying the city. Nonetheless, having much more money than you know what to do with always eases the stresses and strains of travel, and San Francisco has at least a few locations which should be known to the affluent jet-setter.

Heads of state, royalty and the simply mind-bogglingly rich have been regulars at the **Westin St. Francis Hotel** (Union Square) since it opened in 1904. The addition of a modern wing in the 1970s may have upset architectural purists but it delighted the guests, who expect top-notch facilities in their $1,000-a-night suites.

Afternoon tea at the **Ritz-Carlton** (see page 133) is a fixture on the social circuit. At the **Big Four** restaurant (1075 California Street), you do not need to be as wealthy as the 19th-century railroad tycoons for whom it is named, though it helps. The curious but financially embarrassed might sneak in for breakfast and escape with change from $20.

The St. Francis and the Big Four might well be considered overbearingly traditional by design-conscious, money-laden individuals under 40. For such folk, **Hotel Triton** (342 Grant Avenue), with its artistic fixtures and in-room VCRs and CD players—and its roller blades for rent—is tailor-made. Come dinner time, **Aqua** (252 California Street), serving gourmet seafood to a chic crowd in subdued surroundings, is the place to be seen if you are photogenic and have $100 to spend.

Sharing space with the Big Four in the Huntington Hotel is the **Nob Hill spa**, a luxurious place to spend a relaxing, decadent afternoon.

Classy: the Garden Court, Palace Hotel

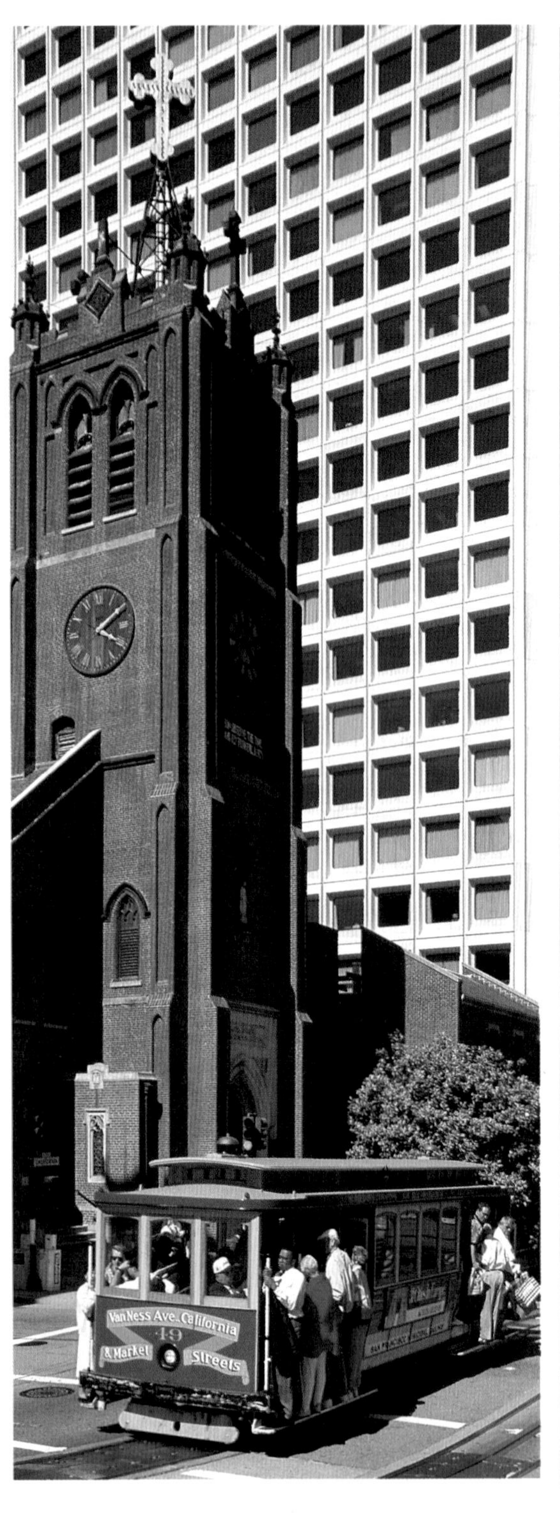

Travel Facts

Arriving and departing

By air San Francisco International Airport (tel: 650/821-8211) is approximately 14 miles (23km) south of the city. Domestic carriers serving the city are **Alaska Air** (tel: 1-800/252-7522), **American** (tel: 1-800/433-7300), **Continental** (tel: 1-800/523-3273), **Delta** (tel: 1-800/221-1212), **United** (tel: 1-800/241-6522) and **USAir** (tel: 1-800/428-4322). International carriers include **Air New Zealand** (tel: 1-800/262-1234), **British Airways** (tel: 1-800-AIRWAYS), **Air Canada** (tel: 888/247-2262), **China Airlines** (tel: 1-800/227-5118), **Japan Air Lines** (tel: 1-800/525-3663), **Lufthansa** (tel: 1-800/645-3880), **Mexicana** (tel: 1-800/531-7921) and **Qantas** (tel: 1-800/227-4500). Several domestic airlines serve Oakland International Airport (tel: 510/563-3300), which is across the bay from downtown San Francisco (via I-880 and I-80), although traffic on the Bay Bridge may at times make travel time longer. Traveling to and from San Francisco International Airport is easy. The best options for first-time arrivals, and anyone encumbered with luggage, are the numerous privately run minibuses, such as SuperShuttle (tel: 415/558-8500), which collect passengers from the traffic island directly outside the terminal; simply wait for one to show up. The one-way fare into the city is around $14 and $8 for a second passenger.

A cheaper alternative is the SFO Airporter (tel: 650/246-8942), a bus that runs every 20 minutes between 5am and 11pm from the airport to the hotels near Union Square; the fare costs around $14. Less expensive is BART (tel: 415/989-2278), which connects the airport directly to the city in around 30 minutes for $4.95. Even cheaper, if slower and with baggage restrictions, is route 292 of the local SamTrans bus service (tel: 1-800/660-4287), for a flat-fare of $1.25 to San Francisco's Transbay Terminal. Exact change is required. The SamTrans bus calls at marked stops outside the airport's United and Delta terminals. Buses are wheelchair accessible. Depending on traffic, a taxi into the city will cost approximately $35–$45.

MUNI
29 SUNSET
To 3rd St/Paul
Daily Approx 7AM-6:30PM
INFORMATION:
DIAL 673-MUNI

By bus Greyhound buses (tel: 1-800/229-9424) into the city finish their journeys at the Transbay Terminal (First and Mission streets). This is also the destination of local long-distance buses, including the Golden Gate Transit (tel: 415/455-2000), that serve Marin and Sonoma counties.

By train If taking Amtrak (tel: 1-800/872-7245) to San Francisco disembark at Emeryville, between Berkeley and Oakland, and continue to the city on one of the free shuttle buses that meet arriving trains. The buses carry passengers to the Transbay Terminal (First and Mission streets), a trip of around 40 minutes. The 511 website, www.511.org, details all transit services and routes in the Bay Area and can also be accessed by toll-free phone, tel: 511.

Buses are inexpensive and generally reliable

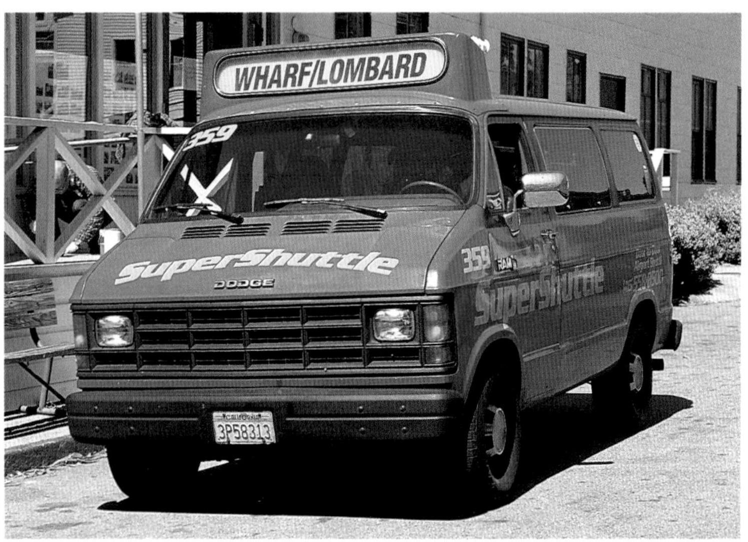

Shuttle vans are an easy option between the airport and city

Insurance
Before leaving home, itemize your bags' contents and their worth in case they get lost. Label them inside and out with your name, address and phone number. (If you use your home address, cover it so potential thieves can't see it.) Put a copy of your itinerary inside each bag, so that you can be easily located. If your bags do not arrive with you, or if you detect damage, file a written report with the airline before you leave the airport.

In the event of loss, damage or theft on domestic flights, the airline's liability is $2,500 per passenger, excluding fragile or perishable items and valuable items such as jewelry or cameras that are listed in the fine print on your ticket. Excess-valuation insurance can be bought directly from the airline at check-in. Your homeowner's policy may fill the gap; or baggage cover is usually included in travel insurance packages.

Airline security procedures have been tightened up. Airlines now have to screen all checked luggage as well as carry on bags, so it is advisable to arrive at least two hours before your flight to allow for the long lines.

When to go
San Francisco is enjoyable at any time. The weather is rarely extreme, and numerous festivals and events take place throughout the year. The peak tourist months are July and August, when accommodations reservations should be made as early as possible and when prices may be slightly higher than usual.

Insurance for overseas visitors should, at the very least, include coverage for medical treatment up to $1,000,000 but fuller travel insurance is sensible. Anything stolen should be reported to the police and a written record acquired from them for a claim once home.

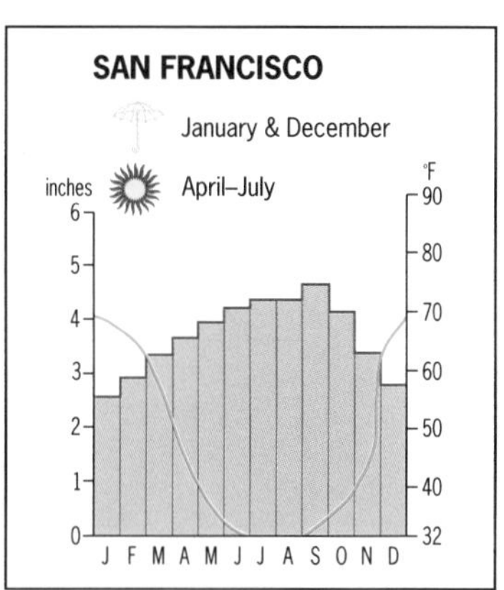

Fog: a frequent visitor, but seldom staying long

Essential facts

Climate Any time of the year is the right time to go to San Francisco, which is one of the most beautiful cities in the world. The fog rolls in during the summer, but it seems less an inconvenience than part of the charm of this never-mundane place. As long as you remember to bring along sweaters and jackets, even in August, you can't miss.

San Francisco is on the tip of a peninsula, flanked by the Pacific Ocean and San Francisco Bay. Its climate is quintessentially marine and moderate: It never gets very hot—above 80°F is reported as a heat wave—or very cold (as far as the thermometer is concerned, anyway).

For all its moderation, however, San Francisco can be tricky. In the summer-time fog often rolls in from the ocean, blocking the sun and filling the air with dampness. At times like this you'll want a coat, jacket or warm sweater instead of the shorts or lightweight summer clothes that seem so comfortable in most American cities during July and August. Mark Twain is credited with observing that the coldest winter he ever spent was one summer in San Francisco. He may have been exaggerating, but it's best not to expect a hot summer in this city. If you travel north, east or south of the city, you will find warmer summer temperatures. Shirtsleeves and thin cottons are usually fine for the Wine Country.

Be prepared for rain in winter, especially December and January. Winds from the ocean can add to the chill factor, so pack some warm clothing to be on the safe side. For current local weather information, check out www.sfgate.com/weather.

Money matters Many automated-teller machines (ATMs) are tied to international networks such as **Mastercard** (which owns Cirrus) and **Plus** partnered with **Visa**. You can use your bank card at ATMs to withdraw money from an account and get cash advances on a credit card account if your card has been programmed with a personal identification number, or PIN. Check in advance on limits on withdrawals and cash advances within specified periods. On cash advances you are charged interest from the day you receive the money from ATMs or tellers. Transaction fees for ATM withdrawals outside your home area may be higher than those at home.

For specific Mastercard or Cirrus locations in the United States and Canada, call 1-800/424-7787. For US Visa-Plus locations, call 1-800/THE-PLUS and press the area code and first three digits of the number you're calling from (or of the calling area where you want an ATM).

You don't have to be a cardholder to send or receive a **MoneyGram from American Express** for up to $20,000: Go to a MoneyGram agent in retail and convenience stores and American Express travel offices. Fees range from 3 percent to 10 percent, depending on the amount and how you pay.You can also use Western Union (www.westernunion.com) and MasterCard or Visa.

Overseas visitors should carry spending money as US dollar travelers' checks, which can be used as cash (sign the check then wait for change) throughout in hotels, restaurants and larger shops. Most hotel cashiers will also exchange travelers' checks for cash; banks may too but will require ID and may charge a commission. Changing foreign currency, or foreign currency travelers checks, is an ordeal worth avoiding. Cash advances can be obtained using a credit card at the appropriate ATM, though these may a entail a poor exchange rate and possibly other charges. The details should be checked with card providers before leaving home.

National holidays Banks and all public offices will be closed on all the following holidays; stores may be open on some of these days: New Year's Day (January 1); Martin Luther King's Birthday (third Monday in January); Presidents' Day (third Monday in February); Cesar Chavez Day (March 31); Memorial Day (last Monday in May); Independence Day (July 4); Labor Day (first Monday in September); Columbus Day (second Monday in October); Veterans' Day (November 11); Thanksgiving Day (fourth Thursday in November); Christmas Day (December 25).

Time differences San Francisco is on Pacific Standard Time, as is the rest of California.

Cash is easily available from a variety of ATMs—but use the right card

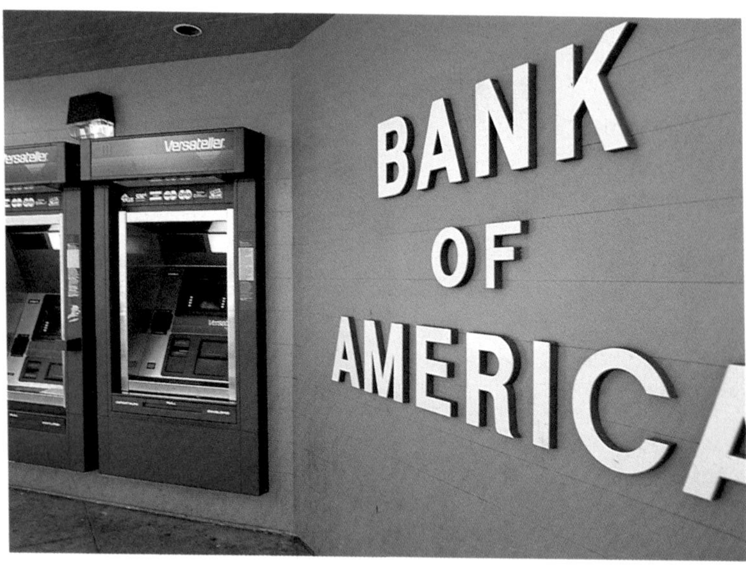

Getting around

Public transportation San Francisco is a fine city to explore on foot, but even the most dedicated walkers will want to make use of the excellent public transportation system during some part of their stay (but preferably not during rush hour), either to experience the delight of a cable-car ride or to avoid having to climb another hill.

Traveling across the bay to Berkeley or Oakland will likely involve a trip on the highly efficient BART system, while a visit to Sausalito, Alcatraz or Tiburon can require a ferry across San Francisco Bay. You will only need to use a taxi if you are in a rush, or for late-night journeys when public transportation services are skeletal.

BART The Bay Area Rapid Transit (known as BART; for information, tel: 415/989-2278) system is chiefly useful for crossing the bay to Berkeley and Oakland, though it also runs through the city and forms a speedy link between the Financial District, the Civic Center and the Mission District.

Fares are priced according to distance traveled. Tickets can be bought from machines at BART stations, where there are also easy-to-read maps. BART runs from 6am to midnight (from 8am on Sundays).

BART moves people below ground...

...while above-ground options include quaint cable cars

Buses The buses and, to some extent, the streetcars that are run by Muni (tel: 415/673-MUNI) are a much more useful—if more mundane—mode of transport for getting around San Francisco than the cable cars.

All Muni routes are shown in the telephone directory and at most bus stops. Historic street cars from

Cable cars cover a limited route—but everybody wants to hop aboard

around the world provide service on the F Line, which travels from the Transbay Terminal to the Castro District.

The standard bus fare is $1.25. Exact change in coins is necessary and should be fed into the machine next to the driver when boarding; free transfers (onto other routes) are issued on request. Muni buses run from 5am to 1am. Through the early hours of the morning, Muni's "Owl Service" buses provide a reduced-frequency service on the main routes.

Cable cars A first-time visitor might well expect to find San Franciscans shuttling around the city aboard the famous cable cars. In truth, the much-loved cable cars, restored to function in the early 1980s, are more of a tourist attraction than a practical means of getting around.

Cable cars operate on just three routes: two (Powell and Market, Powell and Mason) from Market Street to Fisherman's Wharf, and one (California) from the Financial District to the far side of Nob Hill; this one is usually the least busy. Buy your ticket, which costs $2, from self-service machines at the end of each route or from the conductor when you board. During the summer, expect a lengthy wait to board at Market Street and Fisherman's Wharf.

Cabs It is unlikely that you will need to use taxis in San Francisco, except perhaps during the early morning hours when buses may be scarce.

If you have to move in a hurry, you will usually be able to hail a cab on a major street within a few minutes (expect a longer wait during rush hours). Cabs can also be ordered over the phone; many cab companies are listed in the Yellow Pages. Average cab fares are around $2.85 for pick-up and around $2.40 for each mile.

Ferries Few people visit San Francisco and manage to resist the temptation to take a bay cruise or a ride on one of the ferries that sail across the bay to Sausalito, Tiburon or Oakland. Such trips provide great views of the city and its two major bridges. Complete ferry details are given on page 89.

Muni Passports If you are using public transportation a lot, a Muni Passport (available from outlets around the city) is likely to save a considerable amount of money.

A city driving hazard: complex parking laws

The passports are valid on all Muni services (including cable cars) for 1, 3 or 7 days, and currently cost $9, $15, and $20, respectively.

Driving While public transportation more than adequately serves San Francisco and much of the immediate Bay Area, a car is a near-essential accessory for distant explorations.

Car rental The nearest locations of major car rental companies can be found by calling the following numbers:
Avis (tel: 1-800/230-4898);
Alamo (tel: 1-800/462-5266);
Budget (tel: 1-800/527-0700);
Dollar (tel: 1-800/800-4000);
Hertz (tel: 1-800/654-3131);
Thrifty (tel: 1-800/847-4389).

Unlimited-mileage rates range from approximately $35 per day for an

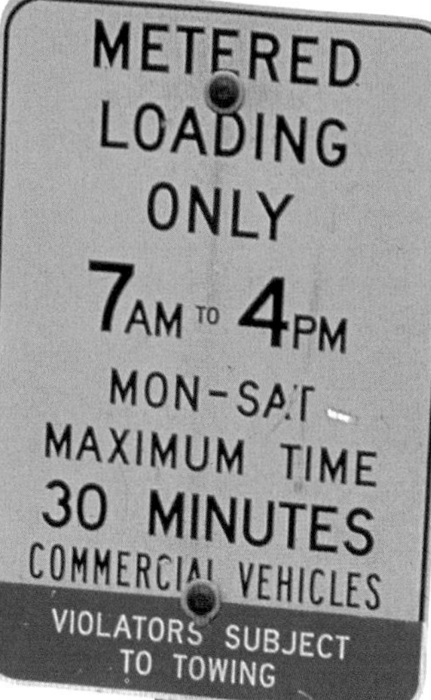
METERED
LOADING
ONLY
7AM TO 4PM
MON-SAT
MAXIMUM TIME
30 MINUTES
COMMERCIAL VEHICLES
VIOLATORS SUBJECT
TO TOWING

economy car to $60 for a large car; weekly unlimited-mileage rates range from approximately $170 upward. This does not include tax, which in San Francisco is approximately 8 percent on car rentals. You should be careful to read the small print.

Picking up the car in one city and leaving it in another may entail substantial drop-off charges or one-way service fees. The cost of a collision or loss-damage waiver can be high also. Some rental agencies will charge you extra if you return the car before the time specified on your contract. Ask before making unscheduled drop-offs. Fill the tank when you turn in the vehicle to avoid being charged for refueling at what you'll swear is the most expensive pump in town.

Major international companies have programs that discount their standard rates by 15–30 percent if you make the reservation beforehand (anywhere from 24 hours to 14 days), rent for a minimum number of days (typically three or four) and prepay the rental.

More economical rentals may come as part of fly/drive or other packages, or even bare-bones deals that only combine the rental and an airline ticket.

Before you rent a car, find out exactly what coverage, if any, is provided by your personal car insurance and by the rental company. Don't assume that you are covered. If you do want insurance from the rental company, secondary coverage may be the only type offered. You may already have secondary coverage if you charge the rental to a credit card, so be sure to check your level of coverage.

Arrivals from overseas should pay particular attention to the Collision Damage Waiver (or CDW), a form of insurance against damage to the car, usually costing at least $12 a day; while this may not be compulsory it is strongly advisable to take it out. More generally, without reserving ahead, any non-US citizen under 25 and/or without a credit card, may encounter problems renting a car in the US.

Breaking down In the unlikely event that your rental car breaks down, phone the emergency number that should be prominently displayed on or near the dashboard (if it is not, simply phone the regular number for the car rental agency). With luck, a rental company representative will shortly arrive with another car in which you can continue your trip. If you are unlucky enough to break down far from a phone, stay with your car and wait for a Highway Patrol vehicle to come by. If any other passing driver stops to offer help—there is every chance that they are genuine—you should treat their interest with caution. Usually, the best help such a person can provide is to drive to a public phone and make a call on your behalf.

Driving tips In San Francisco, your major driving problem is most likely to be parking. Most hotels have designated parking spaces for guests, but general parking in the city's busier areas is notoriously difficult. Many parking lots charge by the hour or by the day. On certain streets, parking is forbidden during

City buses are more useful, if less attractive to visitors, than streetcars

the rush hour. It is important to remember to look for the warning signs, as illegally parked cars will be towed away.

When parking on hilly streets of San Francisco, the law requires you to curb your front wheels, resting the tires firmly against the curb (angle them outward if facing uphill, inward if facing downhill) and to set the emergency brake.

Long-distance public transportation There is currently a much needed major move afoot throughout environmentally concerned Northern California to wean devoted drivers away from their cars and develop less polluting forms of mass transportation.

By bus Greyhound serves San Francisco from the Transbay Terminal at First and Mission streets (tel: 1-800/229-9424).

By plane The Sunday travel section of most newspapers is a good place to look for bargain airfares. When you are making a reservation, particularly through an unfamiliar company, pay with a credit card if you can, and consider trip-cancellation and default insurance.

From within the US and Canada less expensive fares, called promotional or discount fares, are round-trip and involve restrictions, which vary according to the route and season. You must usually buy the ticket in advance (7, 14 or 21 days is standard), although some of the major airlines have added no-frills, cheap flights to compete with new bargain airlines on certain routes.

With the major airlines the cheaper fares generally require minimum and maximum stays (for instance, over a Saturday night or at least seven and no more than 30 days). Airlines generally allow some return date changes for a fee, but most low-fare tickets are nonrefundable. Moreover, some consolidators sometimes give you your money back. Carefully read the fine print detailing penalties for changes and cancellations. If you doubt the reliability of a company, call the airline once you've made your reservation to confirm it.

Travel clubs offer members unsold space on airplanes, cruise ships and package tours at as much as 50 percent below regular prices. Membership may include a regular bulletin or access to a toll-free hot line giving details of available trips departing from three or four days to several months in the future. Other clubs also offer discounts on hotel rack rates, but double-check with the hotel to make sure it isn't offering a better promotional rate independent of the club, plus money-off coupons for restaurants, stores and so on.

Clubs include **Entertainment Publications** (www.entertainment.com; tel: 1-888-231-SAVE; **Privilege Card** (237 E. Front St., Youngstown, OH 44503; tel: 800/236-9732; domestic and international membership available; **Travelers Advantage** (39 Lindeman Drive, Trumball CT 06611; tel: 1-877/259-2691; www.travelersadvantage.com).

From Europe, a rising number of airlines have non-stop flights to San Francisco; from Britain these include Virgin and BMI as well as British Airways. Fly-drive deals and flight-and-accommodations packages are offered by airlines and many major tour operators, though independently arranged trips are relatively easy to plan and will often save money, particularly if done on the internet. Travel sites such as www.ebookers.com offer a wide range of flight options and also hotel reservations, though it is often better to book the latter or any other form of accommodations, directly with the establishment via email.

By rail Emeryville is the nearest stop for Amtrak (tel: 1-800/872-7245). The *Zephyr* travels from Chicago via Denver, the *Coast Starlight* between Los Angeles and Seattle. From Oakland, buses will take you across the Bay Bridge to the Ferry Building on the Embarcadero located at the north end of Market Street in San Francisco.

Student and youth travel Students carrying International Student Identity Cards (ISICs) are entitled to reduced admission to many museums and numerous other attractions throughout the city.

While not exclusively for young and student travelers, San Francisco's hostels (see under Accommodations, pages 268-274) offer good budget-priced accommodations, and several have kitchens where guests can prepare their own meals as well as common rooms.

Travelers under age 25, especially those without credit cards, may have difficulty renting a car.

Communications

Media San Francisco has two daily newspapers, the morning *San Francisco Chronicle* and the weekday-only free tabloid *San Francisco Examiner* and two major free weekly newspapers, the *SF Weekly* and *San Francisco Bay Guardian*. Two other long-established free publications provide news, views and information to the city's large gay and lesbian population: *Bay Times* and *Bay Area Reporter*. All of the above are easy to find in vending machines on the street.

Standard tourist information can be found in free magazines readily available in most hotel lobbies, such as *San Francisco Key* and the *Bay City Guide* and the bigger *San Francisco Tourist Guide*. These are usually financed by advertising revenue, and unsurprisingly their editorial opinions reflect this. Nevertheless, they are worth picking up for their many discount coupons, which may save you money when you are shopping or visiting major tourist attractions.

In all but the very cheapest hotel rooms you will find a TV linked to national networks. The main San Francisco TV channels are 2 (KTVU/FOX), 4 (KRON/ NBC), 5 (KPIX/CBS), 7 (KGO/ABC) and 9 (KQED/PBS). Many hotels also offer selected cable TV channels, and some have a further choice of six or so pay-to-view movies. Most hotel rooms also have a radio, with which you will be able to sample some of the Bay Area's 80-odd (sometimes extremely odd) radio stations.

More comprehensive media details are given on page 154.

Post offices

There are plenty of post offices around the city, and you can find the nearest one by looking in the telephone directory or asking at your hotel reception.

Most post offices are open Monday to Friday 8–6 and Saturday 8–1. For postal service information, tel: 800/ASK-USPS.

Telephone and fax

Some budget-range hotels offer free local calls, but hotel room phone charges are generally considerably higher than those of public phones. A particular hotel's phone charges should be displayed in the room somewhere.

Throughout this book, the area code for San Francisco (415) has been included for all telephone numbers within the city.

Almost all hotels are equipped with fax machines, and most will

Get your news from a vending machine or newsstand

allow guests to send and receive faxes, but the charges for this service vary considerably.

Although all hotels charge to send faxes, some will waive charges for faxes received, while others bill guests as much as $5 per page in addition to imposing a $5 or more "handling" fee.

Email and websites

A city at the forefront of the internet revolution, San Francisco is well served by dedicated cyber cafés as well as many ordinary businesses and libraries that offer internet access. Hotels often offer email access for guests, and many have hi-speed wireless inernet access from guest rooms. Most tourist-related businesses have their own websites, as do the majority of museums and institutions, print media and city bodies.

Among the most useful are:
San Francisco Convention & Visitor Bureau (www.sfvisitor.org);
San Francisco Airport (www.flysfo.org);
city buses (www.sfmuni.com);
BART trains (www.bart.gov);
city government (www.ci.sf.ca.us).

A source of general information is www.sanfranciscocitysearch.com.

Newspaper websites are given on page 154.

Cameras, camcorders and laptops

If your camera is new or if you haven't used it for a while, shoot and develop a few test rolls of film before you leave home. Remember to store your film in a cool, dry place—never in the glove compartment of the car, or on the shelf under the rear window.

Airport security X-rays generally aren't harmful to film with ISO below 400. To protect your film, carry it with you in a clear plastic bag and ask for a hand inspection. Such requests are honored at US airports. Don't depend on a lead-lined bag to protect film in checked luggage—the airline may increase the radiation to see what's inside.

Before your trip, test that your camcorder functions work, invest in a skylight filter to protect the lens and check all the batteries. Airport security personnel may ask you to turn on the camcorder to prove that it is what it appears to be, so make sure the battery is charged.

Videotape is not damaged by X-rays, but it may be harmed by the magnetic field of a walk-through metal detector, so be sure to ask for a hand-check.

Security X-rays do not harm hard-disk or floppy-disk storage, but you may request a hand-check, at which point you may be asked to turn on the computer to prove that it is what it appears to be. (Be sure to check your battery is charged before departure.) Most airlines will allow you to use your laptop in flight except during takeoff and landing (so as not

Calling home: It is cheaper to use a pay phone than the one in your hotel room

San Francisco's police are seldom far away

to interfere with their navigation equipment).

Emergencies

Crime and police San Francisco may have its problem areas—the Tenderloin, the Western Addition and parts of the Mission District—but overall it rates as one of the country's safest major cities.

In its compact neighborhoods, where the main streets are nearly always bustling with pedestrians, you will seldom be alone. It goes without saying, though, that short cuts through dimly lit alleys or across open areas after dark are reckless and potentially dangerous undertakings.

At all times, you should be careful not to carry easily snatched bags and cameras, or to stuff your wallet into your back pocket. In a bar or restaurant, always keep your belongings within sight and within easy reach. When not in use, cameras and other valuables should be left in the hotel's safe (some hotels provide in-room safes), and you should never carry more money than you need.

In order to make an insurance claim, you should report any item stolen to the nearest police precinct (the address of which will be in the phone book). It is highly unlikely that your stolen goods will be recovered, but the police will be able to fill out the forms that your insurance company will need to expedite your claim on your return home.

Emergency telephone numbers
For fire, police or ambulance, dial 911 and ask for the relevant service. Other emergency numbers include **Rape Crisis Hotline** (tel: 415/647-7273) and **Victims of Crime Resource Center** (tel: 1-800/842-8467).

Traveler's checks
Although you will want plenty of cash when visiting small cities or rural areas, traveler's checks are usually preferable. The most widely recognized are **American Express** and **Thomas Cook**, and those issued by major commercial banks. American Express also issues Traveler's Checks for Two, which can be countersigned and used by you or your traveling companion. Some checks are free; usually the issuing company or the bank at which you make your purchase charges one percent of the check's face value as their fee.

It is always useful to buy a few checks in small denominations to cash toward the end of your trip. You can exchange any used checks for cash; Americans can have them credited to their bank account, on their return home. Unlike cash, once lost or stolen, traveler's checks can be replaced or refunded if you can produce the purchase agreement and a record of the checks' serial numbers (especially of those you've already cashed). Sign all the checks when you buy them; you'll endorse them a second time to exchange them for cash or make purchases. Common sense dictates that you keep the purchase agreement separate from your checks. More cautious travelers will even give a copy of the purchase agreement and checks' serial numbers to someone back home. Most issuers of traveler's checks promise to refund or replace lost or stolen checks within 24 hours. In a safe place—or several safe places—record the toll-free or collect telephone number to call in case of emergencies.

See pages 250–251 for more information on money matters.

Most hospitals will accept emergency patients

Health and pharmacies

If you need a doctor or dentist while you are on vacation, look under "Physicians and Surgeons" or "Dentists" in the Yellow Pages. Alternatively, telephone the **San Francisco Medical Society** (tel: 415/561-0850) for doctor referral or the **San Francisco Dental Society** (tel: 415/928-7337) to find a dentist.

City hospitals with well-equipped 24-hour emergency rooms include **San Francisco General,** 1001 Potrero Avenue (tel: 415/206-8000) and **California Pacific Medical Center,** corner of Castro and Duboce streets (tel: 415/565-6000). For general non-emergency medical needs, try **Downtown Medical**, 450 Sutter Street, suite 1723 (tel: 415/362-7177; www.downtownmedical.com). Visitors from Europe should be sure to have taken out insurance against medical costs before leaving home.

Walgreen Drug Stores have 24-hour branches at 498 Castro Street (tel: 415/861-3136) and 3201 Divisadero Street at Lombard (tel: 415/931-6417).

Lost property

For any property lost at San Francisco International Airport, tel: 650/821-7014.

For property lost on Muni public transportation, tel: 415/923-6168.

For possessions lost anywhere else, call the police station; the local precinct's number will be in the phone book.

For an ambulance, dial 911

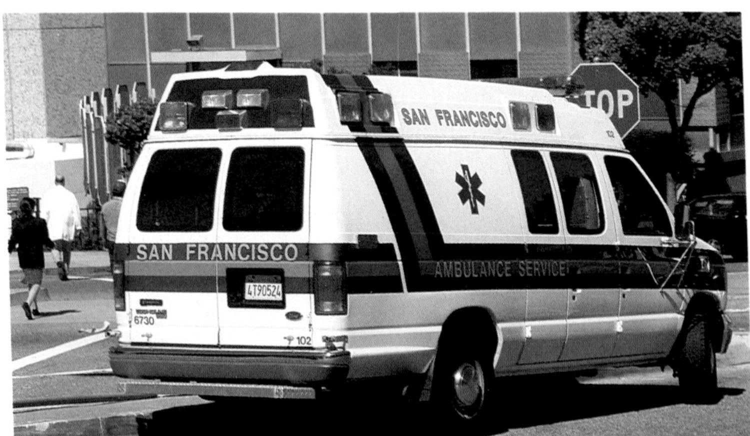

Other information

Children Children are always warmly welcomed. Hotels and motels will usually provide a crib or extra bed in their parents' room for children under 12 (sometimes for older children) at no extra charge, and restaurant staff are likely to appear with games, crayons, the children's menu and, if necessary, a high chair as soon as they spot youngsters.

The California Academy of Sciences and the Exploratorium are just two of the city's major attractions to entertain and educate children. See pages 242–243 for more suggestions.

Travelers with disabilities In San Francisco, facilities for travelers with disabilities are better than in many other cities. A useful publication is *San Francisco Access*, a free booklet published by Access Northern California (www.accessnca.com), available from the Convention & Visitors Bureau.

By law, public buildings must be at least partially wheelchair-accessible, and all must provide lavatories for the disabled.

The majority of street corners have dropped curbs, and nearly all city buses have lifts for wheelchair users, designated wheelchair space on board and can usually "kneel" to make access easier from the curb. All BART stations are equipped with a wheelchair-accessible elevator between the street level and the platform level.

For fuller details of handicapped-accessible public transportation in San Francisco, write for the free *Muni Access Guide* to: Muni Accessible Services Programs, 949 Presidio Avenue, San Francisco, CA 94115 (tel: 415/923-6142). Golden Gate Transit also publishes a free brochure describing access on its ferries and buses (tel: 415/923-2000).

Provided they receive sufficient notice, trains and airlines are legally required to provide services for travelers with disabilities, and Amtrak also offers a 15 percent discount. Though less comfortable than the trains, and particularly uncomfortable for wheelchair users, Greyhound buses allow a companion to travel free provided a letter from your doctor can be produced stating

Facilities for the disabled are many

that this is necessary.

Some major car rental companies are willing to arrange vehicles with hand controls.

Maps The most useful map of San Francisco is the Visitor Map, available from the Visitor Information Center (see Tourist Offices, page 266) and from many hotels. For travel elsewhere around California, use the free map issued by the California Office of Tourism, which is also available from the Visitor Information Center.

Older travelers The **American Association of Retired Persons** (AARP, 601 E. St. NW, Washington, DC 20049, tel: 1-888/687-2277; www.aarp.org) provides independent travelers who are members (open to those aged 50 or older; $12.50 annual fee) with the Purchase Privilege Program, which offers discounts on lodging, car rentals and sightseeing, and the AARP Motoring Plan, which furnishes domestic trip-planning information and emergency road-service aid. AARP can also arrange group tours, cruises and apartments.

Another organization offering discounts on lodgings, car rentals and other travel products, along with such nontravel perks as magazines and newsletters is: **Alliance for Retired Americans** (888 16th St. NW., Washington DC 20006; tel: 1-800/333-7212; www.retiredamericans.org).

Note: For reduced rates, mention your senior-citizen identification card when booking hotel reservations, not when checking out. At restaurants, show your card before you're seated; discounts may be limited to certain menus, days or hours. If you are renting a car, ask about promotional rates that might improve using your senior-citizen discount.

A number of domestic airlines and hotels offer discounts for older travelers (typically those aged 60 or older), though frequently changing details mean that finding out about the latest offers can be difficult. Your local travel agent may have up-to-date information, but you are more likely to glean the latest facts by contacting the airline directly.

The following tour operators offer special services for older travelers. If you want to take your grandchildren, look into **Grandtravel** (6900 Wisconsin Avenue, Suite 706, Chevy Chase, MD 20815, tel: 301/986-0790 or 1-800/247-7651). **SeniorTours** (508 Irvington Road, Drexel Hill, PA 19026, tel: 1-800/227-1100) arranges bus tours throughout the United States and Nova Scotia, as well as Caribbean cruises.

In Britain, leading a very limited field specifically for the over-50s, is **Saga Holidays** (The Saga Building, Middelburg Square, Folkestone, CT20 1AZ, tel: 0800/096 0078; www.sagaholidays.co.uk).

Opening hours The majority of San Francisco's stores open on weekdays and Saturdays from 9 or 10am to 5 or 6pm. Major department stores, shopping centers and the stores in Fisherman's Wharf and Chinatown keep longer hours and are also open on Sundays. Smaller or specialized stores, some of which may be closed on Mondays but open every other day, frequently begin business as late

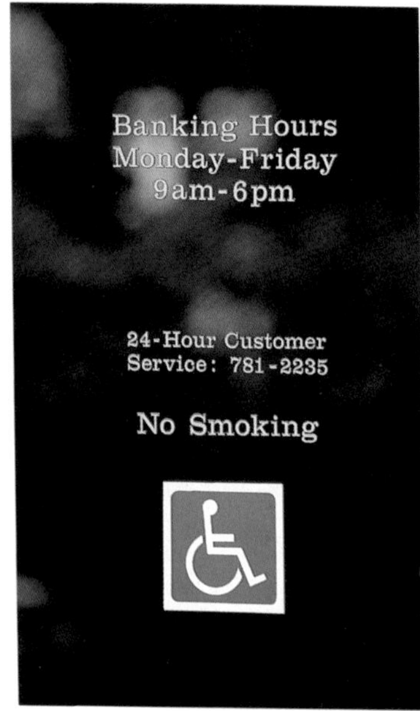

CONVERSION CHARTS

FROM	TO	MULTIPLY BY
Inches	Centimeters	2.54
Centimeters	Inches	0.3937
Feet	Meters	0.3048
Meters	Feet	3.2810
Yards	Meters	0.9144
Meters	Yards	1.0940
Miles	Kilometers	1.6090
Kilometers	Miles	0.6214
Acres	Hectares	0.4047
Hectares	Acres	2.4710
Gallons	Liters	4.5460
Liters	Gallons	0.2200
Ounces	Grams	28.35
Grams	Ounces	0.0353
Pounds	Grams	453.6
Grams	Pounds	0.0022
Pounds	Kilograms	0.4536
Kilograms	Pounds	2.205
Tons	Tonnes	1.0160
Tonnes	Tons	0.9842

MEN'S SUITS

UK	36	38	40	42	44	46	48
Rest of Europe	46	48	50	52	54	56	58
US	36	38	40	42	44	46	48

DRESS SIZES

UK	8	10	12	14	16	18
France	36	38	40	42	44	46
Italy	38	40	42	44	46	48
Rest of Europe	34	36	38	40	42	44
US	6	8	10	12	14	16

MEN'S SHIRTS

UK	14	14.5	15	15.5	16	16.5	17
Rest of Europe	36	37	38	39/40	41	42	43
US	14	14.5	15	15.5	16	16.5	17

MEN'S SHOES

UK	7	7.5	8.5	9.5	10.5	11
Rest of Europe	41	42	43	44	45	46
US	8	8.5	9.5	10.5	11.5	12

WOMEN'S SHOES

UK	4.5	5	5.5	6	6.5	7
Rest of Europe	38	38	39	39	40	41
US	6	6.5	7	7.5	8	8.5

as 11am or noon and close at 9 or 10pm.

Typical bank hours are Monday to Friday from 9 to 3.30, 4 or 5, with some branches staying open until noon or 2 on Saturdays.

Museum opening hours vary according to the size and popularity of the museum. Larger ones generally open daily from 9 or 10 to 5 or 6, though smaller museums keep shorter hours and may be closed on one or more days during the week (and may only open during the afternoon). Where a museum has unusual opening hours, the details are given in the A–Z section of this book.

Places of worship As you might expect in a city with such an ethnically diverse population, San Francisco's places of worship are many and varied, reflecting many faiths. Some of the most interesting churches are detailed in the A–Z section of this book. Your hotel will be able to advise on those in your neighborhood, and the telephone book carries a comprehensive list.

Rest rooms Every public building in San Francisco is required to provide public rest rooms. These are almost always maintained in immaculate condition. Clean and convenient pay rest rooms are now present in all of the most busy business and tourist districts, as are those in hotel lobbies, restaurants and most bars.

Sales tax Added to the marked price of everything you might purchase in the city is an 8.5 percent sales tax. Elsewhere in California the sales-tax may be slightly lower.

Tipping How much you tip is entirely up to you, but the general rule in a restaurant or coffee shop is to leave the server 15 percent of the total bill, or slightly more—generally up to 20 percent, though there is no hard-and-fast rule—for particularly good service.

It is customary to tip drivers around 15–20 percent of the fare. The amount need not be exact, however, and if the sum is appropriate, most people simply tell the driver to keep the change as they hand over the fare.

Tip hotel porters, especially if they are red in the face and short of breath after carrying your bulging suitcases up several flights of stairs. Again, the amount is entirely discretionary, but you should probably plan on an average of $1 per bag.

Wine and beer Many visitors to San Francisco put aside time to sample the produce of the neighboring Wine Country (see the excursions described on pages 204–209 to Sonoma Valley and Napa Valley), but California's native beers are also worth seeking out.

San Francisco's Anchor Steam Beer is now enjoyed in bars across the world, and there are numerous microbreweries in the area making exceptionaly good brews that are a totally different experience from the weaker mass-market domestically produced beers.

Women travelers In San Francisco, as in any city throughout the world, women on their own—whether they are residents or visitors—may attract unwelcome attention. However, this is more likely to be annoying than threatening, and it can usually be dealt with simply by ignoring it or alternatively by delivering a sharp verbal rebuff.

Common sense dictates that women on their own should avoid isolated, poorly lit areas at night and not choose to stay in cheap hotels in seedy districts.

Aging in barrels at Sterling Wineries in Calistoga

Tours and tourist offices

Organized tours San Francisco lends itself to being discovered at your own pace, perhaps with the aid of the guided walking tours detailed on pages 94–95. If you are pressed for time, however, you might consider a whistle-stop guided tour of the city and surrounding area.

Among numerous companies offering such trips, **Tour Tours** (tel: 415/434-8687) has a half-day city tour and a tour crossing the Golden Gate to Sausalito and Muir Woods, either of which can be combined with a cruise on the bay. **Gray Line Tours** (tel: 1-888/428-6937) offers much the same as Tour Tours for a slightly higher price, but the company also has an evening tour that includes a walk around Chinatown and optional dinner.

If you want to see some more of California, **Tower Tours** offers a Wine Country trip and a tour around the Monterey Peninsula.

San Francisco Seaplane Tours (tel: 1-888/SEAPLANE; www.seaplane.com) offer half-hour tours of the Golden Gate costing $120 per person, departing from Pier 39 (mornings) and Sausalito (afternoons).

Other tours, such as those to Alcatraz Island and the opportunity for a guided cavort around the city's nightclubs, are detailed at appropriate points in the A–Z section of this book.

Tourist offices Find the time during your stay in San Francisco to drop by the Visitor Information Center, on the lower level of Hallidie Plaza by the corner of Market and Powell streets (open Mon–Fri 9–5, Sat–Sun 9–3; tel: 415/391-2000). The center carries a large number of hotel and restaurant leaflets (many of which entitle the holder to discounts) and free publications issued by the Convention and Visitors' Bureau (which runs the center). The multilingual staff is ready to answer visitors' questions. You should also be able to pick up the two maps recommended under Maps, pages 262–263.

A variety of maps, brochures, magazines and other useful material can be obtained through the Convention and Visitor Bureau's website, www.sfvisitor.org.

The well-stocked Visitor Information Center

Accommodations & Restaurants

ACCOMMODATIONS

Note that phone numbers prefixed 800 are toll-free numbers accessed by first dialling "1." These numbers can usually be dialed from anywhere in the US or Canada, though in some cases there is an additional toll-free number for calls made within California. Omit the 415 area code if dialing from within San Francisco.

The following recommended hotels and restaurants have been divided by area and into three price categories:

- **budget ($)—under $119**
- **moderate ($$)—$120–$225**
- **expensive ($$$)—over $225**

Chinatown

Astoria ($)
510 Bush Street tel: 800/666-6696 415/434-8889
Slightly pricier than Chinatown's other budget-rate options, the Astoria boasts a laundry and round-the-clock room service, and will pick up its guests from the airport.

Grant Plaza ($)
465 Grant Avenue tel: in California 800/472-6805 elsewhere in US 800/472-6899 415/434-3883
Located in the bustling heart of Chinatown, the Grant Plaza offers small but nicely furnished rooms all with private bathrooms, TVs and phones—and at an unbeatable price.

Hilton San Francisco Financial District ($$)
750 Kearny Street tel: 800/424-8292 415/433-6600
This branch of the well-known chain rises high above Chinatown and is the biggest and best-equipped hotel in the neighborhood; its large size tends to make guests feel anonymous.

Obrero Hotel ($)
1208 Stockton Street tel: 415/989-3960
On a perennially crowded section of Stockton Street with compact rooms lacking private bathrooms, this clean hotel nevertheless offers accommodations which will barely dent your budget—and breakfast is included.

Civic Center and Tenderloin

Albion House Inn ($$)
135 Gough Street tel: 415/621-0896
An inviting bed-and-breakfast alternative in an area dominated by run-of-the-mill hotels, with nine cozy rooms and a relaxing lounge dominated by a colossal fireplace.

Gates Hotel ($)
140 Ellis Street tel: 415/781-0430
Plain but clean, this makes an adequate very low-cost base for a night or two.

The Gaylord ($)
620 Jones Street tel: 800/336-8445 415/673-8445 www.gaylordhotel.com
Only weekly rates are offered at this combination hotel/apartment facility in the Tenderloin's Theater District. Guests have kitchens in studio apartments; no maid service. Meet other "residents" during Friday night happy hour.

Inn at the Opera ($$$)
333 Fulton Street tel: 800/325-2708 415/863-8400
Opera and ballet stars, classical musicians and top-billed thespians are among the fellow guests with whom you might be sharing the breakfast buffet at this extremely cozy and tastefully decorated hotel. Each room has a microwave oven for after-theater feasts.

New Central Hostel ($)
1412 Market Street tel: 415/703-9988
Provides competitively priced single and double rooms, and an even less costly option of small, shared dorms. Also has a few shelves of books on San Francisco and its environs for guests to browse through.

Pension San Francisco ($)
1668 Market Street tel: 888/864-807 415/864-1271
A popular spot for its prime location; cable TVs and phones, shared bathrooms and bargain rates.

Phoenix Hotel ($$)
601 Eddy Street tel: 800/CITYINN 415/776-1380
While other hotels stuff themselves with antiques, the Phoenix uses contemporary Bay Area artwork and a bright upbeat color scheme to make its guests—many of them are visiting rock musicians—feel welcome and relaxed. Facilities include in-room massage, outdoor heated swimming pool, good restaurant and a modest complimentary breakfast.

Renoir Hotel ($)
45 McAllister Street tel: 800/567-3388 415/626-5200
The triangular 1909 building alongside busy Market Street has ornate flourishes, and a Brazilian restaurant and lounge inside. Rooms are small-to-medium-sized, and the staff is multi-lingual.

Roadway Inn ($)
860 Eddy Street tel: 415/474-4374
This budget-priced hotel now has a few more expensive rooms boasting Jacuzzis; the standard rooms are not large but they are clean and tidy.

YMCA Central ($)
220 Golden Gate Avenue tel: 415/885-0460
With plain and simple single and double rooms with shared bathrooms, and a TV room, this makes a reasonable budget option for both men and women.

Financial District and Embarcadero

Galleria Park ($$)
191 Sutter Street tel: 800/792-9639 415/781-3060
Adjacent to the shops of Crocker Galleria, this is one of the city's best boutique hotels—establishments which pride themselves on attentive service and congenial surroundings—offering a choice of nicely furnished standard rooms and exceptionally attractive suites.

Hyatt Regency ($$–$$$)
5 Embarcadero Center tel: 800/233-1234 415/788-1234
Design themes of open space and crisp contours become apparent as soon as you enter

the enormous glass-ceilinged lobby and continue into the guest rooms—efficiently furnished and with first-run movies on the TV—and up to the revolving rooftop restaurant.

Mandarin Oriental ($$$)
222 Sansome Street tel: 800/622-0404 415/276-9888
Occupying the top 11 floors of a towering modern high-rise, the Mandarin spares no effort in pampering its predominantly business-traveler guests. All the rooms are quiet and extremely comfortable, and some of the rooms, including bathrooms, have fabulous views across the city. Excellent restaurant.

Park Hyatt ($$$)
333 Battery Street tel: 800/223-1234 415/392-1234
Squarely aimed at the high-flying business traveler, with complimentary Mercedes service to Financial District addresses and a fax machine and photocopier available. Guests can gaze from their windows across the city or the bay.

Fisherman's Wharf and Fort Mason

Comfort Inn by the Bay ($$)
2775 Van Ness Avenue tel: 415/928-5000
Slightly better-than-average motel rooms at lower-than-average prices are the main reasons for choosing this over its neighborhood rivals; set on a busy street but within easy reach of the main tourist areas. A buffet breakfast is included.

Hilton at Fisherman's Wharf ($$)
2620 Jones Street tel: 800/228-8408 415/885-4700
Another branch of a nationally known mid-range chain, the Hilton easily holds its own with its neighborhood rivals; for a family of four or more, the unusually spacious and well-equipped suites can prove a good option.

Holiday Inn Fisherman's Wharf ($$)
1300 Columbus Avenue tel: 800/465-4329 415/771-9000
A high-quality and very up-to-date link in the worldwide chain within easy walking distance of North Beach as well as the tourist spots of Fisherman's Wharf. If you are hungry but too lazy to go out, the restaurant serves a decent array of fish and meat dishes.

Hostelling International ($)
Fisherman's Wharf, Building 240, Fort Mason tel: 415/771-7277
One of the largest hostels in the US has small dormitories, laundry facilities and a maximum stay of 21 days, though this restriction may be waived if space is available. Good view across the Golden Gate.

San Francisco Marriott at Fisherman's Wharf ($$$)
1250 Columbus Avenue tel: 800/228-9290 415/775-7555
Well-to-do tourists and on-the-road Financial District dealers have both taken a shine to this efficient and well-presented hotel. Besides large, well-furnished and generously equipped rooms, the price includes maid service twice a day and free morning newspaper.

Sheraton at Fisherman's Wharf ($$$)
2500 Mason Street tel: 800/325-3535 415/362-5500
Everything you would expect to find in a hotel run by this competent upscale chain is provided in this 500-room property, which is a very easy walk to the area's main stores and attractions.

Travelodge near Ghirardelli Square ($$)
1201 Columbus Avenue tel: 415/776-7070
Not the most luxurious of the area's accommodations, but an attractively priced base for exploring the neighborhood and nearby North Beach. Only 25 rooms, so be sure to reserve early.

Tuscan Inn at Fisherman's Wharf ($$–$$$)
425 North Point tel: 800/648-4626 415/561-1100
Probably the most attractive lodging in Fisherman's Wharf, with cheerfully furnished rooms and an armchair-filled lobby where complimentary sherry can be sipped beside the fireplace.

The Wharf Inn ($$)
2601 Mason Street tel: 800/548-9918 415/673-7411
Redecorated to create warm, relaxing rooms and a two-bedroom penthouse suite, the Wharf Inn also presents guests with complimentary tea, hot cocoa or coffee and a morning newspaper.

Haight-Ashbury and Western Addition

Alamo Square Inn ($$)
719 Scott Street tel: 888/886-8803 415/922-2055
Located on the west side of scenic Alamo Square a few blocks from the heart of Haight-Ashbury, this atmospheric, rambling Victorian house, with fabulous views, offers bed-and-breakfast in a choice of 12 rooms decorated in widely varying but appealing styles.

Archbishop's Mansion ($$–$$$)
1000 Fulton Street tel: 800/543-5820 415/563-7872
From 1904, this sprawling home really was an archbishop's residence. Transformed into an antique-filled bed-and-breakfast inn, it now has 15 rooms individually decorated with themes pertaining to particular 19th-century French operas.

Grove Inn ($–$$)
890 Grove Street tel: 800/829-0780 415/929-0780
An affordable bed-and-breakfast inn where the cheaper rooms have shared bathrooms; located within easy reach of Haight-Ashbury but in a dreary and sometimes intimidating section of the Western Addition.

Metro Hotel ($)
319 Divisadero Street tel: 415/861-5364
Small, simple and suitably priced, this friendly hotel is located just two blocks away from Buena Vista Park and a short walk from Haight Street.

The Red Victorian ($–$$)
1665 Haight Street tel: 415/864-1978
There can be few experiences more quintessentially Californian than spending a night in this delightful 1904 bed-and-breakfast inn, situated directly above a gallery of Meditative Art and a healthfood café. Some of the variously themed rooms are decorated with original 1960s psychedelic posters, and some of the four-poster beds are draped with tie-dyed canopies.
Stanyan Park Hotel ($$)
750 Stanyan Street tel: 415/751-1000
The staff of this charming, characterful 36-room Edwardian hotel, which faces Golden Gate Park, strive to create an intimate atmosphere similar to that of a small bed-and-breakfast inn; another contributing factor to the B&B ambience is indeed the breakfast: rolls, muffins and fruit laid out in a spacious dining room.
Victorian Inn on the Park ($$)
301 Lyon Street tel: 415/931-1830
Wind your way up the staircase—lined with historic posters and photos of San Francisco—of this imposing 1897 house and you will find 12 cozy rooms decorated with antiques; some have original, working fireplaces. Fruit, croissants and fresh-brewed coffee are served for breakfast.

Japantown

Hotel Majestic ($$$)
1500 Sutter Street tel: 800/869-8966
415/441-1100
Dating from 1888 and said to be the city's oldest hotel, the five-story Majestic helped house the homeless following the 1906 earthquake; a thorough remodel and modernization has created a stylish and relaxing place, filled with French and English antiques and period furnishings.
Miyako Inn ($$)
1800 Sutter Street tel: 800/528-1234
415/921-4000
Not to be confused with the similarly named—and more expensive—hotel (see entry below), the Best Western-owned Miyako Inn offers fairly standard accommodation except for steam baths and a few other Japanese touches.
The Queen Anne ($$)
1590 Sutter Street tel: 800/227-3970
415/441-2828
This handsome and extremely spacious Victorian building dates back to 1890 and originally served as a school for girls. The Queen Anne now offers reposeful nights in elegantly furnished rooms with high ceilings. Breakfast is included, as are afternoon tea and sherry, which are served in the drawing room.
The Radisson Miyako ($$$)
1625 Post Street tel: 800/333-3333
415/922-3200
British rock star David Bowie is just one former guest who has appreciated the luxury-class Miyako's clever fusing of Western and Japanese ideas; all rooms have sliding shoji screens and marble bathrooms with furo tubs, while the traditional Japanese rooms have tatami mats and futons. Excellent restaurant.

Marina District

Cow Hollow Motor Inn and Suites ($–$$)
2190 Lombard Street tel: 415/921-5800
Large, modern hotel with bigger than average rooms, some with views of the Golden Gate Bridge. The suites have hardwood floors, Oriental carpets, antique furnishings, marble fireplaces and kitchens. Covered parking.
Edward II Inn & Pub ($–$$)
3155 Scott Street tel: 800/473-2846
415/922-3000
The finest four-poster beds and whirlpool baths to be found in Pacific Heights are a feature of the pricier rooms (the cheaper ones share a bath) at this bed-and-breakfast inn, which is combined with an English-themed bar.
Hotel del Sol ($$)
3100 Webster Street tel: 877/433-5765
415/921-5520 www.thehoteldelsol.com
With its convenient location between lively Union and Chestnut streets, this colorful, cheerful former motor lodge has 57 rooms, a swimming pool and free parking. Rates include a continental breakfast and cable TV.
Marina Inn ($$)
3110 Octavia Street tel: 800/274-1420
415/928-1000
If the comparative tranquility of the Marina District is what is required, this modestly sized and attractively priced inn is a prudent choice. There is also a light breakfast included.
Marina Motel ($)
2576 Lombard Street tel: 800/346-6118
415/921-9406
A budget-priced option in a busy street in the largely residential Marina District, with a choice of regular and kitchen-equipped rooms.

Mission District and the Castro

El Capitan ($)
2361 Mission Street tel: 415/695-1597
Small, no-frills hotel for students or international travelers only, in the heart of the Mission District; unmatched for price but do not expect peace and quiet on the neighborhood's lively main thoroughfare, which can feel intimidating after dark.
24 Henry ($)
24 Henry Street tel: 800/900-5686
415/864-5686
Five-room Edwardian non-smoking guesthouse on a tree-lined Castro District side street; a small, friendly and affordable base chiefly aimed at gay men.
Willows Inn ($$)
710 Fourteenth Street tel: 800/431-0277
415/431-4770
Some of the 12 rooms may lack private bathrooms, but the friendly atmosphere and the warm furnishings of this 1904 bed and breakfast do much to win the admiration of its guests, many of whom are gay or lesbian visitors to the city.

Nob Hill

Fairmont Hotel ($$$)
950 Mason Street tel: 800/527-4727
415/772-5000
A home-away-from-home for rich and famous

visitors since 1907, the Fairmont still has sky-high standards of service and decadently decorated rooms large enough to park a 747 in; the best of them also offer stunning city views.

Huntington Hotel ($$$)
1075 California Street tel: 800/227-4684 415/474-5400
Quietly sophisticated, this elegant hotel provides a luxurious setting without the flashiness of other leading Nob Hill hotels. There is a wood-paneled piano bar befitting the understated atmosphere, and the new Nob Hill Spa on the premises is a heavenly addition.

InterContinental Mark Hopkins ($$$)
1 Nob Hill tel: 800/662-4455 415/392-3434
Another long-serving Nob Hill landmark and treated to a $10-million facelift in the late 1980s, the Mark Hopkins, sometimes known as "The Mark," offers a choice of "traditional" or "contemporary" rooms—neither of which should ever give cause for complaint—or a penthouse suite complete with grand piano. Its rooftop cocktail bar is a legendary venue for skyscraper partying.

Nob Hill Lambourne ($$$)
725 Pine Street tel: 800/274-8466 415/433-2287 www.nobhilllambourne.com
A boutique hotel that's part of the Joie de Vivre chain, Nob Hill Lambourne has 20 rooms equipped with kitchenettes, fax machines, down comforters and buckwheat pillows. Don't be surprised by the nightly turndown service: Guests receive vitamins instead of mints.

Ritz-Carlton ($$$)
600 Stockton Street tel: 800/241-3333 415/296-7465
Although service has deteriorated somewhat at this plush hotel situated in a distinguished neoclassical building, the Ritz-Carlton still has sumptuously furnished rooms with minibars and TVs with a range of movies; other features include a fully equipped fitness center and swimming pool, an impressive art collection lining the corridors and two excellent restaurants.

Stanford Court ($$$)
905 California Street tel: 800/227-4736 415/989-3500
The epitome of understated elegance, the Stanford Court's mix of good-sized rooms with tasteful and traditional furnishings, and friendly and ultraefficient service, has won it many friends among jet-setting aristocrats. Sauna and fitness center available.

North Beach

Hotel Bohème ($$)
444 Columbus Avenue tel: 415/433-9111
Tidy and welcoming European-style inn in the pulsating heart of North Beach, with each of the comfortable rooms themed on particular flowers.

San Remo Hotel ($)
2237 Mason Street tel: 800/352-7366 415/776-8688
Located on the borders of North Beach and Fisherman's Wharf, the impressively priced San Remo is a fully renovated 1906 Italianate villa with small but serviceable rooms (although the bathrooms are shared) grouped around a central atrium. Good value in a good location.

Washington Square Inn ($$)
1660 Stockton Street tel: within California 800/388-0220 415/981-4220
Facing Washington Square, the inn's simple furnishings do their best to re-create the mood of a rural French family-run hotel. Breakfast is included, as is early evening tea, wine and snacks.

Pacific Heights

Cathedral Hill Hotel ($$)
1101 Van Ness Avenue tel: 800/622-0855 415/776-8200
This big, fully equipped modern hotel with dependable service and comfortable rooms also offers an outdoor heated pool.

Days Inn near Fisherman's Wharf ($)
2358 Lombard Street tel: 800/325-2525 415/922-2010
An inexpensive chain option, about 2 miles (3.5km) from Fisherman's Wharf, this is a convenient and affordable base for the rest of the city.

Hotel Drisco ($$$)
2901 Pacific Avenue tel: 800/634-7277 415/346-2880 www.hoteldrisco.com
Built in 1903 and renovated in 1997, the hotel may look a little different than when President Eisenhower was a guest. Extras include a continental breakfast, afternoon tea or wine, and an in-house fitness room.

Laurel Inn ($$)
444 Presidio Avenue tel: 800/552-8735 415/567-8467
Located in an out-of-the-way section of the city, the inn received a much-needed facelift several years ago. The addition of a bar even added a trendy, Southern California flavor.

Monarch Hotel ($–$$)
1015 Geary Street tel: 800/777-3210 415/673-5232
On the southern fringes of Pacific Heights and just a few blocks from Japantown and the Civic Center, the stylish, moderately sized Monarch is neatly furnished and boasts splendid views from its rooftop terrace.

Pacific Heights Inn ($)
1555 Union Street tel: 800/523-1801 415/776-3310
A reasonably priced inn close to the neighborhood's premier shopping and dining strip and offering adequate if unelaborate motel rooms. Some rooms and suites have kitchens, which can come in handy.

Union Street Inn ($$)
2229 Union Street tel: 415/346-0424
Innkeepers Jane Bertorelli and David Coyle (who was a chef for the Duke and Duchess of Bedford) turned this 1902 Edwardian into a delightful B&B equipped with candles, fresh flowers, wine glasses and fine linens. The Carriage House, with its whirlpool tub, is set off from the main house by an old-fashioned English garden with lemon trees. An elaborate breakfast is included, as are afternoon tea and evening hors d'oeuvres.

SoMa

Argent Hotel ($$$)
50 Third Street tel: 877/222-6699 415/974-6400
This ultra-urban hotel offers comfortable, stylish rooms with floor-ceiling windows; many with spectacular views. In addition to its other merits, it boasts a full workout room, complete with a sauna.

European Guest House ($)
761 Minna Street tel: 415/861-6634
A backpacker-aimed hostel with four-bed dormitories and an easygoing atmosphere; within a few minutes' walk of lively Folsom Street and convenient for the long-distance bus links from the Transbay Terminal.

Globe Hostel ($)
10 Hallam Place tel: 415/431-0540
Aimed at globetrotting backpackers (everyone must show proof of recent travel overseas), this is a down-home hostel just off the nightlife strip of Folsom Street with a number of attractive features—such as safety deposit boxes, free coffee, and no curfew.

Harbor Court ($$)
165 Steuart Street tel: 800/346-0555 415/882-1300
Occupying a characterful early 1900s building just south of Market Street, this is a cozy and stylish option offering all the usual top-notch facilities—plus use of the neighboring YMCA's Olympic-sized pool—and some fine bay views.

Hotel Griffon ($$)
155 Steuart Street tel: 800/321-2201 415/495-2100
A luxurious small hotel a few steps from Market Street; many of the guests are Financial District brokers enjoying the well-stocked minibars and views across the bay. Guests have free use of the adjoining YMCA fitness center.

Marriott Courtyard San Francisco Downtown ($$–$$$)
299 Second Street (at Folsom Street) tel: 800/321-2211 415/947-0700 www.courtyard.com
Opened in October 2001, this Marriott is actually in SoMa, despite the name. The 400-room property is near Union Square and Pac Bell Park, but caters primarily to business travelers.

Mosser Hotel ($–$$)
54 Fourth Street tel: 800/227-3804 415/986-4400
Skimps on the luxuries but with excellent rates and a great location—close to Yerba Buena Gardens and Market Street; good value.

Palace Hotel ($$$)
2 New Montgomery Street tel: 800/325-3535 415/512-1111
Long before the fine hotels of Nob Hill were pampering the great and good, the Palace was firmly established as the city's most luxurious place to stay. Following a $60-million renovation, this restored landmark hotel reopened in 1991, setting a high standard for comfort, service and decor; stop by, if only to stare at the sumptuous Garden Court. Indoor lap pool and health club.

The Pickwick ($$)
85 Fifth Street tel: 800/227-3282 415/421-7500
Unpretentious refurbished French provincial lodgings at a very reasonable price close to Market Street and within a few blocks of Yerba Buena Gardens.

San Francisco Marriott ($$$)
55 Fourth Street tel: 800/228-9290 415/896-1600
Locally derided as the "Jukebox Marriott" because of its architecture, there is no denying that this distinctive high-rise offers top-class accommodations chiefly for convention-goers and business travelers; all the facilities you would want, including a health club.

Union Square

Andrews Hotel ($$)
624 Post Street tel: 800/926-3739 415/563-6877
The pastel peach color scheme of this hotel will enliven the most fog-shrouded San Francisco morning, as will the fresh-brewed coffee, croissants and fruit waiting outside your room.

Campton Place ($$$)
340 Stockton Street tel: in California 800/235-4300 415/781-5555
Travelers used to luxury living but weary of large, impersonal hotels will love this medium-sized, well located place with stylish rooms and where the staff embody professional and personal service. Exceptional restaurant.

Cartwright Hotel ($$)
524 Sutter Street tel: 800/227-3844 415/421-2865
The rooms can be small but are comfortable and very competitively priced for this central neighborhood; complimentary afternoon tea and cakes are offered in the book-lined study.

Chancellor Hotel ($$)
433 Powell Street tel: 800/428-4748 415/362-2004
This Euro-style boutique hotel offers spacious rooms with classic San Francisco vistas, as well as a health club and a staff that displays an admirable attention to detail.

Clift ($$$)
495 Geary Street tel: 800/652-5438 415/775-4700
Designed by the legendary Philippe Starck, the renovated Clift caters to the whims and fancies of the rich and powerful, and accommodates them in spacious, gracefully furnished rooms. Now managed by ultrachic hotelier, Ian Schraeger, the property, which also houses the Redwood Room, attracts a more urban clientele.

Commodore Hotel ($$)
825 Sutter Street tel: 800/338-6848 415/923-6800
This faux-deco hotel with a funky modern design is home to the hip cocktail lounge, the Red Room. With a distinctly youthful feel, this is a perfect place to get simple comfort without stuffiness or pretension.

Four Seasons ($$$)
757 Market Street tel: 800/332-3442 415/633-3000 www.fourseasons.com

While the elegant hotel focuses on business travelers, it remains a luxurious choice in a convenient location, close to downtown shopping, SFMOMA, and the Moscone Center. Along with the expected amenities, access to spa services and workout equipment in the fancy Sports Club/LA, located in the same complex, is an added perk.

Golden Gate ($)
775 Bush Street tel: 800/835-1118 415/392-3702
The original 1913 "birdcage" elevator lifts you to hallways lined with historical photographs and guest rooms individually decorated with antiques and wicker pieces. Most rooms have private baths, some with claw-foot tubs. Continental breakfast and afternoon tea and cookies are served in the cozy parlor by a fire.

Halcyon Hotel ($)
649 Jones Street tel: 800/627-2396 415/929-8033
This should be every bargain-seeker's first stop in the neighborhood; the remarkably inexpensive efficiency apartments, painted in bold and joyful shades, are equipped with microwave ovens and coffee makers, and local phone calls are free. Daily and weekly rates.

Handlery Union Square ($$)
351 Geary Street tel: 800/843-4343 415/781-7800
A most dependable boutique hotel, with friendly service and comfortable rooms.

Hotel Bijou ($$)
111 Mason Street tel: 800/771-1022 415/771-1200
A tiny theater off the lobby treats you to screenings from the hotel's collection of 64 San Francisco-themed films—from *The Maltese Falcon* to *What's Up Doc?* The smallish but cheerful rooms are decorated with black-and-white movies stills.

Hotel Diva ($$)
440 Geary Street tel: 800/553-1900 415/885-0200
Sculpted in chrome and stainless steel, the Diva's striking high-tech Italian design style sets it well apart from most San Francisco hotels. The futuristic fittings continue in the rooms, where virtually everything electrical is remote-controlled, including the VCRs.

Hotel Metropolis ($$)
25 Mason Street tel: 800/553-1900 415/775-4600 www.hotelmetropolis.com
Metropolis is loaded with unique character, though it's located on an unsavory block. The decor is playful, with each room representing earth, wind, fire, or water. Amenities include a continental breakfast, a cardio room and use of the hotel's library.

Hotel Monaco ($$$)
501 Geary Street tel: 800/214-4220 415/292-0100
A graceful marble staircase and floor-to-ceiling fireplace dominate the lobby of this sumptuous hotel. The rooms, though small, are exquisitely appointed with canopy beds and colorful furnishings, and the staff is always on hand and committed to please.

Hotel Nikko ($$$)
222 Mason Street tel: 800/645-5687 415/394-1111
The two-story marble lobby complete with waterfall is just the start; ascend on the ultra-smooth elevators and you will find your room tastefully furnished and fitted with a fully stocked minibar. From the higher floors, the views can be exceptional.

Hotel Rex ($$)
562 Sutter Street tel: 800/433-4435 415/433-4434 www.thehotelrex.com
Restored in 1996, this delightful hotel boasts an ideal location, 94 stylish rooms and a lovely wood bar in the lobby. Guests receive a complimentary newspaper, a glass of wine each afternoon and have access to the Club One gym. Service is top-notch.

Hotel Triton ($$$)
342 Grant Avenue tel: 800/433-6611 415/394-0500
Custom-made designer furnishings, pastel shades and artwork by contemporary Bay Area artists help make this the hippest place to stay in San Francisco; the rooms are all equipped with CD players.

Hotel Union Square ($$)
114 Powell Street tel: 800/553-1900 415/397-3000
Cable cars rumble and clang evocatively past the entrance to this affordable and well-run boutique hotel; the complimentary breakfast features croissants and herbal teas.

Kensington Park ($$–$$$)
450 Post Street tel: 800/553-1900 415/788-6400
An impressively presented boutique hotel with Queen Anne-style furnishings and decorations; breakfast is included, and complimentary afternoon sherry is served to the sound of a pianist.

King George ($$)
334 Mason Street tel: 800/288-6005 415/781-5050
This mid-sized hotel in the heart of the theater area has just undergone a year-long renovation. Serves "English-style" afternoon tea to piano accompaniment.

The Maxwell Hotel ($$–$$$)
386 Geary Street tel: 1-888/734-6299 415/986-2000
Convenient to several theaters, the Maxwell's rooms can be slightly small but most are plushly furnished.

Monticello Inn ($$)
127 Ellis Street tel: 800/669-7777 415/392-8800
An enterprising and entertaining attempt to re-create a southern plantation home, complete with replica Federal-period furnishings, book-lined parlor and fireplace.

The Olympic ($)
140 Mason Street tel: 800/643-5333 415/982-5010
A front-runner among the area's budget-priced possibilities, offering compact but clean rooms with a choice of shared or private bathroom. Popular with backpackers.

Pan Pacific Hotel ($$$)
500 Post Street tel: 800/533-6465 415/771-8600
From the massive open-plan entrance court and its glass-sided elevators, this hotel is strikingly designed offering first-rate facilities.

Savoy ($$)
580 Geary Street tel: 800/227-4223 415/441-2700
The reposeful Savoy is designed to suggest a small hotel in rural France. Breakfast is included, as is afternoon wine and cheese.

Sheehan ($)
620 Sutter Street tel: 800/848-1529 415/775-6500
Formerly a YWCA, transformed into a very good-value hotel with Olympic-sized pool and gym; the tidy, if sometimes slightly spartan, rooms are available with or without private bathrooms.

Sir Francis Drake ($$)
450 Powell Street tel: 800/227-5480 415/392-7755
No more than a skip and a jump from Union Square with would-be Tower of London Beefeaters on hand to greet new arrivals as they enter, the Sir Francis Drake provides a taste of Old World grandeur at an affordable price.

Touchstone Hotel ($–$$)
480 Geary Street tel: 800/ 524-1888 415/771-1600
The small but clean rooms are temptingly good value for the budget-minded visitor, and breakfast is included in the rate.

USA Hostels San Francisco ($)
749 Taylor Street tel: 415/673-3277
A mix of dorm rooms with four beds and a bathroom, and private rooms with their own bathrooms. There's a rooftop lounge and patio, a well-equipped kitchen, plus a free all-you-can-eat pancake and waffle breakfast.

Villa Florence ($$)
225 Powell Street tel: 800/553-4411 415/397-7700
Extremely well-located for Union Square shopping, the Villa Florence's public areas are dotted with Italian art and antiques (the lobby also has a fireplace) and the guest rooms are tastefully furnished and provided with coffee makers.

Vintage Court ($$)
650 Bush Street tel: 800/654-1100 415/392-4666
Classy and comfortable, the Vintage Court identifies its rooms with names of selected Wine Country wineries. The oenological theme continues in the lobby, where complimentary early-evening wine is offered beside the fireplace with a copious pile of magazines.

Westin St. Francis ($$$)
335 Powell Street at Union Square tel: 800/228-3000 415/397-7000
A much-loved San Francisco landmark, the Westin St. Francis has been a prestige hotel since it opened in 1904 and became the city's first hotel to put sheets on its beds. The more recent addition of a modern tower wing and the computerization of the check-in desk have done nothing to detract from its elegant and sophisticated ambience.

White Swan Inn ($$)
845 Bush Street tel: 800/999-9570 415/775-1755
Filled throughout with English antiques, furnishings and paintings, the White Swan strives to provide comfortable bed-and-breakfast accommodations with a full range of services. The English theme includes a complimentary afternoon tea, complete with scones and jam. Some rooms are equipped with fireplaces.

York Hotel ($$)
940 Sutter Street tel: 800/808-9675 415/885-6800
This hotel is a must for film buffs who want to see the staircase where Alfred Hitchcock filmed his extraordinary thriller *Vertigo*. The York, an old-style classic, is well located and decent value.

RESTAURANTS

- **budget ($)—under $15**
- **moderate ($$)—$15–$50**
- **expensive ($$$)—over $50**

Berkeley

Blue Nile ($)
2525 Telegraph Avenue tel: 510/540-6777
Delicious Ethiopian food served in a tastefully decorated room; a favorite eating spot of Berkeley's students and many locals, for years.

Chez Panisse ($$$)
1517 Shattuck Avenue tel: 510/548-5525
Credited with being the mid-1970s birthplace of California cuisine, Chez Panisse is still a pivotal part of Berkeley's so-called gourmet ghetto, and its cultured culinary presentations change daily; reservations are essential. Less costly, less formal and just as good is the upstairs Chez Panisse Café.

Zachary's Chicago Pizza ($$)
1853 Solano Avenue tel: 510/525-5950 and 5801 College Avenue tel 510/655-6385
San Franciscans willingly trek to Berkeley for this fabulous deep-dish pizza in a bustling, always jam-packed setting. Be prepared to wait, and keep in mind that credit cards aren't accepted.

The Castro

Café Flore ($)
2298 Market Street tel: 415/621-8579
The salads and light fare at this predominately gay café play a secondary role to people-watching. Open all day long. Expect a line.

Chow ($)
215 Church Street tel: 415/552-2469
Filling fare at phenomenally low prices, with an emphasis on American comfort food prepared with organic ingredients. Vegetarians have a lot of choices here.

Destino ($$)
1815 Market Street tel: 415/552-4451
Opened in 2000, this South American restaurant is hitting its stride. Large mirrors on coral-colored walls try to disguise the small space; small plates like pork-filled empanadas and Chilean sweet corn casserole are crowd-pleasers.

Mecca ($$)
2029 Market Street tel: 415/621-7000
Known mostly for its nightclub decor, potent cocktails, people-watching and live music, Mecca boasts a Mediterranean menu that satisfies. Excellent creative bar snacks.
La Méditerranée ($)
288 Noe Street tel: 415/431-7210
Enjoyable no-frills spot for tasty, filling Middle Eastern and Greek food, none of it liable to harm your budget.
Thailand Restaurant ($$)
438A Castro Street tel: 415/863-6868
Cozy upper-floor restaurant offering a long and impressive menu of Thai favorites including fiery red and green curries.

Chinatown

Bow Hon ($)
850 Grant Avenue tel: 415/362-0601
For the price, there is no better place to sample Cantonese clay-pot stews; also features noodle soups and stir-fried dishes.
Brandy Ho's ($$)
217 Columbus Avenue tel: 415/788-7527
On the North Beach border, Brandy Ho's is popular for outstanding and often spicy Hunan cuisine.
Empress of China ($$)
838 Grant Avenue tel: 415/434-1345
High above Chinatown—take an elevator to the restaurant—the standard Chinese offerings are outclassed by the views of San Francisco, but the opulent setting is still a reason to visit.
House of Nanking ($)
919 Kearny Street tel: 415/421-1429
There's always a line at this extremely small but highly regarded restaurant, which was among the first to bring quality Shanghai and northern regional Chinese cooking to Chinatown. Do beware, however, as the setting is rather bare and the service can be gruff.
Pot Sticker ($)
150 Waverly Place tel: 415/397-9985
Located on a temple-laden side street just off Grant Avenue, this enjoyable restaurant specializes in steamed and pan-fried dumplings with meat, seafood or vegetables.
Sam Woh ($)
813 Washington Street tel: 415/982-0596
An infamously rude headwaiter made this an essential Chinatown stop for years; now, however, only the very low prices and lively atmosphere—the kitchen occupies the entire first floor, and diners usually have to share the upstairs tables—make this a worthwhile local visit.
San Sun ($)
941 Stockton Street tel: 415/296-8228
While "hole-in-the-wall" accurately describes the pervading ambience at this Chinatown Vietnamese eatery, it simply can't be beat for terrific pho (such as with chicken dumplings and leeks) or classic Vietnamese rice noodle dishes.

Civic Center and Tenderlion

Ananda Fuara ($)
1298 Market Street tel: 415/621-1994
A serene atmosphere prevails at this informal and exclusively vegetarian restaurant, where "neatloaf" served with gravy and potatoes is one popular option, and where the chef creates a daily "Peace Special."
CityScape ($$$)
333 O'Farrell Street tel:415/923-5002
On the 46th floor of the Hilton hotel, with a 360-degree view of the city and beyond, this is an elegant aerie with huge picture windows, top-notch cuisine and dancing nightly.
Indigo ($$$)
687 McAllister Street tel: 415/673-9353
Designers aiming for a Manhattan lounge feel created an inviting atmosphere with wood paneling, velvet banquettes and splashes of indigo. The prix fixe menu from 5pm–7pm attracts opera-goers; the fare is New American.
Maharani ($–$$)
1122 Post Street tel: 415/775-1988
Welcoming Indian eatery with good prices and a menu that includes fiery curries and a wide range of vegetarian options.
Shalimar ($)
1409 Polk Street tel:415/776-4642
Order at the counter and wait for some of the tastiest, cheapest Indian-Pakistani food around. Be warned, the atmosphere is non-existent, the service can be gruff and it's cash only.

Financial District and Union Square

Aqua ($$$)
252 California Street tel: 415/956-9662
Painstakingly selected and prepared—and then carefully presented—seafood inevitably draws a style-conscious crowd to one of the city's most modernistically designed dining places.
Asia de Cuba ($$$)
495 Geary Street (Clift Hotel) tel: 415/929-2300
With branches in LA and New York, these ubiquitous Asian-Cuban hotspots draw a hip crowd, though the food gets mixed reviews. Of course, stick around for a cocktail in the Clift's Redwood Room after dinner.
Bix ($$$)
56 Gold Street (at Montgomery Street) tel: 415/433-6300
Situated on a downtown alley, this supper club is a gem reminiscent of the '30s and '40s. Bix classics include chicken hash, steak tartare and Maine lobster spaghetti. Before dinner, order a martini at the bar.
Café Bastille ($$)
22 Belden Place tel: 415/986-5673
Few places in the city offer outdoor dining, so the sidewalk tables alone set this French café apart. Add the ratatouille crêpes, croque monsieur sandwiches and accented waiters and you've got a winning combination.
Campton Place ($$$)
340 Stockton Street tel: 415/955-5555
One of the most elegant and formal rooms in the city, this hotel restaurant also serves some of the most innovative fusion cuisine. While many of the dishes contain seemingly disparate elements, what comes to the table is always flawless and beautifully presented. An excellent choice for a special occasion.

Cortez ($$$)
550 Geary Boulevard tel: 415/292-6360
In the Hotel Adagio and sporting a huge and colorful sculpture/chandelier, this trendy new restaurant serves excellent Mediterranean-inspired small plates, which means you can order several diminutive dishes and taste away the evening.

E&O Trading Co ($$)
314 Sutter Street tel: 415/693-0303
A happy-hour crowd enjoys micro-brewed beers, while others come for reasonably priced Asian fare, such as giant tiger prawn satay, East Indian samosas, Cambodian lettuce cups and Vietnamese lemongrass chicken.

Farallon ($$$)
450 Post Street tel: 415/956-6969
This capricious restaurant takes its seafood theme to the hilt with a wackily hip interior that makes you feel as if you are dining in an underwater Alice in Wonderland tea party. The decor is reflected in the eclectic seafood menu. The oyster selection is always superb and the selection of homemade caviars intriguing.

Fleur de Lys ($$$)
777 Sutter Street tel: 415/673-7779
The dining room and service are set off by an elegant bright red canopy that drapes provocatively overhead. The cuisine of chef Hubert Keller is essentially lightened contemporary French fare, with special attention paid to vegetarian offerings.

Fog City Diner ($$)
1300 Battery Street tel: 415/982-2000
The abundant chrome and neon evoke the 1950s but the food is resolutely current California, with a host of innovative appetizers and main courses based on regional American cooking. It aims to delight the predominantly affluent Financial District diners.

John's Grill ($$)
63 Ellis Street tel: 415/986-0069
It may overdo its mention in Dashiell Hammett's *The Maltese Falcon* (a replica of the sought-after bird sits in the upstairs dining room), but John's Grill also serves some good steak and seafood dishes.

Kokkari Estiatorio ($$$)
200 Jackson Street tel: 415/981-0983
In a city with few Greek tavernas, Kokkari serves Mediterranean cuisine in a roomy, inviting setting with a country inn feel. Specialties include mesquite-grilled octopus salad, and grilled lamb chops with lemon-oregano vinaigrette.

Kyo-ya ($$$)
2 New Montgomery Street tel: 415/546-5090
The suggestive modern Japanese decor, despite its location in the Sheraton Palace Hotel, is the appropriate backdrop for what many consider the best Japanese restaurant in the city. While the price tag can be high, excellent sashimi, authentic dishes and attentive service make the total experience worth it.

Lori's Diner ($)
336 Mason Street tel: 415/392-8646 and 500 Sutter Street tel: 415/981-1950
Both branches of this 1950s-style diner are dependable places to significantly boost your calorie intake: Heavyweight breakfasts, sandwiches, burgers and creamy milkshakes are served around the clock.

Masa's ($$$)
at the Hotel Vintage Court, 648 Bush Street tel: 415/989-7154
Although chef Julian Serrano, who made this the city's premier French restaurant, has fled to Las Vegas, the restaurant continues to impress, with sumptuous cooking elegantly presented and an excellent wine list.

Postrio ($$$)
inside the Prescott Hotel, 545 Post Street tel: 415/776-7825
Celebrity chef Wolfgang Puck opened this shrine to California-style gourmet eating in 1989, and now, with the kitchen in the hands of brother chef team Mitchell and Stephen Rosehthal, San Franciscans have yet to stop raving about it; reservations are essential.

Rubicon ($$$)
558 Sacramento Street tel: 415/434-4100
The popularity of this smartly appointed spot has been assured by the fact that it is owned by New York's super-restaurateur Drew Nieporent and a slew of celebrity investors. Fortunately, Denis Leary's understated American fare lives up to the hype.

Tadich Grill ($$–$$$)
240 California Street tel: 415/391-1849
In business since the Gold Rush and still as popular as ever for its grilled seafood, steak and pleasant atmosphere.

Thai Stick ($)
698 Post Street tel: 415/928-7730
It is far too easy to order more than you can eat—and still spend less than you think—in this enjoyable, good-quality Thai restaurant; be sure to leave space for the delicious tapioca pudding dessert.

Tommy Toy's ($$$)
655 Montgomery Street tel: 415/397-4888
The city's premier upscale Chinese restaurant serves winning French-influenced fare in an ornate setting, attracting the city's most famous faces and its fussiest eaters in similar numbers. Located by the Transamerica Pyramid.

Yank Sing ($$)
101 Spear Street (Rincon Center) tel: 415/957-9300 and 49 Stevenson Street tel: 415/541-4949
Though pricier than their equivalents in nearby Chinatown, both branches of Yank Sing offer some of the finest dim sum in San Francisco. Reservations essential.

Fisherman's Wharf and Fort Mason

Ana Mandara ($$$)
891 Beach Street tel: 415/771-6800
Formerly Loongbar, this French Vietnamese destination is backed by celeb Don Johnson. The food plays second fiddle to the fabulous upstairs bar, which offers jazz on weekends and breathtaking views of Alcatraz and the Bay.

Buena Vista Café ($)
2765 Hyde Street tel: 415/474-5044
A good choice for simple inexpensive sandwiches, burgers and comfort food in this pricey

area, though best known for its punch-packing Irish coffee—they claim to have been the first place in America to serve it, back in 1952.

Café Pescatore ($$)
2455 Mason Street tel: 415/561-1111
Mouthwatering Italian food, mostly wood-fired pizzas and pasta dishes, served in a pleasant airy room and prepared in an open kitchen.

Eagle Café ($)
Pier 39 tel: 415/433-3689
Satiating the ample appetites of longshoremen since the 1920s, the Eagle Café was shifted by crane to its current position in 1978. It maintains its culinary traditions by serving omelets and substantial sandwiches at rock-bottom prices to a mix of wharf workers and tourists, who relish this authentic slice of local life.

Gary Danko ($$$)
800 North Point Street tel: 415/749-2060
This five-star restaurant serves an exquisite, seasonal, prix fixe menu. Patrons choose from three to five courses, which include appetizers, seafood, meat and game birds, cheese and, of course, dessert. The extensive wine list features bottles from 15 different countries.

Ghirardelli Soda Fountain ($)
900 North Point Street, Ghirardelli Square tel: 415/771-4903
Milkshakes, ice cream and decadent sundaes are all on offer in this outlet of the locally revered chocolate manufacturer; specialties include the mighty "earthquake sundae," which serves four.

Greens ($$$)
Building A, Fort Mason tel: 415/771-6222
An outstanding vegetarian restaurant where gourmet-pleasing dishes are created using the produce of an organic farm run by a Zen Buddhist retreat across the bay in Marin County. The bay views are as stunning as the food; reservations are essential.

Piperade ($$)
1015 Battery Street tel: 415/391-2555
Star chef Gerald Hirigoyenm formerly of Pastis and Fringale, has returned to his French Basque roots in the form of Piperade, and outdone himself with expertly executed dishes in a welcoming environment.

Waterfront Restaurant and Café ($$–$$$)
Pier 7, The Embarcadero tel: 415/391-2696
The recent facelift has beautified the inside to match the stunning views of the harbor. The creative, mostly seafood menu also continues to please locals who have rediscovered this restaurant.

Haight-Ashbury

Asqew Grill ($)
1607 Haight Street tel: 415/701-9301 and 3348 Steiner Street tel 415/931-9201
Stick it on a skewer and serve it up. Kebab options range from lamb and chicken to ahi, though they're typically more generous with veggies than chunks of meat, fish or poultry.

Cha Cha Cha ($)
1801 Haight Street tel: 415/386-5758
Delicious Cuban and Caribbean dishes served in a tropically decorated—and frequently packed—room, where the serving staff leaves diners in no doubt as to who is in charge.

Indian Oven ($$)
233 Fillmore Street tel: 415/626-1628
Non-traditional decor, a young and stylish crowd, and the chef's creative interpretation of classic Indian dishes lead many to believe this is the best Indian restaurant in the city. The dishes from the tandoor oven are particularly noteworthy. Expect a crowd.

Kan Zaman ($)
1793 Haight Street tel: 415/751-9656
Middle Eastern food, strong coffee and exotic ambience: Diners sit on cushions surrounded by hookahs and entertained by belly dancers.

Kate's Kitchen
471 Haight Street tel: 415/626-3984
It's fun to join the crowds of Haight Street hipsters at this countrified diner for a satisfying breakfast or lunch of comforting soul food. Be sure to try the biscuits with sausage gravy or the great meatloaf sandwiches.

Pork Store Café ($)
1451 Haight Street tel: 415/864-6981
Dependable purveyor of wholesome American breakfasts—the side dishes include Deep South favorites such as grits—and lunchtime fare that features delicious soups, sandwiches and thick burgers.

Thep Phanom ($)
400 Waller Street tel: 415/431-2526
Top-notch Thai food in a homey setting for dinner only, at a price to suit even the most threadbare of budgets; be sure to arrive early or make a reservation.

Hayes Valley

Absinthe ($$$)
398 Hayes Street tel: 415/551-1590
Along with American-influenced French bistro fare that changes daily, Absinthe boasts an oyster bar and cheese menu. Theatergoers can pay a visit after the show, as the brasserie stays open till 1am.

Citizen Cake ($$)
399 Grove Street tel: 415/861-2228
Though the baked goods are far more famous than the overpriced lunch and dinner fare, this spot is still a good bet for a casual midday meal. Don't miss the incredible cakes, cookies and other pastries.

Fritz Fries ($)
579 Hayes Street tel: 415/864-7654 and 900 North Point Street tel: 415/928-1475
Savory and sweet crêpes are almost a side dish when compared to the café's delectable Belgian-style fries, served with your choice of dipping sauces. The garden out back is an added bonus.

Jardiniere ($$$)
300 Grove Street tel: 415/861-5555
Award-winning chef Traci des Jardins, also a co-owner, serves California-French cuisine in her romantic, two-story Hayes Valley supper club. Jazz music is on tap nightly.

Suppenkuche ($$)
601 Hayes Street tel: 415/252-9289
Bring your appetite. Hearty dinner entrees, typically for carnivores, include pork chops and

grilled pork sausage, both served with sauerkraut and mashed potatoes; shared seating on long wooden tables adds to the Barvarian feel. The welcoming bar pours both German and Belgian brews.

Zuni Café ($$$)
1658 Market Street tel: 415/552-2522
Lives have been changed by the roast chicken with bread salad at this cramped, slightly worn, but beloved American restaurant with a French accent. Many other delicious items issue forth from the wood-burning oven. The food is always satisfying, the service always friendly.

Japantown

Café Kati ($$$)
1963 Sutter Street tel: 415/775-7313
East-west fusion served in an attractive Victorian building near Japantown's Kabuki theater. Entrees include miso-glazed black bass and porcini-dusted ahi tuna. Try the warm and gooey chocolate cake for dessert.

Korea House ($$)
1640 Post Street tel: 415/563-1388
Eating Korean barbecue food in the heart of Japantown may seem peculiar, but this is a reliable outlet for popular Korean dishes such as spicy do-it-yourself barbecued meat and numerous varieties of soup and noodles.

Mifune ($)
1737 Post Street tel: 415/922-0337
Japanese-style fast food, served to fast-moving customers; includes simple but excellent noodle dishes and much more.

Neecha ($)
2100 Sutter Street tel: 415/922-9419
Thai favorites offered at tempting prices in a friendly room. Many vegetarian options.

Mission District

Angkor Borei ($$)
3471 Mission Street tel: 415/550-8417
Excellent Cambodian food served in inventive and stylish ways; distance from the city's fashionable areas helps keep the prices lower than they might otherwise be.

Burger Joint ($)
807 Valencia Street tel: 415/824-3494
This stylish retro diner with checkered floors and comfy booths serves premium hamburgers made with Niman Ranch beef, thick milkshakes and chunky fries. Non-beef eaters can choose veggie or chicken breast burgers.

Delfina ($$$)
3621 18th Street tel: 415/552-4055
Twice the size of its original space, this lauded Italian restaurant still serves simple, fresh dishes to a loud, packed house nightly and now has a bar to ease the wait. Reservations are a must.

El Toro Taqueria ($)
598 Valencia Street tel: 415/431-3351
Popular fill-up stop with locals for meticulously prepared down-to-earth Mexican food costing just a few dollars per huge plateful.

Firecracker ($$)
1007 Valencia Street tel: 415/642-3470
Make your way through the red curtains for the Mission's lively spin on traditional Chinese food. Spicy dishes include garlicky firecracker chicken.

Foreign Cinema ($$$)
2534 Mission Street tel:415/648-7600
In this edgy section of the Mission District, you might be surprised to find one of the best restaurants in the city. Its eclectic and savory offerings compete with the movie classics shown in the inner courtyard.

Pauline's Pizza ($)
260 Valencia Street tel: 415/552-2050
Get a pizza with a conscience at this lively pizzeria that also serves salads and tasty daily specials made with organic ingredients.

La Rondella ($–$$)
901 Valencia Street tel: 415/647-7474
Mexican cuisine a cut above the neighborhood average and enlivened on weekends by strolling mariachi musicians. Tropical decor. Good for late-night sustenance.

Luna Park ($$)
694 Valencia Street tel: 415/553-8584
Fun food like the goat-cheese fondue is perfect for sharing, while entrees like fontina-stuffed ravioli or "pot on fire" (beef brisket, carrots, turnips and potatoes in broth) is better tackled alone. The surroundings are loud, but damage to the pocketbook is minimal.

Saigon Saigon ($$)
1132 Valencia Street tel: 415/206-9635
Black-pepper catfish and coconut chicken are among the specialties of this highly rated and fairly priced Vietnamese restaurant.

Ti Couz ($)
3108 16th Street tel: 415/252-7373
Fabulous crêpes with a cornucopia of savory and sweet fillings, and jars of hard cider are the bill of fare at this cute crêperie. Expect a long wait for a table, or take a seat at the counter, where you can watch the crêpe-makers in action.

Universal Café ($$)
2814 19th Street tel: 415/821-4608
Inventive American fare in a diminutive warehouse-like restaurant near the Mission. Dishes range from comfort food like grilled pork tenderloin to inventive seasonal salads.

Nob Hill

Big Four ($$$)
in the Huntington Hotel, 1075 California Street tel: 415/771-1140
California-style versions of classic French dishes are the staples of this ultra-elegant, very traditional dining place, where the city's rich and powerful regularly indulge themselves. Just come for a drink to soak up the aura of privilege.

Charles Nob Hill ($$$)
1250 Jones Street tel: 415/771-5400
Charles Condy, who also owns Aqua, has created an intimate dining room to complement the delicious contemporary cooking of chef Michael Mina. All the dishes, like Sonoma quail with quince, are exquisitely presented and delicious.

Ritz-Carlton Dining Room ($$$)
600 Stockton Street tel: 415/773-6198
Exquisitely old-fashioned, with lush carpets, sumptuous drapes, wood-paneled walls and

fine silver and china, this formal dining room is a fine choice for a special occasion. Sylvan Portay's contemporary French cuisine is understated and delicious. An impressive cheese cart, one of the few in the city, completes the experience. The wine list is extensive and offers many costly French bottles. The Terrace restaurant is the hotel's less formal dining room.

North Beach

La Bodega ($)
1337 Grant Avenue tel: 415/433-0439
Long-established and much admired Spanish restaurant which serves a ridiculously inexpensive paella special every night except Friday and Saturday; live flamenco music often accompanies the eating.

Buca Giovanni ($$$)
800 Greenwich Street tel: 415/776-7766
Not many out-of-towners know about this dark and romantic basement restaurant which serves some of the best Tuscan-style food (rabbit is a specialty) in the neighborhood; dinner only, reservations essential.

Caffè Trieste ($)
609 Vallejo Street tel: 415/392-6739
Since it opened in the 1950s, the family-run Trieste has been the quintessential North Beach café, drawing writers, poets, artists and anyone seeking a flavorful cup of coffee and a variety of tempting cakes and snacks. The amateur opera performances staged here on Saturday afternoons have become a neighborhood institution.

Capp's Corner ($$)
1600 Powell Street tel: 415/989-2589
Fill up on huge portions of Italian food to the sound of men at the bar rolling dice for drinks at this casual, old-time North Beach favorite.

Enrico's Sidewalk Café ($$)
504 Broadway tel: 415/982-6223
Nightly live music and a heated outdoor patio make for great fun and people-watching. The innovative Italian food will keep you happy, especially the thin-crust pizzas and hearty Tuscan T-bone steaks.

Fior d'Italia ($$)
601 Union Street tel: 415/986-1886
Among San Francisco's oldest Italian restaurants, Fior d'Italia offers wonderfully fresh pasta dishes either in the elegant back room or at the less formal tables overlooking Washington Square.

Helmand ($$)
430 Broadway tel: 415/362-0641
Though this block of Broadway is a bit down-and-out, elegant Helmand serves tasty Afghan dishes like leek and scallion-filled ravioli with ground beef and mint. For dessert, try rice pudding scented with cardamom.

The House ($$–$$$)
1230 Grant Avenue tel: 415/986-8612
For a pasta respite, elbow your way into the House, which serves an Asian fusion menu with a focus on seafood. The Chilean sea bass is superb, and there's a surprisingly decadent array of desserts.

Mama's on Washington Square ($)
1701 Stockton Street tel: 415/362-6421
Breakfast is the specialty (in fact, they don't serve dinner), but patrons must stand in line for a table. The glass case of mouthwatering baked goods only increases the anticipation for eggs, French toast and other traditional fare.

Mario's Bohemian Cigar Store Café ($)
566 Columbus Avenue tel: 415/362-0536
Long-established North Beach café with excellent focaccia bread snacks and great potential for people watching.

Maykadeh ($$–$$$)
470 Green Street tel: 415/362-8286
A surprise in this largely Italian neighborhood is this authentic Persian restaurant specializing in marinated lamb dishes served in a handsome dining room. A favorite is the *ghorme sabzee* (braised lamb shank).

Moose's ($$–$$$)
1652 Stockton Street tel: 415/989 7800
This bustling and fashionable eatery serves quality Mediterranean/Californian fare but is frequented as much for its social cachet as its food; reserve three days ahead.

North Beach Pizza ($)
1499 Grant Avenue tel: 415/433-2444
Famous throughout the city for its thick, chewy pizzas served with a host of toppings, this is a great late-night stop, and the lines which were once a perennial feature have been reduced by the opening of a second branch in Grant Avenue.

North Beach Restaurant ($$)
1512 Stockton Street tel: 415/392-1700
Among the neighborhood's more elegant and formal Italian restaurants, the choices include a fixed-price seven-course dinner, and there is an extensive wine list.

L'Osteria del Forno ($–$$)
519 Columbus Avenue tel: 415/982-1124
Cozy northern Italian dishes served in a decidely non-touristy and welcoming spot in North Beach. The tiny trattoria doesn't take reservations, so prepare to wait.

Rose Pistola ($$–$$$)
532 Columbus Avenue tel: 415/399-0499
This sleek North Beach hotspot is the work of San Francisco favorite, Reed Heron, who serves up delicious, sophisticated versions of Italian dishes. Items cooked in the wood-burning oven are especially enticing.

Tommaso's ($)
1042 Kearny Street tel: 415/398-9696
This quintessential North Beach haunt serves exceptional pies from its wood-burning oven. A great spot for hearty food, cheap red wine and lively conversation.

Pacific Heights, Russian Hill and Marina District

Art Institute Café ($)
800 Chestnut Street tel: 415/749-4567
Part of the San Francisco Art Institute but open to the public, this café serves inexpensive lunches and snacks, it has a patio area with great views of Fisherman's Wharf and Telegraph Hill.

Betelnut Pejiu Wu
2030 Union Street tel: 415/929-8855
In-the-know crowds have discovered this ultra-hip, high-styled, pan-Asian restaurant boasting an international beer list and exotic dishes that span the scope of the Far East—Korea, Singapore, Thailand, China and more.
Café Kati ($$)
1963 Sutter Street tel: 415/775-7313
A popular café that serves down-home American fare liberally sprinkled with global accents. Dinner can include such diverse choices as spring rolls, risotto and a decadent banana sundae.
Café Marimba ($)
2317 Chestnut Street tel: 415/776-1506
Draws plenty of regular visitors for its tempting variety of regional Mexican dishes, premium tequilas and excellent margaritas served amid a clutter of Latin American folk art.
Dragon Well ($)
2142 Chestnut Street tel: 415/474-6888
Reasonable prices and Americanized Chinese food are the hallmarks of this Marina District restaurant. You can't miss with the pot stickers, Chinese chicken salad or walnut prawns.

The Elite Café ($$)
2049 Fillmore Street tel: 415/346-8668
This gourmet-pleasing cajun/creole restaurant serves the spicy favorites of Louisiana in endlessly inventive and mouthwatering ways.
Ella's ($)
500 Presidio Avenue tel: 415/441-5669
A fabulous Sunday brunch is the main draw at this always-packed café. Regulars rave about the baked goods, especially the sticky buns, and the chicken hash.
Frascati ($$–$$$)
1901 Hyde Street tel: 415/928-1406
Parking in the neighborhood is unbearable, but the tasty Mediterranean dishes are worth the headache. Perfect for a romantic evening; outdoor seating when weather permits.
Izzy's Steak & Chops ($$)
3345 Steiner Street tel: 415/563-0487
A haven for carnivores, though seafood provides an alternative and is served in portions as ample as those of the meat dishes. Creamed spinach and potatoes complete the experience.
La Folie ($$$)
2316 Polk Street tel: 415/776-5577
First-class imaginative and stylish French food. A delightful fixed-price three-course meal is served Monday to Thursday, with an *à la carte* menu at other times. Reserve.
Merenda ($$$)
1809 Union Street tel: 415/346-7373
French-California fare prepared by a chef who once worked in the White House. The wine bar and striking red walls add to the intimacy; save room for the profiteroles at dessert.
Osome ($$)
3145 Fillmore Street tel: 415/346-2311
An unpretentious setting for some of San Francisco's best priced and most imaginatively prepared Japanese food.
Pane e Vino ($$)
1715 Union Street tel: 415/346-2111
Enter this trattoria and be treated to a view of an exciting antipasto selection while you inevitably wait for a table. The delicious risottos and other Italian fare make it one of the city's favorites.
Perry's ($$)
1944 Union Street tel: 415/922-9022
A wood-paneled New York-style restaurant and bar which offers ample portions of meat and seafood and has a long-standing reputation as Pacific Heights' premier singles' meeting spot.
PlumpJack Café ($$–$$$)
3127 Fillmore Street tel: 415/563-4755
One of the big draws at PlumpJack's is the excellent and reasonably priced wine list that features a selection of wines from exceptional California producers. Completing the picture here are the excellent Mediterranean fare, elegant interior design and lighting and attentive service.
Spoon ($)
2209 Polk Street tel: 415/268-0140
Opening to rave reviews in Russian Hill, this cozy spot turns tables with unusual dishes like the Waldorf pizza and comfort food like macaroni and cheese. Now the restaurant serves brunch on weekends.
Thai Spice ($)
1730 Polk Street tel: 415/775-4777
Top-quality Thai food served in an airy setting puts this among the city's premier ethnic eating spots; menu includes an impressive number of vegetarian dishes.
Yoshida-Ya ($$)
2909 Webster Street tel: 415/346-3431
Classy Japanese food and lots of it, presented in an enjoyably low-key environment. Yakitori dishes are particularly good.

Richmond District

Jakarta ($$)
615 Balboa Street tel: 415/387-5225
Subtly flavored Indonesian offerings that feature the usual favorites plus a smattering of the chef's specials.
Kabuto Sushi ($$)
5121 Geary Boulevard tel: 415/752-5652
A Kabuto contingent among San Francisco sushi connoisseurs asserts this is the best Japanese food in town. Others just like to watch the intensity of the owner Sachio Kojima at work.
Katia's Russian Tea Room ($$)
600 Fifth Avenue tel: 415/668-9292
Where else in San Francisco can you order blinis and beef stroganoff while listening to a musician who alternatively strums the guitar and plays the accordion? Old World charm and solicitous service are in big supply.
Khan Toke Thai House ($$)
5937 Geary Boulevard tel: 415/668-6654
Lovers of Thai food bemoaning the fact that city restaurants usually serve only mild forms of the dishes to appease American palates will find plenty to stimulate their tastebuds among the authentic spicy options available at this popular Thai eatery.
Mel's Drive-In ($)
3355 Geary Boulevard tel: 415/387-2255 and 2165 Lombard Street tel: 415/921-2867
You really can make a drive-in order at this 1950s

neighborhood landmark, though most customers take a seat and dig into classic coffee-shop fare such as thick, cheese-coated burgers and enormous barbecued meat sandwiches.

Minh's Garden ($)
208 Clement Street tel: 415/751-8211
Serves great-value Vietnamese food; anyone unfamiliar with this type of cuisine will find the friendly staff a great source of information.

Parc Hong Kong Restaurant ($$)
5322 Geary Boulevard tel: 415/668-8998
Certainly not the cheapest local place to eat Chinese food, but this busy Hong Kong-style restaurant offers the finest Cantonese fare in San Francisco; it serves top-notch dim sum at lunchtime too.

Royal Thai ($$)
951 Clement Street tel: 415/386-1795
More expensive and with a more formal ambience than many of the city's Thai restaurants, though widely regarded as among the best of its kind; no lunches are served on weekends.

Star of India ($$)
3721 Geary Boulevard tel: 415/668-4466
A lengthy menu, which includes many mouth-watering vegetarian selections, helps make this low-key spot one of San Francisco's more appealing Indian restaurants; the weekday lunch buffet is a bargain.

Straits Café ($)
3300 Geary Boulevard tel: 415/668-1783
Wonderful and inexpensive Singaporean food, with a variety of vegetarian options and a particularly strong selection of exotic seafood dishes.

Ton Kiang ($)
5821 Geary Boulevard tel: 415/387-8273
This Hakka restaurant serves some of the best dim sum in the country. Asian women carry trays and push carts of fragrant dumplings, stir fries and some unidentifiable dishes around you while you wait on line for your table.

SoMa

Acme Chophouse ($$$)
24 Willie Mays Plaza tel: 415/644-0242
A favorite of basefall fans (it's next to the major-league ballpark) and meat lovers, this is the place for local naturally raised grass-fed beef and free-range poultry, plus many other hearty dishes and a top-notch raw bar.

Bizou ($$)
598 Fourth Street tel: 415/543-2222
This perfect California bistro brings hearty French-inspired cooking to its many fans. While the menu is seasonal, standouts include skate with mashed potatoes, tomato salad with house-cured anchovies and braised beef cheeks.

Boulevard ($$–$$$)
1 Mission Street tel: 415/543-6084
Opened in 1994 in a landmark building, this cavernous Art Nouveau dining room has become a mainstay on the city's power restaurant scene. Chef Nancy Oakes prepares delectable dishes like wood-oven roasted rabbit and potato napoleons. The tarte tatin may be the best ever.

Le Charm ($$)
315 Fifth Street tel: 415/546-6128
As the name suggests, this quaint French café is indeed charming. The understated, simple food, a reasonable wine list and attentive service make it a local favorite.

Fringale ($$–$$$)
570 Fourth Street tel: 415/543-0573
Beautiful Basque food with French accents is served at Gerald Hirigoyen's original restaurant. The dining room is cheery even if the tables are rather close together, and there is also a good, reasonable wine list. Mussels steamed with garlic and pernod are a specialty.

The Fly Trap ($$)
606 Folsom Street tel: 415/243-0580
In one form or another The Fly Trap has been around for a century. Although this is a new version, it evokes an old-style San Francisco ambience and serves commendable Italian-influenced meals.

Hawthorne Lane ($$$)
22 Hawthorne Street tel: 415/777-9779
Everything is well chosen at this husband-and-wife-run restaurant: the neighborhood (which has up and come), the art on the walls and the lovely fixtures included. The cuisine is quintessentially Northern Californian, with special attention paid to seasonal fare.

Lulu ($$–$$$)
816 Folsom Street tel: 415/495-5775
Fashionable and always crowded, come here for top-class Mediterranean fare given a creative California treatment by a widely acclaimed chef. Large family-style portions and very friendly service.

Max's Diner ($$)
311 Third Street tel: 415/546-6297
Meatloaf, turkey sandwiches, cheeseburgers and hunks of fried fish all feature among the meals famously served in large portions in this 1950s, New York-style diner, which is usually packed with hungry local office workers.

Moshi Moshi ($)
2092 Third Street tel: 415/861-8285
Very reasonably priced Japanese food served in a simple setting; the much-praised sushi is an excellent lunchtime choice; the dinner menu features a wider selection of seafood as well as excellent gyoza.

Pazzia ($–$$)
337 Third Street tel: 415/512-1693
The owners hail from Florence, Italy and it's obvious when patrons dive into the pastas and authentic thin-crust pizzas served at this casual Italian trattoria. Cramped quarters are the only drawback.

South Park Café ($$)
108 South Park Avenue tel: 415/495-7275
Brings a touch of culinary sophistication to this attractive park in SoMa; the food as well as the ambience is modeled on that of a French bistro.

Sushi Groove ($$)
1516 Folsom Street tel: 415/503-1950 and
1916 Hyde Street tel: 415/440-1905
DJ music and a scenester setting add to the experience of eating the sashimi combo plate, excellent sushi rolls or appetizers like asparagus in prosciutto. The Russian Hill branch serves only sushi since there is no kitchen.

Index

Museums and galleries are found under "museums and galleries" as well as under their individual names.

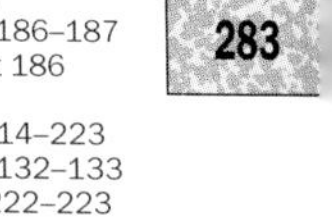

N

O

P

R

S

Picture credits

The Automobile Association would like to thank the following photographers, libraries, and associations for their assistance in the preparation of this book.

BANCROFT LIBRARY 29a, 29b Miwok Indians; MARY EVANS PICTURE LIBRARY 30a Golden Hind, 32a Washing for gold, 32b, 33a, 33b Gold Prospectors, 34a Nob Hill, 34b Fire 1851, 35 Chinatown 1927, 36a First trans-continent link, 36c Norton I, 37a Samuel Brannan, 37b Ambrose Bierce, 38/39 San Francisco Ablaze, 39a Earthquake destruction; GETTY IMAGES 20b Earthquake, 36b John William Mackay, 42b Mario Savio, 111 Hippies; RONALD GRANT ARCHIVES 16a The Maltese Falcon, 16b Clint Eastwood, Dirty Harry, 17a The Convention, 17b Vertigo; MAGNUM PHOTOS 20a Buckled street (Eli Reed); RAY 'SCOTTY' MORRIS 234a, 234b Beach Blanket Babylon; NATURE PHOTOGRAPHERS LTD 21b California gray whale (P. R. STERRY); POPPERFOTTO 42a Hippie couple; DAN REST 232b San Francisco Opera; SAN FRANCISCO CHRONICLE 233b Sleeping Beauty (M. Macor); SAN FRANCISCO CONVENTION & VISITORS BUREAU 10c Chinese Market (Mark Snyder), 165a S. F. Giants Baseball Club (Kerrick James), 252 Cable car Gripman (Mark Gibson); SAN FRANCISCO MUSEUM OF MODERN ART/Richard Barnes 160 Interior view; SAN FRANCISCO SYMPHONY 231b, 232a Herbert Blomstadt & Symphony (T. McCarthy); RON SCHEIL 241 Statue; SPECTRUM COLOUR LIBRARY 28a San Andreas Fault
TOPFOTO 21a Earthquake destruction, 40b General strike, 43 Ron Landberg & Rev Harris, 110b People Haight Street

The remaining photographs are held in the Automobile Association's own photo library (AA PHOTO LIBRARY) and were taken by Rob Holmes with the exception of page 217b, which was taken by H. Harris, page 38a, 50a, 63, 63b, 154, 155, 161a, 164a, 165b, 243b, 246a which was taken by K. Paterson, pages 2, 3, 4, 5a, 9b, 12b, 18c, 19b, 47, 77b, 89a, 89b, 135, 151a, 215, 219, 220, 223, 240, 243, 256, which were taken by B. Smith, and page 12a, which was taken by W. Voysey.

Contributors

Original copy editor: Beth Ingpen
Revision verifiers: Mick Sinclair and Andy Moore
Revision management: Apostrophe S Limited